Adventure Guide to the

Champlain & Hudson River Valleys

Robert & Patricia Foulke

HUNTER

HUNTER PUBLISHING, INC.
130 Campus Drive
Edison, NJ 08818-7816
☎ 732-225-1900 / 800-255-0343 / fax 732-417-1744
E-mail hunterp@bellsouth.net

IN CANADA:
Ulysses Travel Publications
4176 Saint-Denis, Montréal, Québec
Canada H2W 2M5
☎ 514-843-9882 ext. 2232 / fax 514-843-9448

IN THE UNITED KINGDOM:
Windsor Books International
The Boundary, Wheatley Road, Garsington
Oxford, OX44 9EJ England
☎ 01865-361122 / fax 01865-361133

ISBN 1-58843-345-5
© 2003 Patricia and Robert Foulke

This and other Hunter travel guides are also available as e-books in a variety of digital formats through our online partners, including Amazon.com, netLibrary.com, BarnesandNoble.com, and eBooks.com.

For complete information about the hundreds of other travel guides offered by Hunter Publishing, visit us at:

www.hunterpublishing.com

Cover: *Lake Champlain*, Peter Finger
Back cover: *North-South Lake State Park (Catskills)*, Peter Finger

Maps by Toni Carbone, Kim André and Lissa Dailey

Index by Nancy Wolff

4   3   2   1

Contents

■ Maps

Introduction

Abeautiful, large lake and a mighty river, linked together, form a
water corridor with enormous influence on the geography, economy,
politics, history and culture of the northeastern United States. At times it
has been a highway for war between Native American tribes, and later
between Britain and France, and between Britain and its colonies as each
sought control of the continent. It still serves as the political boundary
between New York and New England – a boundary that also has cultural
implications.

The Champlain-Hudson Waterway

Until late in the 19th century the Champlain-Hudson waterway, the
north-south passage through the valleys of Lake Champlain and the Hudson River, was the principal means of transportation and shipping
between the Canadian border and the ocean port of New York. Originally,
a gap in the middle required portages – either into and out of Lake George
or directly from Whitehall to the Hudson. That gap was permanently
closed during the canal-building era in the early 19th century, when the
Champlain Canal connected Whitehall with the Hudson; the navigable
status of the waterway was completed by the **Richelieu Canal** connecting the northern outlet of Lake Champlain with the St. Lawrence River.
Though commerce shifted to railroad and road transportation, the completed waterway remains, now as a resource for recreation.

High in the Adirondacks, **Lake Tear of the Clouds** on the southwestern
slope of Mount Marcy spawns a trickle that eventually turns into the
Hudson. **Feldspar Brook** is the outlet, flowing into the **Opalescent
River** or main branch of the Hudson. It continues south, receiving water
from several branches, past North River, Riparius, Stony Creek, Luzerne
and on to the dam and falls at **Glens Falls**. The distance is 115 miles from
Lake Tear of the Clouds to Glens Falls, via the Hudson River, which for
many years was the major artery of the logging industry. The waterway
bounces along over rapids through Hudson Falls and Fort Edward, meeting the Champlain Canal and continuing on to Troy. The river below the
last dam becomes tidewater, clearly brackish just north of Poughkeepsie
and salty near Newburgh.

Just as important as the waterway itself was the development of the
broad valleys that surround it – full of arable land and opportune sites for
towns and cities. The Champlain Valley and the Hudson River Valley are

essentially one huge slot between the mountain ranges that define their boundaries. The Champlain Valley is bordered on the west by the **Adirondacks** and on the east by the **Green Mountains**.

As the Hudson River flows southward, the **Berkshire Mountains** lie to the east and the **Catskills** to the west. Farther downstream, the **Taconic Range** runs parallel to the river on the east and the **Shawangunk Mountains** on the west. The river cuts through the **Appalachian** chain at Hudson Highlands, then broadens as it nears the New York Bay and the Atlantic.

■ History

 The Champlain Valley was home to Native Americans over 8,000 years ago. The "Champlain Sea" at that time covered an area from Lake Ontario to Whitehall, New York. The waters contained whales, seals, salmon, smelt, crustaceans and shellfish, providing food for the Native Americans, which were a tribe of the Algonquin nation called the **Abenaki.** These "People of the Dawn" still have descendants in the area today, who keep the language, stories and traditions alive.

In 1609, **Samuel de Champlain** arrived from Quebec with a Native American war party intent upon raiding the Iroquois. They defeated a group of Iroquois warriors near Ticonderoga. Champlain was impressed with the beautiful lake and named it for himself. He wrote about the fertile land, mountains, wild game in the forests and fish in the lake. He also described "the Champlain Monster," which he claimed to have seen; four centuries later we haven't heard the last of "Champ."

In the same year, the Dutch sent **Henry Hudson** up the Hudson River looking for a route to the riches of the Far East. As Samuel de Champlain was heading south into Lake Champlain, Hudson was sailing north. Hudson was disappointed to reach the head of navigation in the Albany area, but others followed from Holland to build forts and settlements along the river. Both the French and English tried to settle in parts of the linked valleys at various times. In 1666, Captain Pierre de St. Paul, **Sieur de la Motte**, built a fort and shrine to Sainte Anne on Isle La Motte at the northern end of Lake Champlain, and a British post was built at Chimney Point in 1690. Neither settlement lasted long, though both England and France struggled for possession of the Champlain Valley.

In the middle of the 18th century, that struggle erupted into a major war, replicating the Seven Years War in Europe. In 1755 **Fort Carillon** emerged at Ticonderoga as an important site to guard the portage between Lake Champlain and Lake George. During the 1760s **Fort George** and **Fort William Henry**, both at the head of Lake George, played strategic roles at the next choke point in the nautical highway to the sea. Control of the Hudson-Champlain waterway became a major objective of both sides. The same pattern was repeated with different opponents, during the American Revolution. British land and naval forces unsuccessfully sought to control the waterway and thereby cut off New England from the rest of the rebellious colonies, a strategy that failed at the crucial **Battle of Saratoga**. And in the War of 1812, the British used the waterway to mount another invasion of New York, only to be stopped at the **Battle of Plattsburgh**.

■ Geology

The **Canadian Shield** contains the Champlain Valley, now an eroded plateau of granitic rock. About 400 million years ago, at the end of the Ordovician Period, a large thrust moved the sedimentary rock in the sea against the Canadian Shield. The granitic mass stayed where it was, but the thrust buckled and lifted materials to form the **White**, **Green** and **Berkshire mountains**. The collision produced Logan's Fault, which extends along the eastern shore of Lake Champlain and both French Mountain and Tongue Mountain in the Lake George area.

The Champlain-Lake George Valley remained stable for about 200 million years after the collision on the Canadian Shield. Then, after the dinosaurs disappeared, during the late Cenozoic Period, the land to the west of the Champlain-Lake George Valley crunched into its present state. A river then apparently flowed into the ancestor of the present Hudson, and perhaps these two rivers were connected.

During the Great Ice Age, in the Pleistocene Period, an ice mass moved and receded. Rock and ice contoured the land and the mountain tops. The melting glacier formed **Lake George** and then deposited sand, gravel and rock between Lake George and the Hudson River Valley.

In the Hudson River Valley, the **Palisades** consist of a long mountain ridge perched on the edge of the water. The top section is bare metamorphic basalt rock from 100 to 200 feet in height; the entire ridge measures from 400 to 600 feet in height. The highest point is known as the **High Tor**. The lower section is made up of detritus, or loose stones, that have gathered at the bottom of the cliff.

A gorge cuts through this area, known as the **Hudson Highlands**, for about 20 miles, from Fishkill, in the southwestern corner of Dutchess County, to three miles south of Peekskill, in Westchester County. The rock is gneiss, a coarse-grained stone made up of quartz, feldspar and mica. Rock near Newburgh contains Silurian or Cambrian limestone and slate. From Beacon north to Albany, the rock is mostly sedimentary shale and limestone.

Champlain-Hudson Waterway

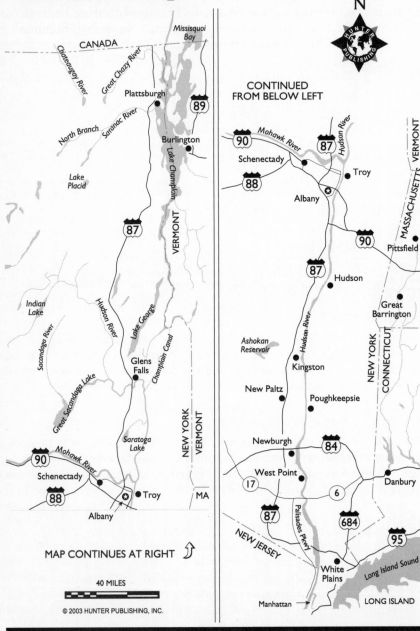

MAP CONTINUES AT RIGHT ⇗

40 MILES

© 2003 HUNTER PUBLISHING, INC.

■ Climate

 The climate along the Champlain-Hudson corridor is a welcome four-season kaleidoscope. Spring, with all of its blossoming and renewal, is often late and short, but beautiful. Wildflowers in spring delight walkers, and gardens bloom all summer. The growing season continues from early spring through late fall and the "brown" period does not begin until November. Summer can be hot, but not as humid as in seacoast regions or the southern part of the country. Hiking, walking, strolling and visiting are then in full swing, but this area is not as crowded as other summer locations, and much of it is woods or untouched wilderness, with little habitation. You can be alone as you head out into the mountains that line the valleys. Fall is magical, with the change of color from green to yellow, orange and red, especially among stands of hardwoods, and the moderately brisk temperatures are great for hiking. Winter can be crisp and clear, but not usually as cold as on the northern plains, and the region's snow sports attract people from all over the East. Storms may come and go but roads are plowed and sanded promptly.

■ Ecology

 The Champlain Valley has a number of watchdog groups that work hard to maintain the integrity of our natural landscape. Six million acres of public and private land are regulated by the **Adirondack Park Agency**, and great patches of woodland and mountains are set aside in state and national parks and preserves. Desecration of the forests here is subject to a fine as well as severe public ostracism. The lakes are monitored carefully to check for contamination from fertilizer runoff. Boats are required to have holding tanks. The water in Lake George is used for drinking water, and area residents want to preserve its quality.

The upper Hudson River is currently the subject of controversy regarding dredging to remove contamination from PCB (polychlorinated biphenyl, a highly toxic compound). Many other stretches of river have been cleaned up in recent years, especially areas affected by toxic materials used in the petrochemical industry. Sections that used to be murky are now clear and enjoyed by canoeists and other boaters. Local governments are focused on preserving the region, with the help of citizens who also play an active role.

The mid-Hudson region has also had problems that spurred the formation of environmental organizations. **Scenic Hudson** was founded in 1963 to fight a proposal by Con Edison, the local power company, to build the world's largest pumped-storage hydroelectric plant on Storm King Mountain. It has since engaged in many other projects involving land preservation, environmental quality, restoring and reinvigorating riverfront communities, and mounting public outreach programs on environmental issues. The organization that owns the **Hudson River Sloop** *Clearwater* is equally active in fighting to preserve the river environment and especially in educating children about its values through direct experience. The sloop itself, a replica of a type common in earlier centuries, is based in Poughkeepsie, but roams the whole navigable river with students and volunteers sailing the vessel to help preserve the quality of the river and foster appreciation of its rich historical and cultural heritage.

About This Book

■ Scope

The scope of the Champlain-Hudson waterway and its broad valleys is, in general, defined by the watershed feeding the lake and the river. We cover primarily the counties with riverfront, from the Canadian border to the Tappan Zee Bridge. Because the valleys are bounded by mountains throughout most of their length, we frequently write about places and activities on their slopes.

There are a number of reasons for writing about the two linked valleys together. One is that it has seldom been done, though there are plenty of travel guides to individual regions like the Adirondacks, the Catskills, or the Hudson Valley from Albany southward. Another is the fact that Lake Champlain and the Hudson River have been linked historically as a water highway – and that was the only kind available – by Native American tribes, then by Europeans once they got into the region. The rich heritage of the valleys cannot be fully understood without reference to the waterway that connects them, a realization that has led to the creation of a number of historical and recreational trails in recent years. And, finally, there is just so much to do in the valleys and the mountains that surround them.

■ Using This Book

The proliferation of Internet sites has raised questions about the functions and usefulness of travel guidebooks in recent years. There is hardly a travel destination, attraction, hotel, B&B, restaurant, or outdoor adventure without its own website. And many of these websites do provide useful information as well as enticing the viewer to come. That information can be as up-to-date as yesterday. Books can never match that because there is always a time lag between writing and publication.

So what is the role of the guidebook now? It was first invented as a popular genre for European travelers. Those who carried around their Baedekers knew they could trust the information in them and create their own tours through strange cities and unknown countryside. Good guidebooks still do that. There is always an editor, and frequently a fact-checker, looking over the writer's shoulder and asking for revisions. In contrast, all travel websites – even those established by regions – are essentially ads. No one vets them for accuracy or honesty.

Gradually the Internet is redefining the nature of guidebooks – what they can and cannot do effectively. For example, no one should turn to a guidebook for restaurant reviews, exact prices, or current schedules of events in any month.

What good guidebooks can do is steer you through the masses of information available about places and activities, making selections through personal experience and research. They can tell you enough to make your choices informed ones as you plan a trip or vacation. They can lead you to sources of information about interesting places and exciting activities, providing addresses, phone numbers and relevant web addresses. There, once you have a plan, you can follow through and get all the necessary details. Entering the Internet first, without that guidance, is like browsing through the Manhattan telephone directory without knowing any names, looking for something without quite knowing what it is.

So there is a role after all for both guidebooks and websites, twin engines for building a good vacation or getaway weekend.

Travel Information

∎ When to Go

No matter what activities you enjoy, there are more than enough to fill a great vacation at any season. The heaviest travel occurs during leaf season, followed by summer and winter in that order. The one time to avoid in the mountains is mud season, which occurs from the time the spring snow melt starts until it is gone.

A WORD TO
THE WISE

Mud season in Vermont usually begins in late March and can last through much of April if there is a heavy snow load. That's when the locals shut down and take their vacations elsewhere.

Our personal preferences for general travel are spring and fall. We like to be home on our beautiful lake in the summer, and in winter we take the time to get away for skiing trips.

■ Clothing & Equipment

Dress is casual for the most part. Dinner out may require an outfit that can be termed "dressy casual" or "business casual." Hikers and other outdoors people know the trick of dressing in layers, with a daypack containing more protective outerwear. Shoes and hiking boots that have been broken in make sense. If you are heading into the forest for a day-hike, the equipment in your pack should include maps, a compass, water bottles and sunscreen. If you are climbing in the mountains, temperature changes can be more radical and you should be carrying some warm clothing even on summer days.

■ Transportation

Rental cars are readily available in the area; it is helpful to have a car for most activities. Train service is available in parts of the Hudson River Valley because commuters depend upon it, but there is limited service north of Albany. See the *Getting Here & Getting Around* section in each chapter for local information.

■ Costs

You can stay in a variety of accommodations in the region. Please be aware that the suggested price key for each entry is influenced by the season, size of room, length of stay, and whether meals are included.

ACCOMMODATIONS PRICE SCALE
Prices for a double room for one or two persons, before taxes.
$ . . . . Under $50
$$. . . . . $50 to $100
$$$ . . . . $101 to $175
$$$$ . . . . Over $175

DINING PRICE SCALE	
Prices include an entrée, which may come with vegetables and salad, but exclude beverage, taxes and tip.	
$	Under $10
$$	$10 to $20
$$$.	$21 to $50
$$$$.	Over $50

Information Sources

■ Heritage Travel

The Independence Trail, ☎ 866-687-8724, www.independencetrail.org. This heritage tourism information source covers Revolutionary War sites from New York City to the Canadian border.

The Northern Campaign, ☎ 518-585-2821, www.thenortherncampaign.org. Another heritage tourism site focused on the crucial campaign of British General Burgoyne from Canada to his defeat at Saratoga in 1777.

■ Connecticut

Connecticut Office of Tourism, 505 Hudson Street, Hartford, CT 06106, ☎ 860-270-8080, fax 860-270-8077, www.ctbound.org.

Berkshire Hills Visitors Bureau, Berkshire Common, Plaza Level, Pittsfield, MA 01201, ☎ 800-237-5747 or 413-443-9186, fax 413-443-1970, www.berkshires.org, bvb@berkshires.org.

Chamber of Commerce of the Berkshires, 66 West Street, Pittsfield, MA 01201, ☎ 413-499-4000, fax 413-447-9641, www.berkshirebiz.org, chamber@berkshirebiz.org.

Litchfield Hills Visitors Bureau, Litchfield, CT 06759, ☎ 860-567-4506, www.litchfieldhills.com.

■ New York

New York State Division of Tourism, Box 2603, Albany, NY 12220-0603. ☎ 800/CALL NYS or 518-474-4116, www.iloveny.com.

New York State Canal System, Box 189, Albany, NY 12201-0181. ☎ 800-4CANAL4, www.canals.state.ny.us.

New York State Parks, Empire State Plaza, Albany, NY 12238. ☎ 518-474-0445, www.nysparks.com.

DEC Public Lands, 625 Broadway, Albany, NY 12233. ☎ 518-402-9428, www.dec.state.ny.us.

Rails to Trails Conservancy, Northeast. ☎ 202-974-5119, www.railstotrails.com.

Rails to Trails, Delaware River & Catskills. ☎ 800-225-4132, www, durr.org.

Hudson River Valley Greenway, Capital Building, Room 254, Albany, NY 12224. ☎ 800-TRAIL92 or 518-473-3835.

Hudson Valley Rail Trails. ☎ 845-483-0428.

New York-New Jersey Trail Conference. ☎ 201-512-9348 or 212-685-9699, www.nynjtc.com.

NYS Outdoor Guides Association. ☎ 518-359-7037, www.nysoga.com.

■ Vermont

Vermont Department of Tourism, 134 State Street, Montpelier, VT 05602. ☎ 802-828-3237, www.800-vermont.com.

Vermont State Parks, 103 South Main Street, Waterbury, VT 05671. ☎ 802-241-3655, www.vtstateparks.com.

■ Massachusetts

Massachusetts Office of Travel and Tourism, 10 Park Plaza, Suite 4510, Boston, MA 02116. ☎ 800-227-MASS, www.massvacation.com.

Massachusetts Department of Environmental Management/Division of Forests and Parks. ☎ 617-727-3180.

Massachusetts Audubon Society. ☎ 781-259-9500.

Lake Champlain

The Vermont Side

You can't go wrong choosing to visit either side of northern Lake Champlain. Starting with a city (Burlington) on the Vermont side that is ripe with Ethan Allen lore, take a trip up into the islands where hikers and bikers restore their souls. Two stunning museums, the Shelburne Museum and the Lake Champlain Maritime Museum, are both treasures.

The New York side offers walking tours in both Essex and Westport. The Battle of Plattsburgh can be explored in the Interpretive Center and Valcour Island, with its 1776 heritage, is visible from shore. Head south to Crown Point where you can climb the bastions for a fine view of the lake.

History of Lake Champlain

 Around 2000 BC the Algonquin Indians lived in the area, traveling back and forth from present-day Massachusetts to New York. Names arising from the Indians include Quechee, Bomoseen, Passumpsic and Winooski.

King Francois I of France laid claim to much of North America after sending Giovanni Verrazano, the Italian navigator, to explore the coast in 1524. In 1608 the paper claim became real when Samuel de Champlain arrived. In 1609 he accompanied the Algonquin Indians as they journeyed to the lake and attacked the Iroquois. Two Iroquois chiefs and warriors were killed, which set the stage for further antagonism.

Ethan Allen and his Green Mountain Boys were active in the area, trying to drive away the "Yorkers." By 1777, Vermont was an independent republic, then a state after 14 more years.

The possible existence of "Champ" intrigues visitors and residents alike – even those who firmly believe that most "sightings" are the stuff of legend rather than fact. Yet Lake Champlain is on the same latitude as Loch Ness in Scotland, famous for similar questions about "Nessie." Both bodies of water have very deep sections and were once connected to the sea, so the possibility of sea creatures lurking in the depths is hard to disprove. People on both sides of the Atlantic claim they have seen "Champ" or "Nessie." Who knows whether these claims are based on illusions?

Lake Champlain
The Vermont Side

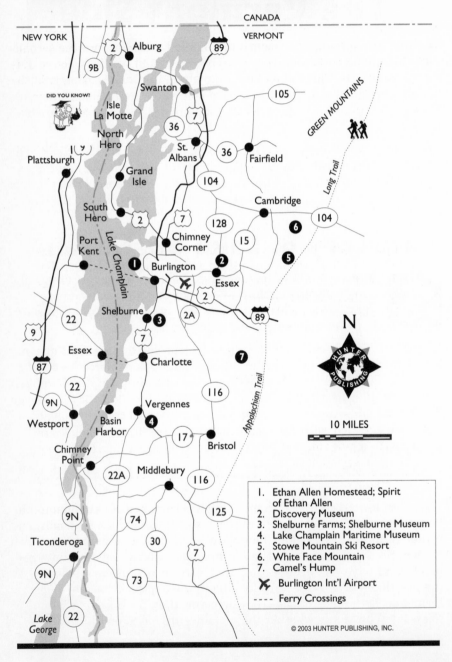

CANADA

NEW YORK | VERMONT

Alburg — (2)

(89)

(9B)

Swanton — (105)

DID YOU KNOW?

Isle
La Motte

(7)

(36)

North
Hero

St.
Albans — (36) — Fairfield

Plattsburgh

Grand
Isle

(104)

South
Hero — (2) — (7) — Cambridge

Port
Kent

(128) — (15) — ❻ — (104)

Lake Champlain

❶ Burlington — ❷ — ❺
Essex

GREEN MOUNTAINS

Long Trail

(2)

Shelburne — (2A) — (89)

(22)

❸ — ❼

(9)

(7)

Essex — Charlotte

(87) — (22)

(116)

(9N)

Westport — Basin
Harbor — ❹ — Vergennes

(17) — Bristol

Chimney
Point

(22A) — Middlebury — (116)

Appalachian Trail

(9N) — (74) — (125)

Ticonderoga — (30) — (7)

(9N) — (73)

Lake
George — (22)

N

HUNTER PUBLISHING

10 MILES

1. Ethan Allen Homestead; Spirit
   of Ethan Allen
2. Discovery Museum
3. Shelburne Farms; Shelburne Museum
4. Lake Champlain Maritime Museum
5. Stowe Mountain Ski Resort
6. White Face Mountain
7. Camel's Hump

✈ Burlington Int'l Airport

---- Ferry Crossings

© 2003 HUNTER PUBLISHING, INC.

DID YOU KNOW?

In 1609 Samuel de Champlain saw a 20-foot-long creature that was thick as a barrel, with a head like a horse and a body like a serpent. Passengers traveling by steamer spotted "Champ" during the 1870s, and in 1985 a local inhabitant captured it on videotape.

Burlington, Vermont, was chartered in 1763 and was once the second-largest shipping port in the country. The waterfront was very active during the American Revolution with English and French soldiers and the colonists moving back and forth. Today the waterfront area is a popular place for strollers in the park, boaters from the Community Boathouse, cyclists and walkers along the paths.

Burlington is the gateway to the Champlain Islands. South Hero, North Hero, Isle La Motte and a number of smaller islands form this group in Grand Isle County.

THE HERO ISLANDS

Ira and Ethan Allen, heroes of the Revolutionary War, are remembered in the names North Hero and South Hero. Ethan Allen and his Green Mountain Boys were indeed very active during the American Revolution, but the origin of the group was anything but heroic. They were especially annoyed after King George II declared that a section of Vermont belonged to New York, and that the land patents granted to them by Governor Wentworth of New Hampshire were invalid. The Green Mountain Boys first gathered as a property-rights group to drive off the "Yorkers" who were coming to claim their land.

Rugged rocks and sandy beaches line the perimeter of the islands, which are rich with farmland in the center. These islands are prized as a quiet place to enjoy boating, fishing, sailing, kayaking, cycling and horseback riding.

After the glaciers receded, about 12,000 years ago, Lake Champlain became an inland sea. Fossils remained and are part of the grey limestone walls of the stone houses in the islands. They are also found along the beaches. Coral reefs grew on Isle La Motte about 450 million years ago.

South of Burlington, **Shelburne** is perhaps best known for its classic Shelburne Museum. You may think of it only as a living history museum, but there is much more. The antiques and historical artifacts inside each of the 37 buildings are varied and deep in content. Each grouping has been carefully put together and all are attractively displayed.

Lake Champlain - Vermont Side

Farther south, **Chimney Point**, at the narrowest point of the big lake, got its name during the French and Indian Wars. The British aggressively threatened the settlers, who burned their homes and fled, leaving sad black chimneys behind. Chimney Point is the site of the Lake Champlain bridge between Vermont and New York.

Getting Here & Getting Around

■ By Air

Albany International Airport. . . . . ☎ 518-869-9611

Burlington International Airport . . . . ☎ 802-863-2874

■ By Car

Interstate 89 is the preferred route from the south, or take scenic **Route 7** from Bennington. If you come through New York State **I-87** is a fast route.

■ By Bus

Adirondack Trailways . . . . ☎ 800-793-5525

Greyhound Lines . . . . ☎ 800-231-2222

Vermont Transit . . . . ☎ 800-451-3292

■ By Train

Amtrak has sparse travel from New York to Burlington. Call ☎ 800-872-7245.

Information Sources

Lake Champlain Regional Marketing Organization, 60 Main Street, Burlington, VT 05401, ☎ 802-863-3489 or 877-686-5253, fax 802-863-1538, www.vermont.org.

Vermont Chamber of Commerce, PO Box 37, Montpelier, VT 05601, ☎ 802-223-3443, www.vtchamber.com.

Vermont Department of Tourism, 134 State Street, Montpelier, VT 05602, ☎ 802-828-3237.

Vermont State Parks, 103 South Main Street, Waterbury, VT 05671, ☎ 800-VERMONT or 802-241-3655.

Adventures

■ On Foot

Walking and hiking are very popular in Vermont. **Camel's Hump Trail** goes between Burlington and Montpelier. The **Long Trail** runs up to Camel's Hump peak and continues for 270 miles. The **Appalachian Trail** runs through the Green Mountains and intersects with the Long Trail. Hikers enjoy the trail between **Mount Mansfield** and **Sterling Peak** at Smugglers' Notch.

Head out to the **Champlain Islands** where there are circle-route trails to be walked.

■ On Wheels

Scenic Drives

Champlain Islands Excursion – From I-89 take Exit 17 west on Route 2 to **South Hero**, **Grand Isle**, **North Hero**, and **South Alburg**. You can extend this trip by following the route described below for bicycles.

Burlington/Vergennes Excursion – Take Route 7 south from Shelburne through rolling countryside with views of Lake Champlain and the Adirondacks in the distance. You can take side trips to the ferry at **Char-**

lotte for a trip across the lake; and to Basin Harbor, site of the **Lake Champlain Maritime Museum** (see *Sightseeing*, page 21).

Bicycling

Vermont is very popular with cyclists, with good secondary roads for bicycles and plenty of dirt roads for mountain biking. Cyclists have many choices, from backcountry lanes and old logging trails to ski area slopes.

 DID YOU KNOW?

It may be helpful to know that north-south roads usually have fewer hills than east-west roads, and roads that follow rivers and streams usually have more gradual inclines than others.

Bicycle clubs welcome riders to come along, and there are many sport shops, resorts and outfitters to get you started in this healthful and pleasurable sport.

BICYCLE TOUR ON NORTH HERO
& ISLE LA MOTTE

Begin this tour by taking I-89 north from Burlington to Exit 17, then go west on Route 2 to the islands. Head along Route 129 where it crosses over onto Isle La Motte; take Shore Road to the right and head for **Sainte Anne's Shrine** on Shrine Road. In 1666, Jesuits celebrated the first Catholic Mass in North America here. Take West Shore Road along Lake Champlain until you reach **Fisk Farm**. Continue on Main Road to the **Isle La Motte Historical Society**. This area is known for the **Chazgan Coral Reef**, which is the oldest coral reef in the world. If you want to explore the fossils up close you must get permission from Tom LaBombard at the RV campground. Head east on Route 129 and onto North Hero, where you will ride south on Route 2 and around to the **North Hero Fire Department**, then turn north on Lakeview Drive and left on Bridge Road back to Route 129.

■ On & In the Water

Boat Rentals & Tours

As you head out on the open water, remember that, whether you call it a "great lake" or not, Champlain is the sixth-largest inland body of water in the nation, stretching 120 miles from the Canadian border nearly to the Hudson and is up to 10 miles wide. We have sailed and paddled on the lake and have great respect for its variability, especially when cold fronts or line squalls swoop down suddenly from the Adirondacks without much warning, churning a formerly placid surface with gale-force winds and steep waves. Our rule of thumb: never start out before listening to the weather radio, and carry it with you on doubtful days. The **NOAA** marine forecasts from Burlington are excellent, the best source of information on lake conditions.

The lake is full of reefs, so be sure you have up-to-date charts with you, and if you are on an extended cruise bring the detailed cruising guide to Lake Champlain along too..

Look for *Cruising Guide to Lake Champlain: The Waterway from New York City to Montreal*, by Alan McKibben, or *Cruising Guide to New York Waterways and Lake Champlain*, by Chris W. Brown and Claiborne S. Young. They provide all sorts of useful information about piloting, neat coves to moor in, sources of gas, food, supplies and repairs, and information on the port towns you will visit. They can be purchased in any marine store.

Burlington Community Boathouse. Rental of sailboats, dinghies or sea kayaks, ☎ 802-865-3377.

PaddleWays. This group offers guided tours in canoes and kayaks, ☎ 802-660-8606.

For sailboat charters and boat rentals, contact the **Lake Champlain Regional Marketing Association**, ☎ 800-262-5226.

Excursion Boats & Ferries

Lake Champlain Cruises offers a Captain's Dinner Cruise, a Sunday Brunch Cruise and other daily lake excursions. This company also operates a ferry service across the lake. Lake Champlain Cruises, King Street Dock, Burlington, VT 05401, ☎ 802-864-9804, fax 802-864-6830.

Lake Champlain Shoreline Cruises offers lunch, brunch, dinner plus variety show dinner cruises on their triple-deck vessel, *Spirit of Ethan Allen II*. College Street, Burlington Boat House, PO Box 605, Burlington, VT 05402, ☎ 802-862-8300, fax 802-860-2261, www.soea.com.

Lake Champlain - Vermont Side

Fishing

Vermont is well known for its cold-water fishing for trout and salmon in Lake Champlain. Shallower bays and flats in the lake provide warm-water fishing for bass and pike. When you plan a fishing trip, contact the **Vermont Fish & Wildlife Department**, 103 South Main Street, Waterbury, VT 05671, ☎ 802-241-3700, www.anr.state.vt.us/fw/fwhome. Ask for a "Vermont Fishing Kit."

Diving

Lake Champlain's Underwater Historic Preserve provides public access for divers and protects each historic wreck. Every diver must register once each season and reserve a time slot by directly contacting the Burlington Community Boat House at ☎ 802-865-3377.

DIVING RULES

Divers must tie their boat to a buoy, with only one boat on a buoy at a time, and leave after the dive. Divers must fly a "diver down" flag on the boat during the dive. Each diver will descend down the buoy line to the anchor pad, then follow the yellow guideline to the wreck. Do not remove anything or touch the wreck.

- The *Phoenix* lies on the northern face of Colchester Shoal reef. Launched in 1815, she burned in 1819. Six of the 46 passengers on board died. The bow remains at a depth of 60 feet and the stern at 110 feet. Underwater lights are necessary, and only very experienced divers should try this dive.

- The *Burlington Bay Horse Ferry* is the only known surviving example of a turntable "team-boat," which used horses for power. She lies two-thirds of the way northwest from the north end of the Burlington Breakwater to Lone Rock Point. The paddle wheels are there, although the paddle blades are missing.

- The *O.J. Walker* dates from 1862. She worked for 33 years hauling heavy cargoes and sank in 1895 during a storm. She was a canal boat providing family living quarters. Her wheel and aft cabin hatch cover are in place but very fragile. Divers must get a diving permit for each dive on this wreck. She is located three-quarters of a mile west of the Burlington breakwater's north end.

- The *General Butler* is a schooner-rigged sailing canal boat. She was built in Essex in 1862 and sank during a winter gale in

1876. A Burlington ship chandler, James Wakefield, rowed out with his son in a 14-foot lighthouse boat to bring the crew to safety. She is located 75 yards west of the southern end of Burlington Breakwater.

■ The *A.R. Noyes* was a canal boat under tow from the steam tug *Tisdale* when she and others broke loose and sank in 1884. Coal still remains in her hold, along with the mules' towing apparatus and coal shovel fragments. She lies just north of the Coast Guard's navigational buoy on Proctor Shoal.

■ The *Diamond Island Stone Boat* was one of many wooden canal boats to take cargo through the lake and the Champlain Canal. She carried quarried stone in the hold; the bottom planks and the stores are still there, although the sides of the boat have fallen to the bottom. She is located off the southeast side of Diamond Island.

■ The *Champlain II* was launched in Burlington in 1868 as the *Oakes Ames*. She ran aground in 1875. Apparently her captain had been taking morphine for his gout. Some of the vessel was salvaged, but the stern section is still there. She lies between Barn Rock and Rock Harbor, north of Westport, NY and across from Basin Harbor, VT.

■ Eco-Travel

Burlington-Lake Champlain Basin Science Center, ☎ 802-864-1848. Displays include "The Sea That Used to Be," "Song of the Wetlands," "Secrets of the Lake," and "Buzz, Croak & Warble." Inhabitants include live turtles, snakes, frogs, fish, and sea urchins. The center offers demonstrations as well as interactive displays.

The **Wetlands Nature Trail** is located adjacent to the Ethan Allen Homestead (see *Sightseeing*, below) off North Road from Route 127, ☎ 802-863-5744. Pick up a trail map in the Visitor Center for the Homestead. Brochures guide visitors as they walk along the trail, hearing bird calls and seeing changes in vegetation from water to swamp to trees on higher ground.

Sightseeing

■ Burlington

Ethan Allen Homestead, North Avenue Exit off Route 127, Burlington, VT 05401, ☎ 802-865-4556. Ethan Allen settled in this house near the end of his life. Your visit begins with a multimedia show inside the tavern, which was the hub of the community for information and news. As the lights dim, you hear the wind whistling and sounds of people talking. Narrators appear on the wall above the fireplace and exchange gossip. After the show, walk over to the house past his wife Fannie's garden, planted with the vegetables and flowers she liked. Inside the house you will see displays on making clothing, from carding wool or flax to spinning and weaving. The four-poster bed in the living room had straw mattresses kept in place on a rope spring with a twister tool – reminding us of the phrase "sleep tight."

Ethan Allen stories get better and better. Remember the one about the night Allen and a friend stopped for a nap after a lot of "elbow bending"? A rattler coiled on his chest, struck, rolled off, staggered, burped and fell asleep. Allen thought it was a mosquito that had bitten him during the night.

■ Essex

The Discovery Museum, 51 Park Street, Essex Junction, VT 05452, ☎ 802-878-8687. Children are especially fascinated with the chance to creep through a simulated animal burrow and peer through openings to see what it might be like to live down there. They will come out into a tree trunk. Much of the museum is interactive so you can touch and hold shells or other objects on display. The planetarium offers astronomy presentations.

■ Shelburne

Shelburne Farms, Harbor Road, Shelburne, VT ☎ 802-985-8686. Dr. and Mrs. William Steward Webb owned 4,000 acres on the water. The farm's main house overlooks Lake Champlain and the Adirondacks and is now a hotel. There's a coach barn and a horseshoe-shaped farm barn. During the summer, concerts are held on the property.

Shelburne Museum, Route 7, Shelburne, VT ☎ 802-985-3346. The SS *Ticonderoga*, the last steam-powered side-wheeler of its type in the country, is on display on the grounds. She dates from 1906 and is 220 feet long. Originally used as a ferry, she later saw service as an excursion boat. Inside, you can see how elegant she was, with paneling in butternut and cherry and gold-stenciled ceilings.

You can view a collection of railcars, including the *Grand Isle*, which has an elegant dining room, mahogany-paneled parlor and staterooms. The railroad station dates from 1890. The lighthouse served as both home and workplace for 11 lighthouse keepers and their families.

Electra Havemeyer Webb created the Shelburne Museum after many years of collecting American antiques. She wrote, "the rooms were over-furnished... then the closets and the attics were filled. I just couldn't let good pieces go by – china, porcelain, pottery, pewter, glass, dolls, quilts, cigar store Indians, eagles, folk art. They all seemed to appeal to me." Her collections now fill 35 buildings.

■ South Hero

Hyde Log Cabin, Route 2, South Hero, VT. Dating from 1783, it is one of the oldest cabins in the country. The Grand Isle Historical Society has furnished the house.

■ Vergennes

Lake Champlain Maritime Museum, 4472 Basin Harbor Road, Vergennes, VT 05491, ☎ 802-475-2022, www.lcmm.org. The museum has built a replica of the *Philadelphia*, of Revolutionary War fame, which sank and lay on the bottom until it was raised in 1935. The original is in the Smithsonian. Visitors can climb all over the replica, even help hoist one of her square sails. Look in the schoolhouse to see illustrations of Native Americans who lived along Lake Champlain's shores during the prehistoric era. A model of Champlain's first steamboat, the *Vermont I*, is on display; she sank in the Richelieu River. The watercraft building houses an Indian birchbark canoe and a "mystery" canoe that probably came from the Amazon. Native Adirondack guideboats are there as well. The *Phoenix* display details the fates of 46 passengers who were on board when fire broke out (see page 18).

Festivals & Events

■ March

Vermont Flower Show, Burlington, VT, ☎ 802-865-5979. The show includes display gardens, exhibitors, children's activities.

■ August

Champlain Valley Exposition, Essex Junction, VT, ☎ 802-878-5545. This fair offers livestock, farm and home products, exhibits, poultry, horse, pony and ox pulling, art show, home crafts, vegetable, fruit and flower competition, horse shows, maple products and exhibits, a midway, food booths, tractor and truck pulls and concerts.

■ October

South Hero Applefest and Craft Show, South Hero, VT, apples@ together.net. The show offers entertainment, music, crafts, flea market, cider pressing contest, petting zoo and lots of apples.

Where to Stay

ACCOMMODATIONS PRICE SCALE
Prices for a double room for one or two persons, before taxes.
$ . . . . Under $50
$$. $50 to $100
$$$ . . . . $101 to $175
$$$$ . . . . Over $175

■ Burlington

Burlington Redstone Bed & Breakfast is on the National Register of Historic Places. There are views of Lake Champlain and the mountains from the house and the perennial garden. 497 South Willard Street, Burlington, VT 05401, ☎ 802-862-0508, www.burlingtonredstone.com. $$$.

Willard Street Inn is located in the Hill District. 349 South Willard Street, Burlington, VT 05401, ☎ 800-577-8712 or 802-651-8710, fax 802-651-8714. $$-$$$.

■ Essex

The Inn at Essex is a contemporary country inn with individually decorated rooms. The New England Culinary Institute (see below) provides the cuisine. 70 Essex Way, Essex, VT 05452, ☎ 802-878-1100, fax 802-878-0063. $$$.

■ Shelburne

Heart of the Village Inn is an 1886 Queen Anne home on Route 7. Each room is decorated with antiques and in a different style. 5347 Shelburne Road, Shelburne, VT 05482, ☎ 802-985-2800, fax 802-985-2870. $$-$$$.

The Inn at Shelburne Farms is a restored 1899 mansion and estate. Shelburne,VT 05482, ☎ 802-985-8498, fax 802-356-8123. $$-$$$.

■ Camping

Charlotte

Mount Philo State Park, Route 7, Charlotte, VT 05445, ☎ 802-425-2390 or 802-372-5060. The site offers camping and picnicking. Take care, as the steep ascent from Route 7 is not recommended for trailers or large RVs.

Ferrisburg

Kingsland Bay State Park, Ferrisburg, VT 05456, ☎ 802-877-3445. The site offers picnic areas and tennis courts on 130 acres.

Grand Isle

Grand Isle State Park, Grand Isle, VT 05458, ☎ 802-372-4300. The site has 155 campsites, a beach, nature trail and recreation building.

North Hero

North Hero State Park, North Hero, VT 05474, ☎ 802-372-8727. The site has 99 wooded tent or trailer sites and 18 lean-tos, a beach, boat launch, boat rentals and picnic area.

Lake Champlain - Vermont Side

Where to Eat

DINING PRICE SCALE
Prices include an entrée, which may come with vegetables and salad, but exclude beverage, taxes and tip.
$ . . . . Under $10
$$ . . . . $10 to $20
$$$. . . . . $21 to $50
$$$$. . . . . Over $50

■ Burlington

 NECI Commons (New England Culinary Institute), 25 Church Street, Burlington, VT, ☎ 802-862-6324. The cuisine is innovative, as one would expect from NECI, and the atmosphere casual. You can also take home freshly baked pastries, soups, salads and rotisserie chicken. Current hours are: 11:30-2 for lunch, 2-4 bistro, 5:30-10:30 for dinner. On Sunday, brunch is 11-3 and dinner 5:30-9. $$.

The Ice House, 171 Battery Street, Burlington, VT, ☎ 802-864-1800. The Ice House is located at the ferry entrance and there's a nice view of Lake Champlain. The menu includes seafood, steaks, and grilled sandwiches. Try the Sunday brunch in season. Current hours are 11:30 am to 10 pm. $-$$.

Sweetwaters, 120 Church Street, Burlington, VT, ☎ 802-864-9800. There's a Southwestern theme in this former bank building. Try one of the wood-grilled specialties. Current hours are 11:30-midnight; Sunday, 10:30-1. $$.

■ Essex

Butler's Restaurant and **The Tavern** (New England Culinary Institute), The Inn at Essex, 70 Essex Way, Essex, VT, ☎ 802-878-1100. An innovative menu that changes nightly with new ways to offer seafood, duck and filet mignon. Current hours are 6:30-10:30 am, 11:30 am-2 pm and 6-9 pm; Sunday, 8-9:30 am and 10 am-2 pm. $$.

The New York Side

Getting Here & Getting Around

■ By Air

Albany International Airport . . . . ☎ 518-869-9611

Burlington International Airport . . . . ☎ 802-863-2874

■ By Car

I-87 leads up the Hudson River all the way north to the Canadian border.

■ By Bus

Adirondack Trailways . . . . ☎ 800-793-5525

Greyhound Lines. . . . . ☎ 800-231-2222

■ By Train

Amtrak. . . . . ☎ 800-872-7245

Information Sources

Lake Placid/Essex County Visitors Bureau, 216 Main Street, Lake Placid, NY 12946, ☎ 800-447-5224 or 518-523-2445.

Plattsburgh/North Country Chamber of Commerce, 101 West Bay Plaza, PO Box 310, Plattsburgh, NY 12901, ☎ 518-563-1000, www.north-countrychamber.com.

Lake Champlain
The New York Side

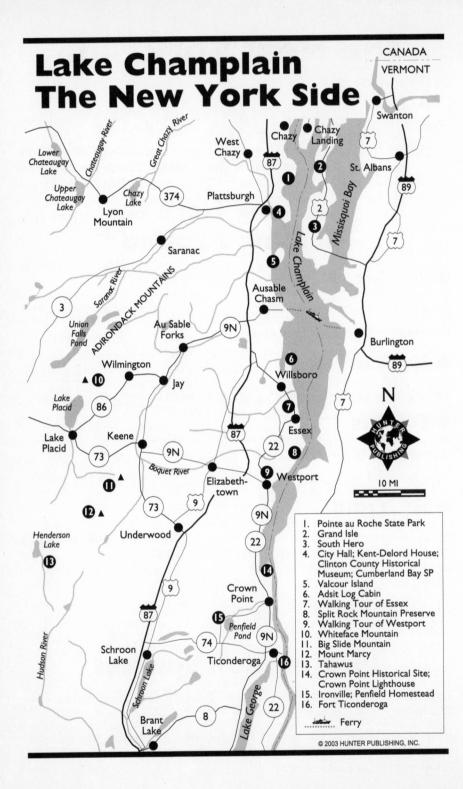

CANADA
VERMONT

Swanton

Lower Chateaugay Lake

Chateaugay River

Great Chazy River

West Chazy

Chazy

Chazy Landing

7

St. Albans

89

Upper Chateaugay Lake

Chazy Lake

374

Lyon Mountain

Plattsburgh

87

1

2

2

89

Saranac

4

2

3

7

Saranac River

ADIRONDACK MOUNTAINS

5

Lake Champlain

Missisquoi Bay

3

Union Falls Pond

Au Sable Forks

Ausable Chasm

9N

6

Wilmington

10

Jay

Willsboro

Burlington

89

Lake Placid

86

7

7

N

Lake Placid

Keene

73

9N

Boquet River

87

Essex

22

8

11

Elizabeth-town

9

Westport

9

9N

10 MI

12

73

9

22

Henderson Lake

Underwood

14

13

9

Crown Point

Hudson River

87

15

Penfield Pond

9N

Schroon Lake

74

Ticonderoga

16

Schroon Lake

Lake George

Brant Lake

8

22

1. Pointe au Roche State Park
2. Grand Isle
3. South Hero
4. City Hall; Kent-Delord House; Clinton County Historical Museum; Cumberland Bay SP
5. Valcour Island
6. Adsit Log Cabin
7. Walking Tour of Essex
8. Split Rock Mountain Preserve
9. Walking Tour of Westport
10. Whiteface Mountain
11. Big Slide Mountain
12. Mount Marcy
13. Tahawus
14. Crown Point Historical Site; Crown Point Lighthouse
15. Ironville; Penfield Homestead
16. Fort Ticonderoga

Ferry

© 2003 HUNTER PUBLISHING, INC.

Adventures

■ On Foot

Walking Tours

A walking tour of **Essex** can begin at Ross Wharf, where Dock House dates from 1812. The Brooklyn Bridge's stones were quarried in Willsboro and shipped from the **Old Dock House**. Today it is a restaurant with a fine view. On the next pier, cars wait for the ferry across the lake to Charlotte, VT. The **Essex Fire House**, colorful in red and yellow with a sunburst pediment, dates from 1800. Across the street the **Essex Community Church** is a grey stone Italianate structure. Up the hill the **Cyrus Stafford House** is a Greek Revival house in red brick.

A **Westport** walking tour begins on the library lawn. You can pick up *A Walking Tour Guide to Westport, New York on Lake Champlain* in the Chamber of Commerce office. **Colonial Cottage**, a brick home built in 1836 on Congress Street, is handsome in Greek Revival style. The rebuilt **Westport Yacht Club**, once the scene of dances and regattas during the 1930s and 1940s, is now a public restaurant with a view. A home on South Main Street, **Rolling Hills**, dates from 1807. Some of its Italianate features were added in the mid-1800s.

The **Split Rock Mountain Preserve** between Essex and Westport in the lake's Palisades region totals 3,800 acres. Once used for logging and granite mining, the region is laced with old roads and some trails, both marked and unmarked. A trail system of 10 to 12 miles, with signs and trail markers, as well as campsites and additional parking lots, is being developed. The existing parking lot is on Lake Shore Road 4.3 miles north of the junction with Route 22 in Westport and 6.1 miles south of the Post Office in Essex. For up-to-date information, contact Jim Papero, senior forester at DEC, PO Box 296, Ray Brook, NY 12977, ☎ 518-897-1200.

■ On Wheels

Scenic Drive

The country road from to **Essex** to **Westport** (not the main road, which is Route 22) provides one of the most rewarding scenic drives in the region. It begins along the shore, then climbs to highlands with truly spectacular views of the high peaks of the Adirondacks; you get a full taste of the beauties of both lake and mountain. With trees on each side, a curving black-topped road, and few houses to mar the view, it is a true pleasure to drive. When we were last there, tiger lilies and Queen Anne's lace bloomed along the roadside just a few miles between the two villages.

Bicycling

 You can rent bicycles for touring the area from **High Peaks Touring Center**, Main Street, Essex NY, ☎ 518-963-7028. Go with a group on Wednesdays and Sundays or head out on your own. Those with a lot of energy can combine bike and boat. The route begins along the Boquet River by bike and then continues from Willsboro by kayak.

Lake Champlain Bikeways, Lake Champlain Visitors Center, RR 1, Box 220, Bridge Road, Crown Point, NY 12928, ☎ 518-597-4646.

Adirondack Coast Bicycling is part of the network linked to the 350-mile route around the lake. Each of the six loops has been named, and the biking conditions are included. The following tours are printed in a brochure which is available locally.

- **Surrounded by Water** (14.5 miles) is appropriate for all levels of cycling ability. It proceeds around Willsboro Point with nice views of Lake Champlain. There is one steep hill just north of the bridge over the Boquet River on Route 22. Begin in Willsboro and head North on Route 22 up the hill, turn right on Point Road/Route 27 and continue on out to the end of the point. Return on East Bay and Frisbie, rejoining Point Road until the turnoff onto Farrell Road/Route 62 and back into Willsboro.

- **Rolling Reber Ramble** (18.6 miles) is rolling, with an occasional steep hill. Begin in Willsboro and head north on Route 22 up the hill, then turn left on Mountain Road/Reber Road North. Pass Route 14 and continue straight at Route 57/Reber Valley Road. Turn left on Route 12/Jersey Street, left on Sanders Road and right on Route 68/West Road. Bear left on West Road at Coonrod Road, left on Route 66/Middle Road and left on Route 22 back to Willsboro. When you cycle along Mountain Road you will see a wollastonite mine. This filler and bonding agent is used in products like pottery, plywood, wallboard, porcelain and paints.

 The area around Reber was once popular for sheep. Some farmers spent several months exporting them to Australia by riding with the sheep on a train to California and then on by ship.

■ **Woman Suffrage Way** (30.8 miles) offers rolling to hilly terrain. Begin in Essex and head South on Route 9/Main Street, turn right on School Street, left on Route 66/Middle Road, right on Christian Road and right on Route 55/Whallons Bay Road. Cross Route 22 and continue on Route 55/Walker Road. Turn right on Power Road, left on Brookfield Road, left on Daniels Road, left on Mason Road, left on Hyde Road, left on Route 10/Lewis-Wadhams Road, and left on Alden Road. The French District School House stands on the corner of Alden and Lewis-Wadhams Road. Dating from 1850, it is like many one-room schoolhouses in Essex County. Turn left on Route 55/Walker Road, cross Route 22, continue on Route 55/Whallons Bay Road, and turn left on Christian Road. From the top of Christian Road there are nice views of Lake Champlain and the Vermont Green Mountains to the east, and Boquet valley and the Adirondacks to the west. Take a left on Route 66/Middle Road, right on School Street, and left on Route 9/Main Street to the Essex Ferry Dock.

The **Meadowmount School of Music**, in the area, was founded by Gregor Piatigorsky and Ivan Galamian of the Juilliard School of Music. Once it was home to John Milholland, whose daughter Inez was a socialist working for peace. She campaigned for underpaid workers, unjustly accused prisoners and suffrage for women. On inauguration day for Woodrow Wilson, Inez Milholland rode a white horse down Pennsylvania Avenue, followed by thousands of women. The suffragettes advocated a constitutional amendment to provide voting rights for women.

■ **Joe's Random Scoot** (38.1 miles) was named after Orson (Old Man) Phelps, called Joe, who used to take parties out bushwhacking in the 1850s. He laid out many of the Adirondack mountain trails. This bike trail is the longest loop, moving through farmlands and woodlands, as well as along the lake. Begin at Essex Ferry Dock and head north on Route 22, turn left on Catholic Church Road, right on Route 66/Middle Road, left on Route 68/West Road, right on West Road at Coonrod Road, left on Sanders Road, right on Route 57/Reber Valley Road, left on Route 14/Deerhead Road, left on Crowningshield Road, left on Moss Road, right on Route 12 and cross I-87. Turn left on Dixon/Redmond Road, right on Route Route 10/Lewis-Wadhams Road, left on Ray Woods Road, left on Route 9 and left on Steele Woods Road. Turn right on Route 10/Lewis Wadhams Road, left on Route 55/Walker Road, cross Route 22 and continue on Route 55/Whallons Bay Road and left on Route 9/Lake Shore Road to Essex Ferry Dock.

Lake Champlain - New York Side

DID YOU KNOW?

Begin There is an historical marker at Whallons Bay that details the demarcation line between the nations of the Iroquois and Algonquin Indians and the French and English. **Steele Woods Road** is the place where Boquet River log drivers used to skid logs by horse teams to the river and wait until spring for the flow.

■ **Coon Mountain Circuit** (18.5 miles) is a route that can combine biking and hiking. The trailhead to Coon Mountain is near the half-way point on Halds Road. Begin in **Essex** by heading south on Route 9/Main Street, then turn right on School Street, left on Route 66/Middle Road, right on Christian Road, right on Route 55/Whallons Bay Road, left on Route 22 and left on Merriam Forge Road. Then turn left on Halds Road, head up Coon Mountain, left on Route 9/Lakeshore Road and back to Essex Ferry Dock. The trail up Coon Mountain heads through wildflower ravines, hardwoods and pines to the top.

DID YOU KNOW?

On the west side of Merriam Forge Road is the house of Gaylord DuBois, who created the "Lone Ranger."

Webb Royce Swamp on the Coon Mountain Circuit is the largest hardwood swamp in the area and an important stopping place for waterfowl in the Lake Champlain Flyway.

■ Last in our list is the **Mountain-Coast Connector** (28 miles), which is rolling, with a few steep hills. Begin in Westport at Library Lawn, turn left on Camp Dudley Road, left on Route 9N/Route 22, right on Napper Road, right on Stevenson Road, left on Mountain Spring Road, right on Macmahon Road and left on Ledgehill Road, which turns into Megsville Road. Turn left on Route 9N and head into Elizabethtown. Turn right on Route 9, right on Route 8/Elizabethtown-Wadhams Road, right on Route 22, right on Sam Spear Road and left on Route 9N back to Westport.

■ On Water

Excursion Boats

In this area Lake Champlain is the favorite place for water activity. *Philomena D.*, Westport Marina, Washington Street, Westport NY, ☎ 800-626-0342. This vessel will take people on a tour of the lake, with narration on the former residents and past history. It is very well done.

Kayaking

If you'd like to get out on the water in a kayak, head for **High Peaks Touring** on Main Street in Westport, next to The Dock , ☎ 518-963-7028. Before you head out on your own you will be given a short explanation of the procedures, and they will be sure you know what to do.

Sightseeing

■ Plattsburgh

Walk into **City Hall** and look straight ahead to see a mural that depicts a plucky rooster standing on a cannon. Another mural in the hall shows both the land and sea engagements in the Battle of Plattsburgh. In the land battle, 13- and 14-year-old boys in the Militia were able to keep the British from advancing. The **Kent-Delord House** (see page 32), which was occupied by the British at the time of the battle, is seen in the distance.

THE ROOSTER OF PLATTSBURGH

Have you heard about the rooster who was involved in the Battle of Plattsburgh? On September 11, 1814, the British fleet rounded Cumberland Head from the north as the American fleet remained at anchor in the bay. Captain George Downie, on the *Confiance*, commanded the British fleet and Commodore Thomas Macdonough, on the *Saratoga*, commanded the Americans.

The British lobbed a shot that shattered a hencoop on the deck of the *Saratoga*; a gamecock inside was delighted to be freed. "He jumped up on a gun-slide, clapped his wings, and crowed lustily." The men on board laughed and cheered, Macdonough fired the first shot from one of the long guns and the battle was on. The rooster may have saved the day – he was seen as a good omen and became the mascot of the battle.

Battle of Plattsburgh Interpretive Center is in City Hall at 41 City Hall Place, ☎ 518-562-3534, www.battleofplattsburgh.com. Take the stairs to the left and head for the Battle of Plattsburgh Interpretive Center. In the center of the room a large diorama of the battle has buttons that you can push to light up parts of the action.

One of the most fascinating items in the room is a framed letter containing the "secret orders" that were discovered long after the battle. The British plan for North America was to keep Americans out of the way of the British moving southward from Canada. After the defeat of Napoleon the British had enough troops to reinforce their army in Canada. Governor General Sir George Prevost in Canada was sent the plan for North America by the Earl of Bathurst. It was marked secret until 1922 and refers to the burning of Washington and the raid on Baltimore as diversions to keep American attention away from the invasion from the North.

There's a model of the *Saratoga* in a glass case and prints depicting the battle on the walls. A model of the replica bateau named *Rooster*, similar to those discovered in Lake Champlain and Lake George and dating from the late 1700s, sits on a table. The full-size replica bateau can be seen on the Plattsburgh Air Force Base. A real bateau dating from 1787 to 1820 was found in Lake Champlain and brought up in 1999. It now sits in a tank at the Base.

The **Clinton County Historical Museum**, 48 Court Street, ☎ 518-561-0340, has exhibits of items dating back to 1600. The Battle of Plattsburgh in 1814 and the 1776 Battle of Valcour are featured. Collections include Redford glass, Staffordshire china, portraits and photographs. There is even a cigar store Indian. Local memorabilia includes snuff boxes, mourning jewelry from the Platt family, wedding slippers, knit silk stockings and a tortoiseshell hair comb worn by Sarah Addoms, a traveling "bonnet" trunk and walking sticks made from the salvaged timbers of the *Royal Savage*, which burned off Valcour Island during the Revoluationary War.

Valcour Island was the site of an important naval battle on October 11, 1776. The Americans were clearly outnumbered when the British gunboats sailed into Valcour Bay. They agreed to retreat to Crown Point, and Benedict Arnold managed to slip the American boats right through the British line by hugging the shore in a dense fog. He muffled his oars with clothing and headed south. The British commander was furious that they had escaped. Because the British thought he had gone north, at first in chasing the escaped fleet they headed in the wrong direction.

For a fine view of Valcour Island, you can have lunch at the Harborside Restaurant, which looks directly at the tower on the Island. A boat trip around the island provides narration on what happened there.

The **Kent-Delord House**, 17 Cumberland, ☎ 518-561-1035, is chock full of furniture and possessions belonging to the Delord family. Collections include Canton porcelain, Royal Crown Derby dinner service, Sandwich glass goblets and monogrammed silver. The house was in the possession of the family until a Delord granddaughter, Fanny, died in 1913.

Fanny married the Rev. Francis Bloodgood Hall in 1856. In his study there is a map laid out on a table indicating his love of the Adirondack wilderness and his hiking excursions there. This love of the wild was not shared by Fanny, who preferred entertaining guests in her home. She sent a letter to her husband in 1895:

"Your letter from the Episcopal Rectory at St. Hubert's [in the Adirondack high peaks area] has just been read and enjoyed. I am delighted that you are having a grand time. We jog along at our usual pace. I enjoy it here very much more than I should there. It is simply a mystery to me beyond my comprehension how any one can enjoy camping. Thine, Fannie Fair"

■ Willsboro

This area was settled by William Gilliland in 1765; settlers dammed the river and built a sawmill near the falls. British General Burgoyne camped with 7,000 men during the Revolutionary War and destroyed the town. Afterward, the Willsboro Iron Works became known for fabricating military anchors and parts for steam boats. After the forge closed in 1883 a paper pulp mill was built. Pollution from the forge and paper mill decimated the salmon in the river until the New York State Department of Environmental Conservation built a fishway at the falls to provide for spawning. There is a glass viewing window there.

DID YOU KNOW? The Phoenix Grist Mill was made of "blue" limestone from the quarry at Willsboro Point. The quarry also provided stone for the Brooklyn Bridge and the Capitol Building in Albany.

THE ADSIT LOG CABIN

On Willsboro Point, this cabin was probably constructed in the early 1790s. It was erected by one Samuel Adsit, who came to the area from Dutchess County, NY. Samuel and his wife Phebe came north to find land and cut out a life for themselves in the northern reaches of New York State, where large tracts of land were established for sale. The settled in the Town of Willsboro, then a relatively peaceful area in the aftermath of the Revolutionary War, and acquired a parcel of land along the west shore of Lake Champlain. It was here, high on a ridge overlooking the lake, that the couple built their first home. The small log cabin remains intact in its original setting to this day.

Heavy lime and sand chinking filled in the spaces between the logs to keep the weather out. The broad gable roof was covered with hand-hewn shakes laid over wide pine boards. A large fireplace in the south gable end of the building (not the original structure, but added) would have been ample to heat and use for the preparation of meals. The original fireplace outline can be seen in the floor and would have been made of brick or local stone.

The building was passed through generations of the Adsit family until 1906 when Mrs. Mary Adsit Fowler left to live in Burlington, VT. The cabin sat empty for many years until in 1927 the farm was purchased by Dr. Earl Van DerWerker to build a "summer camp." Dr. Van DerWerker was in the process of having what had become a group of "old shacks" torn down when the original cabin was discovered. Amazingly many of the farming implements and interior finishes were still intact. The Doctor initiated a restoration that has continued to this day.

In 1942, the property was sold to John Kiehl of Burlington. Soon afterward, Mr. Kiehl opened the cabin to the public. After being passed to family members, today the cabin is undergoing stabilization and preservation by the town, and is open to the public during the summer months.

The Adsit Cabin is reputed to be one of the oldest surviving log cabins in its original location in the United States and is listed in the National Register of Historic Places.

For more information, whs@willsborony.com, visit the website at www.willsborony.com/adsitcabin, or ☎ 518-963-4598. It's suggested that you call for an appointment.

■ Essex

The whole village of Essex, New York is on the National Register of Historic Places. Homes were built in a variety of styles – Federal, Greek Revival, Carpenter Gothic, Italianate and French Second Empire. During the War of 1812, Essex was noted for shipbuilding, with 250 bateaux and two sloops, the *Growler* and the *Eagle*, created for the American effort. Commodore Thomas MacDonough used them in his fleet in the War of 1812.

■ Westport

Today the town of Westport is a popular, yet quiet, place to vacation. William Gilliland was granted 2,300 acres in 1764, which he called Bessboro, for his daughter. Edward Raymond, one of the colonists, built a home in

1770, then a sawmill and a gristmill. His mill produced timber for Benedict Arnold's boats.

Commerce increased when ferries began running from Rock Harbor to Basin Harbor and from Barber's Point to Arnold's Bay in 1790. Although Westport was destroyed during the Revolutionary War, it was rebuilt in 1804. In 1808, the second steam-powered vessel in the world was launched on Lake Champlain. Two blast furnaces were active until they closed around 1855 and Westport changed into a resort area. Nearby Elizabethtown also had mills and forges until the mid-1800s; it is now a summer arts colony. Things really moved along after the Hudson Canal was finished in 1823, connecting Westport to Albany and New York City. In 1876, the Delaware and Hudson Railroad came to town, reducing some of the need for water transportation and allowing an increase in summer visitors.

Vacation for many people means water activity – or shoreside inactivity. You can enjoy just looking at mountains across the lake, watching sailboats tacking back and forth and relaxing on the shore. Or you can take out a kayak, canoe, sailboat or a powerboat yourself. Tours are also available on the *Philomena D.* from Westport Marina (see page 31).

The Westport dock area once provided a nightly berth for the old *Ticonderoga*, from 1906 to 1924. She carried freight and passengers from Plattsburgh to Burlington and Westport, with more stops to the south. After she docked briefly at Basin Harbor, she steamed around North Point at 6 pm every evening. Today she rests in the Shelburne Museum in Shelburne, Vermont (see page 31).

▪ Crown Point

In 1731, France maintained a force of 30 men at Crown Point. By 1734 they had begun to build Fort St. Frederic, which became the first fortification in the Champlain Valley. French patrols from the fort attacked Deerfield, Massachusetts and Fort Number Four (now Charlestown, New Hampshire) in 1746. In 1757 General Montcalm's men headed south to attack Fort William Henry on Lake George.

However, the British, who also claimed Crown Point, tried to take it between 1755 and 1758 and finally did so in 1759. They began to build "His Majesty's Fort of Crown Point," along with a series of blockhouses. With all of this strength, they proceeded to attack Montreal, the last bastion of the French. Lake Champlain became a link between Albany and Montreal, with active maneuvers up and down the lake. British settlers moved into the Champlain Valley and used Crown Point as a place to trade. The Americans also favored Crown Point and captured the British garrison in 1775.

Lake Champlain – New York Side

The Crown Point Visitor Center, ☎ 518-597-3666, has a model of Fort St. Frederic as it was in 1752 and collections of artifacts displayed in glass cases. You can see shards of Delft, Italianware, earthenware and part of a French faience wall font. There's a Perrier gun that was taken from the ruins. A British light 12-pounder dates from 1748.

DID YOU KNOW?

Madame de Lusignan, the wife of the French commanding officer of Fort Frederic, was a very forceful lady. She bought goods, paid for them with brandy, and insisted that no one else be allowed to sell within the fort. Her monopoly finally came to an end but presumably not without a fight.

There's a slide show with musical narration so you can understand the events that took place in this crucial military region. A map lights up as each area is discussed.

Take a walk outside and climb up to the bastions for a wonderful view of the lake as well as the fort. You can walk through the barracks where men slept with up to 18 in a room.

The **Champlain Memorial Lighthouse**, ☎ 518-298-8620, stands just south of the Champlain Bridge. It is a memorial to Samuel de Champlain, who took two of his men and left with Algonquian-speaking Native Americans to head up Lake Champlain from the St. Lawrence River area. They engaged in battle, probably near the lighthouse site, were victorious, and Champlain named the lake for himself.

On the lighthouse site a windmill stood in 1737, but the French blew it up in 1759, along with the fort. Next, the site was chosen by the British for one of the outer forts, the Grenadier Redoubt, and part of that redoubt remains today.

Penfield Homestead Museum, Ironville Road, Crown Point NY, ☎ 518-597-3804. The Penfield Homestead, part of the Ironville Historic District, was built in the Federal style and was occupied by three generations of the Penfield family. Original Penfield furnishings are in the house, along with pieces from other homes in the area.

The museum also displays items used locally in daily life in the 19th century. You'll see spinning wheels used for flax and wool. There's a replica of a large electromagnet that is now in the Smithsonian Museum. Allen Penfield bought one from Professor Joseph Henry, who conducted experiments with electric current at the Albany Academy in the late 1820s. Penfield used the magnet in the ironworks.

Where to Stay

ACCOMMODATIONS PRICE SCALE	
Prices for a double room for one or two persons, before taxes.	
$	Under $50
$$.	$50 to $100
$$$	$101 to $175
$$$$	Over $175

■ Plattsburgh

The Inn at Smithfield is a new residence right in town. 446 Route 3, Plattsburg, NY 12901, ☎ 800-243-4656 or 518-561-7750, fax 518-561-9431. $$-$$$.

Point Au Roche Lodge is next to the State Park of the same name. Some rooms have jacuzzis and fireplaces. 463 Point Au Roche Road, Plattsburgh, NY 12901, ☎ 518-563-8714, fax 518-563-6310. $$-$$$.

■ Westport

All Tucked Inn is a charming inn with a comfortable common room. 53 South Main Street, Westport, NY 12993, ☎ 888-ALL-TUCK or 518-962-4400. $$-$$$.

The Inn on the Library Lawn overlooks the lake through its handsome bay window. One Washington Street, Westport, NY 12993, ☎ 888-577-7748 or 518-962-8666. $$-$$$.

The Victorian Lady is filled with collections belonging to the owners and their families. 57 South Main Street, Westport, NY 12993, ☎ 518-962-2345. $$-$$$.

Westport Hotel has stenciled walls and a great restaurant. The hotel overlooks the Northwest Bay of Lake Champlain and the Green Mountains of Vermont. 114 Pleasant Street, Westport, NY 12993, ☎ 518-962-4501. $$.

■ Camping

Barber Homestead RV Park, Barber Road, Westport, NY 12993, ☎ 518-962-8989. 40 sites, fireplace/table, laundry facility.

Lake Champlain - New York Side

Carpenter's Campground, Point Au Roche State Park, Plattsburgh, NY 12901, ☎ 518-563-4365. 50 sites, fireplace/table.

Cumberland Bay State Park, 152 Cumberland Road, Plattsburgh, NY 12901, ☎ 518-563-5240. 200 sites, table, hot showers.

Plattsburgh RV Park, 56 Plattsburgh RV Park Road, Plattsburgh, NY 12901, ☎ 518-563-3915. 200 sites, fireplace/table, playground, laundry facility.

Shady Oaks RV Park, 70 Moffitt Road, Plattsburgh, NY 12901, ☎ 518-562-0561. 103 sites, fireplace/table, playground, laundry facility.

Snug Harbor, 3962 Route 9, Plattsburgh, NY 12901, ☎ 518-563-5140. 21 sites, table, laundry facility.

Where to Eat

DINING PRICE SCALE
Prices include an entrée, which may come with vegetables and salad, but exclude beverage, taxes and tip.
$ . . . . Under $10
$$ . . . . $10 to $20
$$$. . . . . $21 to $50
$$$$. . . . . Over $50

▪ Plattsburgh

Anthony's Restaurant & Bistro serves Continental-American cuisine. Route 3, Plattsburgh, ☎ 518-561-6420. $$.

Butcher Block offers seafood, pasta, vegetarian dishes, chicken and pork. 15 Booth Drive, Plattsburgh, ☎ 518-563-0920. $$.

Café Mooney Bay offers a varied menu. 15 Mooney Bay Drive, Plattsburgh, ☎ 518-561-0140. $-$$.

Harborside Restaurant has great crab cakes and other seafood. 4016 Route 9, Plattsburgh, ☎ 518-562-2580. $$.

Lindsey's Restaurant in The Inn at Smithfield (see *Where to Stay*, above) has themed specials for both food and drinks. Lindsey's Café offers specialty coffee, espresso, cappuccino and tea, ☎ 518-561-7750. $$.

■ Westport

The Galley at Westport Marina. Dine right on the lake outside, or inside. Saturday night barbecues are popular. Washington Street, Westport, NY, ☎ 518-962-4899. $$.

The Westport Hotel offers gourmet cuisine. This historic inn has a varied menu served inside or open-air. Pleasant Street, Westport, ☎ 518-962-4501. $$-$$$.

Westport Yacht Club is on the water in Westport. It is open to the public and offers casual dining. It is open during the summer season for lunch and dinner., ☎ 518-962-8777. $$.

Lake Champlain - New York Side

Green Mountains

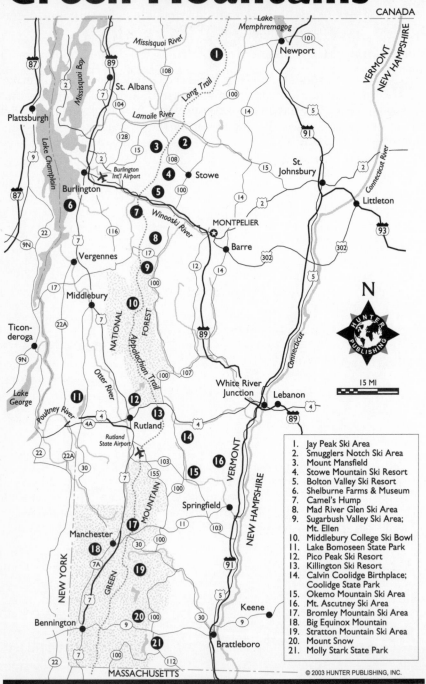

CANADA

Lake Memphremagog

Missisquoi River

Newport ⑩⑪

1

Long Trail

100

St. Albans

Lamoille River

Plattsburgh

Missisquoi Bay

Lake Champlain

Burlington Int'l Airport

Burlington

6

3 **2**

108

4 Stowe

5

100

Winooski River

7

MONTPELIER

8

Barre

9

100

Middlebury

10

NATIONAL   FOREST

Appalachian Trail

Otter River

Ticonderoga

Lake George

Poultney River

11

12

13 Rutland

Rutland State Airport

14

16

15

Springfield

GREEN   MOUNTAIN

Manchester

17

18

19

20

21

Bennington

Brattleboro

Keene

St. Johnsbury

Littleton

Connecticut River

White River Junction

Lebanon

VERMONT

NEW HAMPSHIRE

NEW YORK

MASSACHUSETTS

N

HUNTER PUBLISHING

15 MI

1.   Jay Peak Ski Area
2.   Smugglers Notch Ski Area
3.   Mount Mansfield
4.   Stowe Mountain Ski Resort
5.   Bolton Valley Ski Resort
6.   Shelburne Farms & Museum
7.   Camel's Hump
8.   Mad River Glen Ski Area
9.   Sugarbush Valley Ski Area;
      Mt. Ellen
10. Middlebury College Ski Bowl
11. Lake Bomoseen State Park
12. Pico Peak Ski Resort
13. Killington Ski Resort
14. Calvin Coolidge Birthplace;
      Coolidge State Park
15. Okemo Mountain Ski Area
16. Mt. Ascutney Ski Area
17. Bromley Mountain Ski Area
18. Big Equinox Mountain
19. Stratton Mountain Ski Area
20. Mount Snow
21. Molly Stark State Park

© 2003 HUNTER PUBLISHING, INC.

Green Mountains of Vermont

With the Adirondacks in New York, the Green Mountains of Vermont form the outer boundaries of the broad Champlain basin. They may be the remains of the oldest mountain range in New England, dating back 440 million years. Over time they have eroded along a north-south axis, smoothing out into a "peneplain" or flat plain without valleys and peaks. However, there are some isolated monadnocks left that did not disappear.

Monadnock is a geological term for a residual mountain, often isolated, that survives erosion. Mt. Monadnock has a rounded, rocky top reached by a relatively easy climb. Because the surrounding hills are much lower on the peneplain, the fine views from the summit (3,165 feet) are not blocked by adjoining mountains.

The Green Mountains are higher in the north than in the south; they include **Mount Mansfield**, **Mount Ellen**, **Camel's Hump** and **Mount Killington**. The Green Mountain National Forest became a reality in 1932 when President Hoover signed a Proclamation Boundary to establish it. Skiers and hikers flock to these mountains to enjoy a string of ski areas, and to hike sections of major paths like the Appalachian Trail and Long Trail.

A WORD TO
THE WISE

The main trails are marked with white blazes. Look for blue blazes on secondary trails. Hikers will find overnight shelters spaced along both the Long Trail and the Appalachian Trail. There are cabins in some places, lean-tos in others.

The **Long Trail** is a 270-mile path on the crest of the Green Mountains – the backbone of Vermont. It extends from the Canadian border to the Massachusetts state line and is maintained by the Green Mountain Club. The lowest elevation is 200 feet in southern Vermont and the highest is 4,393 feet at the summit of Mount Mansfield near Stowe. The trail crosses three arctic-alpine zones, four federal wilderness areas, a national forest and eight ski areas.

Getting Here & Getting Around

■ By Air

Burlington International Airport. . . . . ☎ 802-863-2874

Albany International Airport . . . . ☎ 518-869-9611

■ By Car

Interstate 89 is the preferred route from the south with crossovers leading to each destination that are slower but often scenic. **Route 7** or **Route 100** are also suggested on a north/south line.

 Winter driving in Vermont can be arduous in bad conditions. We always pack a winter box in the trunk of the car, containing extra clothing and boots, a shovel, sand or kitty litter, a coffee can with candle and matches inside, blanket, a few snacks in case you're snowed in on the highway, flashlights, and perhaps a cell phone. Be sure to put snow tires on in late fall.

■ By Bus

Greyhound Lines. . . . . ☎ 800-231-2222

Vermont Transit . . . . ☎ 800-451-3292

■ By Train

Amtrak. . . . . ☎ 800-872-7245
Call for information on a connection with bus service from Rutland to Killington.

Green Mountain Railroad . . . . ☎ 800-707-3530
Seasonal only.

Information Sources

Vermont Chamber of Commerce, PO Box 37, Montpelier, VT 05601, ☎ 802-223-3443, fax 802-223-4257, www.vtchamber.com, skruthers@vtchamber.com.

Vermont Department of Tourism, 134 State Street, Montpelier, VT 05602, ☎ 800-VERMONT or 802-828-3237. Public Information Coordinator: ☎ 802-828-3683, fax 802-828-3233, www.1-800-VERMONT.com, dkonrady@dca.state.vt.us.

Vermont State Park, 103 South Main Street, 10 South, Waterbury, VT 05671, ☎ 802-241-3651, fax 802-244-1481, www.vtstateparks.com.

Adventures

■ On Foot

Hiking Trails

Of the 700 miles of hiking trails in Vermont, 512 miles are on State and National Forest Lands. The rest are on private property. When hiking on mountain tops, be careful to stay on the trail and not trample fragile alpine vegetation. During "mud season," usually from the time of snow melt until around Memorial Day, hikers are asked to stay off the trails.

TRAILS ON STATE LANDS

- **Bomoseen State Park**, Castleton, ☎ 802-265-4242. Five trails offer seven miles of hiking and walking. Trails are easy to moderate with some wet places.

- **Calvin Coolidge State Park**, Plymouth, ☎ 802-672-3612. Four trails totaling 15 miles range from moderate to difficult. There are trails up **Killington** and **Shrewsbury** peaks, as well as access to the Appalachian and Long Trails.

- **Camp Plymouth State Park**, Plymouth, ☎ 802-228-2025. The Echo Lake Vista Trail is 1.5 miles long and travels up a dif-

ficult 340-foot pitch. Gold panning is popular at Buffalo Brook
and there's a view of Echo Lake.

- **Gifford Woods State Park**, Sherburne, ☎ 802-775-5354. The
  Kent Brook Trail is easy at 0.5 miles long. The Appalachian
  Trail goes through this park and connects near here to the Long
  Trail.

- **Groton State Forest**, Groton. Seventeen miles of trails, ranging from easy to difficult, include nature trail loops and trails to
  most of the major mountains in the forest. The Cross-Vermont
  Trail is being developed on the old Montpelier-Wells River Railroad bed.

- **Molly Stark State Park**, Wilmington, ☎ 802-464-5460. There
  are two miles of trails in the park. One of them, to the summit of
  Mount Olga, is difficult.

Vermont developed the first public hiking trail in 1825 near Windsor on
Mount Ascutney. In fact, an annual summer picnic had drawn Wind-
sorites up the mountain since the turn of the 19th century, and sometimes
they even had a brass band up there. The Green Mountain Club was created in 1910 and the Long Trail was finished in 1931. It is the oldest long-
distance hiking trail in the country. Now the Long Trail meets the Appalachian Trail at the Massachusetts border and continues up to Sherburne.
This trail goes up and over the highest peaks in Vermont, over 40 of them
more than 3,000 feet high. There are 70 shelters along the way.

Sterling Mountain Summit Hike. The Long Trail can be accessed from
Route 108 South at the Smugglers' Notch Pass parking lot. Look for two-
by-six-inch white blazes on trees and sometimes on rocks. Sterling Pond
is on the summit, and it is the highest trout pond in the state. You will
need a valid Vermont fishing license to fish there (see page 51). The elevation is 3,010 feet and the distance is 2.7 miles to the top, usually taking
about three hours of climbing. You can continue along the ridge on the
Long Trail up to the 3,540-foot elevation to reach **Madonna Mountain**,
the highest peak in the Smugglers' Notch Resort. The trail is challenging,
with lots of ascents and descents.

Stowe Summit Hike. Drive Route 100 into Stowe and turn east onto
School Street; bear right onto Stowe Hollow Road, continuing onto Upper
Hollow Road until you find Pinnacle Road. Head through an apple
orchard and into the forest. Hardwoods illuminate the trail in the fall
with brilliant colors. You can see the summit on a side trail to the left.
Eventually you will see a sign for Skyline Trail to the left and Pinnacle
Trail to the right.

TRAIL INFORMATION

- **Appalachian Trail Conference**, PO Box 807, Harpers Ferry, WV 25425, ☎ 304-535-6331.

- **Green Mountain Club, Inc.**, Route 100, Waterbury Center, VT 05677, ☎ 802-244-7037.

- **Backcountry Publications, Inc.**, PO Box 175, Woodstock, VT 05091, ☎ 802-457-1049.

- **Huntington Graphics**, PO Box 163, Huntington, VT 05462, ☎ 802-434-4330.

- **USDA Forest Service**, Green Mountain National Forest, PO Box 519, Rutland, VT 05702, ☎ 802-773-0300 or 0324.

Hiking Tours & Contacts

You can head out on your own for a day of hiking or join a group and leave the planning to someone else. Some tours have scheduled overnights in local inns. Others are based in resorts and you can get information and hike as long as you like. Call the numbers below for specific information.

1860 House B&B Inn, Stowe, ☎ 800-248-1860. This inn offers maps and suggestions so individuals can hike on their own.

Adventure Guides of VT, Statewide, ☎ 800-425-7747. This group offers organized trips.

American Expeditions, Burlington, ☎ 802-864-7600.

Back of Beyond Expeditions, Statewide, ☎ 800-841-3354 or 802-860-9500.

Balloon Inn Vermont Vacations, Fairlee, ☎ 800-666-1946 or 802-333-4326. Silver Maple Lodge offers self-guided hiking under this name.

Bike Vermont offers hikes in a variety of areas. Ask about their multi-adventure tours which include a day of cycling, a day of hiking and a day of kayaking, ☎ 800-257-2226 or 802-457-3553.

Catamount Family Center, Williston, ☎ 802-879-6001. This center offers individual walking and hiking on their 500 acres.

Country Inns Along the Trail, Brandon, ☎ 800-838-3301.

Country Walkers, Waterbury, ☎ 800-464-9253 or 802-244-1387.

Craftsbury Outdoor Center, Craftsbury, ☎ 800-729-7751. Craftsbury Outdoor Center offers hiking as well as cross-country skiing on trails.

Four Seasons Touring, Townshend, ☎ 802-365-7937. Four Seasons offers cross-country skiing, snowshoeing, hiking and a personally designed tour for you.

Green Mountain Expeditions, Wilmington, ☎ 802-368-7147. Green Mountain Expeditions offers hiking on their trails, guided llama treks in summer (they carry the lunch, not people) and snowshoe rentals in winter.

Middlebury Mountaineer & Green Mountain Adventure, Middlebury, ☎ 802-388-1749. Green Mountain Adventure offers hiking, fly fishing, kayaking and snowshoeing.

Mount Snow Hiking Center, Mount Snow, ☎ 802-464-3333.

North Wind Touring, Waitsfield, ☎ 800-496-5771. North Wind Touring offers organized walking and hiking holidays.

Northern Vermont Llama Co., Smugglers' Notch, ☎ 802-644-2257.

Outdoor Experience, Inc., Williston, ☎ 802-879-6001.

Quechee Outdoor Adventures, Quechee, ☎ 800-438-5565. This group offers organized and individual walking and hiking.

Stratton Mountain Resort, Stratton Mountain, ☎ 800-STRATTON or 802-297-2200. Stratton allows individuals to walk or hike on their ski trails in summer. You can also ride the gondola up.

Sugarbush Cycling & Hiking Center, Warren, ☎ 802-583-6572. You can access the ski trails through state forest. The Long Trail crosses the area. You can also ride the gondola.

Technica Hiking Center, Killington, ☎ 8802-422-6708 or 3333. You can ride the gondola up on this hiking excursion.

Umiak Outdoor Outfitters, Stowe, ☎ 802-253-2317.

Walking Tours of Southern Vermont, Arlington, ☎ 802-375-1141.

Walking-Inn-Vermont, Ludlow, ☎ 802-228-8799.

White River Valley Trails Association, Randolph Center, ☎ 802-728-4100.

Wild Heart Journeys of Discovery, North Pomfret, ☎ 888-890-WILD or 802-457-9367.

Wilderness Trails, Quechee, ☎ 802-295-7620. Wilderness Trails is located at the Quechee Inn at Marshland (☎ 800-235-3133 or 802-295-3133). They offer hiking, snowshoeing, fly fishing, biking, canoeing and kayaking.

Wildwaters Outfitters, Brattleboro, ☎ 802-254-4133.

■ On Wheels

Scenic Drives

 Brandon to Proctor. Head south from Brandon on Route 7 and you will come across five historic covered bridges on the Otter Creek. Take Route 3 south in Pittsford towards Proctor, where there is a marble exhibit and also Wilson Castle to visit. You can then head west on Route 4A, north on Route 30 and east on Route 73 back to Brandon.

Middlebury to Ripton. Route 125 goes east from Middlebury along a brook to the hamlet of Ripton. Middlebury College's Breadloaf Campus is near the Robert Frost Wayside Memorial. You can take a gravel road to Lincoln, then Route 17 to Bristol and Route 116 back to Middlebury.

Mount Equinox. From Manchester, drive south on Route 7A to reach one of the most spectacular routes in Vermont. Before starting the climb up Mount Equinox to Big Equinox, be sure that you have enough gas, and be prepared to pull over and let your car rest if it seems to be laboring or overheating.

 DID YOU KNOW?

Big Equinox is the peak at the top of that spectacular drive (3,816 feet); you pass Little Equinox (3,315 feet) along the way. Like many Vermont mountains, Equinox is a complex rather than a single peak.

The view on the way up, as well as down, is stunning. The road is steep in some places and there are hairpin turns, but for us it was not a white-knuckle drive like the one up the Mount Washington Toll Road in New Hampshire. When you reach the summit, park and walk around to survey the view in all directions – into New York and Massachusetts as well as Vermont. From just south of our home on Lake George, we see the west face of Equinox quite clearly and can still visualize this drive up the other side of the mountain. The road is open from May to October, but telephone first for the latest weather report – there's no point in going up into fog or clouds. ☎ 802-362-1405.

Bicycling

Stowe Recreation Path

 A favorite tour of ours begins in Stowe on the Stowe Recreation Path. It is 5.3 miles. The paved path is open to walkers and runners, rollerbladers, bicyclers and baby carriages. The access is behind the Stowe Community Church, off of Luce Hill Road. You will have views of Mount Mansfield and the West Branch River.

Smugglers' Notch

During the War of 1812 Americans smuggled cattle and other supplies into Canada through Smugglers' Notch, Route 108. It is closed in winter except to cross-country skiers. During the summer you can drive or cycle through; in fact, the Stowe Bicycle Race draws cyclists who enjoy the 50-mile course. Cliffs rise 1,000 feet on both sides of the road and ice-age plants thrive up there.

 Pick up a copy of the *Long Trail Guide* by the Green Mountain Club, Route 100, Waterbury Center, VT 05677, ☎ 802-244-7037, for more information.

Sugarbush Valley

This valley is pretty, with sugar maple trees, winding roads and ski trails. You can begin this tour on Route 100 just north of the junction with Route 17. Make a right turn onto Bridge Street, which begins at the Waitsfield Town Library. Cross the Big Eddy covered bridge, which dates from 1833. It spans the Mad River. The road continues on East Warren Road and heads uphill in a steady climb. When you reach a fork, continue uphill on East Warren Road. You will see the Joslin round barn, which dates from 1910. The **Inn at the Round Barn Farm** is listed in our accommodation section (see page 63). Next you will come to the **Kristal Art Gallery and Sculpture Garden**. It offers both American and European works of art. Get ready to head downhill on Common Road and follow signs into Warren, where you can make the choice to head north on Route 100 back to your starting point or go across Route 100 onto West Hill Road.

The second alternative provides a longer trip, with a challenging ride uphill and then an exhilarating downhill shoot. From West Hill Road, take Golf Course Road, then Sugarbush Access Road and German Flats Road. Turn right onto Route 17 and head downhill. Turn left on Route 100 and ride back to your starting point.

BICYCLE TOURS

- **Adventure Guides of Vermont**, ☎ 800-425-8747. They provides travel planning assistance in 70+ activities statewide.

- **Bicycle Holidays**, ☎ 800-292-5388. This is the national center for bicycling.

- **Bike Vermont**, ☎ 800-257-2226 or 802-457-3553. Bike Vermont runs cycling trips in Vermont, Ireland and Scotland. Kayaking is also offered on Lake Champlain, Kingsland Bay or Caspain Lake, along the Battenkill, Connecticut or Winooski Rivers. They lead hiking trips in a number of areas as well.

- **POMG Bike Tours of Vermont**, ☎ 802-434-2270. POMG offers vehicle-supported luxury camping and B&B bicycle tours.

- **Vermont Bicycle Touring**, ☎ 800-245-3868. This group offers organized vacations throughout North America, Europe and New Zealand.

■ On Water

Canoeing & Kayaking

Vermont has 333 square miles of water surface to play in and on. You can row, canoe, kayak, scull, motor, water ski, tube, sail or cruise. Lakes **Champlain** and **Memphremagog** are popular for kayaking. The **Green River Reservoir**, near Morrisville, is a favorite with canoeists. Both the **Mad River** and the **West River** are used for recreational and competitive kayaking and canoeing. **Otter Creek** and the **Lamoille**, **Missisquoi** and **Winooski** Rivers are nice for canoeing. Tubing is popular on the **White River** and **Wells River**.

- **Adventure Guides of VT**, Statewide, ☎ 800-425-8747. They offer organized or individual canoeing and kayaking.

- **Back of Beyond Expeditions**, Burlington, ☎ 800-841-3354.

- **Balloon Inn Vermont Vacations**, Fairlee, ☎ 800-666-1946 or 802-333-4326. Silver Maple Lodge will help you plan self-guided water experiences.

- **Battenkill Canoe Ltd.**, Arlington, ☎ 800-421-5268 or 802-362-2800. They have day-trip canoe rentals and two- to 12-day trips with stays in inns.

- **Clearwater Sports**, Waitsfield, ☎ 802-496-2708. All sorts of canoeing and kayaking; organized or individual trips as well as rentals.

- **Craftsbury Outdoor Center**, Craftsbury, ☎ 800-729-7751. Canoeing, kayaking and sculling.

- **East Burke Sports**, East Burke, ☎ 802-626-3215.

- **Green Mountain Flagship**, Wilmington, ☎ 802-464-2975. Both canoe and kayaking trips are offered on the Harriman Reservoir.

- **PaddleWays**, Burlington, ☎ 802-660-8606.

- **Pine Ridge Adventure Center**, Williston, ☎ 802-434-5294.

- **Quechee Outdoor Adventures**, Quechee, ☎ 800-438-5565.

- **Raven Ridge**, Richford, ☎ 802-933-4616. Offers both canoeing and kayaking.

- **Reel Vermont**, Calais, ☎ 802-223-1869. Canoeing, kayaking and fishing on lakes and ponds.

- **Smugglers' Notch Canoe Touring**, Cambridge, ☎ 888-937-6266 or 802-644-8321.

- **Stratton Mountain Resort**, Stratton Mountain, ☎ 800-STRATTON or 802-297-2200.

- **Trailside Shop at Burke Mountain**, East Burke, ☎ 802-626-3944.

- **Umiak Outdoor Outfitters**, Stowe, ☎ 802-253-2317.

- **VT Touring Center**, Brattleboro, ☎ 802-257-5008.

- **Wilderness Trails at Quechee Inn at Marshland**, Quechee, ☎ 802-295-7620. Canoeing and kayaking are offered, along with fly fishing, biking and hiking.

- **Wildwater Outfitters**, Brattleboro, ☎ 802-254-4133.

Fishing

 The grandfather of fishing is the **Orvis Company** in Manchester Center, VT. Fishermen order from their mail-order catalog and look for an opportunity to visit the original store or one of its branches. You can also sign up for a fly-fishing course, perhaps on the Battenkill River or elsewhere. Head up the hill on Route 7A from Manchester Center (all of the factory outlet stores are down there), and before you reach The Equinox in Manchester Village, look on the left side for the brand new Orvis store. To order merchandise, ☎ 888-235-9763.

Vermont is known for its "cold-water" fishing in streams that come down the mountains and feed lakes and ponds. Cold-water fish include brook trout, lake trout, rainbow smelt and landlocked salmon. Lakes **Seymour**, **Willoughby** and **Caspian** are famous for trout and salmon. Rivers include the **Battenkill**, **Mettawee**, **White**, **Dog**, and **Upper Connecticut**.

"Warm-water" fish include largemouth and smallmouth bass, walleye, northern pike, muskellunge, chain pickerel, shad, yellow perch, white perch, black crappie, rock bass, sunfish, bullhead, bowfin, sheepshead, turbot, cisco, whitefish, sauger and channel catfish.

When you plan a fishing trip, contact the **Vermont Fish & Wildlife Department**, 103 South Main Street, Waterbury, VT 05671, ☎ 802-241-3700, www.anr.state.vt.us/fw/fwhome. Ask for a "Vermont Fishing Kit." You will also need a fishing license ($20 for residents; $38, non-residents).

■ On Horseback

 Most of the riding facilities listed below are not open in winter; some are, weather permitting. They all offer guided trail rides and most use Western saddles.

Riding Stables

- **Pond Hill Ranch**, Castleton, ☎ 802-468-2449. Offers lessons and guided trail rides in summer, Western saddle.

- **Cavendish Trail Horse Rides**, Cavendish, ☎ 802-226-7821.

- **West River Stables**, Newfane, ☎ 802-365-7668.

- **Kedron Valley Stables**, South Woodstock, ☎ 802-457-1480.

- **Edson Hill Riding Stables**, Stowe, ☎ 802-253-8954. Guided trail rides in summer, Western saddle. A 55-minute trail ride costs $35 at current prices.

- **Topnotch at Stowe**, ☎ 802-253-8585. Lessons and guided trail rides in summer, both English and Western saddles. Current prices for a one-hour ride are $30. They are offered by appointment only.

- **Stratton Mountain Resort**, Stratton Mountain, ☎ 802-297-2200.

- **Sunbowl Ranch**, Stratton, ☎ 802-293-5837. Lessons, guided trail rides, picnics and overnight rides. Current prices are $27 for one hour, $50 for two hours and $55 for a 1¾-hour picnic ride.

- **Mad Mountain Ranch**, Waitsfield, ☎ 802-496-5396.

- **VT Icelandic Horse Farm**, Waitsfield, ☎ 802-496-7141. Guided trail rides year-round, depending on weather. English saddles are used on the Icelandic horses. Current prices (per person, any age) are $40 for one hour, $60 for two hours and $80 for three hours.

- **Flames Stables**, Wilmington, ☎ 802-464-8329.

- **Mountain View Stables**, Wilmington, ☎ 802-464-0615.

■ On Snow

 Winter sports are thriving in Vermont and downhill skiing attracts visitors all winter long. Many people enjoy both downhill and cross-country skiing, as well as skating and snowshoeing. You can have it all in Vermont.

Downhill Skiing

Many of the major ski areas in the Northeast are spread along the spine of Vermont, which is the eastern boundary of the Champlain Valley. Because some are quite sensibly located where snow piles up on the leeward or eastern side of that spine – technically outside the Champlain watershed – we fudge a bit and include them anyway. Who would not want to go to Stowe or Killington just because these signature areas are geographically located on the "wrong" side of the mountain? However, the following list does not include many fine Vermont ski areas located farther east in the Connecticut River watershed.

 Phone number key: I=information, S=snow conditions, R=reservations and F=fax.

- **Bolton Valley Resort**, Bolton, VT 05477. I=☎ 802-434-3444, S=802-434-7669, R=800-877-9BOLTON, F=802-434-2131, www.boltonvalleyvt.com. Bolton Valley has a vertical drop of 1,625 feet, with 51 trails served by six lifts. The resort is a bit off the beaten path, offering a mountain-top village as the center for both Alpine and Nordic skiing, with the highest base elevation in the East. Founded by the Deslauries family in 1966, it closed in 1987 and two years later was purchased by a group that began extensive renovations. More than 300 inches of average annual snowfall support Alpine trails that are nicely balanced to serve all levels of skiing ability and a cross-country network of 100 km.

∎ **Bromley Mountain Resort**, PO Box 1130, Manchester Center, VT 05255. I=☎ 802-824-5522, S=802-824-5522, R=800-865-4786, F=802-824-3659, www.bromley.com. Bromley has a vertical drop of 1,334 feet, with 35 trails served by nine lifts. They started in the 1930s with a collection of rope tows that had been used on other ski hills, but soon evolved into one of Vermont's earliest major ski resorts – and the only one facing dead south. That distinction worked against Bromley before the advent of snowmaking, but the resort is now valued for its warmth on cold winter days. It is also rated highly for family skiing and has an even distribution of greens, blues and blacks to suit every age and level of skill, with the added advantage that all trails ultimately feed into a single, relatively compact base area.

∎ **Jay Peak Resort**, PO Box 152, Jay, VT 05859. I=☎ 802-988-2611, S=802-988-9601, R=800-451-4449, F=802-988-4049, www.jaypeakresort.com. Jay Peak has a vertical drop of 2,153 feet, and 74 trails served by seven lifts. Near the Canadian border, it gets an average annual snowfall of 351 inches – the greatest amount in the East and more than prime Colorado ski areas like Vail and Steamboat. Originally developed by the Weyerhauser Corporation, it has a dramatic Alpine-looking summit approached by a 60-passenger aerial tram. It has a wide variety of single black trails spread over all three faces of the mountain complex, and is especially noted for extensive glade skiing. But there are enough blue trails to satisfy intermediates and a green area on the lower mountain.

∎ **Killington/Pico**, Killington Road, Killington, VT 05751. I= ☎ 802-422-3333, S=802-422-3261, R=800-621-6867, F=802-422-4391, www.killington.com. The complex has five entrances. Route 4 on the west side of Sherburne Pass for Pico; Killington Road off Route 4 on the east side of the pass for the center of the complex; Route 4 north of West Bridgewater for both the Skyeship Base Station and Bear Mountain Road; and Route 100 just south of West Bridgewater for Sunrise Mountain. Killington/Pico has a vertical drop of 3,150 feet, with 200 trails on seven mountains served by 32 lifts. By far the largest ski area complex in Vermont and the entire East, it is now spread over seven mountains – Killington Peak (4,241 feet), Snowdon Mountain (3,592 feet), Rams Head Mountain (3,610 feet), Skye Peak (3,800 feet), Bear Mountain (3,296 feet), Sunrise Mountain (2,456 feet) and Pico Peak (3,967 feet). Only the last, Pico, is not yet connected to the others via an elaborate network of trails and links, but that possibility has been looming since Killington acquired the financially ailing Pico in 1996.

Long before Killington became part of the American Skiing Company, it began spreading through the lesser peaks surrounding Killington Mountain, the highest in central Vermont. In that sense it resembles the groupings of ski terrain that are common in France, Austria and Switzerland more than the typical single mountain developments of American skiing. Killington Peak and Skye Peak have trails for the full range of abilities, from green to double-black, as does Pico Peak, except for double-black. Snowdon and Rams Head are mostly blue with some green trails, while Sunrise is almost entirely green, with a few blue and even black sections. Bear Mountain has only single- and double-blacks.

We sometimes hear skiers complain that Killington / Pico is too big, too complicated and too crowded to be fun. We disagree. We have skied Killington since the 1960s, watching it grow. The main entry lifts may be crowded at 10 or 11 on a sunny weekend morning, but that's not unique. What is unusual is the fact that you can almost always find lifts that are not crowded, once you learn where to go. Take a hint from European skiing practice and never head into the system without a trail map.

■ **Mad River Glen**, PO Box 1089, Waitsfield, VT 05673, www.madriverglen.com. I=☎ 802-496-3551, S=802-496-2001, R=800-451-4574, F=802-496-3562. It has a vertical drop of 1,600 feet, with 45 trails served by five lifts. Mad River Glen is proud of its unique heritage as the tough and ecologically sound ski area that represents itself with the feisty slogan, "Ski it if you can." Although you won't come closer to the original narrow, winding steep trails of classic New England skiing anywhere else, the "Glen" now has a nice set of more hospitable blues and greens to offset the rigorous blacks. Founded in 1948, it became a cooperative in 1995, owned by loyal skiers who kicked in less than $2,000 each to purchase a share. That communal spirit did not surprise us because we remember pleasant weekends in a lodge owned by the Hartford Ski Club, one of many ski club lodges near the base.

■ **Middlebury College Snow Bowl**, Service Building, Middlebury College, Middlebury, VT 05753. I=☎ 802-388-4356, S= 802-388-4356, R=802-388-7951, F=802-388-2871. Middlebury College Snow Bowl has a vertical drop of 1,050 feet, and 15 trails served by three lifts. This is an unpretentious, relatively small and inexpensive ski area with a renowned racing program and a lot of family appeal. Like Mad River Glen, it prides itself on some old-fashioned, winding trails, the first of which were cut in 1934. Trails and slopes are evenly split between blacks, blues and greens.

■ **Mount Snow Resort**, Route 100, Mount Snow, VT 05356, www.mountsnow.com. I=☎ 800-245-7669, S=802-464-2151, R= 800-245-7669, F=802-464-4141. Mount Snow has a vertical drop of 1,700 feet, with 130 trails served by 23 lifts. The major ski area farthest south in Vermont, this has evolved through a number of phases since it first opened with two chairlifts, two rope tows and seven trails in 1954. At the outset, founder Walter Schoenknecht had a different vision of what the base area should look like, with structures resembling a theme park more than the austere, rustic lodges common at the time. Now one of the largest ski areas in Vermont, the extensive base area has a different look, with four base lodges, a resort hotel and conference center, a clock tower and a number of subsidiary buildings. On the mountain, development of lifts, trails and new areas has been equally vigorous, with North Face and Sunbrook added on the back sides of the mountain, and Carinthia (originally a separate ski area) on the flank. All these areas are interconnected by lifts, but another acquisition, Haystack, is about five miles south of Mt. Snow. In the complex, more than half of the trails are rated blue, but there are enough greens to keep novices happy, and the whole of the North Face is black.

■ **Okemo Mountain Resort**, 77 Okemo Ridge Road, Ludlow, VT 05149, www.okemo.com. I=☎ 802-228-4041, S=802-228-5222, R=800-786-5366, F=802-228-4558. Okemo has a vertical drop of 2,150 feet, and 98 trails served by 14 lifts. Their success proves that an imaginatively run family-owned ski resort can still compete in an industry dominated by large corporate groups. Founded in 1955 with support from Ludlow residents, it grew slowly but steadily for two decades. Tim and Dianne Mueller purchased the resort in 1982 and immediately began adding lifts, trails, lodges and snowmaking until 95% of the trails were covered – the highest percentage in New England. Twenty years later they are still expanding the resort's terrain and facilities, while maintaining a low-key, relaxed atmosphere for staff and skiers. The largest number of trails are on the face of the mountain above the base area, with additional trails and lifts on the South Face and Solitude. There's also a 10-year plan to expand onto an adjacent peak, Jackson Gore. All areas of the mountain are loaded with blues, the South Face has a number of blacks, and broad green slopes serve novices just above the base.

- **Smugglers' Notch Resort**, Route 108, Smugglers' Notch, VT 05464, www.smuggs.com. I=☎ 802-644-8851, S=802-644-1104, R=800-451-8752, F=802-644-1230. Smugglers' Notch has a vertical drop of 2,610 feet, with 67 trails served by nine lifts. Smugglers' Notch Resort has been selected as the most "family-friendly" ski resort in the country by various ski magazines, and it certainly deserves that reputation. Although there is plenty of focus on good skiing on the resort's three linked mountains, the compact village offers everything else children or teenagers could desire – tubing, sledding, skating, swimming, sleigh rides, crafts, centers to gather in, parties for all ages. And their parents will appreciate restaurants, a day-care center, a fitness center, indoor tennis, and other services. We remember skiing all day during a three-generation trip, then adding an evening of snowboard lessons – until the elder two generations (but not the youngest) faded away. Even the mountains are neatly graded and situated, with Morse just above the village almost all green terrain, ideal for beginners; higher Sterling full of blue trails for intermediates with a sprinkling of single-blacks; and Madonna, the highest, a mixture of blues and blacks, including one triple-black for crazies.

- **Stowe Mountain Resort**, 5781 Mountain Road, Stowe, VT 05672, www.stowe.com. I=☎ 802-253-3000, S=802-253-3600, R=800-253-4754, F=802-253-3406. Stowe has a vertical drop of 2,360 feet, and 48 trails served by 10 lifts. Stowe Mountain Resort, the grand dame of all Eastern ski resorts, is built on the face of Vermont's highest mountain, Mount Mansfield (4,393 feet) and its facing mountain, Spruce Peak (3,320 feet). The main mountain area contains a score of trails with names that ring in ski history, including the double-black Nosedive and National, the blue Lord, and the green Toll Road, where a classic cross-country ski race all the way to the center of town begins. One of us remembers cutting his teeth as a skier by running the Stowe Standard and coming out with a silver medal. The main mountain has a mixture of blues and blacks, while the adjoining area below the Cliff House restaurant is mostly blue. Spruce Mountain has a network of blues, with some greens at the bottom. Although there are famous toughies for experts, blues dominate the mountain complex, accounting for 59% of the trails.

- **Stratton Mountain Resort**, RR 1, Box 145, Stratton Mountain, VT 05155, www.stratton.com. I= ☎ 802-297-2200, S=802-297-4211, R=800-787-2886, F=802-297-4300. Stratton has a vertical drop of 2,003 feet, with 90 trails served by 11 lifts. Built on the highest mountain in Southern Vermont by skier investors, it became a major resort quickly after its opening in 1961. From the beginning it was stylish, with a compact base village modeled after Austrian ski villages and an initial plan for slopeside chalets. There was no change in direction when the Intrawest Corporation bought the resort in 1994 and began expanding luxury lodging, but developing the mountain has received equal attention, especially with the addition of a mountaintop lodge and many lifts, including four high-speed six-person chairs and a 12-person gondola. Although the trails on the various faces of the mountain seem to form a continuous whole, five areas can be distinguished: Lower Mountain, Upper Mountain, Bear Basin/Snow Bowl, Sun Bowl and Kidderbrook. The spread of trail difficulty tilts slightly toward green and blue, but the mountain has a number of single-blacks and some double-blacks.

■ **Sugarbush Resort**, RR 1, Box 350, Warren, VT 05674, www.sugarbush.com. I=☎ 802-583-6300, S=802-583-7669, R= 800-537-8427, F=802-583-6303. The highest vertical drop is a healthy 2,650 feet and 115 trails are served by 18 lifts. The resort, which consists of the original Sugarbush plus nearby Glen Ellen, renamed Sugarbush North, is one of the largest and most varied skiing complexes in the East. In different eras it has been renowned as an enclave of the jet set and a training ground for professional skiers; it remains both and much more, with major development after it became a part of the American Skiing Company. We found the 12-minute high-speed chairlift ride between Lincoln Mountain and Mount Ellen a pleasure in itself as we swooped up and over ridges between the two halves of Sugarbush – a link that used to require driving. With lift systems developed on five peaks, three in the south and two in the north, you can find an area to suit every taste, from relaxed family skiing to tough, old-fashioned, largely ungroomed trails, like those in nearby Mad River Glen. In both Sugarbush South and Sugarbush North you can find trails for the full range of skiing abilities.

Cross-Country Skiing

Downhill ski areas also offering cross-country skiing include Bolton Valley, Jay Peak, Middlebury College Ski Bowl, Okemo, Smugglers' Notch, Stowe and Stratton. Call the numbers above for detailed information. Additional cross-country ski areas along the spine of Vermont include the following:

■ **Stowe/Mount Mansfield Touring Center** has the highest trails in the Stowe cross-country network, with 35 km groomed and 40 back-country. 5781 Mountain Road, Stowe, VT 05672, ☎ 802-253-3000, www.stowe.com.

■ **Edson Hill Manor**, perched on a hillside and surrounded by forest, has 40 km of trails. 1500 Edson Hill Road, Stowe, VT 05672, ☎ 802-253-7751.

■ **Topnotch at Stowe**, a resort and spa, has 40 km of trails. Mountain Road, Stowe, VT 05672, ☎ 802-253-8585, www.topnotchresort.com.

 Come to Stowe for the largest connected cross-country trail network in the East. Four major centers – Trapp Family Lodge, Stowe/Mount Mansfield Touring Center, Edson Hill Manor and Topnotch at Stowe – all lie between Stowe Village and Mount Mansfield, with links between their trail systems.

■ **Sleepy Hollow Inn Ski & Bike Center**, southeast of Burlington near Camel's Hump Mountain, has 40 km of trails, 30 of them groomed. 1805 Sherman Hollow Road, Huntington, VT 05462, ☎ 802-434-2283, www.skisleepyhollow.com.

■ **Ole's Cross Country Center** has 50 km of groomed trails with scenic views of the Mad River Valley. Located on Airport Road, Warren. Mail PO Box 1653, Waitsfield, VT 05149, ☎ 802-496-3430, www.olesxc.com.

■ **Blueberry Hill**, in the Green Mountain National Forest, has 60 km of trails, 50 of them groomed, including the Romance Mountain trail, highest in Vermont. Forest Service Road 32 off Route 73 (see website for detailed directions), Goshen, VT 05733, ☎ 802-247-6735, www.blueberryhillinn.com.

■ **Mountain Top Cross Country Ski Resort** has 80 km of trails, all groomed, with lake and mountain views in the Green Mountain National Forest. 195 Mountain Top Road, Chittenden, VT 05737, ☎ 802-483-6089, www.mountain-topinn.com/xcski.html.

■ **Mountain Meadows XC Ski Area** has 57 km of groomed trails meandering through white birch and hemlock forest. 209 Thundering Brood Road, Killington, VT 05751, ☎ 802-775-7077, www.xcskiing.net.

- **Okemo Valley Nordic Center** has 28 km of groomed trails in the meadows of the Black River Valley. 77 Okemo Ridge Road, Ludlow, VT 05149, ☎ 802-228-1396, www.okemo.com.

- **The Equinox Ski Touring Center**, part of Manchester's historic resort, has 35 km of groomed trails on resort grounds and Mount Equinox. Union Street, PO Box 46, Manchester Village, VT 05254, ☎ 802-362-3223, www.equinox-resort.com.

- **Viking Nordic Center**, one of the oldest in the country, has 40 km of trails in gentle rolling terrain and woodland, 30 of them groomed. 615 Little Pond Road, Londonderry, VT 05148, ☎ 802-824-3933, www.vikingnordic.com.

- **Hermitage XC Touring Center** has 50 km of trails, 30 of them groomed. Coldbrook Road, PO Box 457, Wilmington, VT 05363, ☎ 802-464-3511, www.hermitageinn.com.

- **Trapp Family Lodge**, Stowe, ☎ 802-253-5719. This was the first commercial Nordic center in the East, dating back to 1967. It now has 100 km of trails, 60 groomed and 40 back-country, in 2,200 acres of forest and meadows.

Sightseeing

■ Middlebury

 Morgan Horse Farm, Weybridge Road, Middlebury, VT 05753, ☎ 802-388-2011. The Morgan horse is the state animal of Vermont. The University of Vermont operates this farm, which offers detailed information on the lineage of this stately animal. Visitors may walk around the farm as well as watch a video presentation.

Vermont State Craft Center, Frog Hollow, Middlebury, VT 05753, ☎ 802-388-3177. This center has exhibitions and classes, as well as crafts to purchase, including handwoven fabrics, hand-fired clay pots, carvings, stained glass, jewelry and wooden toys.

■ Castleton

Hubbardton Battlefield State Historic Site, East Hubbardton, VT, ☎ 802-759-2412. The only Revolutionary battle to be fought on Vermont land was here. The battle is illustrated with a relief map, diorama and interpretive display.

■ Plymouth

President Calvin Coolidge State Historic Site at Plymouth Notch, Route 100A, Plymouth, VT 05056, ☎ 802-672-3773. The birthplace, boyhood home and grave of Calvin Coolidge are on the site, along with the Calvin Coolidge Visitor Center. Other buildings there include the Wilder House, where his mother lived as a child; the Wilder Barn, containing 19th-century farm implements; the Plymouth Cheese Factory; an 1840 meeting house; an 1850s general store; the office of the 1924 Summer White House; Union Christian Church; and Aldrich House, with exhibits on the village and on Coolidge.

PRESIDENTIAL TRIVIA

After President Harding died on August 3, 1923, the local telephone operator's husband hand-carried the news to the Coolidge home because the family didn't have a telephone. Colonel John Coolidge, the vice president's father, administered the oath of office in the front parlor by the light of a kerosene lamp. When queried as to how he knew he could do this for his own son, he replied, "I didn't know that I couldn't."

■ Manchester

American Museum of Fly Fishing, Route 7A and Seminary Avenue, Manchester, VT 05255, ☎ 802-362-3300. This museum offers fishing equipment used by Winslow Homer, Daniel Webster, Ernest Hemingway, Bing Crosby, Jimmy Carter, Grover Cleveland, Dwight Eisenhower and Herbert Hoover.

The Equinox Hotel, Manchester Village, VT 05254, ☎ 800-362-4747 or 802-362-4700. This historic hotel dates from 1769. In 1777, before the Battle of Bennington, a group of Ethan Allen's Green Mountain Boys met there. Mrs. Abraham Lincoln and two of her sons stayed there in 1863. A second visit was anticipated by the hotel and they decorated a suite for the occasion, but the assassination of President Lincoln took place shortly beforehand.

Hildene, Route 7A, Manchester, VT 05255, ☎ 802-362-1788. Walk up to this Georgian Revival mansion and feast your eyes on the lovely gardens with a background of the Green and Taconic mountain ranges. Robert Todd Lincoln, Abraham Lincoln's only son to live into maturity, built this home to use in summers. He kept precise records of the construction, fabrics, wallpaper and furnishings so that the 1978 restoration proceeded with a workable plan. Inside the home you may be treated to one of the piano rolls on the 1908 Aeolian pipe-organ. Lincoln operated his Pullman

Company from an office in the house and his records are still there. One treasure in a glass case is Abraham Lincoln's stovepipe hat.

Southern Vermont Art Center, West Road, Manchester, VT 05255, ☎ 802-362-1405. The center features 10 galleries of art and offers programs and concerts. The sculpture garden and a botany trail are popular.

■ Bennington

Bennington Battle Monument, 15 Monument Circle, Bennington, VT 05201, ☎ 802-447-0550. This monument is the tallest in Vermont. Take an elevator up to the lookout chamber for a fine view. A diorama illustrates the victory of General Stark over the British.

Bennington Museum, Route 9, Bennington, VT 05201, ☎ 802-447-1571. Grandma Moses is the focus in the museum, with the largest public collection of her paintings. The schoolhouse she attended as a child stands next door. The museum houses one of the oldest Stars and Stripes flags in existence, a collection of American glass from the 18th and 19th centuries, Bennington pottery, and the Wasp, a 1925 touring car designed by a local resident, Karl Martin.

Festivals & Events

 Vermont is alive with activity year-round. Some of the highlights include the following events.

■ January

Stowe Winter Carnival, ☎ 802-253-7321. The carnival features snow golf, snowshoe races, a pond party, cross-country race, chicken pie supper, parade and fireworks.

■ February

Vermont State Downhill Ski Championships at Mount Snow, ☎ 802-464-3333.

■ March

Reggae Festival at Mount Snow, ☎ 802-464-4191. Bands, parties, island food and drink and great après-ski fun.

■ May

Covered Bridges Half Marathon, Woodstock to Quechee, ☎ 800-295-5451.

■ June

Balloon Festival, Quechee, ☎ 800-295-5451.

Hildene Antique and Classic Car Show, ☎ 802-362-1788.

Stowe Bicycle Race, Stowe/Smugglers' Notch, ☎ 800-247-8693 or 802-253-7321. Cyclists race through the Notch on the 50-mile course.

■ August

Vermont Festival of the Arts in the Mad River Valley, ☎ 802-496-7907.

Where to Stay

ACCOMMODATIONS PRICE SCALE	
Prices for a double room for one or two persons, before taxes.	
$	Under $50
$$.	$50 to $100
$$$	$101 to $175
$$$$	Over $175

■ Stowe

Edson Hill Manor is on 225 acres in the woods – nice for walking and cross-country skiing. The dining room offers American cuisine with an extensive wine list. 1500 Edson Hill Road, Stowe, VT 05672, ☎ 800-621-0284 or 802-253-7371, fax 802-253-4036. $$$-$$$$.

Fiddler's Green Inn is a Vermont farmhouse with a nice fieldstone fireplace. Route 108, Stowe, VT 05672, ☎ 800-882-5346 or 802-253-8124, fax 802-253-2546. $$.

Inn at the Mountain is at the base of Mount Mansfield. 5781 Mountain Road, Stowe, VT 05672, ☎ 800-253-4SKI or 802-253-3000, fax 802-253-2546. $$$-$$$$.

Stoweflake is an all-season resort with health spa. Mountain Road, Stowe, VT 05672, ☎ 800-253-2232 or 802-253-7355, fax 802-253-4419. $$$-$$$$.

Stowehof is on a hilltop and has a variety of rooms. Edson Hill Road, Stowe, VT 05672, ☎ 800-932-7136 or 802-253-9722, fax 802-253-7513. $$$-$$$$.

Ten Acres Lodge is an 1840 lodge with fireplaces and views to the mountains. American cuisine is served with candlelight. Luce Hill Road, Stowe, VT 05672, ☎ 800-327-7357 or 802-253-7638, fax 802-253-4036. $$-$$$.

Timberholm Inn offers a secluded mountain setting. Cottage Club Road, Stowe, VT 05672, ☎ 800-753-7603 or 802-253-7603, fax 802-253-8559. $$-$$$.

Topnotch at Stowe is a conference center and resort with lots of activities and a health spa. Mount Mansfield Road, Stowe, VT 05672, ☎ 800-451-8686 or 802-253-8585, fax 802-253-9263. $$$$.

Trapp Family Lodge offers the charm of its *Sound of Music* beginnings. Photos of the family bring it to life. Austrian cuisine is featured in the dining room and in a tea room across the road. 42 Trapp Hill Road, Stowe, VT 05672, ☎ 800-826-7000 or 802-253-8511, fax 802-253-7864. $$$-$$$$.

■ Waitsfield

1824 House is a restored farmhouse on 22 acres. Route 100, Waitsfield, VT 05673, ☎ 800-426-3986 or 802-496-7555, fax 802-496-4558. $$$.

Inn at the Round Barn Farm is an 1810 farmhouse with a round barn and lots of charm. East Warren Road, Waitsfield, VT 05673, ☎ 802-496-2276, fax 802-496-8832. $$$-$$$$.

Tucker Hill Lodge is an 1810 farmhouse, which has been restored as an inn and restaurant of renown, Georgio's Café. Route 17, Waitsfield, VT 05673, ☎ 800-543-7841 or 802-296-3983, fax 802-496-3203. $$-$$$$.

Sugarbush Inn has rooms in the main lodge as well as condominiums. Box 33, Warren, VT 05674, ☎ 800-451-4320 or 802-583-4600, fax 802-583-3209. $$-$$$$.

The Sugartree Inn offers canopy beds and quilts. Sugarbush Access Road, Warren, VT 05674, ☎ 800-666-8907 or 802-583-3211, fax 802-583-3203. $$$.

■ Middlebury

The Middlebury Inn is an 1827 Georgian red brick building. There are two dining rooms, and afternoon tea is served. 14 Courthouse Square, Middlebury, VT 05753, ☎ 800-842-4666 or 802-388-4961, fax 802-388-4563. $$$-$$$$.

■ East Middlebury

Waybury Inn was once a stagecoach stop. There's a seniors' menu and a Sunday brunch. Route 125, East Middlebury, VT 05740, ☎ 800-348-1810 or 802-388-4015, fax 802-388-1248. $$-$$$.

■ Goshen

Blueberry Hill is right in the Green Mountain National Forest, with a secluded setting. Prices are per person, double occupancy: $125 mid-week and $160 weekends. They are on Goshen-Ripton Road, Goshen, VT 05733, ☎ 802-247-6735, fax 802-247-3983.

■ Killington

Cortina Inn has a great pool for after skiing or hiking. There's an art gallery upstairs. Route 4, Killington, VT 05751, ☎ 800-451-6108 or 802-773-3331, fax 802-775-6948. $$$-$$$$.

The Inn of the Six Mountains is right on the mountain so you can enter the Killington complex for skiing there. Killington Road, Killington, VT 05751, ☎ 800-228-4676 or 802-422-4302, fax 802-422-4321. $$$-$$$$.

The Summit is casual, with hand-hewn beams and four fireplaces. Mountain Road, Killington, VT 05751, ☎ 800-635-6343 or 802-422-3535, fax 802-422-3536. $-$$$$.

■ Plymouth

Hawk Inn is a resort offering tennis, swimming, boating, skating and ski trails. Box 64, Route 100, Plymouth, VT 05056, ☎ 800-685-HAWK or 802-672-3811, fax 802-672-5067. $$$$.

■ Dorset

Barrows House is about 200 years old and accommodations are scattered on the grounds. Dining is available, with regional American cuisine.

Route 30, Dorset, VT 05251, ☎ 800-639-1620 or 802-867-4455, fax 802-867-0132. $$$$.

Cornucopia of Dorset has rooms in the house and a cottage, Owls Head, in a woodsy setting. Route 30, Dorset, VT 05251, ☎ 800-867-5500, fax 802-867-5542. $$$-$$$$.

Dorset Inn is on the Green in a historic building. Route 30, Dorset, VT 05251, ☎ 802-867-5500, fax 802-867-5542. $$$.

The Inn at West View Farm offers rooms in a Vermont farmhouse. Continental dining is available in the Auberge, and lighter fare in Clancy's Tavern. Route 30, Dorset, VT 05251, ☎ 800-769-4903 or 802-867-5715, fax 802-867-0468. $$$.

■ Ludlow

The Andrie Rose Inn is on a back street in Ludlow, away from the confusion of the main street. The 1829 house is furnished with period antiques. 13 Pleasant Street, Ludlow, VT 05149, ☎ 800-223-4846 or 802-228-4846, fax 802-228-7910. $$$-$$$$.

Echo Lake Inn has a variety of rooms and suites. The dining room offers American and French cuisine. Box 154, Ludlow, VT 05149, ☎ 800-356-6844 or 802-228-8602, fax 802-228-3075. $$-$$$$.

The Governor's Inn is a Victorian home decorated with antiques. The dining room is famous for a gourmet six-course prix fixe menu. 86 Main Street, Ludlow, VT 05149, ☎ 800-GOVERNOR or 802-228-8830. $$-$$$$.

■ Manchester

1811 House was once home to Abraham Lincoln's granddaughter. Guests can play chess in the library and darts in the pub. Manchester Village, VT 05254, ☎ 800-432-1811 or 802-362-1811, fax 802-362-2443. $$-$$$$.

The Equinox is a restored 1769 historic hotel. The Charles Orvis Inn is also in the same complex. 3567 Main Street, Manchester, VT 05254, ☎ 800-362-4747 or 802-362-4700, fax 802-362-4861.$$-$$$$.

The Reluctant Panther can't be missed – it's painted purple. Box 678, Manchester Village, VT 05254, ☎ 800-822-2331 or 802-362-2568, fax 802-362-2586. $$$$.

Wilburton Inn is a 1902 mansion built by a friend of Robert Todd Lincoln. River Road, Manchester Village, VT 05254, ☎ 800-648-4944 or 802-362-2500, fax 802-362-1107. $$-$$$$.

■ Manchester Center

The Inn at Ormsby Hill is a 1760 home on the National Register of Historic Places. Route 7A, Manchester Center, VT 05255, ☎ 800-670-2841 or 802-362-1163, fax 802-362-5176. $$$-$$$$.

■ Arlington

The Arlington Inn is an 1848 Greek Revival mansion built by Martin Chester Deming, who owned railroads. Diners drive for miles to enjoy a candlelit dinner here. Route 7A, Arlington, VT 05250, ☎ 800-443-9442 or 802-375-6532, fax 802-375-6534. $$-$$$$.

■ Bennington

The Four Chimneys Inn is a 1910 estate. Most rooms have whirlpools and fireplaces. The restaurant serves Continental fare. 21 West Road, Old Bennington, VT 05201, ☎ 800-649-3503 or 802-447-3500, fax 802-447-3692, www.fourchimneys.com, innkeeper@fourchimneys.com. $$-$$$.

■ Camping

Vermont is a very popular place to camp, with all of its natural beauty and opportunity for sports and recreation. National forest and state campgrounds, as well as private sites, are available. Contact **Vermont State Parks**, 103 South Main Street, Waterbury, VT 05671-0603, ☎ 800-VERMONT or 802-241-3655, www.vtstateparks.com. Information is also available from **Green Mountain National Forest**, 231 North Main Street, Rutland, VT 05701, ☎ 802-747-6700.

Fair Haven

Half Moon Pond State Park, Fair Haven, VT 05743, ☎ 802-273-3848 or 483-2314. The site offers wooded campsites around a pond; canoes are available for rent.

Lake Elmore State Park, Lake Elmore, VT 05657, ☎ 802-888-2982. The site has 709 acres with a beach, rental boats and 64 sites.

Plymouth

Calvin Coolidge State Forest, Plymouth, VT 05056, ☎ 802-672-3612. This site has 60 campsites, 35 lean-tos, a picnic area and hiking trails.

Poultney

Lake St. Catherine State Park, Poultney, VT 05764, ☎ 802-287-9185 or 802-483-2314. The site offers 52 campsites, a sandy beach, fishing and boat rentals.

Rutland

Bomoseen State Park, Route 4, Rutland, VT. 05701, ☎ 802-265-4242. The site offers 60 campsites in a wildlife refuge with a beach, picnic area, boat ramp and rentals

Sherburne

Gifford Woods State Park, Sherburne, VT 05751, ☎ 802-775-5354. The site offers 47 campsites, a picnic area, and access to fishing on Kent Pond or hiking on the Appalachian Trail

Stowe

Smugglers' Notch, Route 108, Stowe, VT 05472, ☎ 802-253-4041. The site has 38 campsites.

Where to Eat

DINING PRICE SCALE
Prices include an entrée, which may come with vegetables and salad, but exclude beverage, taxes and tip.
$ . . . . Under $10
$$ . . . . $10 to $20
$$$. $21 to $50
$$$$. Over $50

■ Stowe

Edson Hill Manor features American cuisine in a dining room with murals. 1500 Edson Hill Road, Stowe, VT, ☎ 802-253-7371. $$-$$$.

Maxwell's in Topnotch at Stowe has Continental cuisine. 4000 Mountain Road, Stowe, VT, ☎ 802-253-8585. $$-$$$.

Mr. Pickwick's in Ye Olde England Inne provides a pub atmosphere with pub food and drink. Route 108, Stowe, VT, ☎ 802-253-7558. $$.

Ten Acres Lodge offers American cuisine with an extensive wine list. Luce Hill Road, Stowe, VT, ☎ 802-253-7638. $$-$$$.

Trapp Family Lodge has a fixed price menu of three or four courses featuring Austrian cuisine. The Austrian tea room across the road serves lighter fare. Luce Hill Road, Stowe, VT, ☎ 800-826-7000 or 802-253-8511. $$$.

■ Waitsfield

Giorgio's Café at Tucker Hill Lodge has homemade bread, soups and desserts, as well as entrées. Route 17, Waitsfield, VT, ☎ 802-496-3983. $-$$.

■ Warren

Chez Henri serves classical French cuisine in a bistro atmosphere. Sugarbush Village, Warren, VT, ☎ 802-583-2600. $$-$$$.

Sam Rupert's features regional American fare in a casual atmosphere. Sugarbush Access Road, Warren, VT, ☎ 802-583-2421. $$-$$$.

■ Killington

Grist Mill has light fare in an attractive setting. Killington Access Road, Killington, VT, ☎ 802-422-3970. $$.

Hemingway's Restaurant is in an 1860 restored home. The cuisine is Nouvelle American and there is an extensive wine list. Route 4, Killington, VT, ☎ 802-422-3886. $$$.

Zolas at the Cortina Inn serves gourmet American Mediterranean cuisine, and **Theodore's Tavern** has lighter meals. Route 4, Killington, VT, ☎ 800-451-6108. $$$

■ Dorset

Auberge at the Inn at West View Farm offers Continental cuisine in the dining room, lighter fare in **Clancy's Tavern**. Route 30, Dorset, VT, ☎ 802-867-5715. $$-$$$.

Barrows House has a garden motif in the dining room. Route 30, Dorset, VT, ☎ 802-867-4455. $$-$$$.

■ Ludlow

Echo Lake Inn features regional American cuisine. There is also a menu for health-conscious diners. Route 100 in Tyson Village, Ludlow, VT, ☎ 802-228-8602. $$-$$$.

The Governor's Inn has a six-course dinner with elegant settings and presentation for a fixed price. People drive great distances to partake. 86 Main Street, Ludlow, VT, ☎ 800-GOVERNOR or 802-228-8830. $$$.

■ Manchester

The Equinox Hotel offers dining in several locations, including Sunday Brunch in the **Colonnade**. 3567 Main Street, Manchester, VT, ☎ 802-362-4700. $$-$$$.

■ Arlington

The Arlington Inn serves regional American cuisine in a fireside candle-lit setting. Route 7A, Arlington, VT, ☎ 800-443-9442 or 802-375-6532. $$-$$$.

■ Bennington

Four Chimneys Inn features Continental cuisine. 21 West Road, Bennington, VT, ☎ 800-649-3503 or 802-447-3500. $$$.

The Adirondacks

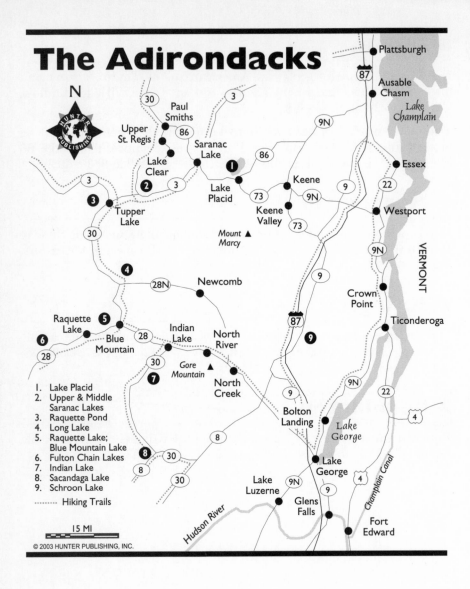

N

Plattsburgh

87

Ausable Chasm

Lake Champlain

30

3

Paul Smiths

Upper St. Regis

86

9N

Saranac Lake

86

Essex

Lake Clear

2

3

1

Keene

9

22

3

3

Lake Placid

73

9N

Westport

Tupper Lake

Keene Valley

73

30

Mount Marcy ▲

9N

VERMONT

4

28N

Newcomb

9

Crown Point

Raquette Lake

5

Indian Lake

North River

87

Ticonderoga

6

Blue Mountain

28

9

28

30

Gore Mountain ▲

9N

7

North Creek

9

1. Lake Placid
2. Upper & Middle Saranac Lakes
3. Raquette Pond
4. Long Lake
5. Raquette Lake; Blue Mountain Lake
6. Fulton Chain Lakes
7. Indian Lake
8. Sacandaga Lake
9. Schroon Lake

Bolton Landing

Lake George

22

4

8

8

30

Lake George

4

8

Lake Luzerne

9N

9

.... Hiking Trails

Glens Falls

Champlain Canal

Fort Edward

15 MI

Hudson River

The Adirondacks

Elsewhere are mountains more stupendous, more icy and more drear, but none look upon a grander landscape... none show a denser or more vast appearance of primeval forest stretched over range on range to the far horizon, where the sea of mountains fades into a dim, vaporous uncertainty."

In these words **Verplanck Colvin**, chief surveyor of the Adirondacks from 1872 to 1900, described what he saw. Earlier, the literati of Boston – including **James Russell Lowell**, **Louis Agassiz** and **Ralph Waldo Emerson** – had trekked to the Adirondacks in 1857 and 1858 as part of the Adirondack Club. In his narrative poem *The Adirondacks*, about the latter journey, Emerson saw members of the group as "lords of this realm" who "trode on air, contemned the distant town" and planned to build "a spacious lodge" for themselves and their sons.

History

Thus began the discovery of the Adirondacks by city folk. In 1864 a New York Times editorial carried it one step further, proclaiming that the mountains were "a tract of country fitted to make a Central Park for the world." The Adirondacks were soon to be easily reached as the railroad headed north from Saratoga, "aiming directly at the heart of the wilderness." Continuing in grandiloquent style, the editorial predicted, "with its completion, the Adirondack region will become a suburb of New York."

Luckily, that did not happen, but after the Civil War this little known tourist destination gradually attracted fishermen and hunters; then families, who summered away from the heat of the city at first in lodges and later in grand hotels; and finally millionaires, who built great camps on vast tracts of land.

Three travel writers created much of this "discovery" of what had always been there. One was **William H. H. Murray**, a Boston clergyman whose best-selling *Adventures in the Wilderness* (1869) recommended the Adirondacks for recreation and health, especially because they had not yet suffered the scars of lumbering that had already marred much of the North woods elsewhere.

A second writer who lured visitors to the Adirondacks and simultaneously built his own fame was **George Washington Sears**, writing under the pen name "Nessmuk." A Pennsylvania shoemaker by trade and a wanderer in spirit, Sears persuaded J. Henry Rushton to build him incredibly light canoes for exploring the wilderness lakes that Verplanck Colvin had written about. His trips on the Fulton Chain and other Adirondack lakes in the 1880s were recounted in *Forest and Stream*, the most prominent outdoor magazine of the day, as well as several books. The most famous of his canoes, now displayed in the Smithsonian Institution, is the *Sairy Gamp*, nine feet long and 26 inches in beam, weighing only 10 ½ pounds.

The third, and perhaps the most influential travel writer, was **Seneca Ray Stoddard**, a man of many talents – landscape photographer, writer, surveyor, cartographer, and lecturer on the Adirondacks. From 1873 to the First World War he wrote and illustrated a series of guidebooks on Lake George, Lake Champlain, and the interior of the Adirondacks, revising them annually. He began publishing maps as an adjunct to his books and later, separately, worked as a photographer for Colvin's surveys; he eventually went on the lecture circuit with his lantern slides.

The eastern edge of this area is a gold mine for history buffs. The waterways of Lake Champlain, Lake George, and the Hudson were highways for Indians, the French, the English, and eventually the Americans who wanted to claim the land. Forts were built, destroyed, and rebuilt at **Crown Point**, **Ticonderoga**, the head of Lake George (now **Lake George Village**) and **Fort Edward**, and the contest for control of this vital waterway system climaxed at the **Battle of Saratoga** in 1777. For more detail about this corridor, see the *Lake Champlain* and *Upper Hudson River* chapters of this book, as well as the *Lake George* section of the current chapter.

In more recent Adirondack history, **Lake Placid** became the venue for the 1932 and 1980 Winter Olympics. You can visit these sites, watch skaters on the speed-skating oval, and quake at the brave jumpers taking off from the 90-meter towers. Nearby, **Mount Van Hoevenberg** offers new Olympic bobsled and luge runs as well as a network of cross-country trails and a biathlon course.

A NOT SO PLACID EXPERIENCE

During a ski writers' weekend at Lake Placid we had a choice of activity at night after the skiing day was over. A few chose the luge, and we marveled at the courage (or craziness) of those who voluntarily placed their prone bodies on these careening sleds. We climbed onto a bobsled between a driver and a brakeman, hanging on to both as we began to move down the course. Hold tighter now! The first curve quickened our grips and we felt the sides of our feet scraping the ice. As we gained speed one of us squeaked "Oh, oh, oh, oh" – and then it was over. It would be nice to try the run once more and feel a bit more relaxed.

■ Preservation Efforts

Disturbed about the worst abuses of lumbering – clear-cutting and the creation of drowned lands – Stoddard presented devastating images in a lecture before the New York State Assembly in February, 1892, and promoted legislation to protect Adirondack forests throughout the state.

In May of that year the legislature established the **Adirondack Park** to complement the **Adirondack Forest Preserve**, which was created in 1885. Two years later the crucial "forever wild" clause was added to protect lands in the Forest Preserve from further incursions. Although created by different legislation, the two entities overlap, and the Adirondack Park Agency was established in 1970 to administer complex rules dealing with an area that includes more private than public land. With six million acres inside the "blue line" that marks its boundaries, the Adirondack Park is the largest wilderness preserve in the United States south of Alaska. It includes most of the land north of a line between Albany and Syracuse and stretches nearly to the Canadian border. It is about the size of Vermont – larger than the Grand Canyon and Yellowstone combined.

We've lived in the Adirondack Park for nearly 30 years – not long enough to be old timers, but more than enough time to know that we don't want to live anywhere else. We moved in just as the Adirondack Park Agency began to enforce rather stringent land use rules (and often saw "Abolish the APA" bumper stickers) but have come to appreciate the net effect of those rules. This vast "suburb" of New York City lacks traffic jams, strip malls, views crammed with housing developments and forests of billboards. It has many scenic roads that are a pleasure to the eye, and a major interstate winding through its eastern fringe that has won awards for its beauty.

We can drink the water from the lake in front of us (Lake George), sail on it, and look across it to a mountainside forest with no ugly clearings. Within easy reach are wild rivers for kayaking and canoeing, many areas for downhill and cross-country skiing, country roads and lanes for cycling, and a vast network of hiking trails along lakeshores and up mountains, 46 of them over 4,000 feet. As travel writers we are off on adventures around the world but have yet to find an environment with more natural amenities easily at hand.

Geography

 Many regions in the northeast are noted for mountains, rivers, or lakes – this one has all three. Geologically, the Adirondacks lie in two pieces. They are one of the five ranges of the Mountain Belt that stretches from Lake Champlain to the southwest, along with the **Luzerne**, **Kayaderosseras**, **Schroon**, and **Boquet**

ranges. The mountains are old, part of the Canadian Shield, and some are pre-Cambrian. The High Peaks area of the Adirondacks is topped by **Mount Marcy** (5,344 feet), with tiny **Lake Tear of the Clouds** – the source of the Hudson River – on its flank. As the Hudson flows south it increases in size, providing wild white water in the Hudson River Gorge and Blue Ledges through the spring. Farther downstream, only slightly milder water is the scene for the annual Whitewater Derby in sections between North River, North Creek, and Riparius. The **Lake Region** lies to the west of the Mountain Belt and is composed of forests and many lakes, including the **Fulton Chain** and the **St. Regis Canoe Area**, linked with the **Saranac Lakes**. At the Adirondacks' eastern edge lies the historically important **Lake Champlain/Lake George** corridor, feeding into the Hudson River and connecting with the St. Lawrence.

Getting Here & Getting Around

■ By Air

If you fly into **Albany**, which has a spanking new airport replacing an old dingy structure, you can easily rent a car from a number of major agencies. You can also fly into **Lake Clear** (near Saranac Lake), **Plattsburgh**, **Burlington** or **Montreal**. Airports in the latter three cities can provide car rentals.

■ By Car

A car is essential in the Adirondacks because bus service is very limited. The major highway in the area is **I-87**, with secondary roads leading off to the east and west. Car rentals are available in some towns but all brands can be found at the airport.

■ By Bus

Adirondack Trailways, ☎ 800-858-8555, serves a number of towns – including Saratoga Springs, Glens Falls, Queensbury, Lake George, Warrensburg, Chestertown, Pottersville, Schroon Lake, Keene, Lake Placid, Saranac Lake and Malone – but you will probably need a car to get around, especially if you are heading for the wilderness areas.

Greyhound Lines. . . . . ☎ 800-231-2222

Information Sources

■ Regional Offices

Adirondack Regional Tourism Council, PO Box 2149, Plattsburgh, NY 12901, ☎ 518-846-8016, www.adk.com.

Central Adirondack Association, Route 28, PO Box 68, Old Forge, NY 13420, ☎ 315-369-6983.

Local Information, ☎ 800-487-6867 or 518-846-8016, www.adk.com.

■ County Offices

Plattsburgh/North Country Chamber of Commerce, 101 West Bay Plaza, PO Box 310, Plattsburgh, NY 12901, ☎ 518-563-1000, www.northcountrychamber.com.

Franklin County Tourism, 63 West Main Street, Malone, NY 12953, ☎ 800-709-4895.

Lake Placid/Essex County Visitors Bureau, Olympic Center, Lake Placid, NY 12946, ☎ 800-44PLACID or 518-523-2445, www.lakeplacid.com, info@lakeplacid.com.

Warren County Tourism, 908 Municipal Center, Lake George, NY 12845, ☎ 800-365-1050, ext.908 or 518-761-6366, www.visitlakegeorge.com, info@visitlakegeorge.com.

Hamilton County Tourism, White Birch Lane, Box 771, Indian Lake, NY 12842, ☎ 518-648-5239, www.hamiltoncounty.com, info@hamiltoncounty.com.

Tourist Information Center (Herkimer County), Route 28, PO Box 68, Old Forge, NY 13420, ☎ 315-369-6983, www.oldforgeny.com.

Franklin County Tourism, 63 West Main Street, Malone, NY 12953, ☎ 800-709-4895, www.adirondacklakes.com, info@adirondacklakes.com.

Adventures

■ On Foot

Hiking

Two or three stops are essential for any newcomer to Adirondack hiking. The first is the headquarters of the **Adirondack Mountain Club**, 814 Goggins Road, Lake George, NY 12845, ☎ 518-668-4447. It is just west of the Northway (I-87) on Route 9N, as you enter the Park area from the south (take Exit 21). There you will find exhibits on the Adirondacks and a bookstore loaded with hiking guides and maps covering the area you are heading for

Look for the excellent series, *Adirondack Mountain Club Forest Preserve Series of Guides to Adirondack Trails*, published by ADK.

The **Adirondack Mountain Club** or **ADK**, as it is called by locals, has been helping to preserve the Adirondacks for more than 75 years, providing all sorts of information, resources, and a number of lodges, as well as taking on the responsibility for clearing and maintaining many trails. Like its sister in New Hampshire, the Appalachian Mountain Club, the ADK is your best first source for information on hiking in this region.

Two **Adirondack Park Visitor Interpretive Centers** are located in the Park, one at Newcomb and one in Paul Smiths, and both have the full range of maps and guides. See page 88 for information on the other exhibits and trails at these centers.

A WORD TO
THE WISE

For advance information, also check the **Adirondack Regional Tourism Council**, Box 2149, Plattsburgh, NY 12901, ☎ 518-846-8016, www.adk.com. Ask for the booklet *Adirondack Great Walks & Day Hikes*, which offers sketch maps of hikes, tips on selecting destinations, a list of licensed Adirondack guides and outfitters, and safety and equipment suggestions.

ADIRONDACK HIKING AREAS

The Adirondack area is loaded with a variety of hiking regions. They are organized into general regions.

- **High Peaks Region** (Essex County)

- **Northern Region** (St. Lawrence and Franklin Counties)

- **Central Region** (Long Lake to Sacandaga Lake in Hamilton County)

- **The Northville-Lake Placid Trail** (a 133-mile trail in Hamilton and Essex Counties)

- **West-Central Region** (south of Stillwater Reservoir, east of the western Adirondack Park "Blue Line," north of NY Route 8 and west of the Northville-Lake Placid Trail in Herkimer and Hamilton Counties)

- **Eastern Region** (from Valcour Island on Lake Champlain through Lake George in Essex, Warren, and Washington Counties)

TRAIL USAGE

As you can imagine, there is concern about overuse of some of the most popular trails, especially in the High Peaks. For the last several years an advertising campaign has attempted to steer hikers away from the High Peaks to less traveled regions of the Adirondacks. It is wise to head for those regions during the height of the season, especially on weekends. In the future there may be some sort of quota system to even out the number of hikers on any one trail.

THE HIGH PEAKS

Peaks of more than 4,000 feet are considered "high peaks." This region is located in the northeastern quadrant of the Adirondack Park. The High Peak regulations described below apply to: "the Johns Brook, Marcy Dam, Lake Colden and Indian Pass areas, along with the summit of Mt. Marcy; the McIntyre Range, which includes the Wright, Algonquin, Iroquois and Marshall Mountains; Phelps; and the Great Range, which includes the Wolfjaws, Armstrong, Gothics, Saddleback, Basin and Haystack mountains, among others." Maps are available from the **Adirondack Mountain Club**, 814 Goggins Road, Lake George NY 12845, ☎ 518-668-4447. Trails are marked with metal disks. Distances are listed in guides.

The Adirondacks

HIGH PEAKS TRAIL RESTRICTIONS

In May of 2000 the **New York State Department of Environmental Conservation** established new regulations for the use of High Peaks trails. They limit the size of day groups (15) and overnight groups (8), prohibit camping above 4,000 feet and limit it between 3,500 and 4,000 feet, severely restrict the use of campfires, and require hikers to sign a trail registry, among other provisions. In July of 2001 the trail registry requirements in the High Peaks were further specified. One member of each hiking group must complete a trip ticket, leaving one copy at the trailhead and carrying the other.

Day hikers need to plan trips carefully, considering the difficulty of the terrain and the length of time needed to finish a round-trip. Check the weather report and bring clothing for various conditions. It makes sense to leave your plan with someone at home, including details about the location of your car. Always sign in at trail registers, now mandated in the High Peaks region but a very good idea anywhere.

Forest rangers recommend a minimum party size of three persons. In case of an accident, at least one person should remain with the injured person while others in the group should carefully note the location and contact the local forest ranger. Pick up a brochure on hiking at an information center or from ADK.

 The park-wide emergency dispatch telephone is ☎ 518-891-0235.

Overnight hikers will need to bring water, rain and wind gear, gloves, hat and sturdy boots, sunscreen, insect repellent and/or a headnet, map, compass, flashlight with extra batteries, first aid kit, tent, extra food, and a portable stove. Lean-tos are available on a first-come, first-served basis. and are occasionally removed or relocated.

Water is not safe to drink here because of the parasite *Giardia lamblia*. Food or water that contains the parasite can infect persons, who then develop sometimes severe gastrointestinal problems. (We speak from direct and painful experience, not in the Adirondacks but in the Colorado Rockies.) It is necessary to boil water and add an iodine-based chemical purifier or a commercial filter.

Mount Marcy: This peak was named in honor of Governor William Marcy in 1837. As the tallest mountain in the Adirondacks, it rises 5,344 feet above sea level, and the view from the summit includes mile after mile of forest and surrounding mountaintops. One of the oldest trails is also the shortest – the **Van Hoevenberg Trail** to **Heart Lake** (7.38 miles; see description below). The **Calamity Brook Trail** leads up to **Lake Tear of the Clouds** – the highest source of the Hudson River at 4,346 feet – then reaches the summit (10.31 miles). Seven other principal trails from **Keene Valley**, **Heart Lake**, **Elk Lake**, and **Tahawus** also reach the summit in distances ranging from 8.8 to 14.16 miles (for approaches from the southern side of the mountain see page 87.

Although this mountain should be avoided during the high summer season and during the spring, you can find good times to stand on the top of the Adirondacks after the spring melt and before the summer droves arrive, and again in the fall. (If you choose late May or June, beware – this is the height of the blackfly season, a moving target each year depending on the weather!) At peak times try some of the other mountains in the High Peaks region, many nearly as high as Marcy and with comparable views.

CARRIED AWAY ON MOUNT MARCY

Many years ago, one of us climbed Mount Marcy with our 10-year-old son a little too early in the spring. Using the short trail, we struggled up a washed-out streambed filled with round rocks. Near the summit, our son rolled his foot on one of these rocks and sprained his ankle. He was able to reach the summit, but on the way down he rapidly lost the use of that ankle, even with a jury-rigged crutch, and had to be carried the last stretch. In spite of his injury, it was a beautiful day on the summit and a grand hike, but not so much fun descending.

Mount Marcy from Adirondac Loj: To reach the Adirondac Loj from I-87, take Exit 30 onto Route 73, toward Keene; turn south about 10 miles beyond Keene when you see the sign for Adirondak Loj and a DEC (Department of Environmental Conservation) sign reading "Trails to the High Peaks." You can stay overnight at Adirondak Loj, have a meal and find useful information on hiking in general and trail conditions in particular. **Heart Lake** is the start of the easiest trail to the summit of Mount Marcy. Henry Van Hoevenberg laid out this trail in the 1880s. Follow the blue markers along the **Van Hoevenberg Trail** to **Marcy Dam**. Lean-tos are available for camping at Marcy Dam. (But don't count on one being available when you need it.) You will pass **Indian Falls** and enjoy a view of the **MacIntyre Range** from flat rocks. The trail heads over bare rock up to Mount Marcy, a distance of 7.38 miles.

Algonquin Peak: Algonquin Peak is the second highest mountain in the state. It is located in the **MacIntyre Range**. From Adirondak Loj, follow the same trail named above, the Van Hoevenberg, toward Mount Marcy

The Adirondacks

until you come to a junction where the Marcy trail and its blue signs go south. You then follow yellow signs on the MacIntyre Trail. (Algonquin has sometimes been called MacIntyre and is so called on some of the DEC trail signs.) You will pass the ski trail, which heads for Whales Tail Notch, but keep right to stay on your trail. Views from the top abound – of Colden, Skylight, Gray Peak, Marcy, Giant, Hurricane, Porter, Cascade, Van Hoevenburg and Whiteface. The distance from Adirondak Loj to the summit of Algonquin is 3.98 miles.

NORTHERN REGION

The northern section of the Adirondacks is the most secluded and isolated region in the Adirondack Park. Most of the hiking trails are unknown to the public. Since the original edition of the ADK guide, changes have been made including the addition of new trails and the abandonment of others. Reasons include excessive flooding due to beavers' dam-building activities, inaccessible trailheads and maintenance difficulties. Some trails were once used for logging, but vehicular traffic is now prohibited and they are open for hiking. Some of these truck trails are also used for cross-country skiing and snowshoeing. They may have missing signs or perhaps DEC orange disks placed there for snowmobilers. Other trails are marked as horse trails or canoe carries. A good topographic map and compass are essential to keep you on track when you encounter junctions with confusing markings.

Major highways in the area are routes **3** and **30**. Villages include **Star Lake**, **Cranberry Lake**, **Tupper Lake** and **Paul Smiths**.

Ampersand Mountain Trail: The view from the top is worth the climb – Ampersand Lake down below, the Seward Range, Whiteface Mountain and the McKenzie Range in the background. In 1873 Verplanck Colvin set a controlled fire to clear the top of Ampersand Mountain, as part of his mountain survey. Paths lead to triangulation lines to more mountain tops. The trailhead is located 8.1 miles west of the village of Saranac Lake on Route 3. You will cross Dutton Brook and head through a shady hemlock forest with striped maple and honeysuckle sprouting up. The foundation of a fire observer's cabin reminds old timers of Walter Rice, "the hermit of Ampersand," who lived there. A plaque to his memory is up on the summit. Yellow markers on the bare rock guide you through the last stages of the ascent. The distance is 2.7 miles.

THE ADIRONDACK CLUB

A literary group from Boston, including Ralph Waldo Emerson, James Russell Lowell and Louis Azassiz, wished to have an Adirondack camp on Ampersand Lake. See Donaldson, *A History of the Adirondacks*, for more information on the camp. Actually, their first camp was on Follensby Pond (also spelled Follansbee and Folingsby in early guide books). The men enjoyed their literary sanctuary so much they decided to organize themselves into the Adirondack Club and add some new members. They bought land on Ampersand Pond that included 22,500 acres called the Ampersand Tract. It was purchased for $600 and the first meeting there was a success. Then one member chose to live abroad, the Civil War disrupted recreation and the club faded away. It was finally acquired by the State for unpaid taxes.

High Falls Loop: If you love the sound of rushing water, head for the scenic **Cataract of High Falls** on the Oswegatchie River. There, water cascades down 20 feet over granite rock. The loop includes **High Falls Trail**, the **Plains Trail** and the **Dead Creek Flow Trail**. Most hikers begin at the High Falls Trail; its trailhead is eight miles west of Cranberry Lake off Route 3. Take Route 3 from Cranberry Lake toward the southwest and then turn south toward the village of Wanakena; after one mile bear right, then take another right over a little bridge that crosses the Oswegatchie River. You will walk past an old mill pond, which was used for lumbering a century ago. Cross several streams, perhaps encountering flooding caused by beaver dams. The distance to High Falls is 9.2 miles. The loop continues on the truck trail to the Plains Trail, then along the base of Three-Mile Mountain. Cross Dead Creek on a bridge at 10.6 miles. Follow the Dead Creek Flow Trail on an old logging trail, and skirt a beaver pond. The total mileage is 16.7 miles.

CENTRAL REGION

Waters in the Central Region of the Adirondacks flow into the Hudson River from the Cedar, Indian, Boreas, Kunjamuk, Miami and Jessup rivers, and from the East Branch of the Sacandaga. The mountains in the area include Snowy Mountain and Blue Mountain. Gore Mountain is a popular downhill ski area with a new gondola to the summit. (One of us remembers skiing at Gore in the early 1950s when the original gondola was being built!) The region also attracts hikers, cross-country skiers and snowshoers. Hunters and trappers arrived in the 18th century, and after the first log drive in 1813 lumbermen made use of all of the Hudson's tributaries. Lumber roads developed between work camps, and stagecoach roads eventually followed to bring city guests to new hotels in the woods.

The Adirondacks

DID YOU KNOW? In 1871 the Adirondack Railroad penetrated the Adirondack woods all the way to **North Creek**, where Theodore Roosevelt rode furiously one night in 1901 after hearing that President McKinley was close to death. He left Tahawus Lodge and arrived in North Creek at 4:39 am, where he was told that he was now President of the United States. In fact, the third relay driver, Mike Cronin, had overheard the telephone call announcing that McKinley was dead but he didn't tell Roosevelt. Mike claimed, "He didn't ask me. All he said was, Hurry!"

Blue Mountain Trail: One of our favorite museums anywhere is the **Adirondack Museum** at Blue Mountain Lake. Every time we visit, it is a treat to look down on the lake. Sometimes it is in brilliant cobalt blue contrast to fall leaves, at other times it is ringed with the bright greens of spring.

Blue Mountain Trail is easily accessible from Routes 30 and 28N in Blue Mountain Lake village. Head up the hill past the Adirondack Museum and look for the trailhead. Follow red trail signs, enter the woods and cross a creek. As the route becomes steeper you will find yourself walking on bare rock. The trail heads through a grove of spruce and reaches the summit at 2.0 miles. Views include Blue Mountain Lake, Eagle Lake, Raquette Lake, Long Lake, Tirrell Mountain, Tongue Mountain, Algonquin Mountain, Ampersand Mountain and the Seward Range.

Tirrell Pond Trail: This trailhead is the same as that for the Blue Mountain Trail, just north of the Adirondack Museum. Hikers pass through private woods, which were lumbered years ago. Follow yellow signs under a high-tension wire and past old lumber roads. During your descent to the pond be careful of loose stones, which could cause a tumble. Head to the Tirrell Pond lean-to, which is 3.6 miles from the trailhead. There's a beautiful beach on the pond.

Northville-Lake Placid (NP) Trail: This trail goes through the center of the Adirondack wilderness as a lowland route. A gradual ascent leads to a plateau and then you will follow streams and several lakes. After passing Long Lake, you will head through a valley between several peaks. (This trail does not ascend the peaks.) Along the way you will cross four roads and walk near three villages. You will find two areas of blacktop and one gravel road. In addition there are two roadless areas. Allow several days to walk these. Along the way, the NP trail intercepts side trails to four mountains: Cathead, Wakeley, Blue and Kempshall. This trail was developed by the ADK in 1922 and at that time there was a railroad at both ends. The NP trail is maintained by the New York State Department of Environmental Conservation (DEC). Markers include diamond-shaped NPT trail signs and also those of the Adirondack Mountain Club.

A car is necessary at the beginning and end of a trek. We suggest purchasing the *Guide to Adirondack Trails* by ADK when planning a trip. Many hikers are now taken by car to the Upper Benson junction with the trail to avoid walking on Route 30. From Northville, the trail stretches 132.2 miles to Lake Placid. From the Upper Benson junction, the distance is 122.6 miles. Some hikers prefer to hike the NP Trail in sections, which are easily accessible from the four roads intersecting it. One caution: Cars may be subject to theft if left in the woods for long periods of time.

WEST-CENTRAL REGION

Trails in the western Adirondacks are reached via Route 28, the major road through the area. The trails in this region border lakes and streams and wind through forests; they are not considered mountainous.

Big Moose: You will find Big Moose Road between the villages of Eagle Bay and Big Moose on Route 1, off Route 28 west of Inlet. Trails create a network that extends east and northeast of Big Moose Road.

DID YOU KNOW? Scandal invaded the area when Chester Gillette apparently drowned the mother of his unborn child. Grace Brown was seen in a boat with Gillette and was next found dead. It happened in the south bay of Big Moose Lake in July, 1906. Gillette was tried and executed in 1908. Theodore Dreiser retold the story in his major novel, *An American Tragedy*.

Cascade Lake Trail: From Route 28 in Eagle Bay drive northwest on Big Moose Road for 1.2 miles and park in the DEC lot. Head northeast to Cascade Lake, go around the lake and back to the road. There is a falls at the east end of the lake.

Old Forge-Thendara: Old Forge stands at the foot of the Fulton Chain of lakes. A triphammer wheel from the old forge still stands in town. Take a walk up the ski slopes of McCauley Mountain for a view of the lower lakes of the Fulton Chain.

Camp Santanoni: Hikers can enjoy an expedition into the forest to visit one of the few surviving Great Camps in the Adirondacks. The Main Camp is located 4.7 miles from the Gate Lodge on Route 28N in Newcomb. For details on what lies at the end of the road see *Sightseeing*, page 99.

The Adirondacks

EASTERN REGION

Much of this region is now called the "Adirondack Coast," a tourism authority name that we at first thought rather silly since **Lake Champlain** – whether one of the Great Lakes or not – is an inland body of water connected to the sea only by rivers and canals. But on reflection the name seemed more appropriate because the mountains do meet the lake throughout large portions of Essex County. Farther south is **Lake George**, 32 miles long and one to three miles wide, snaking through mountains that rise 2,000 feet or more above lake level. Lake George is 220 feet higher than Lake Champlain and connected to it only by a three-mile portage at **Ticonderoga**. Nevertheless, the two lakes served as the main highway through the Adirondacks during centuries of exploration, warfare and trade. Now their high shores provide some of the most scenic hikes in the Adirondacks.

When Thomas Jefferson visited Lake George in 1791, he described it in superlatives as "the most beautiful water... limpid as crystal, and the mountainsides covered with rich groves of thuja, silver fir, white pine, aspen, and paper birch down to the water-edge; here and there precipices of rock to checker the scene and save it from monotony."

Ausable Chasm: Not far from the Champlain shore off Route 9, one of the major rivers of the northern Adirondacks has carved a gorge worthy of the Rockies. Potsdam sandstone layered itself over 500 million years ago and you can see that the Ausable River is still cutting through it to deepen the gorge. There is an easy walkway past Pulpit Rock, Elephants Head, Jacobs Ladder, Mystic Gorge and the Cathedral. The distance is not great so you can stroll along for an hour or so if you wish. Raft rides are available from Table Rock, a natural phenomenon that is well marked, ☎ 518-834-7454 or 800-537-1211, www.ausablechasm.com, ausable@together.net.

Buck Mountain: One of our favorite hikes on Lake George is located just a few miles from our house. The view from the top is memorable as you look down at the sparkling waters of Lake George filled with sailboats tacking back and forth. (This view provided a spectacular Christmas card for our family one year.) You can also see the Green Mountains of Vermont to the east. The round-trip distance of the trail is 6.6 miles, and it takes about four hours to climb up and down. To find the trailhead, leave the Adirondack Northway (I-87) at Exit 21, head east down to Route 9, then take a right on Route 9L. Drive for about seven miles to the Pilot Knob road and turn left; continue for a little more than three miles to the Buck Mountain trailhead. Follow the yellow DEC signs past hemlocks, a couple of logging roads, a stream, and Butternut Brook. As you climb up, glimpses of Lake George appear. Keep following signs and you will eventually come up on bare rock to the summit.

VIEWS FROM BUCK MOUNTAIN

Our son was at Camp Chingachcook back in the 1970s when a fire broke out on the mountain and campers were recruited to help fight it. Since then the foliage has been returning, except for a large expanse of bare rock at the top. A number of mountains rise and overlap each other in the distance, including Gore Mountain to the north and Blue Mountain just beyond. Crane Mountain lies to the west. Look north-northeast from the summit of Buck Mountain to see Sleeping Beauty and Black Mountain behind it along the eastern shore of Lake George.

Tongue Mountain: Early in our residence at Lake George we organized a group of friends to walk the length of the mountainous peninsula that we could see from our front window. We did not understand two important facts: first, the total distance that we wanted to cram into a single day was 16.2 miles, and second, it involved climbing and descending a series of peaks. At about four in the afternoon we came to our senses and bushwhacked across the peninsula to our starting point at Clay Meadows. The ADK describes this as "one of the most strenuous and spectacular routes in the eastern Adirondacks. With the Fifth Peak lean-to midway, this can be a fine backpacking trip, or a one-day trip. It's possible to be picked up by boat from Montcalm Point... " We indeed wished fervently for that.

There are shorter day routes that will allow you to enjoy the spectacular views of the Narrows of Lake George. This is less than a mile wide, encased by mountains on both sides, and overlooks the middle of the lake. This section of the lake is dotted with uninhabited islands that New York State furnishes with rather elegant campsites (☎ 800-456-CAMP). You can undertake shorter day-hikes from the **Clay Meadows** parking lot, walk the shore of **Northwest Bay**, or take a one-mile hike to **Deer Leap** (from the lot near the Sabbath Day Point end of the Tongue Mountain Range on Route 9N). Take the Northway (I-87) to Exit 24, head for Bolton Landing, then turn north on Rout 9N. You will reach the Clay Meadows parking lot first, and the Tongue Mountain Range lot on the other side of the pass. We have also explored sections of these trails on snowshoes. During other (warmer) seasons, be especially careful where you put your hands and feet, since this ridge of mountains is home to the timber rattlesnake. They won't bother you unless you bother them.

The Adirondacks

For more walks in the region, pick up a copy of *Adirondack Great Walks & Day Hikes* (see page 76), one of the pamphlets on trails put out by DEC, or the hiking guidebooks published by the Adirondack Mountain Club.

■ On Wheels

Scenic Drives

 Route 86/Whiteface Mountain: One of our favorite drives leaves Lake Placid on Route 86 heading for Whiteface Mountain, near Wilmington. The Whiteface Mountain Veterans Memorial Highway (Route 86) winds up almost to the top. You can walk up the rest of the way or take an elevator to the **Summit House**, where you can get tourist information as well as look at the view. The **Atmospheric Science Research Center** building stands at the top. There's a nature trail with flora and fauna so you can see what the weather does up there.

Route 30 winds along the Sacandaga River to **Sacandaga**, through Wells and Speculator. The road continues along the shore of Indian Lake through Sabael to the town of Indian Lake and then heads northwest to Blue Mountain Lake, home of the **Adirondack Museum**. You can combine a scenic tour with a visit to the museum.

Route 28 from Old Forge heads along **Fourth Lake** in the Fulton Chain towards Eagle Bay and Inlet, site of **Adirondack Discovery**, a parkwide interpretive program that explores the cultural and natural heritage of the Adirondack Park. The road winds around Seventh and Eighth Lakes before arriving in Raquette Lake. There, **Great Camp Sagamore** was the former summer home of the Alfred Vanderbilt family for 50 years (see *Sightseeing*, page 99).

The Champlain Trail heads north along Route 22 from **Whitehall**, the birthplace of the US Navy. **Fort Ticonderoga** is accessible at the junction of Route 22 with Route 74. Continue north on Route 22 to **Crown Point**. **Port Henry** is notable for the sign at Bulwagga Bay listing the sightings of Lake Champlain's legendary serpent, Champ. The trail continues north through two lovely towns, first (on Route 22) to **Westport** and then (on Route 9) to **Essex** (see page 27 for a more detailed description of this scenic drive between Westport and Essex). Essex is listed on the National Register of Historic Places, and you can enjoy pre-Civil War architecture there. The trail continues north on Routes 22 and 9 to **Ausable Chasm** and **Valcour Island** (see pages 84 and 32).

Scenic drives in the Adirondacks are endless – we have suggested only a few – and it's easy to find your own favorite route on the uncrowded, well-maintained roads that wind through the mountains. That's exactly what we did one day, on a quest to find the sites associated with a major historic event in the Adirondacks and a ghost town we had heard about.

On one of our travel-writing forays we decided to take ourselves on a mystery trip, to explore an area we had never been before. With only sketchy information, we started out from North Creek on Route 28N, passed Minerva, and looked for the first of two markers for Theodore Roosevelt. The first is right on the road next to a boarded-up brown building. It reads, "Theodore Roosevelt September 14, 1901 stopped at Aiden Lair to change horses in a night ride in a surrey from Mt. March to North Creek to take the oath of President at Buffalo."

In about five more miles we came across the second Roosevelt monument, surrounded with red geraniums. This sign reads, "Near this point while driving hastily from Tahawus Club to North Creek at 2:15 am September 14, 1901 Theodore Roosevelt became President of the US as William McKinley expired in Buffalo. Relay drivers David Hunter, Orrin Kellogg, Michael Cronin." Next we looked for County Road 25 and turned north for the seven miles to Tahawus.

ROOSEVELT IN THE WILDERNESS

The Roosevelt family was staying at the Tahawus Club when the following events occurred. Theodore Roosevelt and friends had reached the summit of Mount Marcy on September 13. A wilderness guide found Roosevelt resting on the shore of Lake Tear of the Clouds, where they were having lunch, and told him that President William McKinley was dying.

Roosevelt and his group hurried down to Tahawus and prepared to leave in the morning, until a cable arrived with the news that McKinley was near death. Although his friends wanted him to wait for daylight because the roads were treacherous, Roosevelt said he would go alone on foot. However, a driver was found and off they went into the night, arriving at 4:39 am in North Creek, where a special train waited. Secretary of State Loeb then told him that he was President. The Tahawus Club is private, but you can see the area and get some feeling about the wilderness that Roosevelt treasured.

Next we went in search of the ghost town of **Adirondac**. Turn north on County Road 25 and bounce along until you see a sign for the **High Peaks Trailhead**, then turn left again. If you want to climb Mt. Marcy from this side the distance is 14.3 miles; it is 16.1 miles to Adirondac Loj and 24.6 miles to Keene Valley.

Along the road you can't miss the old 1854 stone blast furnace of the **MacIntyre Iron Works**, once a thriving business, which is huge and was built to last. Look down and you will see the furnace openings. Farther on you will begin to see abandoned houses with shake exteriors, no windows and sagging doors. Several are on the road and more are hidden in the woods. The town of Adirondac is no longer – and it's rather sad to see a once vibrant town so still.

Just beyond the houses you will see the sign for **Upper Works Trailhead** and the distance from that point to the summit of Mt. Marcy is 10.1 miles. A sign here offers advice for winter hikers, "Winter Supplement: bring, wear and/or use: snowshoes or skis, crampons, no 100% cotton clothing, stove, sleeping bag and pad for injuries, wool shirt or sweater, hat, parka, good boots, non-plastic rainwear, map, compass, emergency food and water, matches, whistle, first aid kit, flashlight."

Head back to Newcomb and the **Hudson River Interpretive Center** where there is more information on the MacIntyre blast furnace. Another display shows "river driving," an exciting trip on the river standing on one log after another and guiding them along. It proclaims that a log put in at Newcomb arrives in Glens Falls in a few days.

 The last river drive was conducted in 1950 by Finch Pruyn, a lumber company in Glens Falls.

Also in Newcomb, the **Adirondack Park Visitor Interpretive Center** is the place to go for more information on the area. There is also a trail system starting from the interpretive building. The **Rich Lake Trail** is surfaced for wheelchair travelers. The **Peninsula Trail** passes by 200-year-old hemlocks and follows the high rocky peninsula out into Rich Lake. The **Sucker Brook Trail** goes by cedar wetlands and mixed hardwood stands to an inactive beaver colony. This walk is one mile in length and takes from 60 to 90 minutes.

Head on up Route 30 to the **Adirondack Park Visitor Interpretive Center** in **Paul Smiths** for more great information and displays on the Adirondacks. Walking trails from the building include the **Barnum Brook Trail**, leading for .6 mile to the north end of Heron Marsh and Barnum Brook on four bridges and boardwalks. It is accessible to wheelchairs, with assistance. The **Heron Marsh Trail** is .8 mile in length and has an elevated observation tower as well as boardwalks. The **Shingle Mill Falls Trail** goes by Heron Marsh Dam and a waterfall. The two-mile **Forest Ecology Trail** extends along a 900-foot boardwalk over a peatland bog. The one-mile **Silviculture Trail** illustrates how and why forests are managed for human use.

Bicycling

Friends say, "Hang in there until you get to the top – the view is worth the climb." True enough, and ardent cyclists keep moving up hills steadily. They come to the mountains by choice to get a big dose of the wonderful scenery that is always seen more clearly on a bike than in a car.

You can also choose to cycle on special bike paths like our local **Warren County Bikeway**, which extends from Glens Falls to Lake George Beach State Park. Built on an old Delaware and Hudson railroad bed right-of-way for part of the route, its terrain is mostly flat or evenly graded. It parallels Route 9 and can be entered along the way. As more people take up cycling for fun and exercise, the system of bike paths is expanding. For information contact **Warren County Tourism Department**, Municipal Center, Route 9, Exit 20 from I-87, ☎ 518-761-6366. For tours and bicycle rental contact any of the following outfitters.

Beach Road Outdoor Supply Co., 47 Canada Street, Lake George, NY 12845, ☎ 518-668-4040.

High Peaks Cyclery, 331 Main Street, Lake Placid, NY 12946, ☎ 518-523-3764.

Inside Edge, 643 Upper Glen Street, Queensbury, NY l2804, ☎ 518-793-5676.

Mount Van Hoevenberg Mountain Bike Center, Route 73, Lake Placid, NY 12946, ☎ 800-462-6236 or 518-523-4436.

Whiteface Mountain Biking, Route 86, Wilmington, NY 12997, ☎ 800-462-6236 or 518-946-2223.

■ On Water

Excursion Boats

Scenic trips are available in a number of places in the Adirondacks. Some are on old-time vessels, others on new ships. All have individual character and are popular with tourists. Some cruises offer lunch, dinner or brunch. Prices range from $8.50 for a one-hour cruise to $13 for longer cruises. Call for information on prices for dinner and lunch cruises.

Blue Mountain Boat Livery, Route 28, PO Box 229, Blue Mountain Lake, NY 12812, ☎ 518-352-7351. Scenic boat trips are offered in 1916 wooden launches.

Indian Pipes Charter Cruises, Sagamore Resort, 110 Sagamore Road, Bolton Landing, NY 12814, ☎ 518-644-9400, extension 6040. Take a cruise on the 72-foot *Morgan* or the 36-foot *Albin Trawler*.

Lake George Shoreline Cruise, 2 James Street, Lake George, NY 12845, ☎ 518-668-4644 or 518-894-CHARTER, www.lakegeorgeshoreline.com, shoreline@netheaven.com. Shoreline operates five cruise boats including its flagship, *Horicon*, a wooden vessel that replicates many features of a classic 19th-century lake steamer of the same name.

Lake George Steamboat Company, Steel Pier, Beach Road, Lake George, NY 12845, ☎ 800-553-BOAT or 518-668-5777, www.lakegeorgesteamboat.com, info@lakegeorgesteamboat.com. This is the oldest continuously operating steamboat company in the region, dating back to 1817. Vessels include the steamboat SS *Minnehaha*, the 1908 MV *Mohican*, and the elegant flagship MV *Lac du Saint Sacrement*.

Lake Placid Marina, Lake Street, Lake Placid, NY 12946, ☎ 518-523-9704. Cruises are on turn-of-the-century wooden boats.

Juniper Boat Tours, 2 Dock Street, Plattsburgh, NY 12901, ☎ 800-388-8970 or 518-561-8970. Cruises are offered on the MV *Juniper*.

Old Forge Lake Cruises, Route 28 Main Street, PO Box 1137, Old Forge, NY 13420, ☎ 315-369-6473, www.oldforgecruises.com. Cruises are on large double-decked boats.

Raquette Lake Navigation Company, Pier 1, PO Box 100, Raquette Lake, NY 13436, ☎ 315-354-5532, info@raquettelakenavigation.com, www.raquettelakenavigation.com. Cruises are offered for lunch, dinner and brunch on the *W.W. Durant*.

Schroon Lake Boat Tours, South Avenue, Schroon Lake, NY 12870, ☎ 518-532-7675. One-hour scenic narrated cruises.

Westport Marina, Washington Street, PO Box 410, Westport, NY 12993, ☎ 800-626-0342, marina@shipstore.com, www.shipstore.com. Narrated cruises on the *Philomena D*.

Canoeing, Rafting & Kayaking

Canoe waters are not in short supply in the Adirondacks. You can plan a trip in various regions, including the north flow through the **Oswegatchie River**, **Grass River**, **Raquette River**, **St. Regis River**, **Salmon River**, **Chateaugay River**, **Great Chazy River**, **Saranac River**, **Ausable River** and **Bouquet River**. The south and west flow moves through the **Black River**, upper **Hudson River** and **Mohawk River**. See *Festivals & Events*, page 102, for details about the annual Hudson River Whitewater Derby.

The **Adirondack Regional Tourism Council** (see page 75) offers a booklet titled *Adirondack Waterways*, with sketch maps and route descriptions, regulations, guidelines, lists of outfitters, guides, equipment and supplies. And the **Adirondack Mountain Club**, listed on page 76, also has information on canoe and kayak routes.

The **Fulton Chain of Lakes**, beginning at Old Forge, is popular among canoeists because only two carries connect the lakes. At the edge of **Eighth Lake** you can carry for one mile into **Raquette Lake,** where you can paddle past a Great Camp.

The **Raquette River** winds along at a pace that bird watchers enjoy, as well as fishermen. At **Raquette Falls** there's a 1.3-mile carry around the falls. Head for **Stony Creek Ponds** and get into **Upper Saranac Lake** and routes to the north. One of our October canoe trips to Raquette Lake had a surprise ending. About 20 of us packed up our canoes, tents, food and gear and drove to the put-in spot for this trip. The day was clear and beautiful, warm and windless for a great paddle. After pitching our tents and making dinner we climbed into sleeping bags for the night and still felt somewhat cold by early morning. The first person out of his tent whispered loud enough for all to hear, "Who's ready for a snowball fight?" Several inches of snow had fallen on our tents – and no one had bothered to tune into a weather radio before departure.

The **St. Regis Wilderness Area** is accessed from **Upper Saranac Lake**. There are several loop trips in Fish Creek, Floodwood and Follensby Clear ponds. Or you can head up to Paul Smiths, which is nine miles from **Little Clear Pond**. The **St. Regis Lakes** offer a loop trip with several Great Camps to see.

From **Bolton Landing** on Lake George, you can explore the wilderness area on the islands in the center of that lake. Farther inland, there are many lake and river opportunities for canoes and kayaks, and the **Blue Ledges** area of the upper Hudson is a mecca for rafters, especially during the wild water season each spring. In recent years outflows from a number of dams have also provided warm-water opportunities for rafting and whitewater canoeing or kayaking.

WHITEWATER TALES

Every Memorial Day Weekend the Glens Falls Canoe Club, about 15 canoes strong, used to set up camp on **Schroon Lake** on Fridays. We even had a banner proclaiming our existence to the world. On Saturday morning we would spot cars along the Upper Schroon River and begin our paddle at North Hudson. It was advisable to carry around the four-foot Schroon Falls, and no one was even tempted to try shooting it!

On Sunday we would paddle through the lake – arduously with a strong headwind against us one year – and it was easy to look forward to relaxing in camp that night. On Monday we continued down the Lower Schroon River, culminating in the "Big Drop" below the Starbuckville dam through a long stretch of Class III whitewater. On the next day we put in just below the drop and headed for Warrensburg. One year we managed to dump all of us in a patch of Class IV whitewater just before the Schroon joins the Hudson.

One year we found that an open canoe was no match for the Class IV "haystacks" (standing waves formed by steep declines) on the **Schroon River** as it roars through broken mill dams in Warrensburg before joining the Hudson. Four canoes and one kayak – paddled by an 11-year-old girl – entered the watery turmoil and started down the course. All went well until we encountered a series of three haystacks, each one larger than the last. One canoe rose in the air over a haystack and capsized, then another flipped with our teenaged son, who calmly pointed his feet downriver and headed for shore. We were the next to fill and capsize, came up spluttering, then gathered our wits and remembered to angle towards shore. Meanwhile the young kayaker blithely paddled alongside with not a care in the world.

CANOEING & RAFTING OUTFITTERS

Adirondack Canoes and Kayaks, 96 Old Piercefield Road at Route 3, Tupper Lake, NY 12986, ☎ 800-499-2174 or 518-359-2174, adkcanoe@ capital.net, www.capital.net/com/adkcanoe.

Adirondac Rafting Company, 7 Patch Lane, Lake Placid, NY 12946, ☎ 800-510-RAFT or 518-523-1635, riverfun@northnet.org, www.raftonline.com.

Adirondack River Outfitters, Whitewater Rafting, Route 28, Old Forge, NY 13420, ☎ 800-525-RAFT, aro@aroadventures.com, www.aroadventures.com.

Adventure Sports Rafting Company, Main Street, PO Box 775, Indian Lake, NY 12842, ☎ 800-441-RAFT or 518-648-5812.

Beaver Brook Outfitters, PO Box 96, Wevertown, NY 12886, ☎ 888-454-8433 or 518-251-3394, pete@beaverbrook.net, www.beaverbrook.net.

High Peaks Touring, Essex, NY 12936, ☎ 518-963-7028, or in Lake Placid ☎ 518-523-3764.

Hudson River Rafting Company, 1 Main Street, North Creek, NY 12853, ☎ 800-888-RAFT, 518-251-3215. In Lake Placid, ☎ 518-523-3706, www.hudsonriverrafting.com, hudson@netheaven.com.

Middle Earth Expeditions, Box 37, Lake Placid, NY 12946, ☎ 518-523-7172, www.adirondackrafting.com, wayne@adirondackrafting.com.

Northern Pathfinders, PO Box 214, Lake Clear, NY 12945, ☎ 800-882-PATH, nplrafting@aol.com, http://members.aol.com/raftingguy/npl.html.

Raquette River Outfitters, PO Box 653, Tupper Lake, NY 12986, ☎ 518-359-3228, www.raquettelakenavigation.com, info@raquette-lakenavigation.com.

St. Regis Canoe Outfitters, Inc. Floodwood Road, Lake Clear, NY 12945, ☎ 518-891-1838, http://canoeoutfitters.com.

Whitewater Challengers, Route 28, 13th Lake, North Creek NY, 12853, ☎ 800-443-RAFT or 518-251-3746.

INTERNATIONAL SCALE OF RIVER DIFFICULTY

- **Class I** – Moving water with a few riffles and small waves. Few or no obstructions.

- **Class II** – Easy rapids with waves up to three feet and wide, clear channels that are obvious without scouting. Some maneuvering is required.

- **Class III** – Rapids with high, irregular waves often capable of swamping an open canoe. Narrow passages that often require complex maneuvering. May require scouting from shore.

- **Class IV** – Long, difficult rapids with constructed passages that often require precise maneuvering in very turbulent waters. Scouting from shore is often necessary, and conditions make rescue difficult. **Generally not possible for open canoes**. Boaters in covered canoes and kayaks should be able to Eskimo-roll.

- **Class V** – Extremely difficult, long, and very violent rapids with highly congested routes, which must nearly always be

The Adirondacks

scouted from shore. Rescue conditions are difficult and there is a significant hazard to life in the event of a mishap. Ability to Eskimo roll is essential for kayaks and canoes.

■ **Class VI** – Difficulties of Class V carried to the extreme of navigability. **Nearly impossible and very dangerous**. For teams of experts only, after close study and with all precautions taken.

Fishing

With all of the lakes dotting the Adirondack landscape – many of them replenished with native stocks – fishing is very popular. Licenses are required for anyone 16 years and older (see below). Some New York residents may apply for free licenses: those over 70, the blind, some native Americans living in New York, and veterans with a 40 percent or more service-connected disability. For more information contact the **Department of Environmental Conservation** (DEC) Regional Office, Hudson Street, Warrensburg, NY 12885, ☎ 518-623-3671. DEC publishes a pamphlet, *New York State Boat Launching Sites*, a directory of access and launching areas.

Fishing licenses are available at town and county offices, bait and tackle shops, local sporting goods stores and some state campsites. Licenses for the season cost residents $14, non-residents $35 or $11 for a day. You can also receive a license by mail if you send the fee to New York State Department of Environmental Conservation, 50 Wolf Road, Albany, NY 12233. The DEC Region 5 Hot Line gives fishing conditions, ☎ 518-623-3682. Licensed fishing guides can also be found in the yellow pages of the phone directory or through local sporting goods stores.

If you bring your own boat with a motor it must be registered with the **New York State Department of Motor Vehicles**. An out-of-state craft may operate for up to 90 days in New York State if registered with the proper agency in its home state. You must clean your propellers and bottom before putting your boat in the water to remove any unwanted weeds. Zebra mussels and milfoil are major problems in some lakes, including most of Lake Champlain and some of Lake George, so marinas are mandated to inspect incoming boats with great care, and if you launch on your own you should follow the same practice.

■ On Horseback

 Horseback riding is a traditional and popular activity in the Adirondacks, and a number of ranches offer accommodations. There is a particularly large collection of dude ranches between Lake George and Lake Luzerne. Many of them are open year-round, and all provide guides on tours. Prices range from about $22 for one hour to $125 for a day. Please call for exact prices and times.

Adirondack Saddle Tours, Box 470, Uncas Road, Eagle Bay, NY 13331, ☎ 315-357-4499. Open year-round, but call in winter as there are steep sections that may be difficult. Guides on tours, no lessons.

Bennett's Riding Stable, Route 9N S, 91 Gage Hill, Lake Luzerne, NY 12846, ☎ 518-696-4444. Open year-round, guides on tours; specialty is a 2½-hour ride to Beach Mountain at $48 per person. One-hour rides are currently $22. Riders need to be at least seven years of age, but pony rides are offered for younger children. Call about Lake Vanare Snowmobile rides.

Bit N Bridle Riding Ranch, Ticker Road, Stony Creek, NY 12878, ☎ 518-696-2776. Seasonal, guides on tours, mostly adults. The current price range is $25-40 per person. The facility has been closed for six years and hopes to reopen in 2003.

Cold River Ranch, Route 3, Tupper Lake, NY 12986, ☎ 518-359-7559. Open year-round, guides on tours, offers all-day tours with lunch currently at $95 per person, or 4½-hour tours with lunch at $75.

Emerald Springs Ranch, RFD 1, Box 189A, Saranac Lake, NY 12983, ☎ 518-891-3727, www.emerald.springs.com. Open year-round, lessons, guides on tours. Current prices are $46 for one person, $35 each for two to four and $32 each for five to six.

Riding-Hy Ranch Resort, Sherman Lake, Warrensburg, NY 12885, ☎ 518-494-2742. Horseback riding is only for guests and is part of a package.

Roaring Brook Ranch & Tennis Resort, Route 9N South, PO Box 671, Lake George, NY 12845, ☎ 800-882-BROOK (7665) or 518-668-5767, fax 518-668-4019, www.roaringbrookranch.com, mail@roaringbrook-ranch.com. The price for one hour is $21 and you need to be a guest at the ranch.

Thousand Acres Ranch Resort, 465 Warrensburg Road, Stony Creek, NY 12878, ☎ 518-696-2444, www.l000acres.com. Open during the season and on weekends in winter. Guides on tours. The current price for one hour is $30.

■ On Snow

Downhill Skiing

The State of New York has been providing downhill skiing facilities for a long time at three major areas: **Whiteface Mountain** and **Gore Mountain** in the Adirondacks, and **Belleayre** in the Catskills. Trails on Whiteface were first cut for the 1932 Winter Olympics, and Gore's predecessor was a ski bowl on the other side of the mountain. Both areas came under the aegis of the Olympic Regional Development Authority (ORDA), which continues to manage them, in the early 1980s. For more information, contact Olympic Regional Development Authority (ORDA), 218 Main Street, Lake Placid, NY 12946, ☎ 518-523-1655, www.orda.org.

Gore Mountain – Gore has been a favorite with locals and skiers from afar since the 1930s. Over the years the area has added more quads and increased snow making to 95%. And the new gondola is appreciated in this frosty north country. The elevation is 3,600 feet and the vertical drop 2,100 feet. A network of 60 trails is served by the gondola and seven chairlifts, including two quads. Gore Mountain, North Creek, NY 12853, ☎ 800-342-1234 or 518-251-2411, www.goremountain.com.

Whiteface Mountain – Also called the "Olympic Mountain," Whiteface has quite a heritage, including hosting two Olympic Winter Games (in 1932 and 1980) and a number of other major downhill skiing events. When you approach the mountain from the east, you will immediately understand how its hoary upper slides suggested the name. It's a mountain that inspires respect, a likely site for races – including the World Cup – with 44% of its trails rated black. The summit elevation is 4,867 feet, the highest lift terminus 4,381 feet, and the vertical drop 3,430 feet – the greatest in the East. But there are plenty of blue trails for intermediates, from Little Whiteface (3,676 feet), and one from the Summit lift, as well as a series of greens on the lower mountain and an adjacent, connected novice area. The network of 72 trails on the two linked mountains is served by a gondola and nine chairlifts, including one quad and two triples. Whiteface Mountain, Wilmington, NY 12997, ☎ 800-462-6236, www.whiteface.com. For the Olympic Regional Development Authority, www.orda.org.

Cross-Country Skiing

Cunningham's Ski Barn, Inc., 1 Main Street, North Creek, NY 12853, ☎ 518-251-3215, www.cunninghamsskibarn.com, ski@cunninghamsskibarn.com. There are 40 km of trails in North Creek and just outside North Creek. The trails follow the Hudson River Gorge and run through Beaver Meadows.

Friends Lake Inn, Friends Lake Road, Chestertown, NY 12817, ☎ 518-494-4751. There are 32 km of trails in meadows and woods surrounding an inn noted for its cuisine and wines.

Garnet Hill Lodge Cross Country Skiing, 13th Lake Road, North River, NY 12856, ☎ 518-251-2444 or ski shop 251-2150, www.garnet-hill.com. With unusual altitude for a cross-country area, snow comes early and stays late on 55 km of trails through wooded hillsides.

Gore Mountain, North Creek, NY 12953, ☎ 518-251-2411. There are 10 km of cross-country trails adjacent to the downhill ski area.

Lapland Lake Nordic Vacation Center, 139 Lapland Lake Road, Northville NY 12134, ☎ 800-453-SNOW (24-hour taped ski report) or 518-863-4974, www.laplandlake.com or www.xcski.org/lapland. There are 50 km of woodland trails designed and maintained by Olavi Hirvonen, former Olympic skier.

Mount Van Hoevenberg Recreation Area, Lake Placid, NY 12946, ☎ 800-462-6236 or 518-523-2811. This highly developed venue for Olympic competition has 50 km of trails.

Warrensburg Cross-Country Ski Trail System, Golf Course Road (County Road 40), Warrensburg NY, ☎ 518-792-9951, ext. 245; ski phone ☎ 518-793-1300. A trail system along the shore of the upper Hudson River, with easier trails on the golf course and some more difficult ones in the woods.

Whiteface Club, Whiteface Inn Road, Lake Placid, NY 12946, ☎ 800-422-6757 or 518-523-2551. The Club, located on the west shore of Lake Placid, has 20 km of trails.

■ In the Air

Balloning

Try **A Beautiful Balloon**, 47 Assembly Point Road, Lake George, NY 12845, ☎ 518-656-9328 or 973-335-9799, www.balloon-rides.com, balloonsnj@aol.com. Reservations are required for hot air champagne flights over Lake George and Glens Falls. Flights take place at sunrise and two hours before sunset. They are weather-dependent, of course. The sensation aloft is tranquil and romantic. Price vary from $225 to $295 per person.

Sightseeing

■ Northern Adirondack Region

Lake Placid

 Lake Placid is well known for its **Olympic** sites and facilities developed for the 1932 and 1980 Winter Games. They have been improved and developed over the years and now are in active use for training and competition throughout the year. You can visit a number of them to watch Olympians in training and try out a few venues for yourself. Contact the Visitor's Bureau in Lake Placid (see *Information Sources*, page 75) for detailed information and schedules of events.

John Brown Farm and Grave, John Brown Road, Route 73, Lake Placid, NY 12943, ☎ 518-523-3900. The farm is two miles south of Lake Placid. John Brown came to Lake Placid in 1848 and some of his personal possessions are still on the farm.

Saranac Lake

Robert Louis Stevenson Memorial Cottage, 11 Stevenson Lane, Saranac Lake, NY 12983, ☎ 518-891-1462. Stevenson lived in this cottage from 1887 to 1888 during his rest cure in the Trudeau Clinic. He enjoyed writing up here in the woods, and some of his personal memorabilia remain in the cottage.

Paul Smiths

White Pine Camp, White Pine Road, Paul Smiths, NY 12970, ☎ 518-327-3030, www.whitepinecamp.com. White Pine Camp was the summer white house for President Calvin Coolidge from July 7 to September 18, 1926. During a two-hour tour you will see the owner's cabin, dining hall, boat houses, bowling alley, a Japanese tea house and the tennis house. Cabins on the lake are available during the summer season. One cabin is also available year-round.

Wilmington

High Falls Gorge, Route 86, Wilmington, NY 12997, ☎ 518-946-2278, info@highfallsgorge, www.highfallsgorge.com. These granite cliffs are over a billion years old, and waterfalls cascade down 700 feet. There are self-guided tours on groomed paths and steel bridges.

Newcomb

Hikers can enjoy an expedition into the forest to visit **Camp Santanoni**, one of the few surviving Great Camps in the Adirondacks. The Main Camp is located 4.7 miles from the Gate Lodge in Newcomb. Camp Santanoni's first owner was Robert C. Pruyn, an Albany banker and businessman. He also acted as secretary for his father, Robert H. Pruyn, the minister to Japan appointed by President Lincoln in 1861. The main camp was built from 1891 to 1893, with farm buildings and the Gate Lodge added in 1902. The Gate Lodge is located on Route 28N at the edge of Newcomb. One mile into the estate the farm grouping includes barns, three farmhouses and workers' cottages, a stone creamery, workshop, chicken house, kennels, smoke house, root cellar and other buildings. Located in the middle of wilderness, the estate was designed to be self-sufficient.

The Main Camp has six buildings, including the living and dining lodge, four sleeping cabins, and a kitchen with staff bedrooms. Log grillwork on the eaves, birch-bark wall covering, handhewn beams in the ceiling of the main building, and fieldstone fireplaces provide genuine Adirondack rustic architecture. An artist's studio was used by Edward Lansing Pruyn, the owner's son. The porch roof, stepped in the Japanese fashion, resembles a bird in flight, the phoenix.

Camp Santanoni was sold to the Melvin family of Syracuse, then bought by the Nature Conservancy and is now owned by the New York State Forest Preserve. Since 1993, the New York State Department of Environmental Conservation, Adirondack Architectural Heritage, and the Town of Newcomb have combined to preserve the camp. The public is encouraged to help. Contact Friends of Camp Santanoni at Santanoni Gate Lodge, PO Box 113, Newcomb NY 12852, ☎ 518-582-5472.

■ Central Adirondack Region

Raquette Lake

Great Camp Sagamore, Sagamore Road, off Route 28, Raquette Lake, NY 13436, ☎ 315-354-5311, www.sagamore.org. Built by William Durant in 1897, it is a Great Camp very much in use through a variety of short-term residential programs. The Vanderbilt family owned it from 1903 to 1954 and their children's heights are marked on a doorjamb in the Main Lodge. Today, Camp Sagamore is open seasonally for conferences and workshops. A variety of topics entice visitors to this historic camp.

The Adirondacks

GREAT CAMPS

Adirondack Great Camps are not the sort of camp you went to as a child. William Dix wrote, "An Adirondack camp does not mean a canvas tent or a bark wigwam... a permanent summer home where the fortunate owners assemble for several weeks each year and live in perfect comfort and even luxury, though in the heart of the woods, with no near neighbors, no roads and no danger of intrusion."

Most were made of logs and decorated with rough woodwork, often with the bark in place. Rustic deécor was in fashion. Guests were housed in cabins or perhaps on the second floor of a boathouse. The dining room was often in a separate building. Chimney construction was precise in order to ensure smoke going up instead of out into rooms. Some of the fireplaces were large enough to stand in. Furniture tended to be rustic and was often made on the site.

Blue Mountain Lake

Adirondack Museum, Route 30, PO Box 99, Blue Mountain Lake, NY 12812, ☎ 518-352-7311, www.adkmuseum.org. Adirondack Museum is a prize, with exhibits nicely displayed. It has collections both indoors and outdoors, covering logging and mining as well as recreation, folklore and local culture in the Adirondacks. The Adirondack guideboat collection is highly regarded, as is *El Lagarto*, George Reis's Gold Cup winner on Lake George during the 1930s.

Crown Point

Crown Point State Historic Site, four miles East of Route 9N/22 at Champlain Bridge, RD 1, Box 219, Crown Point, NY 12928, ☎ 518-597-3666. The original Fort St. Frederic was built by the French in 1731 and the British Fort Crown Point replaced it in 1759. You can walk on the grounds to see the restored ruins after viewing a video on the historic episodes that took place here.

Fort Ticonderoga

Fort Ticonderoga, Route 74, PO Box 390, Ticonderoga, NY 12883, ☎ 518-585-2821. The French built the fort in 1755 during the French and Indian War. It was called Fort Carillon at that time. In May 1775, Ethan Allen, Benedict Arnold and the Green Mountain Boys arrived. According to legend, Allen shouted at the commanding officer, Captain Delaplace, "Come out, you damned old rat."

One favorite diorama here is colorful; it depicts the Black Watch wearing their red jackets and distinctive kilts. This famous regiment was decimated in the English attempt to capture the fort from the French in 1758. Collections on display include an original American flag, perhaps made by Betsy Ross. During the summer season you can attend encampments of the French and Indian War, the Revolutionary War, and special events on the Place d'Armes.

■ Southern Adirondack Region

Bolton Landing

Marcella Sembrich Opera Museum, 4800 Lakeshore Drive, PO Box 417, Bolton Landing, NY 12814, ☎ 528/644-9839 or 644-2492. This museum was home to the famous opera singer during summers. Her musical scores and personal collections are here. Classes and performances are given during the summer.

Up Yonda Farm Environmental Education Center, Route 9N, Bolton Landing, NY 12814, ☎ 518-644-3823. Up Yonda was opened in 1997 on 78 acres. The memorial flower garden is spectacular, and there's a nature trail to follow. Programs are given by naturalists. Members of the Garden Club of Lake George spend hours weeding the garden and gave a bench for the benefit of those who would like to rest and savor the beauty in the garden.

Lake George

Prospect Mountain Veterans Memorial Highway, Route 9, PO Box 220, Warrensburg, NY 12885, ☎ 518-668-5198. The drive leads up to the top of Prospect Mountain for a great view down half the length of Lake George. You can also climb up on a path from Lake George Village.

Fort William Henry, 36 Canada Street, Lake George, NY 12845, ☎ 800-234-0267 or 518-668-5471. This fort has had a bloody history, especially as the site of a massacre of prisoners by the Indians in 1757. Their greed encouraged them to open recent graves; the men had died of smallpox, which then spread to those who opened the graves. Demonstrations are held during each day so you can visualize life at the fort during the French and Indian War.

Lake George Battlefield Park is noted for its collection of bronze monuments, including that of Father Isaac Jogues, the first white man to see Lake George. The ruins of Fort George lie in the park and are now being carefully excavated.

Lake George Historical Association Museum, Canada and Amherst Street, PO Box 472, Lake George, NY 12845, ☎ 518-668-5044. The museum is housed in the Old Court House and Jail. You can peruse the displays about this historic village; they include items from cannonballs to photographs of old steamships.

Festivals & Events

■ May

 Adirondack Paddlefest, Fourth Lake, Route 28, Inlet, NY 13360, ☎ 315-357-6672, www.mountainmanoutdoors.com. This event claims to be the largest on-water canoe and kayak exposition in the world, with more than 2,000 boats for sale and available for demonstration. The weekend also includes lectures on wilderness conservation, paddling clinics and water safety demonstrations.

Round the Mountain Canoe Race, Saranac Lake, ☎ 800-347-1992 or 518-891-1900, www.saranaclake.com.

Hudson River Whitewater Derby, North Creek, ☎ 518-251-3777.

THE HUDSON RIVER WHITEWATER DERBY

This event makes news during the first weekend of May every year. You can enter the slalom events at North River on Saturday and run the seven-mile downriver race from North Creek to Riparius on Sunday. When the water is low contestants paddle hard to avoid wrapping their canoes around rocks. When it is high those in open canoes try to avoid swamping in standing waves, while kayakers just plunge right through them. One of us participated every year – after trying to get in shape for the strenuous exertion. A wet suit became a necessity because the water from the snowmelt is very cold! Spectators line the shores with their picnics and cameras, providing a great sense of camaraderie.

■ June

Americade Motorcycle Rally, Lake George, ☎ 518-798-7888. This rally is very popular and draws hundreds of people every year.

No-Octane Regatta, Blue Mountain Lake, ☎ 518-352-7311. This event is great – all sorts of watercraft and no noise!

Larac June Arts Festival, Glens Falls, ☎ 518-798-1141.

Feeder Canal Canoe Race, Queensbury, ☎ 518-792-5363.

Adirondack Ensemble Chamber Music Series, Queensbury, ☎ 518-251-5484. See their website at www.adirondackensemble.org for schedules.

■ July

Arts and Crafts Festival, Warrensburg, ☎ 518-623-2161.

Adirondack Waterfest, Lake George, ☎ 518-623-3291 or 518-668-4881. Displays, educational activities, demonstrations, music, entertainment.

■ August

Warren County Fair, Warrensburg, ☎ 518-623-3291.

Double "H" Hole in the Woods Ranch Gala, Lake George, ☎ 518-696-5676.

Antique & Classic Boat Show, Lake George

■ September

Adirondack Balloon Festival, Queensbury, ☎ 518-761-6366.

 For more information on events in Warren County call ☎ 800-365-1050.

Where to Stay

ACCOMMODATIONS PRICE SCALE
Prices for a double room for one or two persons, before taxes.
$ . . . . Under $50
$$. . . . . $50 to $100
$$$ . . . . $101 to $175
$$$$ . . . . Over $175

■ Northern Adirondack Region

Lake Placid

 Adirondack Loj, Box 867, Lake Placid, NY 12946, ☎ 518-523-3441, fax 518-523-3518, adkinfo@northnet.org, www.adk.org. $. The Adirondack Mountain Club operates this lodge on Heart

Lake. It is ideally located as a base for hiking in the High Peaks.

Best Western Golden Arrow, 150 Main Street, Lake Placid, NY 12946, ☎ 800-582-5540 or 518-523-3353, fax 518-523-3353, info@golden-arrow.com, www.golden-arrow.com. $$-$$$. It is located right on the main street and also fronts on Mirror Lake. There's a beach plus canoes, paddle boats and row boats.

Interlaken Inn, 15 Interlaken Avenue, Lake Placid, NY 12946, ☎ 800-428-4369 or 518-523-1124, fax 518-523-0117, interlkn@northnet.org, www.innbook.com/intr.html. $$$-$$$$ MAP. Victorian furnishings make this house attractive. Don't miss the bears and dolls waiting in the entry.

Lake Placid Lodge, Whiteface Inn Road, Lake Placid, NY 12946, ☎ 518-523-2700, fax 518-523-1124, info@lakeplacidlodge.com, www.lakeplacidlodge.com. $$$$. This luxurious lodge looks very rustic with its Adirondack furnishings.

Mirror Lake Inn, 5 Mirror Lake Drive, Lake Placid, NY 12946, ☎ 518-523-2544, fax 518-523-2871, info@mirrorlakeinn.com, www.mirrorlakeinn.com. $$$-$$$$. The inn was reconstructed after a fire in the 1980s. It is beautifully furnished with antiques, including an 1895 clock that was saved from the fire, and the grand piano.

Keene

The Bark Eater, Alstead Hill Road, PO Box 139, Keene, NY 12942, ☎ 800-232-1607 or 518-576-2221, fax 518-576-2071, barkeater@tvenet.com. $-$$$. It was once a stagecoach stopover.

Paul Smiths

White Pine Camp, White Pine Road, Paul Smiths, NY 12970, ☎ 518-327-3030, wpinecamp@aol.com, www.whitepinecamp.com. Call for weekly rates. This is an historic Great Camp and was also President Coolidge's summer white house in 1926.

Saranac Lake

Hotel Saranac, 101 Main Street, Saranac Lake, NY 12983, ☎ 800-937-0211 or 518-937-0211, fax 518-891-5664, www.hotelsaranac.com. $-$$. Paul Smiths College operates this hotel with the chefs of tomorrow on duty.

Upper Saranac Lake

The Wawbeek, 553 Panther Mountain Road, Upper Saranac Lake, NY 12986, ☎ 800-953-2656 or 518-359-2656, fax 518-359-2475, wawbeek@capital.net, www.wawbeek.com. $$$-$$$$. Located on 40 private acres with 1,700 feet of shoreline. Rooms are available in the log cabins and cottages, some with kitchens.

Tupper Lake

Red Top Inn Motel, Route 30, Tupper Lake, NY 12986, ☎ 518-359-9209. $-$$. Red Top is across the road from the lake and near a golf course and skiing.

■ Central Adirondack Region

Blue Mountain Lake

The Hedges, Blue Mountain Lake, NY 12812, ☎ 518-352-7325, fax 518-352-7672. $$$. Stone and log cottages are furnished with Adirondack-style pieces.

Hemlock Hall, Blue Mountain Lake, NY 12814, ☎ 518-352-7706. $$$. Cottages are located right on the lake.

Hague

Ruah Bed & Breakfast, 34 Lakeshore Drive, Hague, NY 12836, ☎ 800-224-7549 or 518-543-8816, www.ruahbb.com. $$-$$$. The house has landscaped gardens and a view of Lake George. Furnishings include the personal china and antique collections of the owners.

Trout House Village Resort, Lake Shore Drive, Hague, NY 12836, ☎ 800-368-6088 or 518-543-6088, www.trouthouse.com. $-$$$$. Accommodation is available in the lodge as well as cottages. Boats and bikes are on the site.

Chestertown

Friends Lake Inn, 963 Friends Lake Road, Chestertown, NY 12817, ☎ 518-494-4751, fax 518-494-4616, www.friendslake.com. $$$ MAP. This 1860s inn has been renovated with lovely furnishings and every comfort. The wine cellar is one of the finest in New York. There is a restaurant serving gourmet cuisine.

Landon Hill, 10 Landon Hill Road, Chestertown, NY 12817, ☎ 888-244-2599, phone/fax 518-494-2599, landon@bedbreakfast.net, www.bedbreakfast.net. $$. Landon Hill is located at the crossroads of the southern Adirondacks. It is family-run and very cosy.

The Adirondacks

Inlet

Holl's Inn, Inlet, NY 13360, ☎ 315-357-2941, www.hollsinn.com. $$ AP. This is a real Adirondack inn still going strong in the same family since 1935. Holl's is located on the south shore of Fourth Lake, between Old Forge and Raquette Lake.

North Creek

Copperfield Inn, 307 Main Street, North Creek, NY 12853, ☎ 800-424-9910 or 518-251-2500, fax 518-251-4143, www.copperfieldinn.com. $$$-$$$$. This comfortable, modern inn, northwest of Chestertown, is convenient for both winter and summer sports in the area.

North River

Garnet Hill Lodge, 13th Lake Road, North River, NY 12856, ☎ 518-251-2444, fax 518-251-3089, www.garnet-hill.com. $$-$$$. Accommodations are available in the lodge as well as cottages. It is popular for cross-country skiing as well as summer activities.

Schroon Lake

Schroon Lake Bed & Breakfast, Route 9, Schroon Lake, NY 12870, ☎ 800-523-6755 or 518-532-7042, fax 518-532-9820, schroonbb@aol.com, www.schroonbb.com. $$-$$$. White wicker rockers are ready for guests on the porch with a mountain view.

The Silver Spruce Inn, PO Box 426 Route 9, Schroon Lake, NY 12870, ☎ 518-532-7031, www.silverspruce.com. $$. The original house dates from the 1800s; it was expanded to serve as an estate for an executive retreat.

■ Southern Adirondack Region

Lake George

Dunham's Bay Lodge, 2999 State Route 9L, Lake George, NY 12845, ☎ 800-79 LODGE or 518-656-9242, fax 518-656-4019, www.dunhamsbay.com. $$-$$$. The green lawn from the lodge down to the lake sets the stage for relaxation with a view. You can enjoy boating and swimming on the sand beach. The large indoor pool is also popular, and a new restaurant called the Chase House serves breakfast and dinner.

Roaring Brook Ranch & Tennis Resort, Route 9N South, PO Box 671, Lake George, NY 12845, ☎ 800-882-7665 or 518-668-5767, fax 518-668-

4019, www.roaringbrookranch.com. $$. This established resort offers all sorts of sports in a woodsy setting.

Tall Pines Motel, Route 9, Lake George, NY 12845, ☎ 800-368-5122 or 518-668-5122, fax 518-668-3563. $$-$$$. The bike trail is just across the road, and there's a pool on the grounds.

Bolton Landing

Melody Manor Resort, 4610 Lake Shore Drive, PO Box 366, Bolton Landing, NY 12814, ☎ 518-644-9750, fax 518-644-9750, www.melody-manor.com. $$-$$$. This resort offers both pool and lake swimming.

The Sagamore, 110 Sagamore Road, Bolton Landing, NY 12814, ☎ 800-358-3585 or 518-644-9400, fax 518-644-2626, www.thesagamore.com. $$$-$$$$. The Sagamore is an historic building that has been renovated into a luxury resort. Located on Green Island, this place has been the site of presidential conferences of the past.

Warrensburg

Merrill Magee House, 3 Hudson Street, Warrensburg, NY 12885, ☎ 888-MMH-INNI or 518-623-2449, fax 518-623-3990, www.mer-rillmageehouse.com. $$$. The main house is in 19th-century Greek Revival style; a new building has all of the modern conveniences. Don't miss Arabella (a mannequin) in the bathtub; her jewelry is different every time we visit!

Diamond Point

Canoe Island Lodge, Lake Shore Drive, PO Box 144, Diamond Point, NY 12824, ☎ 518-668-5592, fax 518-668-2012, www.mediausa.com/ny/canoeislandlodge. $$-$$$ AP spring and fall, MAP summer. Accommodation is available in the lodge and cottages on Lake George. Many boating activities are on site, as well as an island for barbecues. It has been run by the Busch family since 1946.

Chelka Lodge, 4204 Lake Shore Drive, Diamond Point, NY 12824, ☎ 518-668-4677, www.chelkalodge.com. $$$. Resort with motel and efficiency units on Lake George.

Lake Luzerne

The Lamplight Inn, 231 Lake Avenue, Lake Luzerne, NY 12846, ☎ 800-262-4668 or 518-696-5294, www.lamplightinn.com. $$-$$$$. This 1890 Victorian house is very attractive, with antiques and collections. There's a wrap-around porch for relaxing.

■ Camping

There are more than 500 public and privately-owned campgrounds in New York State. For information, ☎ 800-CALLNYS (225-5697) to reach **New York State Travel Information Center**. To make a reservation through the **New York State Camping Reservation System**, ☎ 800-456-CAMP (2267) during business hours. You can make a reservation online at **www.park-net.com** at any time of day, or mail payment by check, money order or credit card information to New York State Camping Reservation System, 40 South Street, PO Box 199, Ballston Spa, NY 12020. Call one of the numbers above or check the web for fees.

Reservations will be accepted for camping from two days to 11 months in advance of the date of your planned arrival. You can make them for a minimum of one to three nights to a maximum of 14 nights, depending on the campground and the time of year.

Campers may also arrive without a reservation and register if space is available. Sites are assigned at the campground on a first-come, first-served basis.

Northern Adirondack Region

LAKE PLACID

Meadowbrook Campground, Route 86, four miles west of Lake Placid, ☎ 518-891-4351. 62 campsites, coin-operated hot showers, picnic pavillion.

Wilmington Notch Campground, Route 86, eight miles east of Lake Placid, ☎ 518-946-7172. 54 campsites, coin-operated hot showers.

TUPPER LAKE

Fish Creek Pond & Rollins Pond Campgrounds, Route 30, 12 miles north of Tupper Lake, ☎ 315-891-4560 (Fish Creek Pond) and ☎ 518-891-3239 (Rollins Pond). **Fish Creek Pond**: 355 campsites, picnic area, beach, coin-operated hot showers, boat launch, hiking trails, boat and canoe rentals. **Rollins Pond**: open from mid-May through Labor Day, 287 campsites, coin-operated hot showers, boat launch, boat and canoe rentals, hiking trails.

Central Adirondack Region

RAQUETTE LAKE

Eighth Lake Campground, Route 28, five miles west of Raquette Lake, ☎ 315-354-4120. 126 tent and trailer sites, picnic area, hot showers, sand beach, swimming area, bathhouse, hiking trails.

Golden Beach & Tioga Point Campgrounds, Route 28, three miles north of Raquette Lake, ☎ 315-354-4230. 205 tent and trailer sites, picnic area, hot showers, sand beach, swimming area, bathhouse, hiking trails.

LONG LAKE

Lake Eaton Campground, on Route 30, one mile north of Long Lake, ☎ 518-624-2641. 135 tent and trailer sites, picnic area, sand beach, swimming area, bathhouse, coin-operated hot showers, boat and canoe rentals.

NEWCOMB

Lake Harris Campground, Route 28N, Newcomb, ☎ 518-582-2503. 89 campsites, hot showers, boat launch, canoe and boat rentals, picnic area.

INLET

Limekiln Lake, Limekiln Lake Road, three miles east of Inlet, ☎ 315-357-4401. 271 tent and trailer sites, picnic area, hot showers, sand beach, swimming area, bathhouse, nature trail, small boat launch.

SEVERANCE

Paradox Lake, Route 74, four miles east of I-87, Exit 28, Severance, ☎ 518-532-7451. 58 campsites, coin-operated hot showers, boat launch, picnic area, sand beach, bathhouse, canoe and boat rentals.

HAGUE

Rogers Rock, Route 9N, three miles north of Hague, ☎ 518-585-6746. 321 campsites, picnic area, hot showers, boat launch, sand beach, bathhouse.

Southern Adirondack Region

HADLEY

Sacandaga Campsite, Star Route 4, Hadley, NY 12835, ☎ 518-696-4887.

Stewart's Pond Campsite, 4405 S. Shore Road, Hadley, NY 12835, ☎ 518-696-2779.

SPECULATOR

Moffitt Beach Campground, two miles west of Speculator, ☎ 518-548-7102. 261 campsites, picnic area, hot showers, small-craft boat launches, sand beach, swimming area, bathhouse.

Lewey Lake, Route 30, 12 miles north of Speculator and 12 miles south of Indian Lake, ☎ 518-648-5266. 209 campsites, picnic area, hot showers, sand beach, swimming area, bathhouse, boat launch, hiking trails.

The Adirondacks

LAKE GEORGE

Hearthstone Point Campground, Route 9N, two miles north of Lake George Village, ☎ 518-668-5193. 251 tent and trailer sites, hot showers, sand beach, swimming area.

Lake George Battleground, Route 9, ¼ mile south of Lake George Village, ☎ 518-668-3348. 68 tent and trailer sites, hot showers, swimming at Lake George Beach. Day-use facility-charge per person.

Lake George RV Park, 74 State Route 149, just east of Route 9, Lake George, ☎ 518-792-3775. Open May to Columbus Day, 400 RV sites, 15 trailer rental units, hot showers, two outdoor and one indoor pool.

Luzerne Campground, Route 9N, eight miles southwest of Lake George Village, ☎ 518-696-2031. 174 tent and trailer sites, hot showers, picnic area, two swimming areas, two horse corrals, row boats and canoes.

SACANDAGA

Sacandaga Campground, Route 30, three miles south of Wells, ☎ 518-924-4121. 143 campsites, picnic area, hot showers, boat launch.

Island Camping

SARANAC LAKE

Saranac Lake Islands Campground, Route 3, six miles west of Saranac Lake, ☎ 518-891-3170. 87 campsites, five with a lean-to, outhouses, boat launch, five day-use sites.

LAKE GEORGE

Lake George Islands Campground, accessible by boat only, from Bolton Landing, Narrow Island, ☎ 518-499-1288; Glen Island, ☎ 518-644-9696; Long Island, ☎ 518-656-9426; Waltonian, ☎ 518-585-6746. 387 shoreline campsites located on 44 state-owned islands. All have a dock, fireplace, picnic table and toilet facility. For day use, if you are taking your own boat, it is necessary to stop either on Long Island or Glen Island and buy a permit for a full day or half a day.

Where to Eat

DINING PRICE SCALE
Prices include an entrée, which may come with vegetables and salad, but exclude beverage, taxes and tip.
$ . . . . Under $10
$$ . . . . $10 to $20
$$$. . . . . $21 to $50
$$$$. . . . . Over $50

■ Northern Adirondack Region

Lake Placid

Averil Conwell, in Mirror Lake Inn, 5 Mirror Lake Drive, Lake Placid, NY, ☎ 518-523-2544. $$$. Fine dining with a varied menu and also spa entrées. **The Cottage**, also at Mirror Lake Inn, offers healthy spa cuisine.

Goldberries, 137 Main Street, Lake Placid, NY, ☎ 518-523-1799. $$. American cuisine with German, Italian and international specials

Lake Placid Lodge, Whiteface Inn Road, Lake Placid, NY, ☎ 518-523-2700. $$-$$$. New American cuisine served in this Relais & Chateau lodge.

Veranda, 1 Olympic Drive, Lake Placid, NY, ☎ 518-523-3339. $$-$$$. International cuisine in an Adirondack manor house.

Upper Saranac Lake

The Wawbeek, 553 Panther Mountain Road, Upper Saranac Lake, NY, ☎ 518-359-2656. $$-$$$. Have dinner in a Great Camp dining room at The Wawbeek. Regional and international cuisine.

■ Central Adirondack Region

Chestertown

Friends Lake Inn, 963 Friends Lake Road, Chestertown, NY, ☎ 518-494-4751. $$. The Inn is noted for its extensive wine list. New American cuisine.

Rene's, White Schoolhouse Road, Chestertown, NY, ☎ 518-494-2904. $$. The chef offers Swiss-French cuisine with nightly specials.

North Creek

Copperfield Inn, Main Street, North Creek, NY, ☎ 518-251-0822. $$. The Inn's restaurant, **Gardens**, offers a varied menu including home-made breads and desserts.

North River

Garnet Hill Lodge, 13th Lake Road, North River, NY, ☎ 518-251-2444. $-$$. Continental and Mediterranean cuisine; there's a gigantic fireplace in the lounge that is a great place to relax after a day of skiing or hiking.

Schroon Lake

Drake's, Route 9, Schroon Lake, NY, ☎ 518-532-7481. $$. Weekly specials include surf and turf, Alaskan king crab legs, New England lobster, homestyle favorites and prime rib.

Westport

The Galley at Westport Marina, Washington Street, Westport, NY, ☎ 518-962-4899. $$. Dine right on the lake outside, or inside. Saturday night barbecues are popular.

The Westport Hotel, Route 9N, Pleasant Street, Westport, NY, ☎ 518-962-4501. $$. This historic inn has a varied menu served inside or open-air.

■ Southern Adirondack Region

Lake George

East Cove, Route 9L and Beach Road, Lake George, NY, ☎ 518-668-5265. $$. Sunday brunch is special at East Cove.

George's Place for Steak & Seafood, Route 9L, Lake George, NY. ☎ 518-668-5482. $$. Early-bird specials are popular. George's has a great salad bar.

Log Jam, 1484 Route 9, Lake George, NY, ☎ 518-798-1155. $$. Located in a log cabin, it is next door to the Route 149 factory outlets. Prime rib and seafood a specialty.

Mario's, 429 Canada Street, Lake George, NY, ☎ 518-668-2665. $$. Italian cuisine featuring veal and seafood are specialties.

Montcalm, Route 9 at Exit 20 off I-87, Queensbury, NY, ☎ 518-793-6601. $$. Entrées include prime rib, rack of lamb and seafood. There's also a café menu.

Ridge Terrace, Ridge Road, Route 9L, Lake George, NY, ☎ 518-656-9274. $$. Veal, pasta and seafood are specialties.

Shoreline, 4 Kurosaka Lane, Lake George, NY, ☎ 518-668-2875. $$. The salad bar and Sunday brunch are very popular.

TR's, in the Holiday Inn Turf, Route 9, Canada Street, Lake George, NY, ☎ 518-668-5781. $$. Special evenings include Italian night and seafood specials. It is the site of a dinner theater during the summer season.

Bolton Landing

Algonquin, Route 9N, Lake Shore Drive, Bolton Landing, NY, ☎ 518-644-9442. $$. Many people come by boat to this restaurant on the lake. You can eat outside under umbrellas or inside, upstairs or downstairs. Varied menu.

The Sagamore, 110 Sagamore Road, Bolton Landing, NY, ☎ 800-358-3585 or 518-644-9400, www.thesagamore.com. $-$$$. There are several restaurants ranging from a pub to the elegant **Trillium Room**.

Villa Napoli, Route 9N, Lake Shore Drive, Bolton Landing, NY, ☎ 518-644-9047. $$. Northern and classic Italian cuisine in this restaurant at Melody Manor.

Warrensburg

Grist Mill, 100 River Street, Warrensburg, NY, ☎ 518-623-8005. $$-$$$. Some of the original grist mill equipment is still in place. Ask for a window seat beside the rushing river.

Merrill Magee House, 3 Hudson Street, Warrensburg, NY, ☎ 888-MMH-INNI or 518-623-2449. $$. Located in a 19th-century Greek Revival house. Varied menu including a favorite – Maryland crab cakes.

The Adirondacks

Upper River & Foothill Towns

The mighty Hudson River, beginning as a rivulet on the slopes of the highest mountain in the Adirondacks, changes character as it moves southward. It widens and bounces along over rocks and forms steep "haystacks" (standing waves) as it pours down slopes, creating challenges for white-water canoeists. It cascades over a waterfall at Glens Falls, providing power for paper mills on both shores. Then the river, more manageable but not yet fully navigable, snakes along to further drops at Hudson Falls, past Fort Edward and the Saratoga Battlefield. It runs by a number of locks in the parallel Champlain Canal before reaching the confluence of the Mohawk and the head of ocean navigation farther downstream in Albany.

Geologists can trace this tiny beginning of a stream to the Cambrian era, when the river flowed along the path of least resistance through mud, sand and glacial debris. During the glacial period ice sheets slowly ground southward, gouging out valleys and lakes. Waterfalls formed where the grade was steep.

History

The Hudson River provided an important avenue for military action during the French and Indian and Revolutionary Wars. The opponents traveled along Lake Champlain, Lake George and the Hudson River, back and forth, as they sought to defeat the enemy. Whoever garnered strategic points and built forts along the way gained the advantage. Throughout the last half of the 18th century, forts rose and fell, as one battle after another was fought.

■ Glens Falls Area

Until recently, the area's key role – as the major portage in the Champlain-Hudson corridor during the 18th-century wars – was known to historians, but largely forgotten by the rest of us. Today there is tremendous interest in the archaeology of the forts, with digs meticulously in progress at Fort William Henry, Fort George, Roger's Island, Fort Edward and more. Volunteers spend their summer vacations sifting sand with the thrill of a find in their heads, and college students receive credit for archeology lab work.

The Upper River

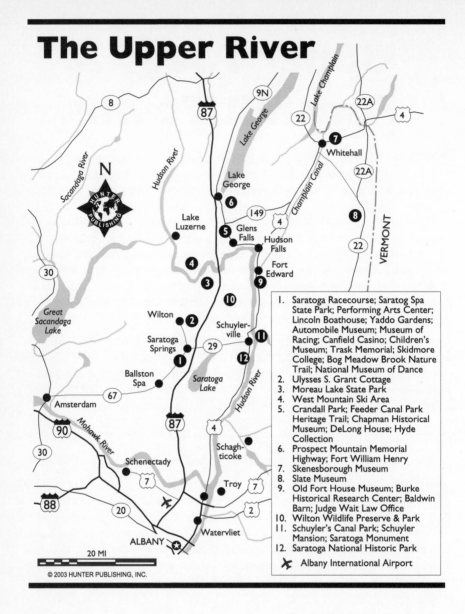

1. Saratoga Racecourse; Saratog Spa State Park; Performing Arts Center; Lincoln Boathouse; Yaddo Gardens; Automobile Museum; Museum of Racing; Canfield Casino; Children's Museum; Trask Memorial; Skidmore College; Bog Meadow Brook Nature Trail; National Museum of Dance
2. Ulysses S. Grant Cottage
3. Moreau Lake State Park
4. West Mountain Ski Area
5. Crandall Park; Feeder Canal Park Heritage Trail; Chapman Historical Museum; DeLong House; Hyde Collection
6. Prospect Mountain Memorial Highway; Fort William Henry
7. Skenesborough Museum
8. Slate Museum
9. Old Fort House Museum; Burke Historical Research Center; Baldwin Barn; Judge Wait Law Office
10. Wilton Wildlife Preserve & Park
11. Schuyler's Canal Park; Schuyler Mansion; Saratoga Monument
12. Saratoga National Historic Park

✈ Albany International Airport

20 MI

© 2003 HUNTER PUBLISHING, INC.

The large Indian population and the constant warfare discouraged settlers until near the end of the French and Indian War, when a group of Connecticut land speculators applied for a patent in 1762. It was named **Queensbury** to honor the Queen of England. This tract was sold to Abraham Wing from Dutchess County, who made the trip north and met the only man who lived in the area, Jeffrey Cowper. He lived on Halfway Brook in an abandoned blockhouse from the war, spending his time fishing for trout. Abraham Wing also reached the waterfalls on the Hudson and knew that it was the best site for a sawmill, grist mill and homes.

GLENS FALLS

Nathaniel Parker Willis, in his 1836 memoir *American Scenery*, writes about the bridge at Glens Falls:

"Miss Martineau [Harriet Martineau, an English traveler in America] observes – 'We were all astonished at the splendour of Glen's Falls. The full, though narrow Hudson, rushes along amidst enormous masses of rock, and leaps sixty feet down the chasms and precipices that occur in the passage, sweeping between dark banks of shelving rocks below, its current speckled with foam. The noise is so tremendous, that I cannot conceive how people can fix their dwellings in the immediate neighbourhood. There is a long bridge over the roaring floods, which vibrates incessantly; and clusters of saw-mills deform the scene. There is stone-cutting as well as planking done at these mills. The fine black marble of the place is cut into slabs, and sent down to New York to be polished. It was the busiest scene that I saw near any waterpower in America.'

Her description is excellent, but, as regards the mills, we cannot agree with her, they certainly add much to the picturesque effect on the scene."

William Henry Bartlett, an English artist and author , came to America four times between 1836 and 1852. He made a series of drawings for steel engravings to illustrate Willis's *American Scenery*; one is entitled *Bridge at Glens Falls*, and it portrays the rushing water falling into a chasm below the rickety wooden bridge.

Today we cross the tame replacement of that bridge, two lanes wide with sturdy railings on each side. The falls below usually roar only during the spring melt in the Adirondacks, when the river rises and sometimes overflows its banks.

James Fenimore Cooper made Glens Falls famous with his rendition of Cooper's Cave in *The Last of the Mohicans*. There's a painting by **Griffith Baily Coale** hanging in the Queensbury Hotel which depicts Cooper's Cave. In it Hawkeye lights the entrance for Cora, Alice and Major Heyward, as well as Chingachgook, his son Uncas, and David Gamut. Since 1961 the cave has been off limits for everyone because it is consid-

Upper River & Foothill Towns

ered unsafe, but now, as the bridge is being revamped, there are various plans to restore it as a historic site and provide access from the bridge.

COOPER'S CAVE

"At the farther extremity of a narrow, deep cavern in the rock, whose length appeared much extended by the perspective and the nature of the light by which it was seen, was seated the scout, holding a blazing knot of pine... At a little distance in advance stood Uncas, his whole person thrown powerfully into view. The travellers anxiously regarded the upright, flexible figure of the young Mohican... 'I could sleep in peace,' whispered Alice, in reply, 'with such a fearless and generous looking youth for my sentinel'... A spectral-looking figure stalked from out the darkness behind the scout, and seizing a blazing brand, held it towards the farther extremity of their place of retreat. Alice uttered a faint shriek, and even Cora rose to her feet, as this appalling object moved into the light, but a single word from Heyward calmed them, with the assurance it was only their attendant, Chingachgook... " James Fenimore Cooper, *The Last of the Mohicans*

In *Bridging the Years,* published by the Glens Falls Historical Association in cooperation with Crandall Library, there is a description by an elderly man of his boyhood, when he acted as a guide for people who got off the stage coach by the bridge and wanted to see the cave. Ten cents was then the going rate for guides.

■ Fort Edward

Fort Edward was a strategic military site for troops traveling north to Fort William Henry and on up to Fort Ticonderoga. The Old Fort House was used as a headquarters by General Philip Schuyler, General John Burgoyne and General John Stark. The tragic murder of Jane McCrea took place nearby (see page 129). George Morris memorialized the event in his 1853 poem, titled *Jane McCrea*:

> *She heard the fight was over,*
> > *And won the wreath of fame!*
> *When tidings from her lover,*
> > *With his good war-steed came:*
> *To guard her safely to his tent,*
> *The red-men of the woods were sent,*
> > *They led her where sweet waters gush*
> *Under the pine-tree bough!*
> > *The tomahawk is raised to crush*
> *Tis buried in her brow!*
> *She sleeps beneath that pine-tree now!...*

■ Whitehall

Whitehall was settled by Captain Philip Skene and others in 1759. Originally called Skenesborough, the name was changed after the Revolutionary War because Skene had supported the British.

■ Schuylerville

Schuylerville was once a Native American camp. French refugees settled here in 1688 and adopted the Mohawk name, Saratoga. In the 19th century it was renamed Schuylerville to honor General Philip Schuyler, who had served with distinction in both the French and Indian War and the Revolutionary War. In 1777, the British army was trapped here after retreating from the decisive Battle of Saratoga, generally regarded as the turning point in the war. For descriptions of the visitor center at **Canal Park** and of **Schuyler House**, see *Sightseeing*, pages 121 and 134.

Saratoga National Historical Park commemorates the serial battles at Saratoga on September 19 and October 7, 1777, when General Horatio Gates defeated British General John Burgoyne. (For a description of the park, see *Scenic Drives*, page 122.)

Getting Here & Getting Around

■ By Air

Albany International Airport . . . . ☎ 518-869-9611

■ By Car

Car rental from all companies is available at the airport. Some cars may be rented in Glens Falls.

■ By Bus

Adirondack Trailways . . . . ☎ 800-858-8555

Greyhound Lines. . . . . ☎ 800-231-2222

Upper River & Foothill Towns

■ By Train

Amtrak. . . . . ☎ 800-872-7245

Information Sources

Fort Edward Chamber of Commerce, Box 267, Fort Edward, NY 12828, ☎ 518-747-3314.

Adirondack Regional Chamber of Commerce, 5 Warren Street, Glens Falls, NY 12801, ☎ 518-798-1761.

Saratoga National Historical Park, Routes 4 and 32, Schuylerville, NY 12171, ☎ 518-664-8721.

Saratoga County Chamber of Commerce, 28 Clinton Street, Saratoga Springs, NY 12866, ☎ 518-584-3255.

Saratoga Springs Urban Cultural Park, 297 Broadway, Saratoga Springs, NY 12866, ☎ 518-587-3241.

Warren County Tourism Department, 1340 State Route 9, Lake George, NY 12845, ☎ 800-365-1050 or 518-761-6366.

Washington County Tourism Department, 383 Broadway, Fort Edward, NY 12828, ☎ 518-746-2290.

Whitehall Chamber of Commerce, 259 Broadway, Whitehall, NY 12887, ☎ 518-499-2292.

Adventures

■ On Foot

Hiking & Walking

The **Saratoga Spa State Park**, built on a grand scale during the Depression, offers a variety of activities, including historical walks through its extensive grounds, which are available during July and August. Other sports include swimming, golf, tennis, cross-country skiing and skating. In 1935 a European-style spa opened, and its pool complex, hotel, and water bottling plant still operate, as well as the **Lincoln Bathhouse**. **The Saratoga Performing Arts Center** and the **Spa Little Theatre** offer performances in season, 19 Roosevelt Drive, Saratoga Springs, NY 12866 (see *Sightseeing*, pages 130-31). Call ☎ 518-584-2535 for information on the park.

Also in Saratoga Springs, the **Bog Meadow Brook Nature Trail** offers walking on an old railroad bed for two miles. The trail has a parking lot on Route 29 and another at the Stafford Bridge Road and Meadowbrook Road junction. It runs through wetlands and woods where plant and animal life flourish. There are 47 species of spring wildflowers, and turtles, frogs and fish live in the brook. There's a boardwalk and a viewing platform with benches along the trail. For information call ☎ 518-587-5554.

At the **Feeder Canal Park Heritage Trail**, PO Box 2414, Glens Falls, NY 12801, ☎ 518-792-5363, hikers, walkers and joggers enjoy a 10-foot-wide, seven-mile-long trail along the spur canal that links Glens Falls to the Champlain Canal. After the old Champlain Canal was begun in 1817 boats could move from Lake Champlain at Whitehall to Fort Edward on the Hudson River. The first feeder canal was dug in 1822, but a flood destroyed part of the dam across the Hudson at Fort Edward. So, in 1824 a new dam was built upstream of the falls in Glens Falls, linking the upper Hudson to the Champlain Canal. Thirteen locks were added to compensate for the 130-foot drop east of Hudson Falls. In the early 1900s the present-day Champlain Barge Canal replaced the old canal. The Heritage Trail has two sections, one beginning at the Haviland Avenue parking area and extending to the Glen Street bridge just below the falls; the second picks up off Warren Street on Shermantown Road and continues eastward through Hudson Falls, where it joins the Old Champlain Canal Towpath.

Schuyler's Canal Park, Route 4, Schuylerville, NY 12871, links the Schuyler House (see page 134) with the New York State Canal Lock 5 on the Old Champlain Canal. The walk is 1½ miles in length. The canal was completed in 1823 and cost $921,011. It is four feet deep and ranges from 28 feet in width at the bottom to 40 feet at the surface. The new visitor center is also part of **Fort Hardy Park**. As you walk you will notice the stone arches of the aqueduct near the pedestrian bridge at Fish Creek, then pass the terminal basin and continue along the towpath.

The 1,200-acre **Wilton Wildlife Preserve and Park** is the result of collaboration between the Town of Wilton, the Nature Conservancy and the New York State Department of Environmental Conservation. It consists of eight parcels and was created to protect the Karner blue butterfly, an endangered species; to provide recreational opportunities; and to "preserve a balance between people, community and habitat" in one of the state's fastest growing towns. There are opportunities for hiking, biking, cross-country skiing and snowshoeing in four of the parcels. To reach the

Upper River & Foothill Towns

most convenient trailhead, leave I-87 at Exit 15, drive northeast for 3.8 miles on Route 50 and look for a parking area on the left. For further information, directions to other parcels with trails, and maps, call ☎ 518-587-1939, ext. 220.

There are networks of trails in other major parks in the region, many of them designed for multiple uses, some designated for a particular activity, such as walking, cycling, horseback riding, cross-country skiing and snowshoeing. They include renowned competition ski trails in **Crandall Park** on Upper Glen Street in Glens Falls (☎ 518-761-3813); and trails for a variety of uses in the **Saratoga National Historical Park** on Routes 4 and 32 in Stillwater (☎ 518-664-9821), and in the **Saratoga Spa State Park** on Roosevelt Drive in Saratoga Springs (☎ 518-584-2535). See *Sightseeing*, page 130, for further description of these three parks.

■ On Wheels

Scenic Drives

Saratoga National Historical Park has a 9.5-mile, one-way driving tour with 10 stops at major battlefield sites along the way. Bicycles are allowed on the same road, and it is used for cross-country skiing in the winter. You can stop at **Free-man Farm**, the American **river fortifications**, **Chatfield Farm**, **Barber's wheatfield**, **Balcarre's redoubt**, **Breymann's redoubt** and **Burgoyne's headquarters**. See *Sightseeing*, page 133, for more details.

The **Saratoga County Heritage Trail**, ☎ 518-664-9821 or 371-7546. This trail has several sections, including Route 9 from Saratoga Springs to South Glens Falls. This was the only major route heading north before I-87 was built. It passes Mount McGregor in Wilton, site of the **Grant Cottage**; crosses under I-87; and heads into South Glens Falls. For an alternative route that becomes more rural after the Wilton malls, take Route 50 northeast from Saratoga Springs to the village of Gansevoort, once home of Herman Melville's relatives, then head north on Route 32 into South Glens Falls. From either route you can head due east on Route 197 to visit the **Old Fort House Museum** in Fort Edward (see page 129).

Our favorite longer driving tour for a day exploring the Upper River and Foothill region is the **Eastern Loop**. It begins in the heart of Saratoga Springs, heading east from Congress Park along Union Avenue (Route 9P) past old mansions, the **Saratoga Race Course**, and the **Yaddo** gardens (see page 133). Cross the Northway (I-87) and keep on 9P along the eastern shore of Saratoga Lake to Snake Hill. Branch off and head due east on Route 423 into rolling hills to join Route 32 and reach the Saratoga National Historical Park.

After leaving the park, take Route 4 north along the Hudson to the **Schuyler Mansion**. From Schuylerville follow Route 29 east to Middle Falls and Greenwich, a classic village with a New England look. Then follow Route 372 southeast into Cambridge, and stop to see its recently renovated historic hotel. From Cambridge, take Route 22 north to Salem and Granville to visit the **Slate Museum**. Then backtrack a short bit and head west on Route 149 through beautiful rolling farm country to Hartford. There, take Route 40 south to 197, then head west into Fort Edward, where you can stop to see the Old Fort House Museum. Finally, take Route 4 south along the Hudson River and parallel **Champlain Canal**, where you can stop to see the locks, to Schuylerville; head west on Route 29 back into Saratoga Springs. If this route seems too long for the time you have, it can easily be split.

The **Northern Loop** is another rewarding route. It also begins in Saratoga Springs and follows Route 9N north through Greenfield, Corinth (pronounced "Co-RINTH" by the natives) to Lake Luzerne. There, it crosses the Hudson and heads northeast past a series of small lakes, well-established dude ranches, and the Hole-in-the-Woods Camp for children with terminal illnesses. When you reach the Village of Lake George, take the time to drive up the **Prospect Mountain Memorial Highway** for a stunning view over the whole southern basin of Lake George. You can visit **Fort William Henry**, centrally important in the wars of the 18th century, at the head of the lake in the village.

Then follow Route 9L along the east shore to Lockhart Mountain Road and head up a steep hill to **Top-of-the-World** golf course for another prized view over the lake. Return downhill to 9L and follow it around the lake's eastern bays, then south until you reach Route 149. There, turn east to Fort Ann, then north on Route 4 into Whitehall. Here, you can visit the **Skenesborough Museum**, which celebrates the town's role as the birthplace of the American Navy in the early years of the Revolution (see page 135). To complete your tour, head back south on Route 4 through Fort Ann, Hudson Falls and Fort Edward to Schuylerville, then take Route 29 west back to Saratoga Springs.

Bicycling

 The **Warren County Bikeway** links Lake George to Glens Falls, and connects with the Feeder Canal Park Heritage Trail to Hudson Falls and the Old Champlain Canal Towpath. This bikeway provides cyclists with a scenic and historic route largely off-road. From its northern terminus in Lake George Beach State Park (off I-87 in the town of Lake George), the bikeway climbs through woods on the steadily graded D&H rail bed to the summit of a low pass, where it runs parallel to Route 9, then drops down to Glen Lake and Round Pond, passes through the semi-rural residential districts of

Queensbury, crosses the heavy traffic of Quaker Road on its own specially built overpass, and jogs through the streets of Glens Falls. It joins the Feeder Canal Park Heritage Trail on Shermantown Road off Warren Street.

The **Saratoga Springs Bikeway System** has at this time only one off-road section, called Railroad Run. It extends between West Circular Street and New Street in Saratoga Springs; it has one paved lane for pedestrians and another for cyclists. Many Saratogians head out to the **Saratoga National Historical Park** (see *On Foot*, page 133) to ride along a quiet, interesting one-way road through a varied landscape loaded with military history. But there is also a great interest in developing more trails and bikeways throughout the region. Current information is available from the **Heritage Trails Committee**, ☎ 518-371-7546, or from one of these outfitters and clubs.

- **Mohawk/Hudson Cycling Club**, ☎ 518-884-2784, www.mohawkhudsoncyclingclub.org. This club organizes rides.

- **Bike Shop**, 35 Maple Avenue, Saratoga Springs, NY 12866, ☎ 518-587-7857. This store sells bicycles and offers information on biking in the area.

- **Inside Edge**, 643 Upper Glen Street, Queensbury, NY 12804, ☎ 518-793-5676. They sell bicycles and offer information on biking in the area.

- **Ricks Bike Shop**, 368 Ridge Street, Queensbury, NY 12804. They offer sales and service plus information on biking in the area.

■ On Water

Canal Boats

 The **Champlain Canal** extends from Whitehall for 60 miles to Waterford, connecting **Lake Champlain** with the **Hudson River**. The canal supplied the missing link in the water route from Montreal to New York City when it was completed early in the 19th century. The impetus for such investment had always been commercial, and between 1905 and 1918 the original canal was replaced by a new and enlarged canal to accommodate the large barges of the **New York State Barge Canal System**; these had an average width of 125 feet and average depth of 12 feet. By the 1990s, as barge traffic decreased, the canal system's potential for tourism was recognized, and a five-year revitalization program aimed at improving boating facilities, encouraging hiking and cycling along towpaths, and developing canalside heritage sites began in 1996. Much of the redevelopment effort has been targeted to improve docks, boat launches and essential marina services, as well to extend the Canalway Trail system.

The navigation season for the Champlain Canal extends from the first Monday in May through early November. The New York State Canal Corporation has published the *Cruising Guide to the New York State Canal System*, available in bookstores and from Northern Cartographic, ☎ 802-860-2886 or ncarto@together.net. The guide includes navigation information, including locations of locks and lift bridges, as well as marinas, restaurants and other public services. For current developments on boating in the canal system contact the **New York State Canal Corporation**, ☎ 800-4CANAL4. For information on tour boats, call **Champlain Canal Tour Boats**, at the end of Towpath Trail, Lock 5, Route 4, Schuylerville, NY 12188, ☎ 518-695-5496. The *Caldwell Belle* and the *Sadie*, operated by Champlain Canal Tour Boats, offer cruises during the season. **Carillon Cruises** of Whitehall, ☎ 518-499-2435, also takes visitors on cruises through Lock 12 to Lake Champlain four days a week.

Those interested in cruising the canal on self-skippered charter boats can contact **Blue Heron "Drive It Yourself" Boating Vacations**, 11 Burkewood Road, Mt. Vernon, NY 10552, ☎ 800-320-1224 (www.blueheronboats.com); or **Erie Canal Cruise Lines**, 714 Union Street, Suite 907, Manchester, NH 03104, ☎ 800-962-1771 (www.canalcruises.com). For charter boats with captain/crew, contact **Premier Charters**, PO Box 161, Feura Bush, NY 12067, ☎ 800-595-1309 (www.premiercharters.com).

Canoeing

Apart from visiting the Hudson, Saratoga Lake and smaller lakes in the region, canoeists and kayakers are likely to head for smaller streams like the **Kayaderosseras** in Saratoga County, and the **Batten Kill** in Washington County. For details, refer to the following organizations:

Saratoga Springs Open Space Project, ☎ 518-584-5554. Call for information on the Kayaderosseras Creek Canoe Trail.

Northern New York Paddlers, ☎ 518-843-8133. Call for information on free weekly canoe lessons and competitive canoe/kayak events.

CANOE & KAYAK RENTALS

- **Battenkill Canoe Ltd.**, Route 7A, Arlington, VT 05250, ☎ 802-362-2800, www.battenkill.com.

- **Battenkill Sports & Campground**, 937 State Route 313, Cambridge, NY 12816, ☎ 800-675-8768, bsq@ixnet.com, www.rvdestinations.com/aca/battenkill.htm.

Upper River & Foothill Towns

- **Lake Lonely Boat Livery**, 378 Crescent Avenue, Saratoga Springs, NY 12866, ☎ 518-587-1721.

- **Lock 12 Marina**, 82 North Williams Street, Whitehall, NY 12887, ☎ 518-499-1663.

- **Saratoga Outfitters**, 268 Broadway, Saratoga Springs, NY 12866, ☎ 518-584-3932, www.saratogaoutfitters.com.

▪ On Snow

Downhill Skiing

West Mountain is very popular with local skiers from the Glens Falls area who can zoom into the parking lot for night-skiing after work, as well as day-skiers from the whole region. The elevation is 1,470 feet and the vertical drop 1,010 feet. There are 22 trails served by three chairlifts and three surface lifts. West Mountain, Glens Falls, NY 12804, ☎ 518-793-6606.

Cross-Country Skiing

Crandall Park International Cross-Country Ski Trails, Upper Glen Street, Glens Falls NY, ☎ 518-761-3813; ski phone ☎ 518-793-1300. A lighted race loop of five km plus a network of adjoining trails in a wooded park.

Lapland Lake Nordic Vacation Center, 139 Lapland Lake Road, Northville NY 12134, ☎ 800-453-SNOW (24-hour taped ski report) or 518-863-4974, www.laplandlake.com or www.xcski.org/lapland. There are 50 km of woodland trails designed and maintained by Olavi Hirvonen, former Olympic skier.

Moreau Lake State Park, Exit 17S from the Northway (I-87), South Glens Falls, NY, ☎ 518-793-0511. Thirteen km of trails for novice and intermediate skiers.

Saratoga National Historical Park, Routes 4 and 32, Stillwater NY, ☎ 518-664-9821. Skiing on the 9½-mile loop road.

Saratoga Spa State Park, 19 Roosevelt Drive, Saratoga Springs NY, ☎ 518-584-2535. Skiing on the golf course.

■ In the Air

Ballooning

The **Adirondack Balloon Festival**, held in Glens Falls during September, is one of the highlights of the fall season. Call ☎ 800-365-1050 or 518-761-6366 for information. It has been held for 28 years and draws huge crowds. Some people gather to walk and talk with balloonists as they spread out their gear. Others keep track of liftoff times and hope for fair weather and kind winds. Photographers ready their cameras and hope to catch lots of color. When the balloons drift over Lake George we can see them from our deck and marvel at the colors against blue water.

People who first come as spectators sometimes decide to sign on as crew and later enter training to be pilots. Tom Ford of Glens Falls has been piloting his own balloon for many years. He describes ballooning as a "pure adrenaline rush. It is an experience that all of Donald Trump's money couldn't buy." He says that he never knows where he is going to land when he takes off. A bottle of champagne is traditionally given to the landowner where a balloonist lands. Some people put a "Land Here" sign in their fields as a friendly signal.

BALLOONING BASICS

As you look at a balloon, note the parts, beginning with the gondola, or basket, made out of strong wicker to withstand brushes with tree limbs. It has a hardwood base and basket handles. Inside the basket, gauges include a thermometer, which takes the temperature from the crown of the balloon and displays it for the balloonist. The altimeter measures altitude above sea level when the balloon takes off and as it ascends. Most balloonists here stay under 7,000 feet. The variometer shows the rate at which the balloon is ascending or descending in feet-per-minute.

Above the basket you'll see the load supports with the fuel lines next to them. The burners and a blast valve are next, then the heating coil. The fabric of the balloon includes a wind guard, a skirt and then the balloon itself. The inside of the balloon is coated with plastic to protect the fabric from the heat.

To ascend, the balloon is inflated by forcing cold air into the interior of the balloon. As propane burners heat the air inside to a temperature greater than the outside, the balloon ascends. To descend, the burner is turned off and the air inside cools, contracts and enters the base of the balloon.

Upper River & Foothill Towns

If you have a yen to try a flight yourself, apart from those offered during the festival, contact **Adirondack Balloon Flights**, 76 Helen Drive, Glens Falls, NY 12801, ☎ 518-793-6342. Balloon takeoff and landing sites vary with wind conditions, so call for information after you have booked a flight. Reservations are required.

Or try **A Beautiful Balloon**, 47 Assembly Point Road, Lake George, NY 12845, ☎ 518-656-9328 or 973-335-9799, www.balloon-rides.com. balloonsnj@aol.com. Reservations are required for hot air champagne flights in Vermont, generally in the Middlebury, Killington, Rutland, Fair Haven, Brandon, Chaplain and Queechee areas. Flights take place at sunrise and two hours before sunset. They are weather-dependent, of course. The sensation aloft is tranquil and romantic. The price is $225 per person.

Sightseeing

■ Glens Falls

 Glens Falls, on Route 9, was called Chepontuc by the Indians. It means "a difficult place to get around." But the waterfall was a treat to the eyes as early as 1780 when the Marquis de Chastellux came to see the falls.

Frances Parkman wrote in 1842, "I journeyed to Glens Falls, and here my wrath mounted higher yet at the sight of that noble cataract almost concealed under a huge, awkward bridge, thrown directly across it, with the addition of a dam above and about 20 mills of various kinds. Add to all, that the current was choked by masses of drift logs above and below." A toll keeper and his family lived at one end of the bridge. A son was born there, Charles Reed Bishop, who went on to become a philanthropist.

FROM GLENS FALLS TO HAWAII

Charles R. Bishop was born in Glens Falls, son of the toll keeper at the bridge over the Hudson. He married Princess Bernice Pauahi, who was the last direct descendant of King Kamehameha the Great of Hawaii. Princess Ruta Keelikolani died in 1883 and willed her estate to her cousin, Bernice. Queen Emma, another cousin, also bequeathed her Hawaiian collection of artifacts to Princess Bernice. After Bernice died, her husband established the Bishop Museum in Hawaii as a memorial to all three royal women.

The **Chapman Historical Museum**, 348 Glen Street, Glens Falls, NY 12801, ☎ 518-793-2826. The **DeLong House**, part of the Historical

Museum, has been restored to the Victorian period. This 1841 home belonged to Zopher Isaac and Catherine Scott DeLong, who lived here with their eight children. There's an outstanding collection of Seneca Ray Stoddard's photographs, plus paintings and manuscripts related to the Adirondacks in the museum. An addition houses galleries with changing displays on the Southern Adirondacks.

The **Hyde Collection**, 161 Warren Street, Glens Falls, NY 12801, ☎ 518-792-1761. The original building is a Florentine Renaissance home dating from 1912. Louis and Charlotte Hyde built the home and furnished it with their priceless art collection. The interior courtyard is an elegant combination of sculpture, fountains and plants, and masterpieces of European painting hang on the walls of sitting rooms. A large 1989 addition provides gallery space for permanent and temporary exhibits, as well as an auditorium with wonderful acoustics. Concerts and other programs are very popular at the Hyde.

Crandall Park, Upper Glen Street, Glens Falls, NY 12801. The park was given to the city by Henry Crandall. A monument near the graves of Mr. and Mrs. Crandall has a five-pointed star on top. This was his log-mark – also a symbol of his wealth gained as a lumberman. It was placed on his logs before they were floated down the Hudson River to the mills in Glens Falls during the log drives of the late 1800s and early 1900s. Today the park is used for walking, fishing in the pond and cross-country skiing in winter.

■ Fort Edward

The **Old Fort House Museum**, 22 and 29 Lower Broadway, Fort Edward, NY 12828, ☎ 518-747-9600. Dating from 1772, the building is one of the oldest frame structures in upstate New York. Both British and American troops used the house as a headquarters during the Revolutionary War. In 1783 George Washington and his friends dined here. You can see the bill in his handwriting on display. There are five buildings in the complex, including the **John P. Burke Historical Research Center** with local genealogical records dating back to the 18th century. The law office of **Judge A. Dallas Wait** is just as it was in 1853, complete with law books and bank ledgers. The **tollhouse** is where the toll collector lived.

Baldwin barn has many collections, including a display telling the story of Jane McCrea, who lived a few miles away from Fort Edward during the Revolutionary War. She was on her way to meet her fiancé, who was a British officer, and stopped to see Mrs. McNeil. A group of American soldiers fled by, followed by some Indians in hot pursuit. The two women dashed inside the house and down a trapdoor. Jane was pulled out by her hair and later killed in a dispute between the Indians.

DID YOU KNOW?

Although there is some confusion about how Jane McCrea died, one version describes her as being placed in the saddle of a horse when a second group of Indians overtook the first and snatched the reins of her horse. Each group of Indians grabbed at the reins while they were moving at breakneck speed, and one of them, wanting to be the person to claim the reward for her and realizing that the other Indian had her, pulled out his gun and shot her.

■ Saratoga Springs

Saratoga Spa State Park, 19 Roosevelt Drive, Saratoga Springs, NY 12866, ☎ 518-584-2535. Iroquois Indians used the area during the 14th century for hunting becaise the high content of salt in the waters attracted animals to the area. When the Indians discovered the springs, they regarded the special healing powers of the waters as a gift from the Great Spirit. Early settlers also used the springs to cure ailments. Bathhouses were built and bathing in the mineral waters became popular. Saratoga was soon called the "Queen of the Spas."

By 1930 the "New Spa" was developed into a complex of buildings, similar to those in Europe. At first people came for medical treatment, then the wealthy came for preventive therapy, as well as for the social life during the racing season that made Saratoga famous. Today the park offers swimming in a pool complex, golf on two courses, mineral baths at **Lincoln Baths**, tennis, walking, and cross-country skiing and skating during the winter.

A DAY AT THE SPA

From personal experience, we can attest that a session at Lincoln Baths is memorable. You will have a private room for soaking in a long tub; there's a little stool to hook your feet under so they won't float. The hot water is dark in color with lots of massaging bubbles. What a way to relax! Afterward the attendant will wrap you in a hot sheet for a sinking spell on the bed in your room. When it is time to leave you will be awakened, rejuvenated and ready to face the world again.

Many people come to Saratoga Springs during the summer to attend performances at the **Saratoga Performing Arts Center**, ☎ 518-587-3330. A shell amphitheater opened in 1966 and there is unlimited seating on the sloping lawn. The **New York City Ballet** is in residence for three weeks in July, and the **Philadelphia Orchestra** performs in August.

Specials, such as **Freihofer's Jazz Festival**, take place at scheduled times. Nearby on the park grounds, the **Spa Little Theatre** offers performances of the **Lake George Opera Festival** and the **Saratoga Chamber Music Festival**.

Canfield Casino, Congress Park, Saratoga Springs, NY 12866, ☎ 518-584-6920. This 1870 casino is host to dances, benefits and a museum. The stained-glass windows are memorable. Among many legendary visitors to the Casino were Diamond Jim Brady and Lillian Russell. Walk up to the second and third floors to see the **Historical Society of Saratoga Springs Museum** and the **Ann Grey Gallery**.

The **Spencer Trask Memorial**, called *The Spirit of Life*, stands in Saratoga Springs' **Congress Park**. It was created by Daniel Chester French (who also sculpted the Lincoln Memorial in Washington, DC). Financier Spencer Trask and his wife, poet Katrina Trask, founded the artists' community called Yaddo, in Saratoga Springs (see page 133). Katrina dedicated the memorial to her husband in 1915.

The **Children's Museum**, 36 Phila Street, Saratoga Springs, NY 12866, ☎ 518-584-5540. Children are treated to one fun activity after another as they learn about science, history, community living and the arts. We watched one little boy, microphone in hand, who was belting out tunes in a Karaoke setting. The preschool circus playhouse is a favorite.

National Museum of Dance and Hall of Fame, 99 South Broadway, Saratoga Springs, NY 12866, ☎ 518-584-2225. This museum is housed in the former Washington Bathhouse. You can wander through the exhibits of sparkling costumes worn in some of the most popular ballets. Photographs of some of the great ballet personalities. such as George Balanchine and Katherine Dunham, are accompanied by a written commentary. There's a photograph of Bill "Bojangles" Robinson with Shirley Temple as a child – he's showing her a new way to dance up a flight of stairs. Shirley said, "I want to do that too!" Fred Astaire and Ginger Rogers in *The Gay Divorcee* tickle the boards with smiles and grace.

Names are added each year to the Hall of Fame, which is housed in the former bathhouse's handsome Beaux Arts foyer. Visitors can also watch dancers in the adjacent **Lewis A. Swyer School for the Performing Arts**. You can even choose to take classes with Pat Peterson of **Dance Alliance** (☎ 518-886-7838).

National Museum of Racing and Thoroughbred Hall of Fame, Union Avenue, Saratoga Springs, NY 12866, ☎ 518-584-0400. The original building has an addition which allows more gallery and display space. We are partial to peering over the shoulders of one dimensional wooden figures who are lounging along the fence watching their favorites. A statue of Secretariat stands in the garden beyond. He won the Triple Crown in 1973, and is a member of the Hall of Fame. You can also look into

Charlie Whillingham's barn and the "Jock's Room," where valets are preparing jockeys for later races. Fan letters to the famous horse, Kelso, are spilling out of a mailbox in one display.

Saratoga Automobile Museum, 10 Avenue of the Pines, Saratoga Springs, NY 12866, ☎ 518-587-1935, www.saratogaautomobilemuseum.org. This new and developing museum has been renovating the 1934 Bottling Plant in Saratoga Spa State Park to display the rich history of automobile building in the region and state, where more than 700 makes of autos originated. One gallery will showcase famous autos that have a Saratoga or New York connection, while another will feature cars that were built or raced in the state, like the 1903 Weebermobile that won its event at Watkins Glen in 1950. In addition to displaying its 29 autos, the museum will hold special exhibitions, lawn days for regional auto clubs, and a three-day major auto show.

Saratoga Race Course, Union Avenue, Saratoga Springs, NY 12866, ☎ 518-584-6200. The town is bursting with vigorous activity during August when the Thoroughbred racing season is on. Dating from 1863, this is the oldest track in the United States. Our favorite way to see the horses is to have breakfast at the track and watch them in the early morning as they gallop around the course in training. You can also have a free tram tour of the backstretch area, tour the grounds of the track, and watch the paddock show and starting gate demonstration.

THOROUGHBRED RACING TERMS

- **Apprentice**: a relatively new jockey. All riders must be at least 16 years old before obtaining a license to ride in sanctioned races.

- **Flat track**: designed for races that are not run over obstacles.

- **Furlong**: the standard measure in US racing, it equals 1/8 mile.

- **Maiden**: a horse that has never won a race.

- **Novice**: a horse in its first full season of racing over fences.

- **Paddock**: the areas where horses are saddled before a race and where they remain until they go onto the course.

- **Purse**: money earned in a race.

- **Scratch time**: usually one hour before the first race, the final time at which entered horses may be withdrawn from a race.

- **Steward**: the presiding judge at a race meet.

- **Stretch**: the straightaway portion of a racetrack.

The **Fasig-Tipton Auction**, George Street, Saratoga Springs, NY 12866, ☎ 518-584-4700. This famous sale of Thoroughbred racehorses takes place during the second week in August. Inside the pavilion, buyers indicate their bids by small gestures such as moving a finger or touching an ear. As the horses are paraded through the pavilion people on the outside can see the action through the windows.

Saratoga Harness Raceway, Route 9, Saratoga Springs, NY 12866, ☎ 518-584-2110. The Raceway is in operation 10 months of the year, not just in August. It also houses the **Saratoga Harness Hall of Fame and Museum**, with memorabilia dating back to the beginning of the sport. Call ☎ 518-587-4210 for more information and hours.

Skidmore College, North Broadway, Saratoga Springs, NY 12866, ☎ 518-580-5000. The college used to be housed in some of the elegant Victorian buildings along Union Avenue and adjoining side streets. Now it is located just off North Broadway on a lovely campus with red brick buildings connected by walkways. Many concerts and performances are open to the public in the **Filene Auditorium** and the **Bernhardt Theater**. The elegant new **Tang Museum** houses the college's art collections and many special exhibits and programs.

Yaddo Gardens, Union Avenue, Saratoga Springs, NY 12866, ☎ 518-584-0746 or 583-0339, www.yaddo.org. Although invited artists and writers are working without disturbance in their houses on the Yaddo grounds, anyone can visit the gardens. A formal rose garden is divided into four beds. Marble statues and terra cotta fountains enhance these beautiful gardens. West of the pergola, the rock garden features an upper and a lower pond with fountains.

Just a few miles north of Saratoga, on Mount McGregor Road in Wilton, stands the **Ulysses S. Grant Cottage**. Ulysses S. Grant and his family lived there until his death. Knowing he had cancer of the throat, he struggled to complete his memoirs to provide for his family, and Mark Twain agreed to publish them. Today the cottage is just as he left it, with his chairs, bed and funeral sprays still intact. You can visit the cottage when it is open. Call ☎ 518-587-8277 for more information and hours.

"When Grant gets possession of a place, he holds on to it as if he inherited it," wrote Abraham Lincoln of his famous general.

■ Schuylerville

Saratoga National Historical Park, Routes 4 and 32, Schuylerville, NY 12871, ☎ 518-664-9821. British General John Burgoyne knew that the Hudson River was an important highway in his plan to separate New

England from the rest of the colonies. On September 13, 1777 he was intent on advancing to Albany and so crossed over to the west bank of the Hudson and began trekking southward. On that date the Americans were entrenched at Bemis Heights on a narrow ridge between the hills and the river. By September 19 the Royal Army was headed for the Americans and an initial battle took place at Freeman Farm.

MILITARY STRATEGY

"I have always thought Hudson's River the most proper part of the whole continent for opening vigorous operations. Because the course of the river, so beneficial for conveying all the bulky neces- saries of an army, is precisely the route that an army ought to take for the great purposes of cutting the communications be- tween the Southern and Northern Provinces, giving confidence to the Indians, and securing a junction with the Canadian forces." – General John Burgoyne, 1775.

After a stop at the Visitor Center head for **Freeman Farm Overlook** where the fighting took place. Continue to the **Neilson Farm** in Bemis Heights. The restored home of John Neilson was used as headquarters by the American staff officers. Continue on to the **American River Fortifi- cations** for great views down on the Hudson River. Retrace your steps on the same road and proceed to **Chatfield Farm** where an American out- post guard first saw the British movement on October 7, the date of the second battle. Head for **Barber Wheatfield** where Burgoyne's troops were forced to flee. **Balcarres Redoubt** at Freeman Farm is where the British retreated after leaving the Barber Farm. Pass **Breymann Redoubt**, now outlined by posts, and head for Burgoyne's Headquarters, which was a large tent at that time. Continue to the **Great Redoubt**, which was designed by the British to guard their hospital, artillery park and supplies. General Fraser was mortally wounded during the second Saratoga battle and is buried at marker 10.

The **Philip Schuyler House**, Route 4, Schuylerville, NY 12871, ☎ 518- 664-9821. Head north along Route 4 from the Saratoga National Histori- cal Park to the Schuyler House. General Schuyler inherited the estate from his uncle, Philip, who was killed in a French-and-Indian War raid in 1745.

Inside, the house has its original wallpaper in the parlor. A tea cup given to the general by George Washington is displayed in the office. Also on view is Schuyler's cane – he had gout from the age of 15. The dining room features a portrait of Cathryn Schuyler. Note the wide chairs there – very handy for the wide dresses of the day.

"My hobby horse has long been a country life; I dismounted once with reluctance, and now saddle him again with a very considerable share of satisfaction, and hope to canter him on to the end of the journey of life." Philip Schuyler in his new house of 1777 (the third on the site).

Saratoga Monument, Burgoyne Road, Victory Mills NY (adjoining Schuylerville). This granite obelisk has been recently renovated. It commemorates the surrender of the British under General John Burgoyne to General Horatio Gates on October 17, 1777. After two battles at Saratoga the British retreated to the Schuylerville area.

■ Whitehall

Skenesborough Museum, Route 22, Whitehall, NY 12887, ☎ 518-499-0716. With the maritime interest in Whitehall alive and well, this museum celebrates the birthplace of the American Navy during the first years of the Revolutionary War, when Benedict Arnold built ships here and commanded fleets to stop the British advance down the Champlain-Hudson corridor. The museum has a collection of ship models from 1776 and 1812, as well as of modern Navy ships and Lake Champlain vessels. There are also models of local shipyards from those eras. Memorabilia of local historical interest and a doll room also intrigue visitors. It is now part of the new **Whitehall Urban Cultural Park**, which has a Visitor Center at the same location.

Festivals & Events

■ May

Dressage Horse Show, Saratoga, ☎ 518-584-0400.

■ June

Annual Feeder Canal Canoe Race, Glens Falls, ☎ 518-792-5363.

LARAC Art Fair, Glens Falls, ☎ 518-793-2006.

Freihofer's Jazz Festival, Saratoga, ☎ 518-587-3330.

Encampment at Saratoga National Historical Park, Stillwater, ☎ 518-664-9821.

■ July

Whitehall Festival, ☎ 518-499-1155.

New York City Ballet, Lake George Opera Festival, Saratoga, ☎ 518-587-3330.

New York State Summer Writers Institute readings, Skidmore College, Saratoga, ☎ 518-580-5879.

Thoroughbred racing, Saratoga Race Course, through August, ☎ 518-584-6200.

■ August

Saratoga Chamber Music Festival, Philadelphia Orchestra, ☎ 518-587-3330.

New York State Summer School of the Arts performances, Saratoga, ☎ 518-580-5897.

Eighteenth-Century Days, Schuylerville ☎ 518-584-3255.

■ September

Adirondack Hot Air Balloon Festival, Glens Falls, ☎ 518-761-6366.

Battle of Saratoga Re-enactments, Saratoga National Historical Park, Stillwater, ☎ 518-664-9821.

■ October

Chronicle Book Fair, Glens Falls, ☎ 518-792-1126.

Encampment at Saratoga National Historical Park, Stillwater, ☎ 518-664-9821.

Head of the Fish Rowing Regatta, Saratoga, ☎ 800-526-8970.

■ November

Festival of Trees, Chapman Historical Museum, Glens Falls, ☎ 518-793-2826.

■ December

First Night Saratoga, ☎ 518-583-9622. This event is very popular every Christmas season, with people strolling the streets amidst lots of entertainment.

Where to Stay

ACCOMMODATIONS PRICE SCALE
Prices for a double room for one or two persons, before taxes.
$ . . . . Under $50
$$. . . . . $50 to $100
$$$ . . . . $101 to $175
$$$$ . . . . Over $175

■ Glens Falls & Queensbury

Crislip's Bed & Breakfast, a Federal-style home, has four-poster beds and period antiques. 693 Ridge Road, Queensbury, NY 12804, ☎ 518-793-6869. $$.

Memory Manor Bed & Breakfast is decorated with family heirloom furnishings. The parlor has a fireplace and there is a library with a nice collection of books, including some for children. The three-season porch has wicker furniture and outside there's a perennial garden. 514 Glen Street, Glens Falls, NY 12801, ☎ 518-793-2699. $$.

Queensbury Hotel is located in downtown Glens Falls across from the park. There is a heated indoor pool. 88 Ridge Street, Glens Falls, NY 12801, ☎ 800-554-4526 or 518-792-1121. $$-$$$.

■ Saratoga Springs

Adelphi Hotel is a Victorian hotel right on Broadway. Guest rooms are individually decorated with period pieces. 365 Broadway, Saratoga Springs, NY 12866, ☎ 518-587-4688, www.adelphihotel.com. $$$.

Batcheller Mansion is in an 1886 home. Some of the guest rooms have whirlpools or fireplaces. 20 Circular Street, Saratoga Springs, NY 12866, ☎ 800-616-7012 or 518-584-7012, fax 518-581-7746, www.batchellermansioninn.com. $$$$.

Brunswick Bed and Breakfast is in an 1886 Victorian Gothic home. 143 Union Avenue, Saratoga Springs, NY 12866, ☎ 800-585-6751 or 518-584-6751, www.brunswickbb.com. $$-$$$.

Gideon Putnam Hotel is located in the Saratoga Spa State Park. It is noted for Sunday brunch as well as breakfast, lunch and dinner every day in the Georgian Room. 24 Gideon Putnam Road, Saratoga Springs, NY 12866, ☎ 800-732-1560 or 518-584-3000, www.gideonputnam.com. $$$$.

The Inn at Saratoga is a Victorian inn right on Broadway. 231 Broadway, Saratoga Springs, NY 12866, ☎ 800-274-3573 or 518-583-1890, www.theinnatsaratoga.com. $$$-$$$$.

Saratoga Arms is a Second Empire brick hotel in downtown Saratoga Springs. 495-497 Broadway, Saratoga Springs, NY 12866, ☎ 518-584-1775. Fax 518-581-4064, www.saratoga-lodging.com, hotel@saratoga-lodging.com. $$$-$$$$.

Union Gables Bed & Breakfast is in a restored 1901 Victorian home. 55 Union Avenue, Saratoga Springs, NY 12866, ☎ 800-398-1558 or 518-584-1558, www.uniongables.com. $$$-$$$$.

Washington Inn is located on four acres on the edge of Saratoga Spa State Park. 111 South Broadway, Saratoga Springs, NY 12866, ☎ 518-584-9807. $$-$$$.

Westchester House Bed & Breakfast is an 1885 Queen Anne Victorian house. Rooms are furnished with antiques. 102 Lincoln Avenue, Saratoga Springs, NY 12866, ☎ 888-302-1717 or 518-587-7613, www.westchester-housebandb.com. $$$$.

Located just outside of Saratoga Springs on 9N, the **Wayside Inn** was once a stop on the underground railroad. It is furnished with pieces from the Middle East, Europe and the Far East. 104 Wilton Road, Greenfield, NY 12833, ☎ 800-893-2884 or 518-893-7249, fax 518-893-2885, www.waysideinn.com. $$$.

■ Camping

Fort Ann

Fort Ann Campground, Clay Hill Road, Fort Ann, NY 12827, ☎ 518-639-8840.

Hadley

Sacandaga Campsite, Star Route 4, Hadley, NY 12835, ☎ 518-696-4887.

Stewart's Pond Campsite, 4405 S. Shore Road, Hadley, NY 12835, ☎ 518-696-2779.

Corinth

Alpine Lake Camping Resort, 78 Heath Road, Corinth, NY 12822, ☎ 518-654-6260.

River Road Campground, 5254 Route 9N, Corinth, NY 12822, ☎ 518-654-6630.

Rustic Barn Campground, 4757 Route 9N, Corinth, NY 12822, ☎ 518-654-6588.

Gansevoort

American Campgrounds, 291 Fortsville Road, Gansevoort, NY 12831, ☎ 518-792-0485.

Care Away Campground, Route 50, Gansevoort, NY 12831, ☎ 518-798-1913.

Cold Brook Campground, 385 Gurnsprings Road, Gansevoort, NY 12831, ☎ 518-584-8038.

Moreau Lake State Park, 605 Old Saratoga Road, Gansevoort, NY 12831, ☎ 518-793-0511.

Saratoga Lake

Lee's Park Campground, 1464 Route 9P, Saratoga Springs, NY 12866, ☎ 518-584-1951.

Cambridge

Battenkill Sports Quarters, 937 Route 313, Cambridge, NY 12816, ☎ 518-677-8868.

Lake Lauderdale, off Route 22, Cambridge, NY 12816, ☎ 518-677-8855.

Where to Eat

DINING PRICE SCALE	
Prices include an entrée, which may come with vegetables and salad, but exclude beverage, taxes and tip.	
$	Under $10
$$	$10 to $20
$$$.	$21 to $50
$$$$.	Over $50

■ Glens Falls & Queensbury

Adirondack Coach House offers steak, seafood and pasta in a rustic building. Route 9, Queensbury, ☎ 518-743-1575. $$.

Montcalm offers lunch, dinner and early bird specials. Route 9 at Exit 20 off I-87, Queensbury, ☎ 518-793-6601. $$-$$$.

The **Log Jam** offers lunch daily in the greenhouse and dinner in the Adirondack log cabin. Route 9, Lake George, ☎ 518-798-1155. $$-$$$.

Davidson Brothers is also a brewery where you can find a variety of ales as well as pub fare. 184 Glen Street, Glens Falls, ☎ 518-743-9026. $-$$.

Carl R's offers breakfast, lunch and dinner with a Mexican flair. At Exit 18 off I-87, Glens Falls, ☎ 518-793-7676. $$.

Sutton's Country Café offers breakfast, lunch and dinner with patio dining in the summer. Route 9, Queensbury, ☎ 518-798-1188. $-$$.

■ Saratoga Springs

Eartha's Kitchen features mesquite grilled specialties in a trendy neighborhood bistro on the east side of town. 60 Court Street, ☎ 518-583-0602. $$-$$$.

Chez Sophie offers a tantalizing menu prepared with French style, which attracts visitors and locals. 2853 Route 9, Malta, south of Saratoga Springs, ☎ 518-583-3538, www.chezsophie.com.

Hattie's has been a popular landmark restaurant with New Orleans style southern cuisine including coconut shrimp. It is open for lunch and dinner. 45 Phila Street, ☎ 518-584-4790. $$.

Inn at Saratoga offers dining in a Victorian inn. Sunday Jazz brunch is popular as well as piano bar on weekends. 231 Broadway, ☎ 518-583-1890. $$-$$$.

Lillian's Restaurant has Victorian atmosphere right on Broadway. Try their famous steaks as well as pasta and Atlantic Salmon fillet. Lillian Russell and Diamond Jim Brady used to dine here. 408 Broadway, ☎ 518-587-7766. $$-$$$.

Longfellows Inn & Restaurant is in a restored 100-year-old barn with a waterfall and pond inside. 500 Union Avenue, ☎ 518-587-9653. $$-$$$.

Maestro's Restaurant has an innovative menu specializing in New Italian cuisine. An à la carte brunch is held on Saturday and Sunday. 371 Broadway, ☎ 518-580-0312. $$-$$$.

Olde Bryan Inn is an historic landmark building. An extensive menu is available seven days a week. 123 Maple Avenue, ☎ 518-587-2990. $$-$$$.

43 Phila Bistro offers creative food with an extensive wine list. 43 Phila Street, ☎ 518-584-2720. $$$-$$$$.

Scallion's Restaurant is a casual place offering soups, salads, pasta and quiche for lunch and dinner. Their carrot cake is a favorite. 404 Broad - way, ☎ 518-584-0192. $$-$$$.

Sperry's is like a New York City bistro. Their grilled fish, Maryland crab cakes and crème brûlée are recommended. 30½ Caroline Street, ☎ 518-584-9618. $$-$$$.

Waterfront is on the shore of Saratoga Lake where you can dine on the deck or inside. Specialty sandwiches are offered at lunch, beef kabobs among the offerings at dinner. 626 Crescent Avenue, ☎ 518-583-2628.

Upper River & Foothill Towns

Capital District

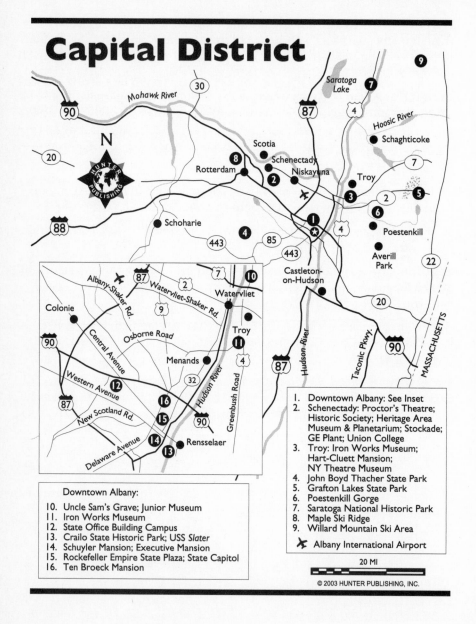

Downtown Albany:
10. Uncle Sam's Grave; Junior Museum
11. Iron Works Museum
12. State Office Building Campus
13. Crailo State Historic Park; USS *Slater*
14. Schuyler Mansion; Executive Mansion
15. Rockefeller Empire State Plaza; State Capitol
16. Ten Broeck Mansion

1. Downtown Albany: See Inset
2. Schenectady: Proctor's Theatre;
   Historic Society; Heritage Area
   Museum & Planetarium; Stockade;
   GE Plant; Union College
3. Troy: Iron Works Museum;
   Hart-Cluett Mansion;
   NY Theatre Museum
4. John Boyd Thacher State Park
5. Grafton Lakes State Park
6. Poestenkill Gorge
7. Saratoga National Historic Park
8. Maple Ski Ridge
9. Willard Mountain Ski Area

✈ Albany International Airport

20 MI

Capital District

The *Half Moon*, under the command of Henry Hudson, sailed 150 miles up the river named after him in 1609. Sponsored by the Dutch East India Company, he was really looking for a short route to the riches of the Far East and hoped this broad river might turn out to be a strait. He was disappointed not to find the hypothetical northwest passage that had lured European explorers throughout the preceding century. Just to make sure, the *Half Moon* stayed in the area that is now Albany and Troy for four days from September 19 to 23, checking all possible navigable routes upstream.

History

 Although Hudson could not have imagined how important an area so far inland yet within reach of the ocean would become in succeeding centuries, there was an immediate incentive for development: the lucrative fur trade. Just five years after Hudson's exploration, Fort Nassau was built on Castle Island in 1614. Hendrick Christiaensen was in charge of this fort, until it was flooded and destroyed in 1617.

In 1624 the Dutch East India Company established a settlement with the specific objective of controlling a fur trading site. Thirty Walloon families (from southern Belgium and France) arrived to build Fort Orange and their homes on Castle Island.

In 1628 the Netherlands offered to give tracts of land to groups of at least 50 adults. Kiliaen Van Rensselaer received a generous tract measuring 24 by 48 miles in the Hudson and Mohawk River valleys, destined to become the hub of the whole region. Although he did not come to the area, it was a business venture from the start. His overseer, Roelf Janssen, arrived and demanded that the tenants purchase their supplies from the commissary.

Van Rensselaer bought more land from the Mohicans and became so powerful that he tried to exact tolls from any vessel on the river that passed his land. Peter Stuyvesant created the town of Beverwyck next to Fort Orange and declared it to be company property under the control of three magistrates instead of the manor of Rensselaerwyck. This became the site of Albany – the second oldest chartered city in the United States – which celebrated its tricentennial in 1986. The Dutch New Netherlands were ceded to British Rule in 1664, so the city was named for the Duke of Albany and York, who had acceded to the throne of England as King James II in 1685.

ON GUARD?

Can you imagine letting two snowmen defend the Stockade as sentries? Just that happened during the night of February 8, 1690, when 114 Frenchmen and 90 Indians came on snowshoes from Montreal to attack **Albany**. Four squaws who lived a few miles away informed them of the situation, and they marched on toward the vulnerable settlement. It was easy to creep past the snowmen and awaken the sleeping inhabitants with warwhoops. Many were killed, some were taken captive, and others fled, escaping into the woods from their burning homes.

■ Albany

Albany became the state capital in 1797 when the New York State Legislature met there. The area continued to prosper as a trade center after the first steamboat arrived in 1807, to be followed by the opening of sections of the **Champlain Canal** in 1822 and the entire **Erie Canal** in 1825. Sitting at the junction of water routes leading south to the port of New York, north to Lake Champlain and eventually Montreal and the St. Lawrence River, and west to Lake Ontario, Albany was destined to become a boom town.

Of these prime routes for transport, the Erie Canal was the most important. Originally conceived by Jesse Hawley, an imprisoned miller from Geneva, New York, the idea of digging a canal across the state became the pet project of New York City mayor DeWitt Clinton. When Clinton became Governor of the state, the legislature appropriated funds to start the big dig of its time in 1817 – an enormous civil engineering project that detractors called "Clinton's big ditch" or "Clinton's folly." When the canal opened on April 26, 1825, the magnitude of the big ditch was apparent: 363 miles long, 40 feet wide, and four feet deep, it had 18 aqueducts to carry it across rivers and 83 locks to change water levels a total of 682 feet throughout its length.

The canal cut road shipping costs by 90%, from $100 to $10 per ton, and created a string of new canal towns across the width of the state. It was the main conduit for developing the midwest, stretching water navigation as far as Duluth, Minnesota. As it was widened and deepened to accommodate larger vessels in 1836 and 1862, and rebuilt between 1905 and 1918, the Erie Canal remained the principal artery of the New York State Barge Canal System – and the Capital District was its heart, pumping goods received from the oceans of the world through the state to the Great Lakes.

■ Troy & Schenectady

The two other major cities in the Capital District received both direct and indirect benefits from the boom in shipping. **Troy** was within the original Kiliaen Van Rensselaer tract from 1629 onwards. At the head of Hudson River navigation, the town originally prospered as a marketplace for settlers and farmers. When the Champlain and Erie canals opened, it was ideally situated to take advantage of the industrial revolution, especially for the production of iron and steel, textiles, precision instruments, even church bells. The population multiplied eight times between 1820 and 1840, primarily to support growing industries. The iron plates of the *Monitor* were made in Troy, and at one point its shirt industry produced 90% of the detachable collars in the US. Industry leaders like Arrow Shirts were located in Troy. Not by accident is Troy the home of one of the country's premier engineering universities, Rensselaer Polytechnic Institute.

UNCLE SAM

Our country's favorite patriotic moniker, "Uncle Sam," can be attributed to Samuel Wilson of Troy, who was an active supplier of meat during the War of 1812. His meat shipments were stamped with the initials "EA-US," which literally stood for Elbert Anderson-United States, the man who accepted the meat, but became associated with "Uncle Sam" Wilson in the popular imagination. Originally a term of derision for government goods – something every GI understands – it later acquired positive connotations. Uncle Sam's red, white and blue costume was derived from one worn by Daniel Rice, an acrobat, clown, and circus manager. In the 20th century the symbol gained new currency through the paintings of Norman Rockwell, and every young man during World War II became familiar with recruiting posters of Uncle Sam pointing his finger and saying "Uncle Sam wants you!"

The third city in the Capital District, **Schenectady**, was founded by Dutch settlers who bought land at the confluence of the Mohawk River and Binne Kill from the Mohawk Indians. A Dutch merchant, Arendt Van Curler, visited the site in 1642 and came back with 15 settlers two decades later. The Stockade was founded in 1661, burned during the French and Indian massacre of 1690, and rebuilt by the Dutch. It has been a residential district for more than three centuries, with a quite marvelous collection of homes representing Dutch, Colonial, Federal, Greek Revival and Victorian architecture. Its residents cherish their restored homes in the heart of the city.

During the early 19th century, Schenectady enjoyed a double-barreled boom as a canal town and railroad center. Soon after the Erie Canal

Capital District

opened, the first intercity railroad route connected Schenectady to Albany in 1831. From 1851 until 1969 it was home of the American Locomotive Company, which built the first steam-powered passenger train in the world and provided the technology for the rapid expansion of America's railroad network after the Civil War. More prosperity was to come in 1886 when Thomas A. Edison brought his Edison Machine Works to Schenectady. It became General Electric, and the company headquarters and major manufacturing plants remained in town for nearly a century. Here many of the major advances in electrical technology were invented or developed, including the application of alternating current, FM radio and television.

Getting Here & Getting Around

■ By Air

Albany International Airport . . . . ☎ 518-869-0611

■ By Car

Car rental from all companies is available at the airport.

■ By Bus

Adirondack Trailways . . . . ☎ 800-858-8555

Greyhound Lines. . . . . ☎ 800-231-2222

■ By Train

Amtrak . . . . ☎ 800-872-231-2222

Information Sources

Albany County Convention & Visitors Bureau, 25 Quackenbush Square, Albany, NY 12207, ☎ 800-258-3582 or 518-434-1217, www.albany.org, accvb@albany.org.

Albany Heritage Area Visitors Center, 25 Quackenbush Square, Albany, NY 12207, ☎ 518-434-0405.

Rensselaer County Tourism, County Office Building, 1600 7th Avenue, Troy, NY 12180, ☎ 518-270-2959, www.capital-saratoga.com/rensselaer.html.

Schenectady County Chamber of Commerce & Visitor Center, 306 State Street, Schenectady, NY 12305, ☎ 800-962-8007 or 518-372-5656, www.schenectadychamber.org, jweyers@wsg.net.

Schenectady Heritage Area Visitor Center, Schenectady Museum, Nott Terrace Heights, Schenectady, NY 12308, ☎ 518-382-7890.

Troy RiverSpark Visitor Center, 251 River Street, Troy, NY 12180, ☎ 518-270-8667.

Adventures

■ On Foot

Hiking

John Boyd Thacher State Park, just outside Albany, offers walking and scenic overlooks of the Hudson and Mohawk Valleys and the Green and Adirondack Mountains. The Indian Ladder Trail contains lots of fossils. Route 157, off Route 85, 15 miles Southwest of Albany, ☎ 518-872-1237.

Grafton Lakes State Park, east of Troy off Route 2 in Grafton, offers hiking trails, a beach, trout fishing and biking, ☎ 518-279-1155.

The **Mohawk-Hudson Bikeway** is a "bike-hike trail" designed for multiple uses; see *Bicycling*, page 149, ☎ 518-386-2225 or 447-5660.

Urban Walks

The Capital District is particularly rich in historical walks in areas of special interest that are unique to each city. These self-guided walks are carefully organized and mapped to allow you to explore the architectural or industrial heritage of each area at your own pace.

WALKING TOURS

- **Albany** – The **Ten Broeck Triangle** is the millionaires' row of mid-19th-century Albany, with homes built by wealthy bankers, merchants and lumber barons. It is the second-oldest residential section in Albany. For a map and more information about this short walk, call the **Albany Heritage Area Visitors Center**, ☎ 518-434-0405.

- **Schenectady – The GE Plot Walking Tour** takes you through the residential area originally planned and reserved by the General Electric Company for its principal officers, scientists and engineers. Begun at the turn of the 20th century, the entire GE Realty Plot was listed on the State and National Register of Historic Places in 1978. The tour takes you by a dozen homes with remarkable architectural variety, many of them associated with prominent Schenectady residents and GE scientists. Get the map from the **Schenectady Urban Cultural Park Visitor Center**, ☎ 518-382-5147.

- The **Stockade Walking Tour** explores the architectural riches of a residential district more than 300 years old. The original Schenectady Stockade was rebuilt after the French and Indian Raid of 1690 and enlarged in 1776. It was declared New York State's first Historic District in 1962. The walk includes two dozen stops, including historic houses and public buildings, parks and the **Schenectady County Historical Society**, where you can get the tour map. Houses have high Dutch gables, colonial doorways, gardens and a variety of architecture styles, ☎ 518-374-0263.

- The **RiverSpark Walking Tour** in the center of downtown Troy takes you through more than 200 years of the city's history. It includes civic buildings, churches, banks, cast-iron storefronts, colleges, a library, markets, statues, squares and parks. It begins and ends at **RiverSpark Visitor Center**, 251 River Street, where you can get a descriptive map, ☎ 518-270-8667.

- There is an unusual concentration of Tiffany windows in Troy, and the **Tiffany Windows Walking Tour** takes you to see half a dozen examples. Get your descriptive map at the RiverSpark Visitor Center.

- **Gateway Tours**, operated by the Hudson Mohawk Industrial Gateway, offers guided tours of the industrial heritage of the region, each one focused on a special topic, ranging from the making of horseshoes or precision instruments to classical architecture and the cemetery plots of prominent Troy industrialists. Call ☎ 518-274-5267 for a current schedule and reservations.

■ On Wheels

Bicycling

The **Mohawk-Hudson Bikeway** continues for 41 miles along the rivers, canal towpaths and railroad roadbeds of the region, passing through both urban and rural landscapes. It begins west of Schenectady in **Rotterdam**, passes through **Scotia**, **Schenectady**, **Niskayuna**, and **Colonie** in the Mohawk Valley to **Cohoes**, where it crosses the Hudson River to **Lansingburg** and **Troy**, then recrosses the river and continues through **Watervliet** and **Menands** to **Albany**. This southernmost section of the trail runs along the flood plain of the river and ends in the **Erastus Corning Riverfront Preserve**.

Interesting sections of the bikeway include the following.

- **Rotterdam Riverfront Bike-Hike Trail**. This seven-mile path is paved and terminates at its eastern end at Lock 8 of the canal system, ☎ 518-356-5344.

- **Niskayuna Riverfront Bike-Hike Trail**. This seven-mile paved path is built on an old railbed along the Mohawk River. It includes Lock 7 of the canal system, ☎ 518-372-2519.

- **Colonie Riverfront Bike-Hike Trail**. This 5.5-mile paved path on an old railbed runs along the Mohawk River and provides fine views, ☎ 518-783-2760.

- **Uncle Sam Bikeway** is a three-mile paved path on an old railbed on the hillside overlooking Troy, ☎ 518-270-8667.

Capital District

■ On Water

 Water activities are very popular in this area, with the Hudson River running through from north to south and the Mohawk River heading west from the Hudson above Troy. The Hudson in the Albany area is full of boat traffic, and not easy for very small craft to navigate.

Excursion Boats

Captain J.P. **Cruise Line**, 278 River Street, Troy, NY 12180, ☎ 518-270-1901, http://captainjp.homestead.com/Directions.html. This 600-passenger paddlewheeler, named *Captain J.P.*, offers a number of cruises on the Hudson River, including lunch and dinner cruises and a downriver trip from West Point to New York City Harbor.

Crescent Cruise Lines, Crescent Bridge, Route 9, Halfmoon, NY ☎ 518-373-1070 or 413-443-2696. Cruises take place on the Erie Canal on board the 76-passenger *Crescent*. Options include sightseeing with narration, a lock cruise, evening dinner cruise, pizza cruise, luncheon cruise and hors d'oeuvres cruise.

Dutch Apple Cruises, Snow Dock, Albany, NY 12201, ☎ 518-463-0220, http://dutchapplecruises.com. Cruises with narration are offered daily. Luncheon, brunch and sunset cruises are popular, and the overnight cruise packages run the length of the Hudson.

Self-Skippered Charter Boats

Collar City Charters, Troy Town Dock & Marina, 427 River Street, Troy, NY 12180, ☎ 800-830-5341 or 518-272-5341. This charter company has a fleet of 41-foot Lockmaster Hireboats (modernized versions of traditional canal boats) available for self-skippered cruises on the Hudson, the Erie Canal and the Champlain Canal.

Canoe & Kayak Rentals

The **Boat House**, 2855 Aqueduct Road, Schenectady, NY 12309, ☎ 518-393-5711. Here's the place to rent a canoe or kayak. You can rent them here and drive north to lakes in the Adirondacks, Saratoga Lake and rivers such as the Kayaderosseras Creek, south of Saratoga Springs. Or you can put in right here on Aqueduct Road at the Boat House and paddle up to Freedom Park in Scotia, to Lock 7 in Niskayuna, or to Lock 8 near a restaurant called Jumping Jacks.

■ On Snow

Downhill Skiing

 Catamount, Hillsdale, NY 12529, ☎ 518-325-3200. Perched on the border between New York and Massachusetts, Catamount is one of the pioneer ski areas in the region. Founded in 1940 with a rope tow and "groomed" by skiers side-stepping down the slope, it now has 96% snowmaking on 27 trails, including two terrain parks and a "snowboard megaplex" served by four double chairlifts and three surface lifts. With a vertical drop of 1,000 feet and a fine set of black diamonds – look up at the double black and you'll believe it – Catamount has always appealed to Capital District skiers looking for challenge close to home. But it also has a lot of blues spread throughout the mountain and fine broad green slopes and trails on the left flank of the mountain.

Maple Ski Ridge, Schenectady, NY 12306, ☎ 518-381-4700. Maple Ridge has a vertical drop of 400 feet and seven trails served by one triple chair, one double chair and two surface lifts.

Willard Mountain, Greenwich, NY 12834, ☎ 518-692-7337. With a history of good junior programs, Willard Mountain has a vertical drop of 550 feet and 14 trails served by two double chairs and three surface lifts.

For other downhill ski areas within easy reach of the Capital District, see *On Snow* in the *Catskills* chapter, page 212.

Cross-Country Skiing

Arctic Circle Ski Center, Gloversville, NY 12078, ☎ 518-725-7699. Arctic Circle has 24 km of groomed trails.

Burden Lake Country Club, Averil Park, NY 12018, ☎ 518-674-8917. Burden Lake has 10 km of trails.

Five Rivers Environmental Education Center, 56 Game Farm Road, Delmar, NY 12054, ☎ 518-475-0291. Five Rivers has 10 km of trails.

Lapland Lake Cross-Country Ski & Vacation Center, Northville, NY 12134, ☎ 518-863-4974. Lapland Lake, a major cross-country skiing center, is located in the woods, lakes, and hills of the lower Adirondacks. It has 50 km of groomed trails, with 38 km also tracked for skating.

Oak Hill Farms, Esperance, NY 12066, ☎ 518-875-6700. Oak Hill Farms, located in western Schenectady County, has 30 km of groomed trails.

Pine Ridge XC-Ski Area, East Poestenkill, NY 12018, ☎ 518-283-3652. Pine Ridge, located in 700 acres of woods along Poestenkill Creek with

Capital District

elevations up to 1,746 feet, has 43 km of trails with 33 km groomed and tracked.

John Boyd Thacher State Park, Route 157, off Route 85, 15 miles Southwest of Albany, ☎ 518-872-1237. Thacher Park has 10 km of trails.

Tree Haven Trails, Hagaman, NY 12086, ☎ 518-882-9455. Located in the midst of a nursery and Christmas tree farm just west of Galway, Tree Haven has 43 km of groomed trails – and you can ski out to cut your own Christmas tree, too.

■ On Ice

Albany County Hockey Training Facility, Albany Shaker Road, Albany NY, ☎ 518-452-7396. Indoor skating.

Empire State Plaza, Outdoor Plaza, Albany NY, ☎ 518-474-2418. Outdoor skating.

Swinburne Rink & Recreation Center, Clinton Avenue below Manning Boulevard, Albany NY, ☎ 518-438-2406. Outdoor skating.

Sightseeing

■ Albany

 Albany Heritage Area Visitors Center, 25 Quackenbush Square, Corner of Broadway and Clinton Avenue, Albany, NY 12207, ☎ 518-434-0405. The source of tourist information, a gallery on area history, and the **Henry Hudson Planetarium**, with special exhibits and group programs.

Albany Institute of History and Art, 125 Washington Avenue, Albany, NY 12210, ☎ 518-463-4478, www.albanyinstitute.org. The Institute is currently undergoing renovation and will reopen soon; call for updates. There will be new exhibitions on the Hudson River School of painting, Colonial Albany and Ancient Egypt. Nineteenth-century paintings will be displayed in the newly restored Lansing Gallery. The original building dates from 1908 and is on the National Register of Historic Places.

Governor Nelson A. Rockefeller Empire State Plaza, Madison Avenue and State Street, Albany, NY 12242, ☎ 518-474-2418. The 98-acre mall is large enough to house a government center, a performing arts center, a state museum and library, the state archives, an observation deck on the Corning Tower Building, a number of memorials, and the adjoining late-19th-century New York State Capitol. A favorite focus for many people is the outstanding artwork displayed in the government buildings. Governor Nelson Rockefeller supervised the collection of art by New York

State artists during the construction of the Plaza during the 1960s. Sculpture is located along the Plaza, and paintings as well as sculpture line the Concourse. Artists represented include David Smith, Alexander Calder, Louise Nevelson and Isamu Noguchi, to name but a few of the more famous.

Known as **The Egg**, the Performing Arts Center on the Plaza is an eliptical, tilting module, a shape not often seen before. Its programs include music, theater, dance, special performances and family entertainment. For current information, ☎ 518-473-1845.

New York State Capitol, Washington Avenue, and Swan, State and Eagle Streets, Albany, NY 12242, ☎ 518-474-2418. Dating from 1867 and 1899, this building is where the New York State Senate and Assembly still meet. The Million Dollar Staircase is carved with renderings depicting famous people in American history – but the sculptors also included some of their own friends and relatives as they carved. Five architects were involved in its design – unusual because it includes a complex roof pattern rather than the conventional dome – and the result was both ridiculed and admired when it was dedicated. Both in its scale and in its detail within individual chambers, it rewards those who take a guided tour, available every day. Call the number above for the daily schedule of tours.

New York State Museum, Empire State Plaza, Madison Avenue, Albany, NY 12230, ☎ 518-474-5877, www.nysm.nysed.gov. The museum is comprehensive, dealing with the history of New York State, including the Adirondack wilderness, upstate New York, and metropolitan New York City. So it's hard to pick a favorite part of the museum, but perhaps the Mohawk longhouse, built inside the museum, is the place to begin and hear stories of an earlier era.

The Mohawk Indian model astride the beams working on the roof of the longhouse was placed there for a practical reason. Because of the fire code, the museum was not allowed to have a full roof close to the ceiling. So some of the roof is left open with the Mohawk working up there, letting visitors see how the roof was made.

The Three Sisters diorama shows people working in their cornfields about 500 years ago. Extinct animals are on display, including the Ice Age mastodon, and you'll feel like a dwarf next to this one. Models of Ice Age hunters are skinning caribou in another setting. For a complete change to a later scene, head for the New York Metropolis Hall where you can wander past scenes of everyday life in various eras. A street scene from New York's Lower East Side includes a peddler, milkman, rag picker and shoeshine boy.

ALL HANDS ON DECK!

The Colonial Commerce exhibit, also inside the New York State Museum, has an overrigged sand-bagger yacht, representing the type raced in New York Bay that generated a betting frenzy in the 19th century. During a race the crew moved sandbags from side to side as the yacht tacked to keep her in balance against the wind. If the wind lightened up too much the sandbags were thrown overboard first, then the excess crew members who had handled them. This dubious practice generated a rule still enforced in yacht racing, requiring that a boat finish with the same crew she started with.

The Executive Mansion, 138 Eagle Street, Albany, is the official residence of the Governor of New York State. It was built as a private home in 1857 and has since served as home to 29 New York Governors, including three – Grover Cleveland, Theodore Roosevelt and Franklin Roosevelt – who later became Presidents of the United States. It has been decorated in a variety of styles to suit the tastes of successive governors but still retains its quiet Victorian charm. Open to visitors by appointment on Thursdays, with two weeks advance notice. Call ☎ 518-473-7521 for reservations.

Historic Cherry Hill, 523½ South Pearl Street, Albany, NY 12202, ☎ 518-434-4791, www.historiccherryhill.org. This home is wonderful because the five generations of the Van Rensselaer family living in the house never threw anything out. Rooms depict the life of the family from the 1780s to the 1960s. As new generations lived in the house, tastes in furnishings changed and new pieces were added. Catherine Van Rensselaer Bonney was a missionary in the Orient, sending home her personal favorite pieces, and Emily Watkinson Rankin, the last resident, maintained the belongings gathered over previous generations.

 Did Jesse Strang shoot the husband of his lover through a window in the Cherry Hill house? Ask while you're there.

Pruyn House Cultural Center of the Town of Colonie, 207 Old Niskayuna Road, Newtonville, NY 12128, ☎ 518-783-1485, www.colonie.org/pruyn. Built by Casparus Pruyn about 1830 as a country home for his wife, Ann, and their eight children, it is a blend of Federal and Greek Revival architecture. Along with his job as land and business agent for Stephen Van Rensselaer III, the last patroon, Mr. Pruyn used a portion of his over 170 acres for farming. The complex includes the house, the Buhrmaster Barn, a one-room schoolhouse, a smokehouse, and gardens.

RiverSpark/Hudson-Mohawk Urban Cultural Park Visitor Center, 58 Remsen Street, Cohoes, NY 12047, ☎ 518-237-7999, www.cdta.org/tourists.html. Exhibits tell the story of the Erie Canal and the industrial revolution that followed its opening, tracing the growth and development of the region surrounding the junction of the two major rivers.

Schuyler Mansion State Historic Site, 32 Catherine Street, Albany, NY 12202, ☎ 518-434-0834, www.pojonews.com/enjoy/stories/0924964.htm. This 1761 English Georgian-style home belonged to Revolutionary War General Philip Schuyler. He missed the Battle of Lake George in 1755 because he was involved in a wedding – his own – but played an important role in attempts to stop the advance of General Burgoyne prior to the Battle of Saratoga. During those years, when he was in command of the Northern Department, George Washington, Benjamin Franklin and Benedict Arnold visited him in this house, which served as his military headquarters.

 Some say that the gash on the stair rail at the Schuyler Mansion happened when one of the daughters in the family dashed downstairs to pick up her baby sister in the parlor. As she ran back up the stairs an Indian tomahawk just missed her and hit the stair rail.

Shaker Heritage Society, Albany-Shaker Road, Albany, NY 12211, ☎ 518-456-7890, www.crisny.org/not-for-profit/shakerwv. The 1848 Shaker meeting house was America's first Shaker settlement. You can visit the museum and take a self-guided tour of the grounds, including the Ann Lee pond and a nature preserve.

Ten Broeck Mansion/Albany County Historical Association, 9 Ten Broeck Place, Albany, NY 12210, ☎ 518-436-9826, www.tenbroeck.org. Revolutionary General Abraham Ten Broeck built this home in 1798. His home had been burned during the Great Albany Fire of 1797, so Ten Broeck leased this land from his father-in-law, Patroon Stephen Van Rensselaer. On one of our visits we saw a bottle from a recently discovered horde of wine in the cellar. Some of it had been purchased in Europe or New York City. The wine was auctioned by Heublein and the proceeds used for restoration of the house.

DID YOU KNOW? A patroon was a landowner with manorial privileges dating from the original Dutch government of New York and New Jersey.

Capital District

USS *Slater*, **DE-766**, Snowdock at Broadway and Quay, Albany, NY 12202, ☎ 518-431-1943, www.ussslater.org. This destroyer escort, one of only three remaining with original armament from World War II, represents the ships that guarded Atlantic convoys and the task forces of the Pacific War. Tours of the ship are often guided by destroyer escort veterans. (Not open during the winter, when the ship is docked at the Port of Albany.)

■ Schenectady

Proctor's Theatre, 432 State Street, Schenectady, NY 12305, ☎ 518-382-3884, www.proctors.org. This 1926 structure was once a vaudeville theatre, the pride of an entrepreneur's chain. F.F. Proctor built it for $1.5 million. It has been restored to its former splendor with gilt and crystal chandeliers, gold leaf on the ceilings and a Louis XV marble fireplace. Proctor's now fills its schedule with plays and musicals by Broadway touring companies, concerts, dance and opera performances, and movies on the big screen.

Schenectady County Historical Society, 32 Washington Avenue, Schenectady, NY 12305, ☎ 518-374-0263, www.schist.org. Here you'll find a genealogical collection, a research library, files of historical documents and many displays of local memorabilia. Indian pieces include Iroquois dolls, a 1720 axe head and arrowheads. One of the elder inhabitants used a special "senility cradle." A Revolutionary War "Liberty flag" hangs upstairs.

Schenectady Heritage Area Visitors' Center at the Museum and Planetarium, Nott Terrace Heights, Schenectady, NY 12308, ☎ 518-382-7890. The Hall of Electrical History, once part of the GE main plant, is now part of the Schenectady Museum. Archives in the Hall house more than one million photographs, plus papers, publications and films documenting the history of the electrical industry. The Museum offers many exhibits, including hands-on experimentation for children and anyone else. You can pick up maps for self-guided walking tours of the GE Plot and Stockade here (see *Urban Walks*, page 148).

Union College, Union & Nott Streets, Schenectady, NY 12308, ☎ 518-388-6000, www.union.edu. Union has the first architecturally planned college campus in the country. Jackson's Garden, on the Nott Street side of the campus, contains sixteen acres of gardens. At the focal point in the middle of the campus, Nott Memorial, a National Historic Landmark, has 16 sides. Call ☎ 518-382-7890 for a brochure describing a self-guided walking tour of the campus.

■ Troy

Burden Iron Works Museum, foot of Polk Street, Troy, NY 12180, ☎ 518-274-5267. The museum is located in the former office of Henry Burden's Iron Works in South Troy, a property listed on the National Register of Historic Places. His factory was powered by the mightiest waterwheel of all time, and he or an employee could make a horseshoe every second. The museum also explores the wider contributions of Troy at the height of its industrial power and examines questions about the uses of technology.

Fort Crailo State Historic Site, 9½ Riverside Avenue, Rensselaer, NY 12144, ☎ 518-463-8738. This museum features the history and culture of Dutch settlements in the Upper Hudson Valley.

Hart-Cluett Mansion, 59 Second Street, Troy, NY 12180, ☎ 518-272-7232, www.rchsonline.org/ar_hc.htm. This Federal-style mansion, built in 1827, houses both original and period furnishings, some of them made in the area. The Carr Building next door has changing exhibits exhibits and one permanent exhibit on resourceful people in the area. The complex serves as headquarters of the **Rensselaer County Historical Society** and its research library.

The **Junior Museum**, 105 8th Street, Troy, NY 12180, ☎ 518-235-2120, www.juniormuseum.org. Exhibits focus on science, history and nature, and children enjoy the hands-on programs in many of them. Live animals are housed in their own habitats. There's a Digistar II planetarium and a Mohican wigwam for kids to explore.

The **New York State Theatre Institute**, Box Office at 155 River Street, Troy, NY 12180, ☎ 518-274-3256, www.nysti.org. This innovative repertory group provides a wide range of drama from October through May, both for children and adults, as well as workshops and educational programs. Most performances are held at the Schacht Fine Arts Center, Russell Sage College, in Troy.

The **Poestenkill Gorge**, a scenic and historic park listed in the National Register of Historic Places, is under development in Troy. It contains Mt. Ida Falls, a series that drops 200 feet from the Prospect Park hillside into the Hudson. The site generated tragic legends about lovers in the Colonial era but the potential water power caught the eye of mill operators as early as 1791. That power was tapped in more elaborate ways from 1840 onwards for a century, as factories were built and operated on both sides of the gorge. A park and walking trail have been developed on the south side, but the north side was still inaccessible at this writing. Call the RiverSpark Visitor Center, listed below, for current information.

RiverSpark Visitor Center, 251 River Street, Troy, NY 12180, ☎ 518-270-8667, fax 518-270-1119, www.troyvisitorcenter.org. Displays include

Capital District

locally made shirt collars, stoves and bells cast in Watervliet and Troy, and a working model of Henry Burden's iron works. An electronic map of the 28-mile Hudson-Mohawk Heritage Trail shows some of the sites in the Heritage Area. Visitors can borrow bikes and return them to the Visitor Center. Ask for maps of the self-guided walking tours, one of downtown Troy and the other of the city's many Tiffany windows (see *Urban Walks*, page 148).

Troy Savings Bank Music Hall, Second and State Streets, (Box office, 88 Fourth Street) Troy, NY 12180, ☎ 518-273-0038, www.troymusichall.org. Conductors maintain that this building has the finest acoustics in America. It is home to the **Troy Chromatic** concert series and hosts the **Albany Symphony Orchestra** and **Siena College Music Series**.

Uncle Sam's Grave, Oakwood Cemetery, 101 Street, Troy NY, ☎ 518-272-7520. Sam Wilson, who was a local meat packer, sold his beef to the US Army in the War of 1812 and has been identified as the source for the "Uncle Sam" character.

Festivals & Events

 Contact the Albany County Convention & Visitors Bureau for more information, ☎ 800-258-3582, www.albanycountycvb.org.

■ February

American Wine Festival, Desmond Hotel, Albany, ☎ 518-464-9466 www.desmondhotel.com.

Mardi Gras Celebration at Proctors, Schenectady, ☎ 518-382-3884 www.proctor.org.

■ March

Fiber Arts Show, Shaker Heritage Society, Albany, ☎ 518-456-7890.

Capital District Garden and Flower Show, Hudson Valley Community College, Troy, ☎ 518-786-1529.

■ April

New York State Chocolate Festival, Empire State Plaza Convention Center, Albany.

■ May

Annual Tulip Festival in Washington Park, Albany, ☎ 518-434-2032 www.albanyevents.org.

Antique Show, Rensselaer County Historical Society, Troy, ☎ 518-270-2959.

Annual Grecian Festival, St. Sophia Greek Orthodox Church, Albany, ☎ 518-489-4442.

■ June

New York Quilts, Russell Sage College, Troy, ☎ 518-244-2018 www.nyquilts.org.

Annual Riverfront Arts Fest, Riverfront Park, Troy, ☎ 518-273-0552.

■ July

Sculpture in the Streets, Albany, ☎ 518-465-2143, www.albanybid-ny.org.

Fleet Blues Fest, Empire State Plaza, Albany, ☎ 518-473-0559 www.ogs,state,ny.us.

Albany Riverfest, Corning Preserve, Albany (water skiing, watersports, entertainment), ☎ 518-434-2032, www.albanyevents org.

■ August

Great Northern Catskills Balloon Festival, Balsam Shade, Route 32, Greenville (south of Albany), ☎ 518- 966-5315, www.balsamshade com.

■ September

Capital District Scottish Games, Altamont Fairgrounds, Route 146, Altamont, ☎ 518-453-2551, www.scotsgames.com.

Shaker Craft & Harvest Festival, Shaker Heritage Society, Albany, ☎ 518-456-7890, www.crisny.org/notforprofit/shakerwv.

■ October

Annual Apple Festival and Craft Show, Goold Orchards, Brookview Station Road, Castelton-on-Hudson, ☎ 518-732-7317.

Capital District

■ November

Crafts Festival, Schenectady Museum, Schenectady, ☎ 518-382-7890, www.schenectadymuseum.org.

Christmas Parade, Downtown Schenectady, ☎ 518-372-5656.

Symphony of Lights, State and Pearl Streets, through December, Albany, ☎ 518-465-2143, www.albanybid-org.

Capital Holiday Lights in the Park, Washington Park, through December, Albany, ☎ 800-258-3582, www.albanybid-org.

■ December

Annual Victorian Stroll, Downtown Troy, ☎ 518-274-7020.

Albany's New Years Eve Celebration, Downtown Albany, ☎ 518-434-2032, www.albanyeventsnys.org.

Where to Stay

ACCOMMODATIONS PRICE SCALE
Prices for a double room for one or two persons, before taxes.
$ . . . . Under $50
$$. . . . . $50 to $100
$$$ . . . . $101 to $175
$$$$. . . . . Over $175

■ Albany

Albany Mansion Hill Inn and Restaurant is in an 1860 building. It is located in the downtown area. 45 Park Avenue, Albany, NY 12202, ☎ 888-299-0455 or 518-465-2038. $$$.

Century House Inn has a Colonial theme. The dining room has an innovative menu including Angus steaks, ocean-fresh fish, veal and chicken. 997 New Loudon Road, Latham, NY 12047, ☎ 888-67-HOUSE or 518-785-0931, fax 518-785-3274, www.centuryhouse.inter.net. $$$-$$$$.

The Desmond looks like a Colonial village with rooms around interior courtyards, complete with fountains, flowers and second-story balconies on the façades of the faux-buildings. The hotel's restaurant, **Scrimshaw** (see *Where to Eat*, page 163), offers all kinds of seafood from all over North America. There is also a casual restaurant with a friendly menu. We usually stop there for a quick meal after arriving home from a trip; it is very near Albany Airport. We also often stay overnight before an early morning flight. 660 Albany-Shaker Road, Albany, NY 12211, ☎ 800-448-3500 or 518-869-8100, www.desmondhotels.com. $$$-$$$$.

The **Morgan State House B&B** is located on Washington Park. 393 State Street, Albany, NY 12210, ☎ 888-427-6063 or 518-427-6063, www.statehouse.com. $$$.

Wingate Inn is a new hotel very near the airport in a suburb of Albany. Rooms are large and well-appointed. The **Calaway Grill** is right next door; you can also order from room service. 254 Old Wolf Road, Latham, NY 12110, ☎ 518-869-9100, fax 518-869-0114. $$$

■ Scotia

Glen Sanders Mansion dates from the 1600s; the mansion has been renovated and more accommodations have been added. The restaurant is very popular with its Continental menu. One Glen Avenue, Scotia, NY 12302, ☎ 518-374-7262, www.glensandersmansion.com. $$$-$$$$.

■ Averill Park

The **Gregory House Country Inn** stands behind a century-old handcrafted iron gate that once welcomed visitors to the area. The restaurant serves continental cuisine. Route 43, Box 401, Averill Park, NY 12018, ☎ 518-674-3774, fax 518-674-8916, www.gregoryhouse.com. $$$-$$$$.

■ Berlin

The **Sedgwick Inn** was once a stagecoach stop; it is located in the Taconic valley. It is furnished with antiques and decorated with fine art. The restaurant serves lunch and dinner, Wednesday through Sunday. Route 22, Box 250, Berlin, NY 12022, ☎ 800-845-4886 or 518-658-2334, fax 518-658-3998, www.regionnet.com/colberk/sedgwickinn.html, sedgwickin@aol.com. $$$-$$$$.

■ Camping

Schaghticoke

Deer Run Campground, Box 120, Schaghticoke, NY 12154, ☎ 518-664-2804, www.deerruncampground.com.

Scotia

Arrowhead Marina, 2 Van Buren Lane, Scotia, NY 12302, ☎ 518-382-8966, www.ohwy.com/ok/a/arromari.htm.

Averill Park

Alps Family Campground, 1928 NY Route 43, Averill Park, NY 12018, ☎ 518-674-5565.

Petersburg

Aqua Vista Valley Campgrounds, 82 Armsby Road, Petersburg, NY 12238, ☎ 877-646-0653 or 518-658-3659, www.fortunecity.com/business/wrigley/256.

Broken Wheel Campground, 61 Broken Wheel Road, Petersburg, NY 12138, ☎ 518-658-2925, www.brokenwheelcampground.net.

Where to Eat

DINING PRICE SCALE
Prices include an entrée, which may come with vegetables and salad, but exclude beverage, taxes and tip.
$ . . . . Under $10
$$ . . . . $10 to $20
$$$. . . . . $21 to $50
$$$$. . . . . Over $50

■ Albany

 C. H. Evans Brewing Company at the Albany Pump Station is a microbrewery and full-service restaurant. It is in the original pump station for the Albany Water Works. 19 Quackenbush Square, Albany, NY, ☎ 518-447-9000. $$-$$$.

Jack's Oyster House dates from 1913 and is now in the hands of the third generation. 42-44 State Street, Albany, NY, ☎ 518-465-8854. $$.

The **Riverfront Bar & Grill** is a floating restaurant on the Hudson River. Corning Preserve, Albany, NY, ☎ 518-426-4738. $.

Cranberry Bog has been family owned for 30 years. Open for lunch, dinner or Sunday Brunch. 56 Wolf Road, Albany, NY, ☎ 518-459-5110. $$.

La Serre is in an 1829 building in downtown Albany. 14 Green Street, Albany, NY, ☎ 518-463-6056. $$.

Nicole's Bistro at Quackenbush House is a French-American bistro. 25 Quackenbush Square, Albany, NY, ☎ 518-465-1111. $$-$$$.

Ogden's Restaurant in an historic building downtown has an award-winning wine list. 42 Howard Street, Albany, NY, ☎ 518-463-6605. $$-$$$.

Scrimshaw (in The Desmond hotel; see page 160) is a great place to relax after arriving at the airport. 660 Albany-Shaker Road, Albany, NY, ☎ 518-869-8100. $$-$$$.

■ Scotia

Glen Sanders Mansion is in an historic building that has been restored. One Glen Avenue, Scotia, NY, ☎ 518-374-7262. $$-$$$.

■ Troy

Allegro Café is attractive with a collection of musical instruments and autographed chef's jackets. 33 2nd Street, Troy, NY, ☎ 518-271-1942. $$-$$$.

Holmes & Watson evokes memories of Sherlock Holmes and Dr. Watson. 450 Broadway, Troy, NY, ☎ 518-273-8526. $$.

Lo Porto Ristorante Caffe specializes in Northern and Southern Italian cuisine with a Continental flair. 85 4th Street, Troy, NY, ☎ 518-273-8546. $$-$$$.

River Street Café is right on the river. 429 River Street, Troy, NY, ☎ 518-273-2740. $$.

Troy Pub & Brewery has been voted the "best brewery in the Hudson Valley." It sponsors an Oktoberfest in late September. 417-419 River Street, Troy, NY, ☎ 518-273-2337. $-$$.

Capital District

The Berkshires

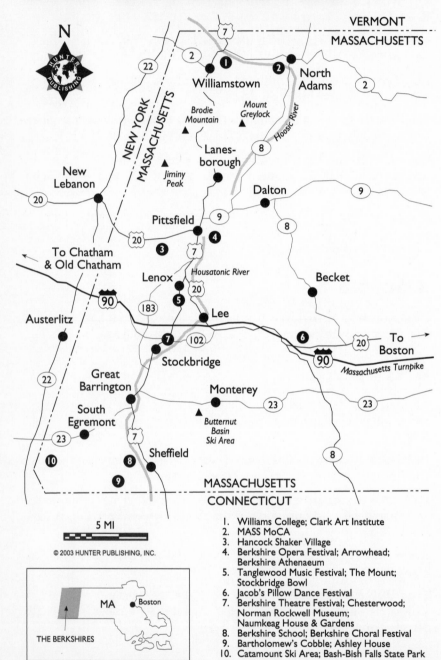

N

VERMONT
MASSACHUSETTS

NEW YORK
MASSACHUSETTS

Williamstown

North Adams

Brodie Mountain

Mount Greylock

Hoosic River

Lanes-borough

New Lebanon

Jiminy Peak

Dalton

Pittsfield

Housatonic River

Becket

To Chatham & Old Chatham

Lenox

Lee

Austerlitz

Stockbridge

To Boston

Massachusetts Turnpike

Great Barrington

Monterey

South Egremont

Butternut Basin Ski Area

Sheffield

MASSACHUSETTS
CONNECTICUT

5 MI

© 2003 HUNTER PUBLISHING, INC.

MA   Boston

THE BERKSHIRES

1. Williams College; Clark Art Institute
2. MASS MoCA
3. Hancock Shaker Village
4. Berkshire Opera Festival; Arrowhead;
   Berkshire Athenaeum
5. Tanglewood Music Festival; The Mount;
   Stockbridge Bowl
6. Jacob's Pillow Dance Festival
7. Berkshire Theatre Festival; Chesterwood;
   Norman Rockwell Museum;
   Naumkeag House & Gardens
8. Berkshire School; Berkshire Choral Festival
9. Bartholomew's Cobble; Ashley House
10. Catamount Ski Area; Bash-Bish Falls State Park

The Berkshires & Taconics

The lure of the rural countryside has long been celebrated in England through landscape painting, pastoral poetry, novels, and the journals of travelers. As many modern travelers know, there is much to please the eye in the valleys of the Cotswolds, the rolling downs of Sussex, the blended hills and lakes of Cumbria, and the coastal villages of Devon and Cornwall.

The source of that appeal is a partial taming of the landscape, a subtle blending of human habitation and nature – meadows carved out of hillsides surrounded by rock walls, houses set on knolls against a background of wooded mountains or beside brooks, roads winding through it all with ever-varying perspectives. Probably no one who cleared the land and built the walls and houses ever saw it quite that way, but visitors from the city did and still do.

The Berkshires

The vastness of much American landscape militates against such a comfortable conjunction of habitation and nature, but some regions seem cast in the same mold. One of them, the southern Berkshires, in southwestern Massachusetts, caught the eye of wealthy Bostonians and New Yorkers at the end of the 19th century, and their presence brought painters, sculptors, writers, and musicians to the mountains. The result is a treasure-trove of nature and culture.

■ Geography of the Berkshires

"The Berkshires" doesn't mean a mountain range but refers to the forest shire, which is mostly Berkshire County. The mountain range that borders New York State is the Taconic and to the east is the Hoosac range. The Housatonic River flows in-between, then through Connecticut and into Long Island Sound. And the Hoosic River runs cross-country in the north, then flows into the Hudson. Glaciers advanced four times over the last 10,000 years ago, creating the landscape we see now.

Getting Here & Getting Around

■ By Air

Albany International Airport . . . . ☎ 518-869-9611

Bradley International Airport. . . . . ☎ 860-623-2533
Windsor Locks, CT

■ By Car

From New York, take the **Taconic Parkway** to the **Massachusetts Turnpike (I-90)**, then watch for the exit you want into the Berkshires. If coming from Connecticut, drive the **Connecticut Turnpike** to **Route 91**, then take 91 north to the **Massachusetts Turnpike (I-90)**.

■ By Bus

Bonanza Bus Line . . . . ☎ 800-556-3815

Greyhound Lines. . . . . ☎ 800-237-8747

■ By Train

Amtrak . . . . ☎ 800-USA RAIL

Information Sources

Berkshire Hills Visitors Bureau, Berkshire Common, Plaza Level, Pittsfield, MA 01201, ☎ 800-237-5747 or 413-443-9186, fax 413-443-1970, www.berkshires.org, bvb@berkshires.org.

Chamber of Commerce of the Berkshires, 66 West Street, Pittsfield, MA 01201, ☎ 413-499-4000, fax 413-447-9641, www.berkshirebiz.org, chamber@berkshirebiz.org.

Lee Chamber of Commerce, 3 Park Place, Lee, MA 01238, ☎ 413-243-0852, fax 413-243-4533, www.leechamber.org, info@leechamber.org.

Lenox Chamber of Commerce, Box 646, Lenox, MA 01240, ☎ 413-637-3646, www.lenox.org, info@lenox.org.

Mohawk Trail Association, Box 1044, North Adams, MA 01247, ☎ 413-743-8127, fax 413-743-8163, www.mohawktrail.com, peter.tomyl@milesmedia.com.

Stockbridge Chamber of Commerce, 6 Elm Street, Stockbridge, MA 01262, ☎ 413-298-5200, fax 413-298-4321, www.stockbridgechamber.org, info@stockbridgechamber.org.

Williamstown Chamber of Commerce, Town Hall, Williamstown, MA 01267, ☎ 413-458-9077, fax 413-458-2666, www.williamstownchamber.com, commerce@williamstown.net.

Adventures

■ On Foot

Hiking

Mount Greylock, Rockwell Road, Lanesborough, ☎ 413-499-4262. From Lanesborough, drive along North Main Street to Quarry Road, turn right, and in 0.4 mile fork left onto Rockwell Road. The visitors center is 0.7 mile on the right at the south end of the reservation. Natural history exhibits provide an introduction to the trails. Then drive along Rockwell Road to Sperry Road and into Sperry Campground. A number of trails are available from this point. The **Deer Hill Trail** begins at an elevation of 2,400 feet and goes downhill to Deer Hill Falls and on to Roaring Brook. The trail heads uphill and meets **Hopper Trail**, then **Overlook Trail** and **Notch Road**, which takes you to the summit of Mount Greylock. When you wish to return to your car, head down, following the white-blazes of the **Appalachian Trail**, until you take the right fork onto the Hopper Trail to Sperry Campground.

Pleasant Valley Wildlife Sanctuary, 472 West Mountain Road, Lenox, MA 01240, ☎ 413-637-0320. The **Massachusetts Audubon Society** parking area is reached from Route 7, four miles south of Pittsfield. Turn west on West Dugway Road and in 1.7 miles you will see the parking area. You can get a trail map in the sanctuary office there. Begin your hike on **Pike's Pond Trail**, continue past **Yokun Trail** and onto **Trail of the**

Ledges, with blue markers. Begin climbing Lenox Mountain past **Farview Ledges** lookout and reach the summit of Lenox Mountain. To descend, take **Overbrook Trail** past **Laurel Trail**, **Great Hemlock Trail**, **Ovenbird Trail** and **Old Wood Road**. Bear left on **Beaver Lodge Trail**. After crossing the boardwalk, take Old Wood Road and Yokun Trail to **Bluebird Trail** and back to the sanctuary.

In 1932, beavers were placed in the Pleasant Valley Wildlife sanctuary and they have made lodges, dammed ponds and changed the contour of the area, providing a habitat for ducks, frogs and birds.

Bartholomew's Cobble, ☎ 413-229-8600. Drive south from Great Barrington on Route 7 for eight miles. Turn west on Route 7A and drive 2.3 miles to Ashley Falls, then right onto Rannapo Road and left on Weatogue Road. The visitors center has exhibits and information on trails. Head out on **Ledges Trail**, then **Bailey Trail**, which goes along the west side of the river. You can take a side jaunt on the **Sterling and Louise Spero Trail** or continue on Bailey Trail. Continue on and turn left onto **Weatogue Road**, then **Tulip Tree Trail** to the summit of **Hurlbut Hill**. To return, retrace your way down to Weatogue Road.

Bash Bish Falls State Park, Falls Road, Mount Washington, ☎ 413-528-0330. From South Egremont, take Route 23, Route 41 and Mount Washington Road. Head for the upper parking lot on Falls Road and walk down a quarter-mile trail to the falls. You can also take the road to the lower parking lot in New York's Taconic State Park for an easier walk to the falls. From Taconic State Park, there is a steep trail to the top of the falls.

HIKING CLUBS & RESOURCES

Appalachian Mountain Club, Lanesborough, MA 01237, ☎ 413-443-0011. Contact the club for information on naturalist programs, trail maps, environmental displays and equipment.

Bascom Lodge, at the summit of Mt. Greylock, Adams, MA 01220. Mailing address: Box 1800, Lanesborough, MA 01237, ☎ 413-743-1591, fax 413-442-9010, www.outdoors.org. The Appalachian Mountain Club offers free hikes, sunset walks, slide shows, and the Lodge provides overnight accommodations.

Berkshire Wildlife Sanctuary, 472 West Mountain Road, Lenox, MA 01240, ☎ 413-637-0320, www.massaudubon.org, berkshires@massaudubon.org.

■ On Wheels

Scenic Drives

The Berkshires are particularly rich in scenic drives that also take you into the area's cultural heritage. You can get a map and more detailed descriptions of the following drives, and four others, from the **Berkshire Hills Visitors Bureau** (see *Information Sources*, page 166).

CENTRAL BERKSHIRES – Begin this tour in **Pittsfield**, where you will drive west on Route 20 just past the intersection with Route 41 for a visit to **Hancock Shaker Village**. Then drive south on Route 41 through Richmond before heading east on Lenox Branch Road and Lenox Mountain Road. Join Route 183 just before the main entrance to **Tanglewood**, where you can pause for a visit to the grounds and perhaps stay for a performance. Continue on Route 183 into **Lenox** village, then head south on Route 7A to Edith Wharton's mansion, **The Mount**, where you can tour the house and gardens and see Shakespeare performances (for information about visiting The Mount, see *Sightseeing*, page 175). Next turn east on Plunkett Street to Route 20 and head south through Lee and east to **Jacob's Pillow**, site of America's oldest dance festival. Continue east on Route 20, to the junction with Route 8, and follow the latter north into **Becket**, where there is an arts center. Farther north off Route 8 you may want to take a side trip east on Route 143 to a cemetery where **Israel Bissell** is buried. He galloped five days to carry the news of the battle at Lexington to Connecticut, New York and Philadelphia. Then continue north on Route 8 to **Dalton**, where the **Crane Museum** has exhibits on the history of paper making. Head back into Pittsfield on South Street from Dalton.

SOUTH BERKSHIRES – Begin this tour in **Sheffield**, which is a mecca for antique dealers in the Berkshires. Take Route 7 north into Great Barrington. The **Newsboy Statue** stands on Route 23 a half-mile west of Route 7. The statue was created by sculptor David Richards and it is a tribute to hard-working newspaper carriers everywhere. Continue west on Route 23 to **South Egremont**. Where Route 23 meets Route 41 at Smiley's Pond, watch for **Mount Everett-Bash Bish Falls** signs and follow the road west to the parking area on the western slope of the mountain. You can take a foot trail to the falls.

DID YOU KNOW? The "Spirit Profile" is a rock that looks like the profile of a maiden through the mist. Here a Native American girl jumped to her death in the pool from the cliff above. The water still calls her name – Bash Bish, Bash Bish.

Head back to South Egremont and follow Route 7A to Ashley Falls, taking a right at signs for **Bartholomew's Cobble**, a jagged limestone outcropping over the Housatonic River (see page 168). There you can walk some interesting nature trails and visit the **Colonel Ashley House**. Retrace your route to rejoin Route 7 and head north back to Sheffield.

SOUTH CENTRAL BERKSHIRES – This tour begins in **Great Barrington**; you will head east on Route 23, also known as the **Knox Trail**. General Henry Knox took this route through the mountains in the winter of 1775-76, hauling cannon captured from the British at Fort Ticonderoga to Boston. In the center of Monterey village, turn north on Monterey Road past the Lake Garfield beach to the **Bidwell House**, an elegant 1750 mansion on the National Register of Historic Places, where you can stop for a visit. Continue north on Monterey Road, which joins the Tyringham Road and leads into a beautiful valley surrounded by mountains. This area was popular with writers and poets in the 19th century; Mark Twain used to summer in the area. Continue north until you reach Route 102 and take it west into **Stockbridge**, where there are many things to do. From Main Street take Pine Street to Prospect Hill Road for a visit to **Naumkeag Museum and Gardens**. **Berkshire Botanical Garden** is at the intersection of Routes 102 and 183. Also on Route 183 you will find the **Norman Rockwell Museum** and **Chesterwood**, home and studio of sculptor Daniel Chester French. When you have finished your visits in this area, head south on Route 183 back to Great Barrington.

MOUNT GREYLOCK – Begin this tour one mile north of **Lanesborough** on Route 7. Rockwell Road will take you up to the summit (3,491 feet) of the highest mountain Massachusetts, a trip of 10 miles. As mentioned in the hiking section, it pays to stop in the Mount Greylock Visitor Center (see page 167) for information. On the way up, a side trip of a mile on Sperry Road leads down to **Stoney Ledge**, which overlooks a wooded canyon called the "Hopper," with Mount Prospect in the background. Continue on Rockwell Road until you see the **War Memorial Tower**, a 90-foot granite tower dedicated to the memory of Massachusetts casualties in all wars. On a clear day, the view from here includes Mount Monadnock in New Hampshire, the Green Mountains in Vermont, the Adirondacks and Catskills in New York, and Mount Everett in the southern Berkshires. One can take Notch Road to Route 2 in North Adams through Williamstown to the starting point in Lanesborough or retrace the original route.

TACONIC-MOHAWK TRAIL – **Williamstown** is the place to begin this tour. Take Route 2 east out of Williamstown to North Adams, where you can visit **MASS MoCA** (see *Sightseeing*, page 174). **Natural Bridge State Park** is east of North Adams off Routes 2 and 8. Continue on Route 2 east to the Mohawk Trail, a very scenic drive following the old Native American trail between Connecticut and the Hudson River Valley. The first scenic stop is the observation point called **Spirit Mountain** at the hairpin turn. Here you will have fine views of southern Vermont and northwestern Massachusetts, including Mount Greylock, Mount Prospect and Mount Williams. Whitcomb Summit, at 2,173 feet has even more distant views. You can continue to Charlemont, Shelburne Falls and Greenfield or turn right into Savoy Mountain State Forest to visit **Tannery Falls**.

■ On Water

Paddlers will find plenty of places to dip an oar in the Berkshires. One of the most popular is **Stockbridge Bowl**, located between Lenox and Stockbridge on Route 183. October Mountain State Forest offers **Buckley Dunton Lake**, which is a little more secluded. **Onata Lake**, in Pittsfield, is another option, followed by **Pontoosuc Lake** on Route 7.

As whitewater enthusiasts we can relate to trips on one of the rivers in the area. The **Housatonic** offers some flat water and also some rapids. The **Deerfield River** is known for great whitewater with some rocks to watch out for. The **Farmington River** is another one for exhilarating rapids.

Boating

Berkshire Sculling Association, 43 Roselyn Drive, Pittsfield, MA 01201, ☎ 413-496-9160, fax 413-496-9160. Instruction and rentals of single rowing shells.

Wild 'n Wet Sport Rentals, Matt Reilly's Restaurant, Route 7, Pontoosuc Lake, Pittsfield, MA 01201, ☎ 413-637-8041, fax 413-637-2370. Jet skis, paddleboats, canoes and parasailing. Winter snowmobile tours.

Rafting

Crab Apple Whitewater, Inc., Route 2, Charlemont, MA 01339, ☎ 800-553-RAFT or 413-625-2288, fax 413-625-6829. Rafting outfitter offering full- and half-day trips.

Zoar Outdoor, Mohawk Trail, Charlemont, MA 01339, ☎ 800-532-7483 or 413-339-8596. Whitewater rafting, canoe and kayak clinics.

Fishing

The state stocks many of the area's ponds and rivers. Fishermen angle for trout, largemouth bass, perch and chain pickerel. For information on guides, contact **MassWildlife**, Field Headquarters, 1 Rabbit Hill Rd., Westboro, MA 01581, ☎ 508-792-7270, www.state.ma.us/dfwele/dfw.

Licenses can be obtained from the **Division of Fisheries and Wildlife**, 100 Cambridge Street, Boston, MA 02202, www.state.ma.us/dfwele/dfw/dfw_toc.htmor (where you can get a license online) or at sporting goods stores.

■ On Horseback

For information on horseback riding, stables and instructors, ☎ 508-881-4766.

Undermountain Farm, 400 Undermountain Road, Lenox, MA 01240, ☎ 413-637-3365, fax 413-637-1008. Licensed instruction, guided trail rides, and a riding day camp.

■ On Snow

Downhill Skiing

Four downhill ski areas in the Western Berkshires have vertical drops of approximately 1,000 feet or more, and highly developed facilities. We list them from north to south.

Brodie Mountain, Route 7, New Ashford, MA 01237, ☎ 413-443-4752. Now under the ownership of nearby Jiminy Peak, Brodie maintains its reputation as a family-friendly area, with a good selection of green and blue trails for novices and intermediates, as well as a number of single-blacks for aspiring young hotshots. Unlike many areas, where the greens are all bunched on the lower slopes, here novices can go to the top of the lifts, enjoy the view of Mount Greylock on a fine day, and find at least one green trail to take them down. Snowmaking covers 96% of the trails, and nearly half of them are lighted for night skiing. Brodie has a healthy vertical drop of 1,250 feet, and its 40 trails are served by four double chairs and two surface lifts. It also has 25 km of cross-country trails linked to the downhill facilities.

Jiminy Peak, Hancock, MA 01237, ☎ 413-738-5500. With a reputation for a wide variety of trails, including some demanding ones, Jiminy Peak claims to be "the largest ski and snowboard resort in Southern New England." The vertical drop is 1,150 feet, and 40 trails are served by seven chairlifts, including a high-speed six-person chair, and two surface lifts. The trails are nicely distributed through the full range of skiing abilities, with 21% rated for beginners, 50% for intermediates, and 29% for experts. Snowmaking covers 95% of the 176 skiable acres, and 18 trails are lighted for night skiing. Two short lifts serve the needs of beginners at the bottom, and most of the easiest trails higher up curve around the perimeter of the mountain. Intermediates will want to explore many of the trails on the right flank of the mountain, as well as ones on the far left. Those who want more demanding terrain will stick closer to the middle, where the straight shots paralleling the lifts are single- or double-black diamond.

Ski Butternut, Route 23, Great Barrington, MA 01230, ☎ 413-528-2000, www.skibutternut.com. Just beyond the eastern edge of Great Barrington, Butternut – like Brodie Mountain in the northern Berkshires – has a family-friendly reputation. You can reach green or blue trails from the top of the four major lifts, which also serve a scattering of single-blacks that take advantage of 1,000 feet of vertical drop. Altogether, 22 trails are served by six chairlifts and two surface lifts. The snowmaking is 100%, covering 110 skiable acres, most of them on trails winding through pleasant woodland. For those who want a different experience, Butternut also has eight km of groomed cross-country trails.

Catamount, South Egremont, MA 01258, ☎ 413-528-1262, www.catamountski.com or www.ridecatamountride.com. Perched on the border between New York and Massachusetts, Catamount is one of the pioneer ski areas in the region. Founded in 1940 with a rope tow and "groomed" by skiers sidestepping down the slope, it now has 96% snowmaking on 27 trails, including two terrain parks and a "snowboard megaplex" served by four double chairlifts and three surface lifts. With a vertical drop of 1,000 feet and a fine set of black diamonds – look up at the double-black and you'll believe it – Catamount has always appealed to Capital District skiers looking for challenge close to home. But it also has a lot of blues spread throughout the mountain and fine broad green slopes and trails on the left flank of the mountain.

Cross-Country Skiing

Bucksteep Manor, Washington Mountain Road, Washington, MA 01223, ☎ 413-623-5535. Surrounding the turn-of-the-century replica of an English manor house are 25 km of groomed trails.

Canterbury Farm, Fred Snow Road, Becket, MA 01223, ☎ 413-623-0100. Twelve miles of groomed and tracked trails are supplemented by wilderness skiing throughout its 2,000 acres.

Cranwell Resort, 55 Lee Road, Route 20, Lenox, MA 01240, ☎ 413-637-1364. The resort tracks cross-country trails on its golf course.

Notchview Reservation, PO Box 792, Sergeant Street, Stockbridge, MA 01262, ☎ 413-684-0148 or 413-298-3239. One of 77 properties of The Trustees of Reservations, Notchview is located on Route 9 in Windsor and has 30 km of trails.

Otis Ridge, Box 128, Route 23, Otis, MA 01253, ☎ 413-269-4444. The oldest Alpine ski camp in the nation also has an extensive cross-country system with 38 km of trails.

Pleasant Valley, 472 West Mountain Road, Lenox, MA 01240, ☎ 413-637-0320. This wildlife sanctuary owned by the Massachusetts Audubon Society has eight km of ungroomed trails. See pages 167-68, for more.

 Note that **Brodie Mountain** and **Butternut**, listed under *Downhill Skiing*, page 172, also have cross-country trails.

Sightseeing

■ Williamstown

 Sterling and Francine Clark Art Institute, 225 South Street, Williamstown, MA 01267, ☎ 413-458-2303, fax 413-458-2318, www.clarkart.edu. The Clarks began collecting in Paris in 1912 and continued adding to their extensive and stunning collection throughout the years. You can see works by Renoir, Monet, Van Gogh, Degas, Homer and Remington, among others.

■ North Adams

MASS MoCA, 87 Marshall Street, North Adams, MA 01247, ☎ 413-664-4481, fax 413-663-8548. This contemporary art center is housed in a renovated 19th-century factory with 27 buildings spread over 13 acres. The galleries are enormous and each has a stunning display on the theme of the exhibiting artist.

■ Pittsfield

Herman Melville's Arrowhead, 780 Holmes Road, Pittsfield, MA 01201, ☎ 413-442-1793, fax 413-443-1449, www.mobydick.org. Herman Melville brought his family to Pittsfield and moved into Arrowhead, where he wrote *Moby Dick*. His study faced the whale-like Greylock range. The house is filled with family and literary memorabilia.

 Melville wrote a letter to a friend: "I look out of my window in the morning when I rise as I would out of a porthole of a ship in the Atlantic. My room seems a ship's cabin; & at nights when I wake up & hear the wind shrieking, I almost fancy there is too much sail on the house, & I had better go on the roof & rig in the chimney."

Herman Melville Memorial Room, Berkshire Athenaeum, 1 Wendell Avenue, Pittsfield, MA 01201, ☎ 413-499-9486. The Athenaeum houses a collection of books, pictures, letters and memorabilia relating to Herman Melville.

Hancock Shaker Village, Route 20, Pittsfield, MA 01201, ☎ 800-817-1137 or 413-443-0188, fax 413-447-9357. Twenty-one buildings are open to visitors in this 200-year-old Shaker village. Hancock Shaker Village is part of the sect created by Mother Anne Lee and her followers in 1776 at Niskayuna, New York. The Shakers held property in common and believed that men and women should be equal and celibate. Their motto was "Do all your work as though you had a thousand years to live and as you would if you knew you must die tomorrow."

■ Lenox

The Mount, 2 Plunkett Street, Lenox, MA 01240, ☎ 888-637-1092 or 413-637-1899, fax 413-637-0619, www.edithwharton.org. The Mount was built in 1901 as a summer estate for Edith Wharton. She considered The Mount her first real home and spent six or seven months a year there. Like many novelists, Wharton wrote early in the day, then worked in her garden and visited with friends. Henry James called the Mount "a delicate French château mirrored in a Massachusetts pond."

THE COTTAGES

In the parlance of the day, The Mount was a "cottage" because it was designed for summer residence, but obviously was not the rustic cabin that the word suggests today. Just as Newport, Rhode Island had its cottages, so did Lenox and Stockbridge. Many of them had 20 to as many as 100 rooms, and some had ballrooms, libraries, and rooms set aside for billiards and musical performances. They all had servants, who were kept busy cleaning, arranging fresh flowers, and serving guests. One servant's only task was winding all of the clocks on one of the estates.

Initially, cottages were not used as primary residences, but as places to entertain guests during "the season." As a guest, you would not be expected to lift a finger and could spend your time talking, listening to music, playing tennis or golf, riding horseback or walking along paths through extensive grounds.

■ Stockbridge

Chesterwood, 4 Williamsville Road, Stockbridge, MA 01262, ☎ 413-298-3579, fax 413-298-3973, www.chesterwood.net. Chesterwood was the summer estate of Daniel Chester French, a prolific sculptor whose works include the "Seated Lincoln" in the Lincoln Memorial and the "Minuteman" at Old North Bridge in Concord. You can visit the house, the studio, and the 19th-century barn, which is now a gallery. Take a walk along the nature trails and enjoy the gardens as well as views of Monument Mountain.

DID YOU KNOW?

The sculptor Daniel Chester French once said, "I live here six months of the year – in Heaven. The other six months I live, well – in New York."

Naumkeag House & Gardens, Prospect Hill Road, Stockbridge, MA 01262, ☎ 413-298-3239, www.thetrustees.org. Naumkeag was the estate of Joseph Choate, an ambassador to England in the late 19th century. The 26-room Norman mansion is filled with beautiful antiques. The china collection includes Lowestoft pieces, Leeds lusterware, Staffordshire and Chinese porcelains.

The gardens are colorful, with fountains, topiary shrubs, and a Chinese pagoda featuring blue tiles made in China. Dragons guard the gardens and a Moon Gate brings good luck to anyone who passes through it. You can enjoy walking along ramps and down steps through Birch Walk. At the bottom, turn around to see symmetrical steps and four pools painted royal blue.

The Norman Rockwell Museum, Route 183, Stockbridge, MA 01262, ☎ 413-298-4100, fax 413-298-4142. If you remember Norman Rockwell's magazine illustrations with fondness, don't miss visiting the museum in Stockbridge devoted to his work. You'll see the originals of magazine covers, posters, and prints that all look very familiar. Guides enjoy pointing out the humor in his work – also the painterly composition that is often overlooked. Some of his well-known paintings also have historical value. The Red Lion Inn and the wide main street in Stockbridge look much the same now as they did in Rockwell's time, except for cars of a different era.

An octagonal gallery inside the museum displays the "Four Freedoms" group, which Rockwell painted to illustrate President Roosevelt's objectives as the country entered World War II.

Rockwell's studio was moved onto the grounds of the new museum, a former country estate. You can walk along a path from the museum to see it and listen to anecdotes from the docent. Looking at the studio, we felt that Rockwell had just gone out for lunch and would soon be back to pick up his brushes again.

Performing Arts

■ Pittsfield

Berkshire Opera Company, Ozawa Hall, Lenox & Koussevitzky Arts Center, Pittsfield, MA 01201, ☎ 413-443-1234, fax 413-443-3030, www.berkop.org. Professional opera in English.

■ Lenox

Tanglewood Music Festival, West Street, Route 183, Lenox, MA 01240, ☎ 413-637-5165 (summer), 617-266-1492 (off-season), fax 617-638-9436, www.bso.org. Tanglewood beckons music lovers to hear the Boston Symphony Orchestra, the Boston Pops, opera companies, chamber players, noted soloists, popular artists, and jazz ensembles. You can bring a picnic supper, then sit in the shed or find a spot on the lawn and drift off to semi-sleep if you wish. Both the setting and the music are magnificent.

Shakespeare & Company, The Mount, Route 7 & Plunkett Street, Lenox, MA 01240, ☎ 413-637-1199, box office 413-637-3353, fax 413-637-4240, www.shakespeare.org. Fourteen plays are performed on five outdoor/indoor stages. At The Mount you can watch a Shakespearean performance at open-air Mainstage, where the actors glide in from every direction; they use the stream, surrounding white pines, and the house as a backdrop. Bring a picnic, insect repellent, and a blanket to enjoy magical theater under the stars.

■ Becket

Jacob's Pillow Dance Festival, George Carter Road, Becket, MA 01223, ☎ 413-243-0745, www.jacobspillow.org. Nine weeks of dance performances include ballet, modern and ethnic dance. Performances take place in the Ted Shawn Theatre and the Doris Duke Studio Theatre.

■ Stockbridge

Berkshire Theatre Festival, Main Street, Stockbridge, MA 01262, ☎ 413-298-5536, fax 413-298-3368. Performances are given on the main stage, Unicorn Theatre and BTF Plays.

■ Sheffield

Berkshire Choral Festival, 245 North Undermountain Road, Sheffield, MA 01257, ☎ 413-229-8526, fax 413-229-0109. Saturday concerts are held at 8 pm on the grounds of the Berkshire School. There's a preconcert talk at 6:30 pm.

Festivals & Events

■ June

 Williamstown Film Festival, Williamstown, ☎ 413-458-2700.

Pittsfield Summerfest, Pittsfield, ☎ 888-838-5337. Music, art and recreation all summer long.

■ July

Berkshire Botanical Garden Antiques Show, Stockbridge, ☎ 413-298-3926.

■ August

Berkshire Crafts Fair, Stockbridge, ☎ 413-528-3346.

■ September

Josh Billings Runaground, Great Barrington, ☎ 413-442-1090. Bike/canoe/run.

■ October

Fall Foliage Festival, North Adams, ☎ 413-663-3735.

■ November-December

Festival of Trees at the Berkshire Museum, Pittsfield, ☎ 413-443-7171.

Where to Stay

ACCOMMODATIONS PRICE SCALE	
$	Under $50
$$.	$50 to $100
$$$	$101 to $175
$$$$	Over $175

■ Williamstown

The 1896 House, Route 7, Cold Spring Road, Williamstown, MA 01267, ☎ 888-666-1896 or 413-458-8125. There is a room dedicated to Christopher Reeve and Dana Morosini. Rooms feature Waverly-Schumaker patterns. $$-$$$.

The Orchards, 222 Adams Road, Williamstown, MA 01267, ☎ 800-225-1517 or 413-458-9611, fax 413-458-3273. Built around a courtyard, the rooms contain four-poster beds and English antiques. $$$.

The Williams Inn, on the green at Williams College, Williamstown, MA 01267, ☎ 800-828-0133 or 413-458-9371, fax 413-458-2767, www.williamsinn.com. A modern Colonial-style building right on the campus. $$$.

■ Lenox

Blantyre, 16 Blantyre Road, Lenox, MA 01240, ☎ 413-637-3556, fax 413-637-4282, www.blantyre.com. An elegant Tudor-style mansion that looks and feels like an English country house. It is complete with gargoyles and turrets. More rooms and suites are avilable in other buildings on the property. $$$$.

Brook Farm Inn, 15 Hawthorne Street, Lenox, MA 01240, ☎ 800-285-POET or 413-637-3013, www.brookfarm.com. Poetry readings are held in this Victorian home. Bedrooms are comfortable, with quilts and canopy beds. $$$.

Candlelight Inn, 35 Walker Street, Lenox, MA 01240, ☎ 800-428-0580 or 413-637-1555, www.candlelightinn-lenox.com. Guest rooms are individually decorated with print wallpaper, antiques, quilts, and paintings. $$-$$$.

Cliffwood Inn, 25 Cliffwood Street, Lenox, MA 01240, ☎ 800-789-3331 or 413-637-3330, fax 413-637-0221, www.cliffwood.com. The ambassador to France built this home in 1890s. Paintings and artwork were brought from Europe by the owners. $$$-$$$$.

Cranwell Resort, 55 Lee Road, Route 20, Lenox, MA 01240, ☎ 800-272-6935 or 413-637-1364, fax 413-637-0571, www.cranwell.com. The original building is a Tudor mansion dating back 100 years; it is surrounded by a golf course. $$$-$$$$.

Gateways Inn, 51 Walker Street, Lenox, MA 01240, ☎ 888-492-9466 or 413-637-2532, fax 413-637-1432, www.gatewaysinn.com. Harley Proctor, of Proctor and Gamble, was the first owner of the house. One of the suites was frequented by Arthur Fiedler, who came to conduct the Boston Pops during the summer. $$-$$$$.

Wheatleigh, Hawthorne Road, Lenox, MA 01240, ☎ 413-637-0610, fax 413-637-4507, www.wheatleigh.com. Wheatleigh looks very much like a European estate. The Great Hall has an ornate marble fireplace. Waterford chandeliers grace the dining room, along with ceramic tile wall plaques made by Doulton. $$$-$$$$.

■ Lee

Applegate, 279 West Park Street, Lee, MA 01238, ☎ 800-691-9012 or 413-243-4451, www.applegateinn.com. Each guest room is different and one has a two-person steam shower. The garden and landscaping on this six-acre estate are spectacular. $$-$$$.

The Inn at Laurel Lake, Lee, MA 01238, ☎ 413-243-9749, www.laurellakeinn.com. This inn has wooded grounds and is right on Laurel Lake. $$-$$$.

■ Stockbridge

The Inn at Stockbridge, Route 7N, Stockbridge, MA 01262, ☎ 888-466-7865 or 413-298-3337, fax 413-298-3406, www.stockbridgeinn.com. This inn reminds one of an English country house. Set on 12 acres, guests can wander on paths in good weather or borrow snowshoes when snow is on the ground.

The Red Lion Inn, Stockbridge, MA 01262, ☎ 413-298-5545, fax 413-298-5130, www.redlioninn.com. This inn is full of collections of china, antiques and pewter. Rooms are available in surrounding buildings as well as the main inn.

Above: Lake Champlain (Peter Finger)

Below: Ethan Allen Homestead, Burlington VT (see page 20)

Below: Ethan Allen Homestead, Burlington VT (see page 20)
Below: Skiing at Sugarbush VT

ove: Robert Louis Stevenson Memorial Cottage, Saranac Lake NY (see page 98)

Below: Sailing on Lake George

Above: Lac du Saint Sacrement *on Lake George (see page 90)*

Below: Canoeing in the Berkshires

Hiking Whiteface Mountain in the Adirondacks.

Above: Bull's Bridge, Litchfield CT (see page 187)

Below: White Flower Farm, Litchfield CT (see page 192)

Above: Kaaterskill Falls (Peter Finger; see page 204)

Below: Looking at Olana from the Hudson (see page 250)

Above: Hunter Mountain in NY's Catskills (see pages 213, 216)

Below: Mohonk Mountain House (see page 238)

Above: *Hasbrouck House, New Palz NY (see page 235)*

Below: *Poet's Walk Park, Poughkeepsie NY (see page 243)*

Bear Mountain Bridge

Above: Hiking on Bear Mountain (see page 280-81)

Below: West Point from the Hudson (see page 289-90)

Above: Boscobel, Garrison NY (see page 274)

Below: Perkins Tower, Bear Mountain (see page 290)

Above: Sunnyside, Hudson River home of Washington Irving (see page 312)

Below: Van Cortlandt Manor, Croton-on-Hudson NY (see page 310)

Above: Kykuit, Rockefeller home at Sleepy Hollow NY (see page 311)

Below: Philipsburg Manor, Tarrytown NY (see page 311-12)

■ Camping

Pittsfield

Bonnie Brae Cabins & Campsites, 108 Broadway, Pittsfield, MA 01201, ☎ 413-442-3754, http://bonniebraecampground.tripod.com.

Lanesborough

Hidden Valley Campground, 15 Scott Road, Box 700, Lanesborough, MA 01237, ☎ 877-392-2267 or 413-4477-9419.

North Egremont

Prospect Lake Park, 50 Prospect Lake Road, North Egremont, MA 02152, ☎ 413-528-4158, www.prospectlakepark.com.

Where to Eat

DINING PRICE SCALE
Prices include an entrée, which may come with vegetables and salad, but exclude beverage, taxes and tip.
$ . . . . Under $10
$$ . . . . $10 to $20
$$$. . . . . $21 to $50
$$$$. . . . . Over $50

■ Williamstown

 The Williams Inn, on the green at Williams College, Routes 7 and 2, ☎ 800-828-0133 or 413-458-9371, www.williamsinn.com. American and continental cuisine. Entrées include New England scrod, cedar plank salmon, roasted maple duck, Yankee pot roast and filet mignon. A great Sunday brunch. $$-$$$.

■ Lenox

Blantyre, Blantyre Road, ☎ 413-637-3556, www.blantyre.com. Each meal is a culinary treat, beginning with breakfast, which is served with elegance. As in English country houses, guests have a glass of wine in the lounge or on the terrace before going in for dinner. The menu features dishes such as ahi tuna, pheasant breast, and Broken Arrow Ranch venison. Allow several hours to enjoy dinner, one of the best anywhere. $$$$ Prix Fixe.

Church Street Café, 65 Church Street, ☎ 413-637-2745. American bistro offering fish, pasta, regional and ethnic dishes. Outdoor seating in season. $$-$$$.

Gateways Inn, 51 Walker Street, ☎ 888-492-9466 or 413-637-2532, www.gatewaysinn.com. Fine dining, featuring modern American gourmet cuisine using fresh local products. Beef tenderloin, rack of New Zealand lamb and Long Island duck are specialties. Extensive wine list and 49 single malts. Picnics prepared, including china and candles or casual fare to take to concerts. $$-$$$.

Spigatina, 80 Main Street, ☎ 413-637-4455. Try the paella Valenciana or Salmon en papillote. $$-$$$.

Wheatleigh, Hawthorne Road, ☎ 413-637-0610, www.wheatleigh.com. Featuring dishes such as Muscovy duck, Copper River salmon and squab. Stepping into the dining room of this beautiful mansion sets the stage for the cuisine to follow. The prix fixe is $82 per person. $$$$. Also try **The Library**, a dining room offering lighter fare at Wheatleigh.

■ Stockbridge

Once Upon a Table, 36 Main, ☎ 413-298-3870. Featuring pork tenderloin and crab cakes. $$-$$$.

Red Lion Inn, 30 Main Street, ☎ 413-298-5545. Contemporary New England cuisine in the antique-filled dining room. $$-$$$. Try **The Lion's Den** or **Widow Bingham's Tavern** in the Red Lion for lighter fare.

■ South Egremont

The Old Mill, Route 23, ☎ 413-528-1421. Dishes include filet of salmon, medallions of pork, New York strip steak and rack of lamb. $$-$$$.

The Taconics

Northwestern Connecticut's Litchfield Hills

One of the jewels of northwest Connecticut is the Litchfield Hills region, a quiet, secluded area – long recognized as just the place to get away from the bustle of cities, but still underdeveloped. Without major highways and cities, inhabitants and visitors alike can enjoy beautiful surroundings without being disturbed. Hikers and walkers glory in finding one more trail or riverside path on a beautiful day. There are villages with English names – Cornwall, Kent, Litchfield, New Milford and Salisbury – reminding us of pleasant walks in Britain. Church spires soar upward on village greens surrounded by white clapboard Colonial homes.

This is the state of the land on the far northwestern border of Connecticut, not far removed from the Hudson River. It was not always so peaceful. Iron ore mining left ruins of forges that once sent cannon, balls and shot to the Continental army. But industrialization did not permanently infringe upon the gorgeous landscape because hardnosed, sensible entrepreneurs of later ages chose flatter lands for manufacturing and distributing their goods. Lucky us!

Friends who told us about the special character of this region cautioned us not to write about it. But how can one fully appreciate the pleasures of travel without sharing them with appropriate listeners? We assume that our readers will be discreet after they have visited the region!

Getting Here & Getting Around

■ By Air

Bradley International Airport . . . . ☎ 888-624-1533
Windsor Locks, CT

■ By Car

From New York City, take the **Taconic State Parkway** north and head east on one of the connecting roads to the Litchfield area. Or take **I-84** from the New York border and then **Route 7** north. From Hartford, take **Route 44** to **Route 202**. From Vermont, head south on **Route 7**.

■ By Bus

Bonanza Bus Line . . . . ☎ 800-556-3815

Greyhound Lines. . . . . ☎ 800-231-2222

■ By Train

Amtrak. . . . . ☎ 800-872-7245

Information Sources

Connecticut Office of Tourism, 505 Hudson Street, Hartford, CT 06106, ☎ 860-270-8080, fax 860-270-8077, www.ctbound.org.

Litchfield Hills Visitors Bureau, Litchfield, CT 06759, ☎ 860-567-4506, www.litchfieldhills.com.

Adventures

■ On Foot

Hiking

Connecticut has 500 miles of blue-blazed hiking trails, most of them on private land – a system that reminds us of the public footpaths in Britain. The state also uses a consistent pattern of blazes (both blue and white), with the top blaze offset like an arrow to indicate the direction of travel. Respect the generosity of the landowners by keeping to the trail's defined footway and carrying out what you carry in. *The Connecticut Walk Book* is the most comprehensive source of information, with detailed maps and trail descriptions. For more

Litchfield Hills

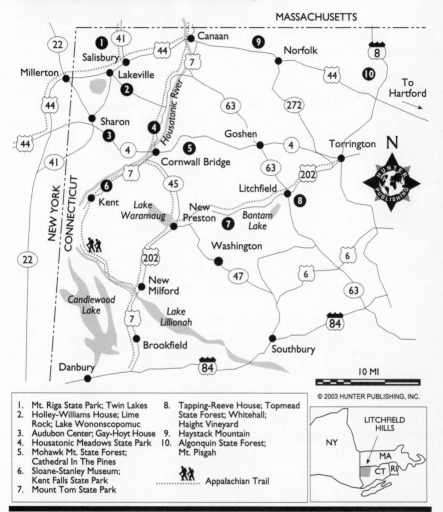

MASSACHUSETTS

The Taconics

1. Mt. Riga State Park; Twin Lakes
2. Holley-Williams House; Lime Rock; Lake Wononscopomuc
3. Audubon Center; Gay-Hoyt House
4. Housatonic Meadows State Park
5. Mohawk Mt. State Forest; Cathedral In The Pines
6. Sloane-Stanley Museum; Kent Falls State Park
7. Mount Tom State Park
8. Tapping-Reeve House; Topmead State Forest; Whitehall; Haight Vineyard
9. Haystack Mountain
10. Algonquin State Forest; Mt. Pisgah

.... Appalachian Trail

10 MI

© 2003 HUNTER PUBLISHING, INC.

information contact the publisher, Connecticut Forest and Park Association, Middlefield, 16 Meriden Road, Rockall, CT 06481, ☎ 860-346-TREE.

Obtain trail maps from the **Bureau of Outdoor Recreation**, State Parks Division, Connecticut Department of Environmental Protection, 79 Elm Street, Hartford, CT 06106-5127, ☎ 860-424-3200.

SALISBURY

Mount Riga, Salisbury, CT. The Appalachian Trail winds through this area, designated Mount Riga State Park. There are many approaches to Mount Riga. On our first visit, we were led by a local friend who knew all the right turns. We arrived, had a picnic, enjoyed the view and headed back down.

To reach Mount Riga State Park, you can drive north of Salisbury on Route 41 to the trailhead for Lions Head, park and take the Appalachian Trail, which winds through this area up 2.3 miles to the summit of Lions Head. The last part is steep but you can follow the blue trail for 100 yards and then, when you reach the ridge, double back to a fairly level trail which leads to the lookout point. You can also continue on this trail for 5.6 miles to the top of Bear Mountain. Along the way, you will reach an Alpine meadow and have a great view of Mount Greylock, which is the highest point (3,491 feet) in Massachusetts. Mount Riga State Park, c/o Burr Pond State Park, 385 Burr Mountain Road, Torrington, CT 06790, ☎ 860-482-1817.

Bear Mountain, Salisbury, CT. From the center of Salisbury take Route 41N for 3.2 miles to the hiker parking lot. Follow the blue-blazed Undermountain Trail and the Paradise Lane Trail to the white-blazed Appalachian Trail. The last part is steep but you will finally reach the summit of Bear Mountain. A monument indicates that this is the highest point in Connecticut, and the panoramic view on top is worth the climb. Follow the white blazes to descend until you reach Riga Junction, where you will turn left onto the blue-blazed Undermountain Trail.

SHARON

Sharon Audubon Center, 325 Route 4, Sharon, CT 06069, ☎ 860-364-0520. The National Audubon Center mains this 890-acre sanctuary. There are 11 miles of self-guided trails that are open dawn to dusk.

Housatonic Meadows State Park, Route 7, Sharon, CT, ☎ 860-672-6772. The Pine Knob Loop Trail joins the Appalachian Trail.

CORNWALL BRIDGE

Mohawk State Forest, Route 4, Cornwall Bridge, CT, ☎ 860-672-6100. Park at the entrance to the forest and walk to the radio tower for great views.

Cathedral in the Pines, Cornwall Bridge, CT. Take Route 4 half a mile from the junction with Route 125 in Cornwall. Turn left on Bolton Hill Road and right on Jewell Street. Turn left after .2 mile and find the white blazes. Although a tornado came through in the late 1980s and toppled the pines, the area is still beautiful. The Appalachian Trail goes through Cathedral Pines.

KENT

Kent Falls State Park, Route 7, Kent, CT 06757, ☎ 860-927-3238. Walkers can take a trail to the head of this 200-foot cascade. Bull's Bridge River Walk heads along the Housatonic River on the Appalachian Trail to Ten Mile Gorge and then to the summit of Ten Mile Hill. Begin with a walk around Bull's Bridge Scenic Loop below the covered bridge. Follow the white-blazed path on the Appalachian Trail into the woods. Bear left at a fork and continue to a bridge where the Housatonic and Ten Mile River merge. Continue and cimb up to the crest of Ten Mile Hill. Retrace your steps back to the parking area.

Issac Bull built a bridge in 1760 to bring iron ore and charcoal across the river. Five bridges later it became covered. Apparently George Washington had an accident on Bull's Bridge in 1781, and one of his horses fell in the river; there was a note in his travel expense record: "getting a horse out of Bull's Bridge Falls, $215.00." That's quite a price for 1781!

LITCHFIELD

White Memorial Foundation, Litchfield, CT, ☎ 860-567-0857. Walkers will find 4,000 acres to explore. Stop in at **Whitehall**, the nature museum on the grounds, for information and a look at the displays. To begin a walk head down the gravel road from the nature museum, turn left onto a blue-blazed trail, cross Bissell Road and meet the white-and-black square trail. Continue through woodlands on the white-and-black trail, which crosses Whites Wood Road. When you see a "Y" in the trail bear left and continue past three boulders. Take a right to the elevated boardwalk. You will see cat-o-nine tails, and Sutton Bridge over the Bantam River. Although the boardwalk ends momentarily, you will bear left and take a path that eventually leads back to the boardwalk. Little Pond is the place to see beavers, swans, ducks, turtles, frogs, fish, songbirds and water fowl. Continue around it and retrace your steps back to the nature museum.

Mount Tom State Park, Route 202, Litchfield, CT, ☎ 860-868-2592. A trail leads up to a circular stone tower, which is 34 feet high. Wooden stairs inside the tower take you up to a cement roof. Theres a 360° view of the Mount Riga Plateau, Mount Bear, Mount Race and Mount Everett.

The Taconics

■ On Wheels

Scenic Drives

NORTHERN LITCHFIELD HILLS

 Begin this tour in **Cornwall Bridge** and head north on Route 7 through **Housatonic Meadows State Park**. In **West Cornwall** you will have a chance to stop and photograph its famed covered bridge. Farther north you can take a side trip on Route 112 west to **Lime Rock Park**, which is called "the road racing center of the east" (see page 191). Or take a tiny detour left from Route 7 on Route 126 into **Falls Village**, which has a marvelous collection of Greek Revival, Italianate, Second Empire and Queen Anne styles of architecture. Continue north on Route 7 to Canaan, where you can see the **Beckly Iron Furnace** – the last operating iron furnace in Connecticut. Then take Route 44 west from Canaan to Salisbury, which offers all sorts of recreational activity. Continue southwest to Lakeville, then take Route 41 (one of the most scenic roads in Connecticut) to Sharon, home of the **Sharon Audubon Center**. Complete your circular tour by taking Route 4 back to Cornwall Bridge.

CENTRAL LITCHFIELD HILLS

Begin this tour in **New Milford** and head north on Route 7 through Gaylordsville. The next section of Route 7 has received a special designation for scenic beauty as it runs beside the Housatonic River. Continue on to Bull's Bridge, which is a covered bridge, and Kent. Route 7 continues on to **Kent Furnace** and **Kent Falls State Park** with its 200-foot-high cascading waterfall. You can continue north to Cornwall Bridge, Housatonic Meadows State Park, West Cornwall and Housatonic State Forest. Or you can choose to turn back southeast when Route 7 hits Route 45 and head to **Lake Waramaug**, which reminds us a bit of Lake Lucerne in Switzerland and Lake Como in Italy. The drive around the lake is eight miles with a state park, vineyard and inns to visit. Route 45 continues to New Preston, where Route 202 takes you four miles east to **Mount Tom State Park**. You can take Route 202 back to New Milford or try Route 47 to Washington Depot and Route 109 to New Milford.

Bicycling

Cycling is popular at **Steep Rock**, **Mohawk State Forest**, around **Lake Waramaug** or in **White Memorial Park** in Litchfield.

The Bicycle Tour Company, Upper Kent Hollow Road, Kent, CT 06757, ☎ 860-927-1742.

Connecticut Cycle Tours, Woodbury, CT 06798, ☎ 860-274-4166.

The Cycle Loft, 25 Litchfield Commons, Route 202, Litchfield, CT 06759, ☎ 860-567-1713.

For more information on cycling contact the **Connecticut Department of Environmental Protection**, DEP-NRC Publication Sales, 79 Elm St., Hartford, CT 06106, ☎ 860-424-3555. Ask for the *Connecticut Bicycle Book*. Also contact the **Connecticut Department of Transportation**, 2800 Belin Turnpike, Box 317546, Newington, CT 06131. Ask for the *Connecticut Bicycle Map*.

■ On Water

The Housatonic River offers fishing, canoeing and kayaking. Dont forget to get a Connecticut fishing license and ask about catch and release fly fishing. Trout fishing is popular.

Lakes offer the chance to sail, row, canoe and kayak. **Lake Waramaug**, located in Lake Waramaug State Park near New Preston, is one that offers a variety of recreation. Also try **Twin Lakes** north of Salisbury, **Wononskopomuc** at Lakeville, **Tyler Lake** near Goshen, **Bantam Lake** near Litchfield and **Candlewood Lake** west of New Milford.

"This body of crystalline water winds like a river around its hilly shores, which at the southern end rise and peer at their own woody shadows in its still mirror.... The lake (Waramaug) turns away westward with a wide sweep, its shores gracefully indented with little coves and crowned with green farms." *Reverend Horace Bushnell, author and theologian, 1802-1876.*

Canoeing, Rafting & Tubing

Clarke Outdoors, 163 Route 7, West Cornwall, CT 06796, ☎ 860-672-6365.

Fishing

 Housatonic Anglers, fly-fishing guide service, 484 Route 7, West Cornwall, CT 06796, ☎ 860-672-4458.

Housatonic River Outfitters, Inc., Route 128 at the Covered Bridge, West Cornwall, CT 06796, ☎ 860-672-1010.

Paradise Valley Farm, 376 Nonnewaug Road, Bethlehem, CT 06751, ☎ 203-266-7800.

Boating

 O'Hara's Landing Marina, 254 Twin Lakes Road, Salisbury, CT 06068, ☎ 860-824-7583. Boat rental, sales and service, launching ramp, dock space by the day or season.

■ On Horseback

 Lee's Riding Stable, Inc., 57 East Litchfield Road, Litchfield, CT 06759, ☎ 860-567-0785.

■ On Snow

Downhill Skiing

 Mohawk Mountain Ski Area, 46 Great Meadow Road, Cornwall, CT 06753, ☎ 800-895-5222 or 860-672-6100. With 650 feet of vertical drop and 23 trails served by five chairlifts and one surface tow, this is the major ski area of the state's northwestern region.

Cross-Country Skiing

White Memorial Foundation, 71 Whitehall Road, Route 202, Litchfield, CT 06759, ☎ 860-567-0857. This ecological foundation, described on page 187, provides 35 km of cross-country trails.

Sightseeing

■ Lakeville

 Holley House Museum, 15 Millerton Road, Lakeville, CT 06039, ☎ 860-435-2878. This museum focuses on the role of women in the 19th century. There is a maze and gardens on the grounds.

Lime Rock Park, Route 112, Lakeville, CT 06039, ☎ 800-RACE-LRP or 860-435-5000. The park offers professional and amateur road racing, car shows and auto festivals.

■ Sharon

Gay-Hoyt House Museum, 18 Main Street, Sharon, CT 06069, ☎ 860-364-5688. The 1775 house has a hands-on history room for children as well as collections of furniture, paintings, photography and textiles.

■ Litchfield

Haight Vineyard & Winery, 29 Chestnut Hill Road, Litchfield, CT 06759, ☎ 860-567-4045 or in CT 800-577-WINE. The winery offers tours, self-guided vineyard walks and complimentary wine tasting.

Litchfield Historical Society Museum, 7 South Street, Litchfield, CT 06759, ☎ 860-567-4501. The museum features the Litchfield History Gallery, portraits, furniture and changing exhibits.

Lourdes in Litchfield Shrine of Our Lady of Lourdes, Route 118, Litchfield, CT 06759, ☎ 860-567-1041. This 35-acre shrine has a replica of the grotto at Lourdes in France.

Tapping Reeve House, 82 South Street, Litchfield, CT 06759, ☎ 860-567-4501. This first law school in the country dates from 1773. Over 100 members of Congress were graduates.

Topsmead State Forest, Buell Road, Litchfield, CT 06759, ☎ 860-567-5694. This English Tudor cottage was the summer home of Edith M. Chase. In 1917, she inherited from her father some 16 acres on Jefferson Hill in Litchfield. She hired the noted architect Richard Henry Dana, Jr. to design the house here, which was completed in 1925. Upon her death in 1972, Edith Chase left the estate to the people of Connecticut, to be known as Topsmead State Forest. In her will, Miss Chase requested that Topsmead State Forest "be kept in a state of natural beauty."

The Taconics

White Flower Farm, Route 63, Litchfield, CT 06759, ☎ 860-567-8789. Here there are 10 acres of display gardens and 30 acres of growing fields. People drive from great distances to select their plants.

▪ Kent

Sloane-Stanley Museum and **Kent Furnace**, Route 7, Kent, CT 06757, ☎ 860-927-3849 or 860-566-3005. Displays include early American woodworking tools, some from the 17th century. The ruins of the 19th-century Kent Iron Furnace are on the grounds.

▪ New Preston

Hopkins Vineyard, 25 Hopkins Road, New Preston, CT 06777, ☎ 860-868-7954. There's a 30-acre vineyard and winery. Wine tasting is complimentary.

▪ New Milford

New Milford Historical Society Museum, 6 Aspetuck Avenue, New Milford, CT 06776, ☎ 860-354-3069. Several buildings include the Knapp House, Litchfield County First Bank, Elijah Boardman Store and a one-room schoolhouse.

Festivals & Events

▪ June

Gallery-on-the-Green, Litchfield, second Sunday, ☎ 860-567-4506.

Litchfield Hills Road Race, Litchfield, second Sunday, ☎ 860-567-4506.

▪ July

Car Racing & Fireworks, Lime Rock Park, 4th of July, ☎ 860-567-4506.

Litchfield Open House Tour, Litchfield, second Saturday, ☎ 860-567-9423.

Canaan Railroad Days, Cannan, second and third weekends, ☎ 860-567-4506.

New Milford Village Fair Days & 8-Mile Road Race, New Milford, last Friday and Saturday, ☎ 860-354-6080.

■ August

Sharon on the Green Arts & Crafts Fair, Sharon, first Saturday, ☎ 860-567-4506.

Kent Summer Festival, Kent, second Saturday/Sunday, ☎ 860-567-4506.

Salisbury Farm Fair, Salisbury, third Saturday, ☎ 860-567-4506.

■ September

Antique Machinery Fall Festival, Kent, fourth Saturday/Sunday, ☎ 860-927-0050.

■ October

Salisbury Antiques Fair & Fall Festival, Salisbury, second Friday/Saturday/Sunday, ☎ 860-567-4506.

■ December

Litchfield Holiday House Tour, Litchfield, second Saturday, ☎ 860-567-4162.

Toy Train Display, New Milford, second week in December, ☎ 860-354-6080.

Covered Bridge Christmas, West Cornwall, through December 24, ☎ 860-672-6545.

The Taconics

Where to Stay

ACCOMMODATIONS PRICE SCALE	
Prices for a double room for one or two persons, before taxes.	
$	Under $50
$$	$50 to $100
$$$	$101 to $175
$$$$	Over $175

■ Salisbury

 Under Mountain Inn, Route 41, Salisbury, CT 06068, ☎ 860-435-0242, fax 860-435-2379, www.innbook.com/undermnt.html. Dating from the 1700s, each room is individually decorated. There's an English pub with paneling that was found under the attic floorboards (the lumber was supposed to have been turned over to the King of England). $$$$.

The White Hart Inn, The Village Green, Salisbury, CT 06068, ☎ 800-832-0041 or 860-435-0030, fax 860-435-0040, www.whitehartinn.com. The original house on the property dates from 1806; it has been an inn since 1867. $$-$$$$.

■ Litchfield

Litchfield Inn, Route 202, Litchfield, CT 06759, ☎ 800-499-3444 or 860-567-4503, fax 860-567-5358, www.litchfieldinnct.com. Each of the guest rooms is different; the Sherlock Holmes Room is a favorite. $$$-$$$$.

■ New Preston

The Birches Inn, 233 West Shore Road, New Preston, CT 06777, ☎ 888-590-7945 or 860-868-1735, www.thebirchesinn.com. This inn has been recently renovated, and guest rooms are decorated individually. It is right on Lake Waramaug. $$-$$$$.

Boulders Inn, New Preston, CT 06777, ☎ 800-552-6853 or 860-868-0541, fax 860-868-1925, www.bouldersinn.com. The house has a view of Lake Waramaug. Cottages have working fireplaces. $$-$$$.

The Hopkins Inn, New Preston, CT 06777, ☎ 860-868-7295, fax 860-868-7464, www.thehopkinsinn.com. This Federal-style inn overlooks Lake Waramaug and is next to a vineyard. Two new apartments have been added. $-$$$.

■ New Milford

Heritage Inn, 34 Bridge Street, New Milford, CT 06776, ☎ 800-311-6294 or 860-354-8883, fax 860-350-5543, www.newmilford-chamber.com. Once an 1800s warehouse, it is now a country hotel. $$$.

■ Camping

Hemlock Hill Camp Resort, Hemlock Hill Road, Litchfield, CT 06759, ☎ 860-567-2267. 125-plus sites. Open April 21-October 15. Swimming, hiking.

Lone Oak Campsites, 360 Norfolk Road (Route 44) East Canaan, CT 06024, ☎ 800-422-2267 or 860-824-7051. 500 sites. Open April 15 to October 15. Swimming, boating, fishing, hiking.

Looking Glass Hill Campground, Route 202, Litchfield, CT 06759. 45 sites. Open mid-April to mid-October, ☎ 860-567-2050.

Mohawk Campground, Route 4, Goshen, CT 06756, ☎ 860-491-2231. 50 sites. Open May 1 to October 3. Swimming.

Valley in the Pines, Lucas Road, Goshen, CT 06756, ☎ 800-201-2267 or 860-491-2032. 32 sites. Open year-round. Swimming, hiking.

White Memorial Family Campground, Bantam Lake, Litchfield, CT 06759, ☎ 860-567-0089. 68 sites. Open early May to mid-October. Boating, fishing, hiking.

Where to Eat

DINING PRICE SCALE
Prices include an entrée, which may come with vegetables and salad, but exclude beverage, taxes and tip.
$ . . . . Under $10
$$ . . . . $10 to $20
$$$. . . . . $21 to $50
$$$$. . . . . Over $50

■ Salisbury

Under Mountain Inn, Route 41, ☎ 860-435-0242. Phone ahead to make sure you can get a table in the dining room; inn guests have priority. The English fare is delicious. $$$

The White Hart Inn, the Village Green, ☎ 860-435-0030. Both restaurants serve seafood, beef and poultry, with specials. Riga Grill, $$$, and Garden Room, $$-$$$.

■ Litchfield

Bistro East, in the Litchfield Inn, Route 202, ☎ 860-567-9040. Contemporary American cuisine includes local produce. The Sunday brunch is memorable. $$-$$$.

■ Kent

The Fife and Drum, Main Street, ☎ 860-927-3509. This restaurant, family-owned since 1972, offers rack of lamb, filet au poivre and 500 wines. It is open for lunch, dinner and Sunday brunch. $-$$$.

■ New Preston

The Birches Inn, 233 West Shore Road, ☎ 888-590-7945 or 860-868-1735. The cuisine is New American with touches of Asian and French influences. The dining room has a view of Lake Waramaug. It is open for dinner. $$-$$$.

Hopkins Inn, 22 Hopkins Road, ☎ 860-868-7295. The Inn specializes in Austrian cuisine, and there is an extensive wine cellar. The garden terrace is open in good weather. $$-$$$.

■ New Milford

Bistro Café, 31 Bank Street, ☎ 860-355-3266. Bistro Café offers specials each day. The menu has a Thai influence; try the spring rolls. $$.

The Catskills

The Catskills cannot match the Adirondacks in height or the White Mountains in grandeur, yet they continue to exert an uncommon influence on the human imagination. From Henry Hudson to Washington Irving and John Burroughs, those who encountered them or lived among them never forgot the experience. Even contemporary travelers speeding down the New York Thruway can be startled – as we always are – if they look west through gaps in the trees at the right moments. What do these strange shapes looming against the western skyline mean?

History

 Henry Hudson's *Half Moon* sailed up the river in 1609 in search of a route to the Orient. Robert Juet, historian and ship's officer, kept a journal that brings some of the details of the river and the mountains to life. Henry Hudson tried for a month to find a northwest passage but gave up in the vicinity of present-day Albany. Although one of the native elders had extended Hudson and his companions an invitation "to goe on land to eate with him" they regretfully sailed away, disappointed in their quest for the riches of the Orient.

"At night we came to other mountaines, which lie from the rivers side. There wee found a very loving people, and very old men; where we were well used. Our boat went to fish, and caught great store of very good fish... This morning the people came aboard, and brought us eares of Indian corne, and pompions, and tabacca; which wee bought for trifles... " Robert Juet

■ The 17th Century

Those who came to the Catskill region a bit later were more pragmatic. Early settlers included Hans Vos, who built a mill on the Vosenkill sometime before 1650. Claes Uylenspiegel, a fur trader, had a cabin on the eastern slope of Hop-O-Nose, also before before 1650. And Jan Jansen van Bremen, from Rensselaerwyck, built a house on the outskirts of Catskill on Old Snake Road. At this time there was a battle for control of the Catskills between the powerful patroonship of Rensselaerwyck to the north and the West India Company in Niew Amsterdam, with the Catskills in the middle. (A patroon was a landowner with manorial privileges dating from the original Dutch government of New York and New Jersey.) In 1652, Peter Stuyvesant, the new governor of New York, temporarily resolved the conflict of land interests by forbidding new settlement in the disputed area.

Yet Pieter Bronck bought a large tract of land in what is now Coxsackie from the Indians in 1661. It extended from the river at Coxsackie back to the Kalkberg ridge. His stone home became a meeting place and traditional site for signing documents. (It still stands today and may be visited.) In 1678 Silvester Salisbury and Marte Gerritse Van Bergen, two

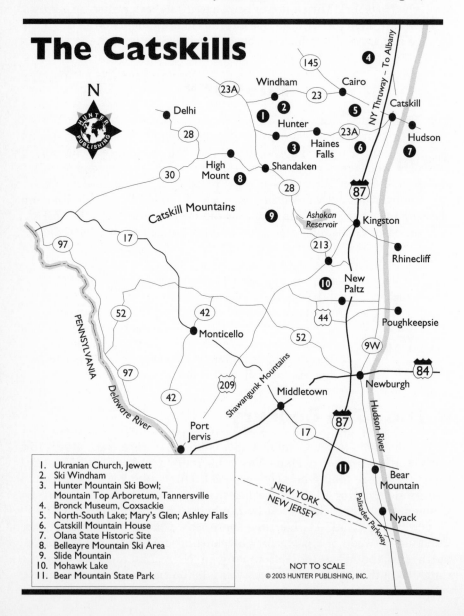

The Catskills

N

1. Ukranian Church, Jewett
2. Ski Windham
3. Hunter Mountain Ski Bowl;
   Mountain Top Arboretum, Tannersville
4. Bronck Museum, Coxsackie
5. North-South Lake; Mary's Glen; Ashley Falls
6. Catskill Mountain House
7. Olana State Historic Site
8. Belleayre Mountain Ski Area
9. Slide Mountain
10. Mohawk Lake
11. Bear Mountain State Park

NOT TO SCALE
© 2003 HUNTER PUBLISHING, INC.

Fort Orange officers, bought land that was four miles west of the Hudson. The village was named Katskill for 100 years until it was expanded to the landing on the river, called Het Strand.

■ The 18th Century

Besides the Dutch, Palatine Germans settled around 1710. After the American Revolution families arrived from New England to farm in the Hudson Valley. With this growth Catskill became a busy port, and many local merchants owned sailing vessels. After Robert Fulton's *Clermont* demonstrated the practicability of marine steam propulsion in 1807, the shift from sail to steam began, spurred by unreliable winds in the narrower stretches of a river surrounded by mountains and high hills. Although the Hudson kept up with the times and became busier with steamboat traffic, and with a railroad along its east bank by mid-century, the Catskills remained self-enclosed and largely impenetrable – almost timeless, a place for legends.

Washington Irving took great delight in presenting the tale of Rip Van Winkle, told by Diedrich Knickerbocker, as sketches in the May 1819 installment of *The Sketch Book*. To set the stage for this classic story of a time warp, he describes the peculiar fascination of the Catskills:

> "Whoever has made a voyage up the Hudson, must remember the Kaatskill mountains. They are a dismembered branch of the great Appalachian family, and are seen away to the west of the river, swelling up to a noble height, and lording it over the surrounding country. Every change of season, every change of weather, indeed, every hour of the day, produces some change in the magical hues and shapes of these mountains, and they are regarded by all the good wives, far and near, as perfect barometers. When the weather is fair and settled, they are clothed in blue and purple, and print their bold outlines on the clear evening sky; but sometimes, when the rest of the landscape is cloudless, they will gather a hood of gray vapours about their summits, which, in the rays of the setting sun, will glow and light up like a crown of glory."

Irving continues to describe a village settled by Dutch colonists, where Rip Van Winkle and his family lived in one of the houses. Rip Van Winkle was one who enjoyed life, was kind to others and had an aversion to work. His wife was a nag and so he escaped into the woods for a stroll.

> "He heard a voice from a distance, hallooing, 'Rip Van Winkle! Rip Van Winkle!... He was a short square built old fellow, with thick bushy hair, and a grizzled beard. His dress was of the antique Dutch fashion – a cloth jerkin strapped round the waist – several pair of breeches, the outer one of ample volume, decorated with rows of buttons down the sides, and bunches at the knees. He bore

The Catskills

on his shoulder a stout keg, that seemed full of liquor and made signs for Rip to approach and assist him with the load... "

"As they ascended, Rip every now and then heard long rolling peals, like distant thunder, that seemed to issue out of a deep ravine... On a level spot in the centre was a company of odd-looking personages playing at nine-pins... By degrees, Rip's awe and apprehension subsided. He even ventured, when no eye was fixed upon him, to taste the beverage, which he found had much of the flavour of excellent Hollands. He was naturally a thirsty soul and was soon tempted to repeat the draught. One taste provoked another, and he reiterated his visits to the flagon so often, that at length his senses were overpowered, his eyes swam in his head, his head gradually declined, and he fell into a deep sleep."

"Even to this day they never hear a thunder storm of a summer afternoon, about the Kaatskill, but they say Hendrick Hudson and his crew are at their game of nine pins... " (Washington Irving, *Rip Van Winkle*)

■ The 19th Century

The Catskills have inspired much more than legends in the painters and writers who found their forms and realities compelling. The **Hudson River School**, one of the first movements in American landscape painting to gain worldwide attention, focused on the dramatic shapes of the mountains. Those shapes appear and reappear in the work of Thomas Cole, Asher Durand, and Frederick Church, who could see them from Olana, his home across the river. In his poems and essays, William Cullen Bryant's imagination was fired by the Catskills, and he invokes them when his friend Thomas Cole is leaving for Europe:

A POEM FOR A PAINTER

"Thine eyes shall see the light of distant skies;
  Yet COLE! thy heart shall bear to Europe's strand
  A living image of our own bright land,
  Such as upon thy glorious canvas lies..."

(From *To Cole, the Painter, Departing for Europe*)

John Burroughs, a nature writer, philosopher and prophet, had an even stronger connection to the Catskills, and much of his nature writing springs from a boyhood spent on a farm at Roxbury in their western foothills. Although he spent most of his life on the Hudson at "Riverby," a house he had built on the west shore south of Esopus, he was never content with riverside life. His son Julian writes that the river was alien to him: "... there had been no rivers like the Hudson in his boyhood country, therefore it could never have a real or lasting interest for him. The great tidal river, almost like an arm of the sea, was wholly unlike anything in nature that he had learned to love." Eventually he purchased Woodchuck Lodge on the Roxbury farm and spent much of his time from June to October there, enjoying its hills and streams.

THE STREAM AT WOODCHUCK LODGE

"A small river or stream flowing by one's door has many attractions over a large body of water like the Hudson. One can make a companion of it; he can walk with it and sit with it, or lounge on its banks, and feel that it is his own. It becomes something private and special to him. You cannot have the same kind of attachment and sympathy with a great river; it does not flow through your affections like a lesser stream." – John Burroughs, *A River View*, 1886.

As the population of New York City multiplied rapidly during the 19th century, the Catskills could no longer withstand the pressure for tourist development. Its most classic hotel, the **Catskill Mountain House**, perched above Palenville from its opening in 1824 until its ruins were razed in 1963. From the end of the Civil War until World War I, this "palace in the clouds" attracted distinguished visitors from Europe and America, as well as affluent city families who could afford to "summer" there. City folk reached Catskill either by steamboat or by railway and ferry, then took carriages to Palenville, until the Catskill Mountain Railway opened in 1881. Starting in 1894, they could even get to the doorstep of the hotel via the Otis Elevating Railway, a cable car.

The success of the Catskill Mountain House spurred the construction of an even more extravagant competitor nearby. In 1881 George Harding of Philadelphia built the Hotel Kaaterskill to accommodate 1,200 guests – once claimed to be the largest resort hotel in the world. It burned in 1924, just as various changes in transportation and lifestyle were making the grand hotels obsolete. As automobiles replaced railroads and steamboats as the preferred means of getting around, and as the habit of summering for two months became less feasible for many families, smaller properties and hotels nearer the city in the Southern Catskills replaced the elegant but relatively inaccessible grande dames sitting on mountaintops. And in the 20th century conventions and transplanted city entertainment – not getting out into nature – became the dominant themes of the survivors.

The Catskills

Getting Here & Getting Around

■ By Air

Albany International Airport . . . . ☎ 518-869-961

Burlington International Airport . . . . ☎ 802-863-287

■ By Car

The Catskills are located a few hours north of New York City and an hour south of Albany. They are reached via the **New York State Thruway**, the **Massachusetts Turnpike (I-90)** and **Interstate Routes 84** and **88**. Rail and bus service is available in a number of places along the river.

■ By Bus

Adirondack Trailways . . . . ☎ 800-858-855

Short Line . . . . ☎ 800-631-840

Greyhound Lines . . . . ☎ 800-231-222

■ By Train

Amtrak . . . . ☎ 800-872-724

Information Sources

Department of Environmental Conservation (DEC) Region 3 Headquarters, 21 South Putt Corners Road, New Paltz, NY 12561-1696, ☎ 845-256-3098.

DEC Region 4 Subregion Office, Route 10 HCR 1 Stamford, NY 12167-9503, ☎ 607-652-7364 (fishing) or 607-652-7367 (wildlife).

Delaware County Chamber of Commerce, 114 Main Street, Delhi, NY 13753, ☎ 800-642-4443 (outside NYS) or 607-746-2281, www.delawarecounty.org.

Greene County Promotion Department, PO Box 527, Catskill, NY 12414, ☎ 800-355-2287 (outside NYS) or 518-943-3223, www.greene-ny.com.

Sullivan County Visitors Association, County Government Center, Monticello, NY 12701, ☎ 800-882-2287 or 845-794-3000, extension 5010, www.scva.net.

Ulster County Tourism Office, Box 1800 CR, Kingston, NY 12402, ☎ 800-342-5826 or 845-340-3566, www.co.ulster.ny.us.

Adventures

■ On Foot

For many years the Catskills remained a remote wilderness, in part because the Indians believed that it was the dwelling place of the Great Spirit. Early Dutch settlers, apart from Rip Van Winkle, concentrated their interest on the Hudson River. Catskill terrain is often rugged and steep, with elevations to 4,200 feet. There are 34 peaks in the Catskills that rise to 3,500 feet in elevation; 20 of these have developed trails to the summit.

DID YOU KNOW?

The Indians named the Catskill Mountains "Onteora," which means "Land in the Sky." However, the Dutch name, Kaatskills, translates into "Wildcat Creek Mountains."

Hiking

NORTHERN CATSKILL TRAILS - EASIER

Catskill Mountain House: Head east of Haines Falls on County Route 18 to the North-South Lake Campground. This easy hike ascends 80 feet in half a mile. Begin at the North Lake Beach parking lot where you can park in the gravel lot beyond it. Look for the blue trail markers and a sign advising you to turn right. Follow the blue markers uphill for .2 mile and you will come out on open ledges and the site of the Catskill Mountain House (see page 201).

Lookout and Sunset Rock: Park in the North Lake Beach lot where you will begin on a yellow-marked trail for .1 mile, then turn left and follow the blue markers. Climb up to a ledge at .2 mile and find the trail register. Walk over flat slabs of rock and through a pitch pine forest until, at .3 mile, you will reach Artists Rock. At .4 mile there's some red shale with a steep climb, then a flatter place and another short climb up to a trail junction at .7 mile. Turn right and continue on the yellow trail to Sunset Rock where the trail ends at .9 mile one way, with the ascent at 300 feet. There are views of North and South Lake and the Hudson River below.

Mary's Glen and Ashley Falls: Parents with young children will appreciate this trail, which does not have open ledges. Walk from the day-use parking lot at North-South Lake, as with the two hikes above, cross over the stone bridge and turn right following the red trail markers. A sign will direct you to North Point and Mary's Glen. The yellow spur trail leads ahead at .2 mile and the sign says Mary's Glen Falls. Walk a short distance to the base of the falls. The ascent is 20 feet in .6 mile. Mary Scribner's husband, Ira, operated a sawmill on the creek.

Kaaterskill Falls Trail: If you're ready for a spectacular falls head out on this short but rugged and moderately difficult walk from the parking lot on Route 23A, 1.3 miles east of North Lake Road at the junction of Route 23A and Kaaterskill Creek. Cross the bridge and at .2 mile turn left on the yellow-marked trail. This trail rises steeply and has several active slide areas. It continues above the stream bed past several 200-year-old hemlocks. The walk is easy to the base of Kaaterskill Falls where the trail ends at .7 mile. The ascent is 340 feet. These two-tiered falls are the highest in New York at 260 feet.

NORTHERN CATSKILL TRAILS - LONGER

The Escarpment Trail: This system of 24 miles begins at Kaaterskill Creek near Haines Falls on Route 23A and continues northerly to East Windham on Route 23. It extends along the escarpments of North and South Mountains. Hikers will pass overlooks and cliffs 1,000 feet above Kaaterskill Clove and the Hudson River Valley.

Begin at the junction of Route 23A and Kaaterskill Creek, following blue markers. Head up beside the stream to the first trail junction and head right unless you want to take the yellow markers to the lower falls. Continue for 2.75 miles until the blue trail meets the old Kaaterskill road, following it to the left up a grade along a laurel-bordered road. You can make a detour by taking the road to the right to Palenville, which is part of the Sleepy Hollow Horse Trail network.

At the next junction you can head left on red markers to the Kaaterskill Hotel site and North Lake Road, or continue on blue to the right. At trail junction 3.70 you can take the red-marked trail to the left to the site of the Catskill Mountain House or keep right on the blue trail along ledges. At

Boulder Rock you can see the village of Palenville and the Hudson Valley from a lookout.

The parking lot for the North-South Lake Campground is at mile marker 4.50 on the Escarpment Trail. Follow the blue markers along the cliff edge to Artists Rock for a view of the Hudson Valley. Head up the steep slope to Newmans Ledge with another great view of the Hudson Valley. Continue on up to North Point, which is the last turn-back point to the campground.

Keep heading up to the North Mountain summit (elevation 3,180 feet) and the summit of Stoppel Point (elevation 3,420 feet), and begin descending from the top of Stoppel Point. Continue on to the summit of Blackhead (elevation 3,937 feet) and of Acra Point. Windham High Peak (elevation 3,524 feet) leads to Maple Crest Road and the end of the trail on Route 23, three miles west of East Windham.

Iindian Head-Hunter-West Kill Mountain Range Trail: This trail heads over rugged country and is known as the "Devil's Path." It begins on Platte Clove road, a half-mile west of the New York City Police Camp near Platte Clove; turn south from the highway following red markers on Prediger Road. Cross the East Branch of the Schoharie Creek (cars may be driven to this place). Take the left fork following red markers and join Overlook Road. Leave Old Overlook Road and reach the summit of Indian Head Mountain (elevation 3,573 feet). Continue on the red markers to Summit Twin Mountain (elevation 3,540 feet) and the summit of Sugarloaf Mountain (elevation 3,800 feet).

Pass Mink Hollow Trail and continue to Plateau Mountain summit (elevation 3,840 feet). Devil's Tombstone Public Campground is located at Stony Clove Notch. For the Forest Fire Observatory (elevation 4,040 feet) pass the Devil's Acre lean-to and take the right trail with yellow markers, which leads to the blue trail junction. After Diamond Notch, the trail heads steeply upward and reaches the top of West Kill Mountain's east ridge and the summit (elevation 3,880 feet). The trail ends at 23.59 miles at Spruceton Road.

Hunter Mountain Forest Fire Observatory: This trail is shorter (2.4 miles) and easier, beginning on Stony Clove Road near Hunter, one mile north of Devil's Tombstone Campground, following blue markers. At the trail junction, mile marker 1.90, turn right for the Observatory. At trail junction mile marker 2.05, turn right again for the Observatory. You will reach it at the 2.40 mile marker.

CENTRAL CATSKILL TRAILS

There are several ways to reach the summit of **Slide Mountain**, the highest of the peaks in the Catskills at 4,204 feet. The shortest trail is from the **Slide Mountain Trailhead** parking area, 10 miles south of Route 28 on County Route 47. Take the yellow-marked Woodland Valley-Denning Trail southwest .70 mile to the junction with the red-marked

Burroughs Range Trail. Turn left and continue east for two miles to the summit rock and Burrough's Plaque. The distance is 2.7 miles one way, 5.4 miles round trip.

Phoenicia-East Branch Trail follows old roads and does not have very steep climbs. It follows mountain streams through woodlands. Begin at the **Woodland Valley Public Campground** on Woodland Valley Road, five miles south of Route 28; check in with the caretaker during the season. Follow yellow markers to the right, going up steps from the parking area. Cross a footbridge over a tributary of Woodland Creek and follow the old road. The trail meets the blue markers of the Giant Ledge-Panther Mountain-Fox Hollow Trail. You follow the yellow markers as the trail turns right off the old road. Join the town highway and turn left up the hill. Continue on the highway past Winnisook Lake.

For Slide Mountain, turn left off the road and follow trail at signs. Meet the old road and turn right. Slide Mountain Trail is on the left with red markers. You continue on yellow markers along Curtiss Trail to Slide Mountain. Pass the junction with Peekamoose and Table Mountains Trail and enter a clearing on Route 19 from Claryville. Cars can be driven up to this point on the East Branch of Neversink Creek. This trail is 10.65 miles in length.

Wittenberg-Cornell-Slide Trail is another way to reach Slide Mountain. Wittenberg at 3,780 feet and Cornell at 3,860 are also way up there. Begin this hike at **Woodland Valley Campground**. Turn left on the red markers over Woodland Creek and continue to the summit of Wittenberg Mountain at 3.40 miles. There's a spur trail to the left, after the junction with the trail from West Shokan, to the summit of Cornell Mountain. Continue on to the summit of Slide Mountain. Continue on red markers, passing an unmarked trail on the right to Winnisook Lake. At the junction with Phoenicia-East Branch Trail turn right for Winnisook and Woodland Valley. Turn left off the jeep road and follow markers. Meet the highway at Slide Mountain parking area. Turn right for Woodland Valley. This trail is 8.85 miles in length.

Peekamoose-Table Mountain Trail: Begin this trail at the junction of the Phoenicia-East Branch Trail near the Denning lean-to on the East Branch of Neversink Creek. Cross the East Branch on a log bridge. Continue to the summit of Table Mountain (3,847 feet), down the saddle of Table Mountain and Peekamoose Mountain and up to the summit of Peekamoose Mountain (3,843 feet). There are nice views at Reconnoiter Rock, which is to the right of the trail. Heading down to the junction with Gulf Road (Peekamoose Road), take a right at Sundown, and left to West Shokan.

■ On Wheels

Scenic Drives

 You can pick up a great brochure put out by the Mountain Top Historical Society, entitled *The Catskill Mountain Heritage Trail, Historic and Cultural Landmarks*, in tourist offices, accommodations and restaurants in the area. Some of our scenic suggestions are along this trail. We selected the best and most attractive roads for the following two tours.

Mountain Tour #1

Begin this tour in Windham, which is home to **Ski Windham** (see *On Snow*, page 213). During the summer you can also take a chairlift ride at Windham Mountain Ski Area.

The **Five State Lookout** is located on Route 23 in East Windham. There is a public parking lot on the way up the hill from the east. Park there and savor the view of the Hudson River and five states. Drive a little farther up the hill and you will come to the **Herb and Perennial Gardens** at **Point Lookout Mountain Inn**. You can park in their lot to see the gardens and maybe drop in for lunch during the summer season. Call for lunch and dinner days and times. See *Where to Stay* (page 220) and *Where to Eat* (page 223), ☎ 518-734-3381.

From Windham, take Route 296 to the south and through the hamlet of Hensonville, turning right on 296 and taking a right fork onto 14 west to Jewett; then take 17 south to **Jewett Center**. Here you will find a striking onion-domed **Ukrainian Church**, which was built without nails. Concerts are held there (see Festivals & Events, page 217).

Turn left on Route 23A and head west to **Lexington**, which was settled by Revolutionary War veterans from the Hudson Valley. During the 1800s there were grist mills, saw mills and a tannery in town. This section of 23A is very pretty as it runs along the Schoharie Creek.

Head south on Route 42, into Ulster County, through the striking Deep Notch to **Shandaken**, where there is an historical museum open year-round.

Turn west on Route 28 through Pine Hill and Highmount, and back into Greene County to Route 30 and the East Branch of the Delaware River. Drive past the Pepacton Reservoir, Margaretville, and continue along Route 30 north to **Roxbury**. This town was founded by Connecticut families in 1790. It was the home of **John Burroughs**, a literary naturalist. Drive along Burroughs Memorial Road to see his grave by Boyhood Rock, where he spent time as a child. Woodchuck Lodge (see page 201) was his summer home from 1910 to 1920.

Head north to the **Grand Gorge**, the headwaters of the East Branch of the Delaware River. The trailhead there is popular with walkers, hikers, bikers, cross-country skiers, snowshoers and snowmobilers. The old train bed of the Ulster and Delaware Railroad has been converted to a trail.

Drive east on Route 23 to **Prattsville**, which was settled by Dutch and Palatines from the Schoharie Valley around 1757. Zadock Pratt built a tannery there in 1824. There's a museum, as well as **Pratt Rock Park**, which has relief sculptures carved into the cliffside. (See *Sightseeing*, page 216). Continue on to Windham on Route 23.

Mountain Tour #2

Begin this tour in **Catskill**, which was settled in the mid-1600s. You can visit the **Thomas Cole house** on Spring Street. Cole lived there from 1836 to 1848, where he painted his series of allegorical paintings. He also tutored Frederic Edwin Church there. (See *Sightseeing*, page 217). Thomas Cole and his wife Maria are buried in the Thompson Street Cemetery. Dont miss the view of the eastern escarpment of the Catskills there.

Dutchmans Landing is a riverside park with boat launch and an interpretive walking path. You can see the Olana estate from there.

Take 23 to Leeds to see the **Stone Arch Bridge** dating from 1792. The site of a 17th- and 18th-century Mohican Village and Burial Ground is at the junction of Routes 23 and 23B. Farther along on Route 23, **Cairo** was settled by English colonists in the early 1700s. **Shinglekill Falls Grist Mill** is located on Mountain Avenue.

Continue on Route 23 on the Mohican Trail, which is a scenic drive from Leeds to Windham, to the spectacular **Five State Lookout** in East Windham. (See information in previous tour on page 207.) Head south from Windham on Route 296 to Hensonville, then Route 40 to Maplecrest and Route 23C to East Jewett, then drive Route 25 along the lovely row of estates and dip down east of Tannersville to 23A. If you wish to visit **Kaaterskill Falls**, head north on Route 18 to the North-South Campground (see page 217), which is the highest waterfall in New York. You can also see the site of the Catskill Mountain House.

The road from Haines Falls to Palenville is also known as the **Rip Van Winkle Trail**. It follows Rip and his dog, Wolf, along their journey. Palenville is known as the home of Rip Van Winkle, and it is believed he walked up to Kaaterskill Clove for his long slumber. Return to Route 23A through Palenville.

Bicycling

 Mountain biking is popular in the Catskills, with breathtaking views and fresh air. As in other mountainous areas, bikers need to consider their stamina level in deciding where to go.

You can choose to bike on easy road rides, or head up into the mountains on an off-road bike.

Easy Rides

Hunter to Ukrainian Church and Back: From the village of Hunter, head out west along Route 23A to the church, which was built totally without nails. The terrain is gently rolling, and there are views of the mountain peaks and valleys. The total mileage is 12.5.

Dolans Lake: From Dolans Lake, ride along Route 23A west to Route 214 south. Turn right on Ski Bowl Road, then onto Riverside Drive and right on Bridge Street. Another right on Main Street and you will be back at the lake. The total is five miles. If you want a little more exercise, head up Route 214 on a steep hill to the Devil's Tombstone recreation area.

Moderate Road Ride

Hunter to West Kill: Ride on Route 23A from Hunter west to a left turn on Route 42. Turn left at the flagpole and take the local road to West Kill. The road dead-ends at a hiking trail. Watch for deer and wild turkeys. Along the way you will pass some of the favorite trout fishing streams in the area. The total distance is 25 miles.

More Challenging

South Mountain: From Haines Falls, take North Lake Road, which is off Route 23A to Scutt Road. Turn right onto Scutt Road into the parking area. The trailhead begins over the foot bridge at the end of Scutt Road. Now you can follow red/blue or yellow trail markers and design your own loops. If you take the red trail you'll find the edge of the Escarpment hiking trail and a view of the Catskill Mountain House site and the Hudson Valley. Do not continue on the road, which is not rideable.

Outfitters

White Birches Mountain Biking, Nauvoo Road, Windham NY 12496, ☎ 518-734-3266. 15 miles of trails, single- and double-track, with challenges for all abilities. Rental bikes available.

The **Bike Shop at Windham Mountain Outfitters**, Route 296 and South Street, Windham, NY 12496, ☎ 518-734-4700. Mountain bike rentals, trail maps for all abilities, guided group mountain bike rides.

Balsam Shade "Innside Out," 6944 SR 32, Greenville, NY 12083, ☎ 518-966-5315. Hike and bike the Catskills, rafting when available. Lodging available.

The Catskills

▪ On Water

Boating

The Hudson River and its tributaries provide plenty of boating opportunities for those who want to launch their own boats or rent from a marina.

Catskill Marina, Greene Street, Catskill, NY 12414, ☎ 518-943-4170. Floating docks, heated pool, showers, restrooms, laundromat, grills, rental cars available.

Clarence D. Lane Park, Maplecrest, NY 12454, ☎ 518-734-4170. Swimming, baseball, basketball, restrooms. Canoe and rowboats only.

Club Nautico of Catskill, 103 Main Street, Catskill, NY 12414, ☎ 518-943-5342. Powerboat and personal watercraft rentals, fishing tackle and ski rentals.

Dutchmen's Landing, Lower Main Street, Catskill, NY 12414, ☎ 518-943-3830. Four launch ramps, BBQs, port-o-lets, picnic tables, playground, benches, snack bar.

Hagar's Harbor, off Route 385, Athens, NY 12015, ☎ 845-945-1858. Showers, dockage, restaurant open all year.

Hop-O-Nose Marina, West Main Street, Catskill, NY 12414, ☎ 518-932-4640. Transient marina with pool, showers, laundry, picnic area, restaurant.

New York State Park System, Coxsackie launch ramp on Route 385. Launch ramp, parking for 36 cars and trailers. Hudson River access. Athens launch ramp, parking for 25 cars.

North-South Lake Campgrounds, County Route 18, Haines Falls, NY 12436, ☎ 518-589-5058. Canoe and rowboat rentals, no motors.

Riverfront Park, Foot of Second Street, Athens, NY 12015, ☎ 845-945-1551. Picnic tables, benches and docking facilities for boats.

Riverside Park, Reed and River Streets, Coxsackie, NY 12051, ☎ 518-731-2718. Gazebo, picnicking, basketball court, swings, launch ramp.

Riverview Marine Services Inc., 103 Main Street, Catskill, NY 12414, ☎ 518-943-5311. Full service marine facility, marine store, boat and motor sales, service, parts and accessories, storage and dockage, travelift, fuel, boat rentals.

Shady Harbor Marina, Route 144, New Baltimore, NY 12124, ☎ 518-756-8001. Dockage, service, storage, ship's store and restaurant.

Fishing

New York State offers these fish in the Catskills: shad; rainbow, brown and brook trout; bass; striped bass; and walleye. For information call ☎ 800-355-CATS and ask for *Get Hooked!* A fishing license is needed for those over 16.

Trout streams: Esopus Creek; East and West Branches and the main stem of the Delaware River; Beaver Kill, Willowemoc Creek, Schoharie Creek, Neversink River, Catskill Creek, East Kill, West Kill and Batavia Kill.

Lake fishing: Colgate Lake, North-South Lake.

A list of licensed fishing guides is available from most **Chambers of Commerce**, Regional **DEC** offices, and by contacting the **New York State Outdoor Guides Association** at PO Box 4704, Queensbury, NY 12804, ☎ 518-798-1253. Local marinas and bait and tackle shops are another good source for locating a guide.

Schoharie Creek and Tributaries, brown trout and brook trout, ☎ 607-652-7366. Schoharie Creek begins at the Schoharie Reservoir and flows past Hunter and along Route 16.

Esopus Creek, rainbow trout and brown trout, ☎ 845-256-3161. Esopus Creek flows through Phoenicia and it jogs around in several directions.

Ashokan Reservoir, rainbow trout, brown trout, bass, panfish and others, ☎ 845-256-3161; special fishing and boating permits are required (see above).

You can visit the **New York State Fish Hatchery** on Hatchery Road in DeBruce; ☎ 845-439-4328. The major species is brown trout. Fish life stages include eggs, October-January; small fish, mid October-June; fingerlings, June-September; yearlings, September-May; and broodstock all year. Their mailing address is RR 1, Box 312, Livingston Manor, NY 12758.

■ On Horseback

Bailiwick Ranch/Catskill Equestrian Center, Castle road next to Catskill Game Farm, Catskill, NY 12414, ☎ 518-678-5665. Horseback riding, scenic mountain trail rides, overnight camping trips, pony rides, English and Western riding instruction, riding camp, boarding facilities.

The Catskills

K & K Equestrian Center, Route 67, East Durham, NY 12423, ☎ 518-966-5272. Guided scenic trail rides, overnight trips, horseback riding, pony rides, lessons and pony parties.

Rough Riders Ranch, Route 23C, East Jewett, NY 12424, ☎ 518-589-9159. Trail rides, pony rides, overnight riding adventures, paddock riding, riding lessons, boarding.

Silver Springs Dude Ranch, Route 25 off 23A, Haines Falls, NY 12436, ☎ 800-258-2624. Dude ranch, year-round horseback riding, overnight horse trips.

Tanglewood Ranch, Cornwallville, NY 12418, ☎ 518-622-9531. Horseback riding, scenic trails, pony rides, horsedrawn hayrides, overnight riding trips.

■ On Snow

Downhill Skiing

 Skiing in the Catskills is within a couple of hours from New York City. Since the three major mountains all have vertical drops of well over 1,000 feet and are highly developed, this makes them extremely attractive to city skiers, who often crowd the slopes on weekends. So our advice is simple: ski them during the week, if you can, and you'll think you're in Vermont.

Belleayre Mountain, PO Box 313, Route 28, Highmount, NY 12441, ☎ 800-942-6904, snow phone; ☎ 845-254-5600, main number; and ☎ 800-431-4555, lodging; www.belleayre.com, belleayr@catskill.net. Belleayre is the oldest active ski area in the Catskills and one of three areas developed and maintained by New York State. Facing northwest at elevations ranging from 2,000 to 3,400 feet, it is relatively high and retains snow late into the season. In many ways its layout is unique, with the main lodge (Overlook) in the center of 37 trails, above an extensive set of novice trails (15% grade) also served by another lodge (Discovery) at their base. Trails above the main lodge are laid out in parallel on the side of a long mountain, so they appear to descend from a ridge. The whole system is served by five major lifts, one leading from the middle of the beginners' area to the summit, and lateral crossover trails to allow skiers to move from one edge of the broad swath of trails to the other. With a lodge, teaching facilities, parking, and a fine set of trails all to themselves, this is one of the friendliest and largest ski areas for novices we have seen anywhere – a great place for people of all ages to enter the sport. Intermediates will also be pleased with the spread of blue trails stretching above the main lodge along the whole side of the mountain. The peculiarity of this mountain system is a relatively short headwall, rated single- or even double-black, at the head of trails that are otherwise predominantly blue.

Belleayre has 1,404 feet of vertical drop and 35 trails served by seven lifts, including two quads, a triple, two double chairs, and three surface lifts.

Hunter Mountain Ski Bowl, PO Box 295, Hunter, NY 12442, ☎ 518-263-4223, main office; ☎ 800-FOR-SNOW, snow conditions; ☎ 800-775-4641, reservation hotline; www.huntermtn.com. Anyone who rides the Snowlite Express, a detachable quad, to the summit of Hunter Mountain will get enough views of huge boulders and rock faces to feel that this is indeed a mountain. And the majority of trails from the summit are black diamond (30%) or double-black (13%), but the area as a whole has a generous supply of blues (27%), including several from the summit, and greens (30%), all lower down. Altogether Hunter's 53 trails, providing 240 acres of skiing, are reasonably balanced for skiers of varying abilities, but the main mountain, with 1,600 feet of vertical drop and challenging trails, has special appeal for advanced and expert skiers. The official name, Hunter Mountain Ski Bowl, reflects a terrain shape that is not always evident on a first visit. If you sweep your eyes from the main mountain to Hunter One you will sense the bowl. Very early, in 1980, Hunter supplemented its 125 inches of average annual snowfall with 100% snowmaking. Novices will want to head for Hunter One, where several lifts reach halfway up and serve a variety of green slopes and trails. Hunter One is not a bad place for intermediates to warm up either, as one lift reaches higher into a set of blue trails. Intermediates can then work their way up to the middle of the main mountain, where more broad blues, named for prominent streets and parkways in Manhattan, await. Advanced skiers and experts can play in a wide range of blacks and double-blacks at the top of Hunter Mountain and throughout Hunter West. Hunter has 1,600 feet of vertical drop and 53 trails served by 14 lifts, including three quads and two triple chairs.

Ski Windham, PO Box 459, Windham, NY 12496, ☎ 800-729-4766, snow report; ☎ 800-754-9463 or 518-734-4300, information; www.ski-windham.com or www.ridewindham.com. Windham consists of two separate but closely linked mountains, offering a healthy 1,600 feet of vertical drop and 39 trails, with a total of 242 skiable acres. Apart from the statistics, it is a mountain complex that offers something for everyone in a family group, including a terrain park and half-pipe for boarders and skiers and an adjacent tubing hill for everyone. Much of the terrain is ideal for intermediate skiers (45%), but there is enough for beginners (30%) and advanced skiers or experts (25%). Beginners should head for the Whiteway triple chair, which serves a wide slope and two winding trails, all thoroughly green. They can also enjoy a fine winding trail from the summit of the eastern mountain, aptly named Wanderer. The main mountain is largely intermediate territory, with a fine range of blue trails on the left flank (looking up), including one from the summit, named Wraparound, that lower intermediates can enjoy. On the right flank the upper mountain is for experts, with an abundance of black double-diamonds, while both advanced skiers and experts will enjoy the three long single-blacks on the eastern mountain, especially Why Not. Seven lifts serve the two mountains, including a high-speed quad, four triple chairs, one double chair, and a surface lift for children.

> **DID YOU KNOW?** *Besides providing fun for everyone, Windham is well known in the world of disabled skiing. Under the leadership of Gwen Allard, it has become the East's most developed area for disabled skiing, with a wide range of equipment and programs. That is a wonderful feeling – to watch someone in a sit-ski grinning from ear to ear flying down a slope.*

Cross-Country Skiing

Belleayre offers five km of marked trails. The area is open daily and there are no trail fees. Belleayre Mountain, Highmount, NY 12441, ☎ 800-942-6904 or 845-254-5600, www.belleayre.com.

Mountain Trails offers 35 km 35 kilometers of quiet nature trails on 300 acres that are groomed, track-set, and marked for their degree of difficulty. The area is open weekends and there is a fee. Mountain Trails, Route 23A, Tannersville, NY 12485, ☎ 518-589-5361, www.mttrails.com.

White Birches has 35 km of track-set trails. The area is open daily and there is a fee. White Birches, off Route 23, Windham, NY 12496, ☎ 518-734-3266.

■ Eco-Travel

Outdoor Education Centers

New York State has a number of Environmental Education Centers. The closest center to the Catskills is **Stony Kill Farm Environmental Education Center**, Route 9D, Wappingers Falls, NY 12590, ☎ 845-831-8780. This year-round center offers teacher workshops, school and youth group activities and programs for adults and families. There are walking trails, exhibits and meeting rooms.

Week-long outdoor residential Environmental Education Camps for 12- to 17-year-olds offer exploration of field, forest and freshwater communities. **Camp DeBruce** at Livingston Manor in the Catskills is one. Contact The Bureau of Environmental Education, 50 Wolf Road, Albany, NY 12233-4500, ☎ 518-457-3720

Regional Environmental Facilities are available such as the one at **Belleayre Mountain Ski Center**, PO Box 313. Highmount, NY 12441, ☎ 845-

254-5600, extension 434. The Catskill Interpretive Program offers weekend hikes and nature activities for families and individuals. Annual events include a Backyard Maple Syruping Day in March, Earth Day Fair in April and Test the Waters in May.

The **Hudson River National Estuarine Research Reserve** conducts interpretive programs in protected tidal wetlands such as Piermont Marsh (south of Nyack in Rockland County), Iona Island Marsh (south of Bear Mountain in Rockland County), Tivoli Bays (near Annandale in Dutchess County) and Stockport Flats (south of Hudson in Columbia County). Contact **Hudson River NERR**, NYSDEC, Bard College Field Station, Annandale-on-Hudson, NY 12504, ☎ 845-758-7010.

Sightseeing

■ Durham

The **Irish American Heritage Museum**, Route 145, East Durham, NY 12423, ☎ 518-634-7497. The museum offers exhibits and educational programs on the Irish in America. Call for information on films and lectures.

■ Cornwallville

Black Walnut Farm, Corner of Stonebridge and Cornwallville Road, Cornwallville, NY 12418, ☎ 518-239-6987. Visitors take a self-guided walking tour through fields of Eastern and Canadian wildflowers. The walk takes about 30 minutes. You may cut your own wildflowers.

■ Windham

Lawrence Carriage Museum, Route 23, Box 67, Windham, NY 12496, ☎ 518-734-4485. The collection includes over three dozen horse-drawn vehicles used on the mountain top from the early 19th century onwards.

Ski Windham Chairlift Ride, Windham, NY 12496, ☎ 518-734-4300. The chairlift goes up to the summit for views of the Northern Catskills.

Five State Lookout, Route 23, East Windham. New York State maintains this public scenic viewing area. Visitors can see the Hudson River and five states.

Herb and Perennial Gardens at Point Lookout Mountain Inn, on the Mohican Trail, Route 23, Windham NY, ☎ 518-734-3381. Culinary herbs, perennials, bulbs, annuals and shrubbery are on view in cliffside gardens.

■ Prattsville

Zadock Pratt Museum, Route 23, Prattsville, NY 12468, ☎ 518-299-3395. The house dates from 1828 and contains artifacts from his life, period furniture, a tannery exhibit and other local exhibits.

Pratt Rock, Route 23, Prattsville, ☎ 518-299-3395. White-painted relief carvings by Zadock Pratt are 150 years old. It is on the National Register of Historic Places.

■ Jewett

Ukrainian Church and Grazhda, Route 23A, Jewett Center, ☎ 518-263-3862. This church is built in the traditional Ukrainian way: without nails. The interior is hand-carved. Call for information on concerts and craft workshops.

■ Hunter

Hunter Mountain Ski Museum, Hunter, NY 12442, ☎ 518-263-4223. Ski columnist and broadcaster Lloyd Lambert founded the museum in 1974. Collections include skis, boots, bindings, ski poles, photographs, books and mementos.

Hunter Mountain Sky Ride, Hunter Mountain Ski Bowl, Hunter, NY 12442, ☎ 518-263-4223. Visitors will ride on the longest, highest chairlift in the Catskills.

Devil's Tombstone, near Hunter on Route 214, ☎ 518-688-7160. This natural rock formation looks like a large tombstone.

■ Tannersville

Mountain Top Arboretum, Route 23C, Tannersville, NY 12485, ☎ 518-734-3592. Six acres of botanically identified plantings of flowering trees, shrubs and evergreens are open to visitors.

■ Coxsackie

Bronck Museum, Route 9W, Coxsackie, NY 12051, ☎ 518-731-6490 or 731-8862. The museum complex is listed in the National Register of Historic Places. The 1663 and 1738 dwellings are furnished with 18th and 19th century art, furniture, textiles, ceramics, silver and glass. This was a working farm for eight generations of the Bronck family.

■ Freehold

W.J.R. Farm, Vly Road, Freehold, NY 12431, ☎ 518-634-2343. Horse-drawn wagon rides, winter sleigh rides. Call for reservations.

■ Catskill

Thomas Cole House, 218 Spring Street, Catskill, NY 12414, ☎ 518-943-6533. Thomas Cole, the founder of the Hudson River School of Painting, lived and worked here. It has recently been closed for renovation – call for current information.

Catskill Game Farm, off Route 32, Catskill, NY 12414, ☎ 518-678-9595. The game farm is divided into sections such as African, birds, animal nursery, equine, reptile and more. Children love the petting and feeding grounds. Exotic animals are in residence as well as tame animals. There is a children's playground and amusement rides.

Sporting Clays at Friar Tuck Inn, 4858 Route 32, Catskill, NY 12414, ☎ 800-832-7600 or 518-678-2271. Develop your skills with sporting clays. Call for reservations.

Cohotate Preserve, Route 385, Athens, two miles north of Catskill NY, ☎ 518-622-3620. This nature preserve offers self-guided tours on nature trails and is open all year.

■ Haines Falls

Kaaterskill Falls, Route 23A, Haines Falls, ☎ 518-589-5058. Kaaterskill is the highest cascading waterfall in New York State.

Festivals & Events

■ February

 Annual Ski Fest, Windham, ☎ 800-Ski-Windham.

■ March

Winter Carnival, Hunter, ☎ 518-263-4524.

Spring Fest, Windham, ☎ 800-Ski-Windham.

The Catskills

■ May

Belleayre Music Festival, through September, ☎ 845-254-5600.

■ June

Round Top's Bavarian Summer Fest, Purling, ☎ 518-622-9584.

■ July

Great Northern Catskills Black Bear Festival, Hunter, ☎ 518-263-4524.

Mountain Culture Festival, Catskill Mountain Foundation, Hunter, ☎ 518-263-4908.

Irish Music Festival, Leeds, ☎ 518-943-3736.

Catskills Irish Arts Week, East Dunham, ☎ 800-434-FEST.

German Alps Festival, Purling, ☎ 518-622-3261.

Street Festival, Athens, ☎ 518-945-1551.

Windham Chamber Music Festival, Windham, ☎ 518-734-3868.

Belleayre Music Festival, July and August, ☎ 845-254-5600.

■ August

German Alps Festival, Hunter, ☎ 518-263-4223.

Celtic Festival, Hunter, ☎ 518-263-4223.

■ September

Native American Indian Festival, Hunter, ☎ 518-263-4223.

Fall Foliage Festival of Events, Hunter, ☎ 518-263-4524.

Irish Festival, Leeds, ☎ 518-943-3736.

■ October

Belleayre Fall Festival, Belleayre, ☎ 845-254-5600.

Harvest Fair, Windham, ☎ 800-Ski-Windham.

Fall Foliage Festival, Catskill, ☎ 518-943-3400.

∎ November

Festival of Trees, Leeds, ☎ 518-943-9350.

∎ December

Kwanzaa Celebration, Catskill, ☎ 518-943-3400.

Where to Stay

ACCOMMODATIONS PRICE SCALE
Prices for a double room for one or two persons, before taxes.
$ . . . . Under $50
$$. . . . . $50 to $100
$$$ . . . . $101 to $175
$$$$ . . . . Over $175

∎ Greenville

The Greenville Arms dates from 1889 when it was built by William Vanderbilt as a retreat. It is furnished with antiques and comfortable pieces. There's an English croquet course on the south lawn and a 50-foot pool. The cuisine is American and the American Bounty Buffet is held on weekends. Route 32, Greenville, NY 12083, ☎ 518-966-5219, ny1889inn@aol.com. $$$.

Sunny Hill Resort is a family-run resort offering boating, swimming, fishing, tennis and a fitness room. In the evening guests are treated to a ride on the Doodle Bug, the Surrey, a trolley, fire engine, five car train, tram or a hay ride. The dining room offers international theme dinners. Sunny Hill Road, Greenville, NY 12083, ☎ 518-634-7642, fax 518-634-7810, www.sunnyhill.com. $$$ per person AP.

∎ Windham

Albergo Allegria dates from 1876 and is a registered historic site. Each room is individually decorated; rooms have various features, such as a mini-cathedral ceiling, stained glass window, porch with mountain view, fireplace and Tiffany lamps. Route 296, Windham, NY 12496, ☎ 518-734-

5560, fax 518-734-5570, www.albergoUSA.com, mail@albergoUSA.com. $$-$$$$.

The **Windham Arms** offers an outdoor pool, fitness center, 18-hole putting green, tennis and croquet. The cuisine is Continental/American. Main Street, Windham, NY 12496, ☎ 800-SKI-WINDHAM or 518-734-3000, fax 518-734-9500. $$-$$$.

Christman's Windham House Country Inn is a Greek Revival inn dating from 1805. Today, five colonial-style buildings house guests. The Inn offers a golf course, driving range and practice area, pool, tennis and hiking. The cuisine is enhanced by herbs from the kitchen garden; breads and desserts are baked daily. The Windham House, Windham, NY 12496, ☎ 888-294-4053 or 518-734-4230. $$ per person MAP.

■ East Windham

Point Lookout Mountain Inn is on a hill with a view of five states. The well-known restaurant offers Mediterranean, Southwestern, and modern American cuisine. Lunch and dinner, Thursday-Monday; brunch, Sunday and Monday. The Mohican Trail, Route 23, East Windham, NY 12439, ☎ 518-734-3381. $$-$$$.

■ Round Top

Winter Clove Inn offers indoor and outdoor pools, tennis a nine-hole golf course, hiking trails and bowling. The inn is family-run and there are rockers on the porch. Winter Clove Road, Round Top, NY 12473, ☎ 518-622-3267. The price is per-person, per-night, including meals ($80 midweek, $90 weekends).

■ Purling

Bavarian Manor Country Inn and Restaurant dates from 1865 and is family-run. The German Alps Festival began there in 1973. The cuisine is German with a variety of specials on weekends. Route 24, Purling, NY 12470, ☎ 518-622-3261, fax 518-622-2338. $-$$$.

■ Hunter

Fairlawn Inn dates to 1904 when it was built as a retreat for a New York family. It is now a Queen Anne Victorian bed and breakfast. Main Street, Hunter, NY 12442, ☎ 518-263-5025. $$-$$$.

Hunter Inn offers rooms and suites, some with whirlpool baths, terraces or cathedral ceilings. Route 23A, Hunter, NY 12442, ☎ 518-263-3777, fax 518-263-3981. $$-$$$.

Scribner Hollow Lodge has some fireplace lofts, some Southwest adobe-style rooms, some balconies, a heated indoor pool and one tennis court. The cuisine is regional American/Continental. 602 Main Street, Hunter, NY 12442, ☎ 800-395-4683 or 518-263-4211, fax 518-263-5266, www.scribnerhollow.com. $$$-$$$$.

■ Tannersville

Deer Mountain Inn is a turn-of-the-century country estate. Some rooms have working fireplaces. Two dining rooms serve guests. Route 25, Tannersville, NY 12485, ☎ 518-589-6268. $$-$$$.

■ Catskill

Friar Tuck Resort offers sporting clay and a pheasant preserve, indoor and outdoor pools, sauna, Jacuzzi, and tennis. The cuisine is Italian-American; there are three restaurants. Route 32, Catskill, NY 12414, ☎ 800-832-7600 or 518-678-2271. $$$ for room or $$ per person MAP.

Green Lake Resort is a family-run resort on the lake. They offer swimming, boating, tennis and hiking. The cuisine is Italian-American served in the Terrace Room. 605 Green Lake Road, Catskill, NY 12414, ☎ 800-762-3162 or 518-943-2880. $$$$ per person AP.

Wolff's Maple Breeze Resort offers swimming in the lake or pool, boating, fishing, tennis and a health club. The cuisine is German/American. 360 Cauterskill Road, Catskill, NY 12414, ☎ 800-777-9653 or 518-943-3648, www.wolffsresort.com. $$$$ per person MAP

■ Camping

Brookside Campgrounds, 4952 Route 32, Catskill, NY 12414, ☎ 518-678-9777. Offers 50 sites, pool, creek, showers, playground, fishing, picnic tables, fireplaces. Open April 15 to October 15.

Catskill Campground, 79 Castle Road, Catskill, NY 12414, ☎ 518-678-5873. Offers heated pool, showers, playground, picnic tables, store, fireplaces. Open May 15 to Columbus Day.

Dohertys Campground, Joseph Chadderdon Road, Acra, NY 12405, ☎ 518-622-8295. Offers 100 sites, pool, shower, laundry, playground, picnic tables, store, snack bar, fireplaces. Open May 15 to October 15.

Earlton Hill Family Campground, Medway-Earlton Road, Earlton, NY 12058, ☎ 518-731-2751. Offers 304 sites, lake for fishing, boating with rowboat rentals, showers, laundry, playground, picnic tables, fireplaces, store, snack bar. Open May 1 to October 15.

Juniper Woods, Box 1, Athens, NY 12015, ☎ 518-945-1399 or 908-689-4911. Offers clothing-optional camping, two lakes, pool, volleyball, shuffleboard. Open early May to late October.

Indian Ridge Campsites, HC 2, Box 23, Leeds, NY 12451, ☎ 518-943-3516. Offers pool, playground, store, snack bar, walking trail, showers, laundry, fireplaces, tables. Open May 1 to October 24.

KJ Western, Ashland, NY 12407, ☎ 518-734-5292. Offers pool, pond, showers, laundry, playground, fishing, picnic tables, hiking, store, snack bar, fireplaces. Open Memorial Day to October 15.

Lynchs Pot O'Gold, Old Route 23, Acra, NY 12405, ☎ 518-622-9229. Offers 140 sites, pool, lake, showers, laundry, playground, fishing, picnic tables, store, snack bar, fireplaces. Open May to December.

Pine Hollow Campground, Route 32A, Palenville, NY 12463, ☎ 518-678-2245. Offers showers, laundry, playground, picnic tables, fireplaces, game room. Open May 14 to October 14.

Torchlite Campsites, Old Route 23, Cairo, NY 12413, ☎ 518 622-9332. Offers 62 sites, showers, laundry, playground, picnic tables, fireplaces. It is open May 1 to October 31.

Whip-O-Will, County Route 31, Round Top, NY 12473, ☎ 518-622-3277. Offers 250 sites, showers, laundry, pool, store, boat rentals, lake. Open April 15 to October 15.

White Birches Campsites, Nauvoo Road, Windham, NY 12496, ☎ 518-734-3266. Offers 140 sites, lake, showers, laundry, playground, fishing, picnic tables, store, snack bar, fireplaces, boating. Open Memorial Day to Columbus Day.

State Campgrounds

North-South Lake Public Campgrounds, County Route 18, Haines Falls, NY 12436, ☎ 518-589-5058 or 800-456-CAMP. Offers lake, swimming, fishing, showers, picnic tables, fireplaces, boating with rentals available. Open April to October.

Devil's Tombstone Public Campgrounds, Route 214, Hunter, NY 12442, ☎ 800-456-CAMP. Offers playground, picnic tables, fireplaces. Open May to September.

Woodland Valley Campground, Woodland Valley Road, Phoenicia, NY 12464, ☎ 845-688-7647. Woodland Valley offers 72 sites, picnic tables, fireplaces and fishing. Open mid-May to early October.

Where to Eat

DINING PRICE SCALE
Prices include an entrée, which may come with vegetables and salad, but exclude beverage, taxes and tip.
$ . . . . Under $10
$$ . . . . $10 to $20
$$$. . . . . $21 to $50
$$$$. . . . . Over $50

■ Windham

Brandywine, Route 23, Windham NY, ☎ 518-734-3838. Northern Italian cuisine. $$.

Chalet Fondue, Route 296, Windham, NY, ☎ 518-734-4650. Swiss, German and American cuisine. $-$$$.

Millrock Restaurant, Main Street, Windham, NY, ☎ 518-734-9719. Wood-fired oven. A family restaurant. $$.

Try the **Catskill Mountain Country Store and Restaurant** for a quick lunch that offers innovative sandwiches and tasty soups. Breakfast also looks creative. Outside, they also have a zoo with animals rescued from local shelters: turkeys, chickens, goats, pot-bellied pigs, peacocks, bunnies and other lucky animals. 5510 Route 23, Windham, NY 12496, ☎ 518-734-3387.

■ East Windham

The Victorian Rose Restaurant at Point Lookout Inn, Route 23, East Windham, NY, ☎ 518-734-3381. Two CIA-trained (that's Culinary Institute of America) chefs will prepare your meal at Point Lookout Inn. Entrées include sautéed medley of jumbo shrimp and sea scallops in a crabmeat Brie sauce with wild rice timbale, pecan-crusted trout with Dijon cream sauce and wild rice pilaf, or grilled salmon served with herbed red potatoes and orange-basil buerre blanc. Open for breakfast, lunch and dinner. $$-$$$.

The Catskills

■ Hensonville

Vesuvio, Goshen Road, Hensonville NY, ☎ 518-734-3663. Italian cuisine. $$.

■ Hunter

The Prospect at Scribner Hollow Lodge, Hunter, NY, ☎ 518-263-4211. Entrées include salmon Veronica with sliced white grapes, capers and Spanish Manzanilla sherry, honey mustard pork chops with local wildflower honey and mustard glaze, veal cutlet Milanese with Japanese panko crumbs and served with loganberry preserves, or grilled ostrich tenderloin with a porcini mushroom and black truffle butter. Open for breakfast and dinner. $$$.

Mountain Brook, Main Street, next to the bridge, Hunter, NY, ☎ 518-263-5351. Contemporary American cuisine includes specialties such as Chilean sea bass with plum wine sauce and jasmine rice, roast rack of lamb with cherry peppercorn sauce, or grilled loin veal chop with port garlic sauce. The restaurant is open for dinner. $$-$$$.

Château Belleview, Route 23A, between Hunter and Tannersville, NY, ☎ 518-589-5525. French country cuisine. Opens at 5 pm for dinner. $$.

■ Catskill

La Conca d'Oro, 440 Main Street, Catskill, NY 12414, ☎ 518-943-3549. Italian cuisine. The restaurant is open for lunch and dinner and closed on Tuesday. $-$$.

■ High Falls

DePuy Canal House, Route 213, High Falls, NY 12440, ☎ 845-687-7700. Located in a registered National Historic Property, the restaurant serves Hudson Valley foods. Entrées include rack of lamb and fingerling potato with zucchini flower or lobster, scallops and oysters in sunburst yellow squash on tortilla hay. The restaurant is open for dinner Thursday through Sunday, and for Sunday brunch from 11:30 to 2. Bistro is open for lunch Wednesday and Thursday; and 8 am-10 pm, Friday, Saturday and Sunday. $$$.

■ Milton

Ship Lantern Inn, 1725 Route 9W, Milton, NY 12547, ☎ 845-795-5400. Entrées include sea scallops with braised leek and wild mushroom fricassee, Panama shrimp creole Ponchartrain or parmesan-crusted swordfish steak. The restaurant is open from noon to 2 am, Tuesday through Friday, opening at 5 pm on Saturday; and from 1 to 8 pm on Sunday. $$.

■ West Hurley

Terrapin Restaurant, 250 Spillway Road, West Hurley, ☎ 845-331-3663. Located in the woods of the Ashokan Reservoir in a historic building that was saved and moved when the reservoir was constructed. Noted for fine food, especially New American cuisine blended with European and Asian flavors. $$-$$$.

Ulster County

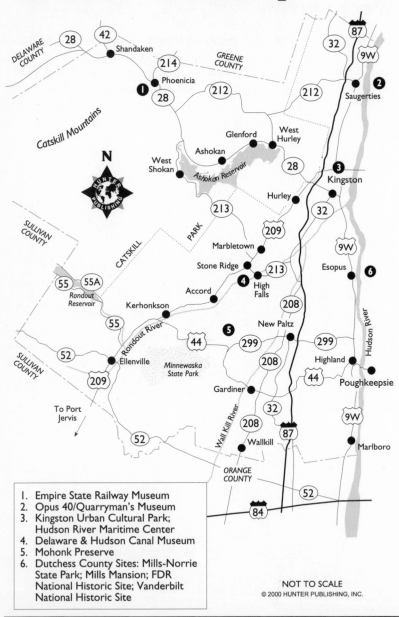

1. Empire State Railway Museum
2. Opus 40/Quarryman's Museum
3. Kingston Urban Cultural Park;
   Hudson River Maritime Center
4. Delaware & Hudson Canal Museum
5. Mohonk Preserve
6. Dutchess County Sites: Mills-Norrie
   State Park; Mills Mansion; FDR
   National Historic Site; Vanderbilt
   National Historic Site

NOT TO SCALE
© 2000 HUNTER PUBLISHING, INC.

The Mid-Hudson

You can have it all in the central part of the Hudson River valley – historic settlements, great estates, and plenty of opportunity for outdoor activity of all kinds. On the west bank in **Ulster County** you'll roll back to 1652 when the Dutch settled in Kingston. Stroll through the Stockade area where a number of 17th- and 18th-century stone houses are still in use today. The **Hudson River Maritime Museum** in Kingston (see page 234) shows what the river has provided for the communities along its banks, and you can even take a cruise from the Maritime Center.

A bit farther west from the shore, New Paltz has a well-preserved Huguenot history with original houses on the oldest street in the country. In 1678, 12 Huguenot families arrived after fleeing French persecution. The nice feeling one gets while wandering is that descendants of the original families still take an active part in the street, donating memorabilia and furniture from their families and returning to visit and make sure all is well in the family home.

If you can't visit the Loire Valley in France you can enjoy similar estates right on the east bank of the Hudson River in **Dutchess County**. Some of them are still owned by the original families and others have been given to New York State or the National Park Service to maintain for us to visit. You can wander through beautiful rooms and learn some of the stories about people who lived there. Although they may have had other houses, many residents considered these mansions overlooking the Hudson River as "home." And you can share their views without owning or paying taxes on these magnificent properties. Some are used as sites for annual festivals and most open their doors between Thanksgiving and Christmas to let you enjoy period decorations.

Getting Here & Getting Around

■ By Air

Albany International Airport	☎ 518-869-9611
JFK International Airport	☎ 718-244-4444
Newark International Airport	☎ 888-EWRINFO

La Guardia International Airport . . . . ☎ 718-533-4300

Stewart International Airport. . . . . ☎ 845-564-2100
Newburgh, NY

■ By Car

One of the most direct ways to get to this area is via **I-87**. Coming from the east, you can use the **Massachusetts Turnpike**; from the west, use the **New York Thruway**.

■ By Bus

Adirondack Trailways . . . . ☎ 800-858-8555

Greyhound Lines. . . . . ☎ 800 231-2222

Short Line. ☎ 800-631-8405

■ By Train

MTA Metro-North Railroad, ☎ 800-METRO-INFO (when outside New York City) or 212-532-4900. This is a commuter railroad with 43 station stops in Westchester. Ask for "One-Day Getaway" packages.

Amtrak, ☎ 800-872-7245. Amtrak offers service from New York to stations on the Boston-Washington Northeast Corridor, including Metroliner service. Passengers can also take Amtrak to upstate New York, Montreal, Chicago and points west. We have enjoyed the waterline trip from Albany to New York City, craning our necks to get a glimpse of passing Hudson River landmarks such as Washington Irving's "Sunnyside" and other mansions, many of which loom above the tracks. There are also wonderful spreads of the western shore to enjoy.

Information Sources

Ulster County Tourism Office, Box 1800 CR, Kingston, NY 12402, ☎ 800-DIAL-UCO or 845-340-3566.

Dutchess County Tourism Promotion Agency, 3 Neptune Road, Poughkeepsie, NY 12601, ☎ 800-445-3131 or 845-463-4000.

Columbia County Tourism, 401 State Street, Hudson, NY 12534, ☎ 800-724-1846 or 518-828-3375.

Ulster County

Ulster County runs along the bank of the Hudson River at the southern end of the Catskills. The mountains and the rivers provide year-round recreational activity. The **Shawangunk Mountains**, also known as the "gunks," offer great hiking, rock climbing and hang gliding. Trout fishing is very popular, as is cruising on the Hudson River or enjoying the white water on the Esopus River.

Historical sites abound, with **New Paltz** offering an authentic street of preserved stone homes, some still held by the original families. **Kingston** was the first capital of New York State, and Revolutionary-War-era figures lived and worked there.

Adventures

■ On Foot

Hiking

IN THE SHAWANGUNK MOUNTAINS

 Minnewaska State Park Preserve (☎ 845-255-0752) is located on the **Shawangunk Mountain ridge**, which runs through Orange, Sullivan and Ulster counties and rises more than 2,000 feet above sea level. The geology is sometimes spectacular, reminding us of the much higher huge, uplifted and tilted sedimentary slabs that are characteristic of the Northern Rockies around Banff and Lake Louise. Carriageways, trails and overlooks throughout this park are adjacent to steep descents and cliffs. Exercise extreme caution in all areas. The park is accessible from Route 44/55. There are 28 miles of hiking trails. Pick up a hiking map and information. Trails on the map are marked with the color of the trail blazes, and distances in miles are also listed. About 20 miles of old carriage roads, including some that have won awards, are open for mountain biking.

Mohonk Preserve is the largest private nature preserve in New York State. It protects over 6,000 acres of the Shawangunk Ridge. The **Visitor Center** on Mountain Rest Road in New Paltz is open daily. There are 56 miles of trails and carriage roads for hiking, cycling, horseback riding and nature observation. Rock climbing cliffs are also in the Preserve.

A reciprocal agreement allows Preserve members to visit the Mohonk Mountain House grounds (excluding the beach, interior and porches of the Mountain House – see page 238) free of charge if entry is on foot from Preserve lands. If you want to park at the resort please call ahead (☎ 845-255-1000, extension 2035) to ask if space is available for Preserve members. There is a **Day Visitor Center** located 1½ miles from the Gatehouse; seasonal shuttle service is available to the Gatehouse.

The **Sky Top Walk**, only a little over a mile long, lives up to its name and is one of our favorite short walks anywhere. Sitting on a balcony at the Mountain House and looking across the lake at the cliffs on the other side, we noticed a number of log projections, some with people on them. Later we discovered that they were "options" on an otherwise easy and pleasant climb to the tower at the top, where you can see six states on a clear day. Telling ourselves that our acrophobia wasn't justified, we got out on about half of the cliffside projections on the way up, and, having got used to the idea, managed the others on the way down.

The **Eagle Cliff Walk**, again short (1.7 miles), takes you on a loop road past the tennis courts and then circles back to the bluffs overlooking the northeast shore of the lake. For more serious hikers, these walks and others can be extended into a number of half-day and all-day hikes.

Cycling is also permitted on roads in the Mohonk Lake region, apart from restricted roads near the Mohonk Mountain House. You can bring as many as four bikes per car. Be sure to get a map from the day visitor center or the hotel showing the routes and the restricted areas.

ALONG THE RIVER

Sleightsburgh Spit: This 79-acre peninsula was conveyed by Scenic Hudson to the town of Esopus to be used as a park. This is a group that protects and monitors the Hudson River area. Their first fight was in 1963 when they saved Storm King Mountain from a Con Edison proposal to build the world's largest pumped-storage hydroelectric plant. A conservation easement held by Scenic Hudson ensures that the property will forever remain parkland. There is a fishing platform, public boat launch and a walking trail. You can reach (by your boat) wooded islands visited by many bird species and the remains of the original **Rondout Lighthouse**. Take Route 9W to North Broadway (toward the river), turn right on First Street and left on Everson. The parking lot is on the right.

Esopus Meadows Preserve: The preserve is adjacent to the Esopus Meadows Environmental Center. It offers two miles of trails, and views of an 1838 lighthouse. Just beyond the shoreline lies one of the Hudson River's most important spawning grounds for striped bass. Take Route 9W in Ulster Park to River Road. The park is located two miles farther along Route 9W, on the right.

Shaupeneak Ridge: This 500-acre recreation area is home to deer, fox, coyotes and wild turkeys. Glacially-carved Louisa Pond houses osprey and beavers. There are 3.5 miles of trails. Look on the opposite side of the river to see the Vanderbilt Mansion and the Mills Mansion. Take Route 9W to Old Post Road and the lower parking area is .25 miles on the right. The upper parking area is 2.5 miles on the left on Poppletown Road (go straight at "dead end" sign).

Black Creek Forest Preserve: Walk over a 120-foot suspension bridge spanning Black Creek to enter this 130-acre nature preserve. The creek is a spawning ground for blue herring and trout. Two miles of trails offer views of Mills-Norrie State Park and Esopus Island. Take Route 9W in Esopus, go east on Winding Brook Acres Road.

RAIL TRAILS

The **D&H Canal Heritage Corridor** is developing from **Kingston** to **Ellenville** along the D&H tow paths and the Ontario & Western Railway. Call for information on guided walks, biking, equestrian, cross-country skiing and running events ☎ 845-331-2102.

The **Hudson Valley Rail Trail** is a nature trail extending for 4.2 miles from the Mid-Hudson Bridge in **Highland** into the Town of **Lloyd**. Walking, mountain biking, cross-country skiing and horseback riding are allowed. Call ☎ 845-483-0428.

The 12.2-mile **Wallkill Valley Rail Trail**, designed for walking and bicycling, is on the railbed of the former Wallkill Valley Railroad through **New Paltz** and **Gardiner**.

GROUP TOURS

High Land Flings Footloose Holidays, PO Box 1034, Kingston, NY 12402, ☎ 800-HLF-6665, www.highlandflings.com, info@highlandflings.com. Guided walking tours are available in New York, as well as New England and abroad. The Hudson River Valley National Heritage Area includes walking in the Great Estates Region on carriage roads as well as a six-mile overhead trail on the edge of the river. More carriage roads in the Olana region almost bring you into one of Frederic Church's paintings. On the western shore, you can walk through a village with stone cottages built by Dutch and Huguenot settlers. Another walk heads through the carriageways in Minnewaska State Park Preserve and out to Castle Point.

■ On Wheels

Scenic Drives

There are many pretty drives in Ulster County through for-ests, rolling hills and villages. From Kingston take Route 209 south to **Hurley** to savor a group of 18th-century houses built of stone. Continue on south past Marbletown to **Stone Ridge**, with more stone houses. Take a left on Route 213 to **High Falls** for a visit to Lock 16, once on the Delaware & Hudson Canal line. The Delaware & Hudson Canal Museum in High Falls (www.canalmuseum.org/museum.htm) houses photographs and boat models of the past. Routes 213 and 32 will return you to Kingston.

Another favorite drive begins in New Paltz along Route 299, taking a right turn onto Routes 44 and 55 leading to **Lake Minnewaska**. There are scenic overlooks along the way. You can turn right on Route 209 through Accord, then taking Route 6 to the right through Alligerville and back to New Paltz.

Bicycling

Delaware and Hudson Canal Heritage Trailway

This is part of a continuous rail trail within a greenway from the City of Kingston to the City of Port Jervis. The trail now runs for 12 miles, with another 18 miles proposed; it is open and unpaved. For information, contact **D & H Canal Heri-tage Corridor Alliance**, ☎ 845-331-7512 or 845-339-4531.

Wallkill Valley Rail Trail - North

The former Wallkill Valley Railroad Line from the New Paltz/Rosendale Town Line to the City of Kingston is in private ownership. The owner allows the property to be utilized as a rail trail. The length is 15 miles and it is open and unpaved.

WORD TO THE WISE

Get a copy of the *Hudson Valley Bikeways and Trailways* map from the New York State De-partment of Transportation, Region 8, Eleanor Roosevelt State Office Building, 4 Burnett Blvd., Poughkeepsie, NY 12603, ☎ 845-431-5723.

Hudson Valley Trailway

This section of the former Maybrook rail line in the town of Lloyd has been developed into a multi-use trailway by the town of Lloyd. The length is 2.4 miles and it is open and paved. For more information, call ☎ 845-691-2144.

Table Rock Tours, 292 Main Street, Rosendale NY, ☎ 914-658-7832, offers bikes for sale as well as guided tours.

>>>>>>> See *On Foot*, above, for descriptions of parks and areas that allow (and encourage!) cycling.

Train Excursion

Catskill Mountain Railroad, Phoenicia, ☎ 845-688-7400. This scenic rail trip travels along Esopus Creek. The route is six miles long, with nice views of the mountains. It is open from Memorial Day to Columbus Day.

■ On Water

Sailing & Cruising

Great Hudson Sailing Center, Dock Street, Kingston, ☎ 845-429-1557. Sailboat rides, evening cruises, sailing lessons and rentals.

Hudson River Cruises, Rondout Landing, Kingston, ☎ 845-255-6515. The *Rip Van Winkle* cruises south past estates and lighthouses. Evening music cruises are popular.

■ On Snow

Cross-Country Skiing

Minnewaska State Park, New Paltz, NY 12561, ☎ 845-255-0752. Here you can enjoy 32 km of cross-country skiing on old carriage trails (see *On Foot*, page 229).

Mohonk Mountain House, New Paltz, NY 12561, ☎ 800-772-6646. There are 45 km of cross-country trails emanating from the Mohonk Mountain House, 35 km of them with set tracks.

Williams Lake Resort, Rosendale, NY 12472, ☎ 800-382-3818. Twenty km of trails, 10 of them tracked, stretch through 600 acres of pleasant woodland overlooking Williams Lake.

The Mid-Hudson

Sightseeing in Ulster County

■ Saugerties

 Opus 40 & **Quarryman's Museum**, 7480 Fite Road, High Woods, Saugerties, ☎ 845-246-3400. In the 1930s, sculptor Harvey Fite was involved with the Carnegie Institute restorations of the Mayan cities of Tikal and Copan in Mexico. He bought this abandoned quarry to provide himself with a source of stone for his own sculpture work. As he began organizing the pieces of rubble he realized that he could display his work in the quarry, and created a six-acre environmental bluestone sculpture.

The name came from his idea that it would take him 40 years to finish. He worked on the stone with hand tools used by quarrymen to develop his sculptures. Pools and fountains were added to enhance the scene. A giant nine-ton bluestone monolith stands as a focus. Quarrymens' tools are on display in the museum. Concerts are held here during the summer; call for a schedule.

■ Phoenicia

Empire State Railway Museum, Phoenicia, ☎ 845-688-7501. The museum is located in the 1899 Ulster & Delaware Railroad Station. There's a 2-8-0 steam locomotive #23, dating from 1910, and a 1913 Pullman dining car stored in Kingston.

■ Kingston

Hudson River Maritime Museum, One Rondout Landing, Kingston, ☎ 845-338-0071. Displays preserve the maritime heritage of the Hudson River. Outside the museum, the *Matilda*, an 1899 steam tug, is on display. Although she sank at the dock at the South Street Seaport in 1976, she was raised and given to the maritime center.

Inside, an 1861 steamboat, the *Mary Powell*, comes to life with photographs and memorabilia. Her lifeboat and bell are there.

People came to recognize the *Mary Powell* along the river as she kept to her daily schedule into Manhattan. Many set their watches by her accuracy. This "Queen of the Hudson" made 27,000 trips in 56 years between 1862 and 1918. She carried nine million passengers over these years.

Kingston Urban Cultural Park Visitors Center, 20 Broadway and 308 Clinton Avenue, Kingston, ☎ 800-331-1518 and 845-331-7517. The center offers displays on the Rondout area, and arranges walking tours by appointment.

Boat tours are offered on the *Rip Van Winkle*. Visitors can also take a boat to see the Rondout Lighthouse, the last and largest lighthouse on the Hudson.

■ High Falls

D & H Canal Museum, Mohonk Road, High Falls, ☎ 845-687-9311. Here you will see dioramas, photos, and the original locks from the D & H Canal.

■ New Paltz

Huguenot Street, New Paltz, ☎ 845-255-1660/1889. Six stone houses date from 1692 to 1890 and they are furnished with original family possessions. We had a tour with one of the Huguenot descendants and loved her descriptions and stories while walking along the street.

DID YOU KNOW?

Abraham Hasbrouck, leader of the French Huguenot settlers, negotiated a piece of land and organized the "Duzine," which means "rule of the elders." One person from each of the 12 original land-grant recipient families was a representative to the Duzine.

Our European friends place small oriental rugs on tables like those in the **Jean Hasbrouck House**. This house is furnished with many pieces that made a house a home, such as a Dutch "kaas" or cupboard with Delft spice jars on the top. Walk up the stairs to the attic and note the hand-hewn beams held in place by wooden pegs. The chimney is unusual in that its main weight rests on the wide stone wall to the back of the house and is balanced on a beam in the front. The bricks were made in New Paltz by hand and are known as "Hudson River Valley thins."

The **French Church** has a cupola on top and it has been recorded that a man or boy would climb up to blow a horn or conch shell for services or to sound an alarm. The French Provincial communion table and a nearby chair date from the early 1700s. Take a walk through the cemetery and look closely at some of the tombstones. We like the one with angels crafted by an itinerant stonecutter. All but two of the patentees, or original land-grant recipients, and their wives are buried in the cemetery.

Locust Lawn, Route 32, four miles south of New Paltz, ☎ 845-255-1660/ 1889. Josiah Hasbrouck lived in this 1814 mansion. He was a lieutenant in the Revolutionary War and a member of the House of Representatives during the terms of Adams and Jefferson. After living in Washington, Hasbrouck decided to build this Federal-style house. Six pilasters rise up for two stories on the front of the house, giving it an elegant appearance. The Terwilliger House next door dates from 1738 and is open for visitors.

WINERY TOURS

Adair Vineyards, 52 Allhusen Road, New Paltz, NY 12561, ☎ 845-255-1377. The winery has tastings, tours and picnics around an historic Dutch barn. It is open March, April, November and December from Friday to Sunday.

Baldwin Vineyards, 110 Hardenburgh Road, Pine Bush, NY 12566, ☎ 845-744-2226. The winery is open for tours and tastings every day from June through October; Friday through Monday in April, May, November and December. During the winter it is open on weekends and by appointment. Special wines include Gold Medal-winning Chardonnay, Riesling and Strawberry wine, plus 10 other varieties.

Benmarl Winery, 156 Highland Avenue, Marlboro, NY 12542, ☎ 845-236-4265. They are high on a hill overlooking vineyards, orchards and the Hudson River. There is an art gallery and museum. It is open year-round.

Brimstone Hill Vineyards, 49 Brimstone Hill Road, Pine Bush, NY 12566, ☎ 845-744-2231. This winery is family-operated and specializes in French-style wines. It is open daily for tours and tastings, May through September. Open weekends, October through April.

El Paso Winery, Route 9W, Ulster Park, NY 12487, ☎ 845-331-8642. They have tastings and are open daily, April through December 31. The winery offers a variety of New York State wines.

Magnanini Farm Winery, 172 Bordens Road, Wallkill, NY 12589, ☎ 845-895-2767. Open Saturday and Sunday, April through December, for free tastings. The Northern Italian restaurant opens on Saturday at 7 pm and Sunday at 1 pm by reservation.

Rivendell Vineyards and Winery, 714 Albany Post Road, New Paltz, NY 12561, ☎ 845-255-2494. Open seven days a week, year-round for tours and tastings. It offers vintage New York wines and other fine wines from boutique wineries around the state.

Royal Kedem Winery, Dock Road, Milton, NY 12547, ☎ 845-795-2240. There is a tasting room with free tastings and a video about the winery and purchasing of wines.

Shawangunk Wine Trail, ☎ 845-744-8399. This includes five Ulster County wineries (Adair, Baldwin, Brimstone Hill, Rivendell and Whitecliff) in a beautiful 30-mile loop. Special festivals are offered throughout the year.

West Park Wine Cellars, Burroughs Drive, West Park, NY 12493, ☎ 845-384-6709. This is an estate winery producing only vintage Chardonnay wines. There is a self-guided tour and video show. It is open March through December, Saturday and Sunday.

Whitecliff Vineyard and Winery, 331 McKinstry Road, Gardiner, NY 12525, ☎ 845-255-4613. This 70-acre farm grows Chardonnay, Merlot, Cabernet Franc and Pinot Noir grapes. It is open June through December, Thursday, Friday and Sunday, from 12 noon to 5 pm; Saturday, from 11:30 am to 6 pm.

Windsor Vineyards, 26 Western Avenue, Marlboro, NY 12542. The wine shop and tasting room are open Friday through Monday year-round. The vineyard offers California premium wines and champagnes.

Where to Stay

ACCOMMODATIONS PRICE SCALE	
Prices for a double room for one or two persons, before taxes.	
$	Under $50
$$	$50 to $100
$$$	$101 to $175
$$$$	Over $175

The Mid-Hudson

■ Stone Ridge

 Baker's Bed & Breakfast is in a 1780 stone farmhouse with a view of Mohonk. Antique furnishings fill the house. 24 Old Kings Highway, Stone Ridge, NY 12484, ☎ 888-623-5513 or 845-687-9795. $$-$$$.

The Inn at Stone Ridge is in an 18th-century stone house, also called Hasbrouck House. Landscaping is attractive and the property has several large old trees. Milliways, the restaurant here, offers Sunday brunch. Route 207, Stone Ridge, 12484, ☎ 845-687-0736. $$$-$$$$.

■ New Paltz

Mohonk Mountain House, which opened in 1870, is located on a spectacular lake with a cliff on the other side. The view is one to remember, and visitors can hike up to gazebos high above the water for a private moment. Besides hiking, guests can enjoy horseback riding, golf, cycling, tennis and special programs. Lake Mohonk, New Paltz, NY 12561, ☎ 800-772-6646 or 845-255-1000. Fax 845-256-2100. AP for two persons $$$$ including afternoon tea and cookies.

■ Highland

Rocking Horse Ranch is a dude ranch with facilities for swimming, water skiing, tennis, fishing and horseback riding. In winter there is both downhill and cross-country skiing, ice skating, snow tubing and sleigh rides. 600 Route 44-55, Highland, NY 12528, ☎ 800-647-2624 or 845-691-2927. MAP for two persons $$$$.

■ Camping

Saugerties

Blue Mountain Campground, 3783 Route 32, Saugerties, NY 12477, ☎ 845-246-7564.

Rip Van Winkle Campgrounds, Inc., 139 Blue Mountain Road, Saugerties, NY 12477, ☎ 845-246-8114 or 800-246-8334.

Saugerties/Woodstock KOA, 882 Route 212, Saugerties, NY 12477, ☎ 845-246-4089.

Phoenicia Area

Hide-A-Way Campsite, 900 Woodland Valley Road, Phoenicia, NY 12464, ☎ 845-688-5109.

Uncle Pete's Campsite, Old Route 28, Phoenicia, NY 12464, ☎ 845-688-5000.

Woodland Valley Campground, 1319 Woodland Valley Road, Phoenicia, NY 12464, ☎ 845-688-7647 or 256-3099.

Kenneth Wilson Campground, Wittenberg Road, Mt. Tremper, NY 12457, ☎ 845-679-7020/6533 or 256-3099.

Lazy Meadow RV Campground, 5191 Route 28, Mt. Tremper, NY 12457, ☎ 845-688-9950.

Kingston Area

Hidden Valley Lake, 290 Whiteport Road, Kingston, NY 12402, ☎ 845-338-4616.

So-Hi Campground, Route 209, Stone Ridge, NY 12484, ☎ 845-687-7377.

Creekview Campsites, 227 Creek Locks Road, Rosendale, NY 12472, ☎ 845-658-9142.

Ellenville Area

Open Well Campground, 326 Briggs Highway, Ellenville, NY 12428, ☎ 845-647-1487.

Skyway Camping Resort, Route 52, Greenfield Park, NY 12435, ☎ 845-688-5471.

Spring Glen Campground, Inc., Lewis Road, Spring Glen, NY 12483, ☎ 845-647-7075.

Yogi Bear Jellystone Park at Birchwood Acres, Route 52, Woodridge, NY 12789, ☎ 800-552-4724 or 845-434-4743.

New Paltz Area

Yogi Bear Jellystone Park Camp-Resort at Lazy River Campground, 50 Bevier Road, Gardiner, NY 12525, ☎ 845-255-5193.

Lembo Lake Park, Route 44/55, Modena, NY 12548, ☎ 845-883-7135.

Marlboro Area

Newburgh/New York City North KOA, Freetown Highway, Plattekill, NY 12568, ☎ 845-564-2836.

The Mid-Hudson

Where to Eat

DINING PRICE SCALE
Prices include an entrée, which may come with vegetables and salad, but exclude beverage, taxes and tip.
$ . . . . Under $10
$$ . . . . $10 to $20
$$$. . . . . $21 to $50
$$$$. . . . . Over $50

■ New Paltz

 The Bakery, 13A North Front Street, New Paltz, ☎ 845-255-8840. $.

Gilded Otter Brewing Company, 3 Main Street, New Paltz, ☎ 845-256-1700. $$.

The Locust Tree Inn Restaurant, 215 Huguenot Street, New Paltz, ☎ 845-255-7888. $$-$$$.

Main Course, 232 Main Street, New Paltz, ☎ 845-255-2600. $$-$$$.

Toscani & Sons, 119 Main Street, New Paltz, ☎ 845-255-2272. $$.

■ Saugerties

Emiliani Ristorante, 147 Ulster Avenue, Saugerties, ☎ 845-246-6169. $$-$$$.

■ Kingston

Hoffman House Tavern, 94 North Front Street, Kingston, NY 12401, ☎ 845-338-2626. The menu is Continental and includes such entrées as fisherman's platter broiled with lemon butter and white wine, grilled Norwegian salmon with chef's sauce of the day or coconut-encrusted chicken. Open from 11:30 am to 10 pm. $$.

Mariners Harbor, 1 Broadway, Kingston, NY 12401, ☎ 845-340-8051. You can have steak or seafood right on the waterfront. The menu includes stuffed flounder with crabmeat stuffing, jumbo king crab legs or Norwegian salmon. Open Tuesday through Sunday for lunch and dinner, and on Monday for dinner. $$.

■ High Falls

DePuy Canal House, 1111 E. New York, Route 213, High Falls, NY, ☎ 845-687-7700. This is a 1797 National Historic Landmark that had its heyday before canal transportation dwindled. Today it is a fine restaurant with five dining rooms, a Sunday brunch and a health-conscious menu. $$-$$$.

■ Highland

Coppola's La Fantasia Ristorante, Route 9W, Highland, ☎ 845-691-7832. $$.

■ Marlboro

The Raccoon Saloon and Restaurant, 1330 Main Street, Marlboro, ☎ 845-236-7872. $$-$$$.

Dutchess & Columbia Counties

The grand estates of millionaires still stand on the east bank of the Hudson. Many of them were influenced by European châteaux and country houses. Fortunately, a number of them have been preserved.

"A class who can afford to let the trees grow is getting possession of the Hudson.... With bare fields fast changing into wooded lawn, the rocky wastes into groves, the angular farmhouses into shaded villas, and the naked uplands into waving forests, our great thoroughfare will soon be seen (as it has not been for many years) in something like its natural beauty. It takes very handsome men and mountains to look well bald." – Nathaniel Parker Willis, 1853.

Adventures

■ On Foot

Hiking

THE APPALACHIAN TRAIL

Appalachian Trail, 166 Wilbur Boulevard, Poughkeepsie, NY 12603, ☎ 845-454-4936. The section of the Appalachian Trail that runs through Dutchess County begins near East Fishkill on **Shenandoah Mountain** and ends in Dover Plains at **Schaghticoke Mountain** before entering Connecticut. In Dutchess County about 2,500 acres of forested land are available for hiking, snow-shoeing and cross-country skiing.

APPALACHIAN TRAIL EMERGENCY CONTACTS

The Appalachian Trail is officially protected by state and local laws and local enforcement agencies even though it is mainly on federal property. If you need emergency help, or to report an incident, contact:

NY State Police . . . . ☎ 845-221-2411

Dutchess County Sheriff . . . . ☎ 845-452-0400

In addition to designated hiking trails, a number of parks offer hiking and nature trails. Some also offer boating, camping, cycling, cross-country skiing, fishing, swimming and golf.

NORTHERN DUTCHESS COUNTY PARKS & TRAILS

Harlem Valley Rail Trail, Millerton, NY 12546, ☎ 518-789-9591. Nine miles of 21 proposed miles have been completed on the railbed from Amenia to Copake Falls. You will travel through farms, wetlands, forest hillsides, historic settlements and villages. Hikers and cyclists are allowed but not motorized vehicles. You can actually begin at the trail-head at the Metro North Station in **Wassaic**, then continue past Amenia, the **Sharon Station**, which has been restored to its original 1870 state, **Coleman Station**, **Millerton**, the **Irondale Furnace** north of Millerton, **Boston Corner** and **Copake Falls**.

Stissing Mountain Fire Tower, Pine Plains, NY 12567, ☎ 518-398-5673. From the base of the mountain you can hike up to an elevation of 1,492 feet where there is a 90-foot tower. From it you can see Albany, Bear Mountain and the Catskills in New York, as well as parts of Massachusetts and Connecticut. From Route 82 south of Pine Plains turn right on Lake Road to the Thompson Pond Sanctuary entrance on the left.

Ferncliff Forest, Rhinebeck, NY 12572, ☎ 845-876-3196. The 200-acre forest is located on Mount Rusten Road. It is open dawn to dusk and admission is free.

Taconic State Park, Rudd Pond Road, Millerton, NY 12546, ☎ 518-789-3059. The 225-acre park is open from 8 am to dusk.

CENTRAL DUTCHESS COUNTY PARKS & TRAILS

Historic Hyde Park Trail, National Park Service, 519 Albany Post Road, Hyde Park, NY 12538, ☎ 845-229-9115 or 8086. Hiking trails connect several parks and historic sites for 8.5 miles. Five sections of the trail can be hiked together or separately. Bicycles are not allowed.

Mills-Norrie State Park, Old Post Road, Staatsburg, NY 12580, ☎ 845-889-4646. The park is open from dawn to dusk and offers golf, camping and a marina on 1,000 acres.

Pinewoods Park, 627 Albany Post Road, Hyde Park, NY 12538, ☎ 845-229-8086. The park is open from dawn to dusk on 25 acres.

Riverfront Park, 627 Albany Post Road, Hyde Park, NY 12538, ☎ 845-229-8086. The 95-acre park is open from dawn to dusk.

Hackett Hill, 627 Albany Post Road, Hyde Park, NY 12538, ☎ 845-229-8086. Open from dawn to dusk and there is a pool.

James Baird State Park, 122D Freedom Road, Pleasant Valley, NY 12569, ☎ 845-452-1489. Open from 6 am to 10 pm on 590 acres.

SOUTHERN DUTCHESS COUNTY PARKS & TRAILS

Fishkill Ridge Conservation Area, Fishkill NY. In Dutchess County, Fishkill Ridge is the northern gateway to the Hudson Highlands. Eagles, falcons and other species inhabit this 1,000 acre area. Trails connect to **Hudson Highlands State Park** and **Mount Beacon**. To reach the Conservation Area from Fishkill, take Business Route 52 to Old Glenham road; turn left onto Maple Avenue. At the end of Maple turn right and cross the bridge, then left onto Old Town Road. Turn right on Sunnyside road, take the last driveway on the left, and go uphill to Sunnyside Parking Area.

Madam Brett Mill Park, Beacon NY. This is a work-in-progress park that offers one mile of easy trail along Fishkill Creek at the moment. Remains of the 1709 **Madam Brett Grist Mill** are still here. There is an elevated boardwalk next to a former hat factory, a fishing pier, views of Tioronda Falls and a viewing deck at the creek's mouth. Take Route 9D to South Avenue (toward the river). Turn left onto Tioronda and go right under the railroad trestle bridge.

Poet's Walk Park, 9 Vassar Street, Poughkeepsie, NY 12601, ☎ 845-473-4440. Among these many good choices, Poet's Walk is our favorite – a great place to unwind if you've had too much sightseeing. Walk along the curving gravel path through a meadow colorful with Queen Anne's lace, clover blossoms, golden rod and inhabited by butterflies and crickets. Wooden benches are conveniently placed for a rest and quiet contemplation, and you eventually reach the river, perhaps to enjoy a sunset at the end of the day.

Bowdoin Park, 85 Sheafe Road, Wappingers Falls, NY 12590, ☎ 845-298-4600. From the entrance to Bowdoin Park on Sheafe Road you will come to Clinton Point Quarry. Continue on to a fork and go to the left, following Old Post Road, then Camelot Drive, South Drive and Mockingbird Lane. Go around a circle to Nassau Drive, then Sheraton Drive and Barnegat Road, and pass an IBM plant. Turn left on Route 9 until you come to the Samuel Morse Estate, Locust Grove.

Hudson Highlands State Park is located off Route 9D, Cold Spring, NY 10512. This undeveloped preserve is a fine fishing and boating area. The park has 25 miles of hiking trails, including mountaintop trails with spectacular views of the Hudson and the Hudson Highland Range. Take Taconic State Parkway to Route 301, west to Route 9D, two miles south of Beacon. It is open from dawn to dusk on 6,500 acres, ☎ 845-227-7207.

THE NATURE CONSERVANCY

The following Nature Conservancy reserves offer hiking trails, woods and ponds, ☎ 845-244-3271.

■ **Nellie Hill Preserve**, Route 22, Dover Plains, NY 12522.

■ **Pawling Nature Preserve**, Quaker Lake Road, Pawling, NY 12564.

■ **Thompson Pond Preserve**, Lake Road, Pine Plains, NY 12567.

■ On Wheels

Scenic Drives

Dutchess County has many scenic driving tours; we have chosen one with meadowland, small streams, and wooded hills with mountain views.

NORTHERN DUTCHESS COUNTY

Begin your drive in the center of **Rhinebeck** village, at the intersection of Routes 308 and 9. Head south on Route 9 and turn left on Mill Road, once the site of early mills. Stone walls still encompass family properties, and there are some attractive gatehouses and gates. Drive through part of the **Wilderstein** estate (see page 252) and on into Rhinecliff.

Rhinecliff was a busy place after Jacob Kip began a ferry service over to Rondout by canoe. You can see **Rondout Lighthouse** from the dock, as well as a nice view of the Hudson River. The earliest house, the **Kip-Beekman-Heermance House** dating from 1700, is near another early 18th-century building, the **Abraham Kip Stone House**, which was once used as a tavern and inn when the ferry operated.

Head up River Road (Route 103) past **Ferncliff**, once William Astor's estate and now a nursing home. You will pass more river estates, including **Valeur** and **The Meadows**. When you reach Poet's Walk (described in *On Foot*, above) pause for a romantic walk. The next estate is **Rokeby**, dating from 1811 and still in the Livingston family. Continue on up to **Montgomery Place** at Annandale-on-Hudson (see page 252). Janet Livingston Montgomery built the house after her husband died.

Bard College is next, near Annandale-on-Hudson, with its two riverfront estates, **Blithewood** and **Ward Manor**. Visitors may tour the campus and attend programs there.

Tivoli Bay, north of Annandale-on-Hudson, is the site of Henry Hudson's 1609 visit. Just after the parking lot for Tivoli Bay, near Routes 9G and 79, is a good place to stop for a fine view of the Catskills.

The **Hudson River Nature Estuarine Research Reserve** includes a network of four coastal sites, open to the public: **Piermont Marsh**, **Iona Island**, **Tivoli Bays** and **Stockport Flats**. These protected reserves are managed as field labs for estuarine research and education. Route 9G near Route 79.

TIVOLI BAY

For the 152 miles below the Federal Dam at Troy to New York Bay the Hudson River is an estuary, a tidal river that rises and falls with twice-daily tides. Its distinctive ecology is created when saltwater meets and mixes with fresh water.

Tivoli Bay is especially interesting as the permanent and seasonal habitat for killifish, blue crabs, snapping turtles, muskrats, Virginia rails, ospreys and an occasional bear. Tivoli North Bay is a cattail marsh with creeks and large open pools. Tivoli South Bay is a shallow wetland cove with mudflats exposed at low tide.

A sign at Tivoli Bay gives distances for short walking trails through the nature reserve, including:

Manor Road . . . . .6 mile

Hogback Trail . . . . .6 mile

North Bay Trail . . . . 1.1 miles

Scenic Overlook . . . . 1.1 miles

The Mid-Hudson

Dutchess & Columbia Counties

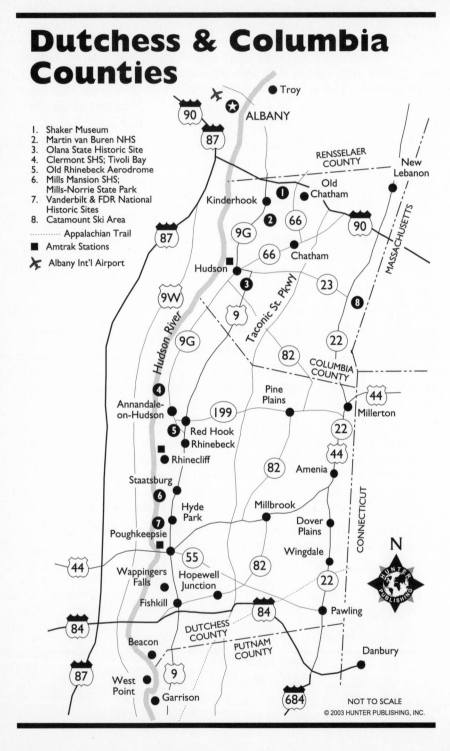

1. Shaker Museum
2. Martin van Buren NHS
3. Olana State Historic Site
4. Clermont SHS; Tivoli Bay
5. Old Rhinebeck Aerodrome
6. Mills Mansion SHS;
   Mills-Norrie State Park
7. Vanderbilt & FDR National
   Historic Sites
8. Catamount Ski Area

---------- Appalachian Trail

■ Amtrak Stations

✈ Albany Int'l Airport

Troy

ALBANY

RENSSELAER COUNTY

New Lebanon

Old Chatham

Kinderhook

Chatham

Hudson

COLUMBIA COUNTY

Hudson River

Pine Plains

Millerton

Annandale-on-Hudson

Red Hook

Rhinebeck

Rhinecliff

Amenia

Staatsburg

Millbrook

Hyde Park

Dover Plains

Poughkeepsie

Wingdale

CONNECTICUT

N

Wappingers Falls

Hopewell Junction

Fishkill

Pawling

DUTCHESS COUNTY

PUTNAM COUNTY

Danbury

Beacon

West Point

Garrison

MASSACHUSETTS

Taconic St. Pkwy

HUNTER PUBLISHING

NOT TO SCALE

© 2003 HUNTER PUBLISHING, INC.

To continue the tour from Tivoli Village, turn right to W. Kerley Corners Road, past early 18th-century farmhouses into **Upper Red Hook**. The brick **Thomas House** was once a stagecoach stop and was the headquarters of General Israel Putnam during the Revolutionary War. Turn onto Route 56, going east past the **Fulton Homestead**, **Torre Rock** and **Jackson Corners** before you come to the Taconic Parkway. Take the Taconic south to the Pine Plains/Red Hook exit and turn right onto Route 199. Continue on Route 199 past Rock City and into Red Hook Village. Turn left on Route 9 and head back south into Rhinebeck, completing your loop.

WORD TO THE WISE

For more driving tours contact **Dutchess County Tourism** at ☎ 800-445-3131 and ask for their pamphlet with maps, *County Scenic & Historic Drive Tours*.

Bicycling

Head for **Pleasant Valley** and the Town Hall on Route 44 to begin your bicycle tour of 26.7 miles. Ride east on Route 44 to Creek Road, turn left and ride three miles to a stop sign. Continue straight to the stop sign at Hibernia Road. Turn right and ride one mile to the Taconic Parkway; cross both southbound and northbound lanes with care and proceed on Hibernia Road to Route 13, which is an unmarked T-junction.

Turn left and ride 1.3 miles to Salt Point Turnpike (Route 17). This is the hamlet of **Clinton Corners**, where there is a country store. Bear right and ride one mile to Pumpkin Lane; turn left and ride 1.9 miles to the stop sign at Taconic Parkway. Cross both lanes again and continue straight on Pumpkin Lane, riding 1.2 miles to Electronic Lane on a long gradual hill. Bear left on Electronic Lane and ride to Nine Partners Road.

Continue to the stop sign at Centre Road (Route 18). This is the hamlet of **Schultzville**. There's another country store here for more sustenance. Ride straight on Fiddlers Bridge Road for 4.1 miles to Pleasant Plains, then continue down Route 16 to Route 41, where you turn left onto 41 and go 1.1 miles to Gretna Road (on right opposite lake) and 2.4 miles to Route 115 (Salt Point Turnpike), left to Wigsten Road, right for one mile to North Avenue (Route 72) and right on Route 44 to the Pleasant Valley Town Hall.

The Mid-Hudson

■ On Water

Excursion Boats

 Hudson Valley Riverboat Tours offers brunch and dinner cruises from the Rinaldi Boulevard dock site in Poughkeepsie. Contact them at 6 Dogwood Road, Peekskill, NY 10566, ☎ 845-788-4000.

Sloop *Woody Guthrie*, Beacon, NY 12508, ☎ 845-297-7697. This wooden sailboat is a replica of a 19th-century Hudson River ferry sloop, built in 1978 by Pete Seeger, the folk singer. It picks up passengers at the Beacon Railroad Plaza. The 300-member Beacon Sloop Club maintains public access facilities in the harbor and hosts a series of public festivals that draw thousands to the Beacon waterfront every year. Groups that take advantage of the free sailing program aboard the *Woody Guthrie* include area homeless shelters, boy scouts, girl guides, schools and summer camps.

Marinas

Chelsea Carthage Landing Marina, Front Street, Wappingers Falls NY, ☎ 845-831-5777. The marina has 200 slips, electricity, water, shower and marine supplies.

Hyde Park Landing Marina, Dock Street, Hyde Park NY, ☎ 845-229-9669. There are 12 slips, with no facilities except restrooms.

Hyde Park Marina, River Point Road, Poughkeepsie NY, ☎ 845-473-8283. There are 150 slips, gas, parts and service, electricitiy, water, showers, a restaurant and marine supplies.

Norrie Point Marina, Norrie State Park, in Staatsburg NY, ☎ 845-889-4200. The marina has 145 slips, electricity, water, showers.

White's Hudson River Marina, 15 Point Street, New Hamburg NY, ☎ 845-297-8520.

■ Eco-Travel

 Stony Kill Farm Environment Center, Route 9D, Wappinger's Falls, NY 12590, ☎ 845-831-8780. Programs are offered for individuals and groups on this 756-acre education center and working farm. Natural history, ecology and farming programs are offered. The trails and grounds are open for hiking, fishing, birding and snowshoeing.

The Hudson River Sloop *Clearwater*, 12 Market Street, Poughkeepsie, NY 12601, ☎ 845-454-7673, www.clearwater.org. "The non-profit organization Hudson River Sloop *Clearwater* was created to defend and restore the Hudson River, one of the great and historic rivers of this nation.... To investigate and conduct research into any causes or sources of contamination and destruction of this river, its tributaries and similar river systems.... To foster the historic and cultural heritage of the Hudson River Valley from the mountains to the sea...." This part of the mission statement indicates the broad environmental interests of the *Clearwater* organization. Its physical centerpiece, a replica of a Hudson River sloop from the age of sail on the river, navigates the whole river to publicize its cause and educate those on board – often groups of school children, who learn how to sail the vessel and simultaneously gain an appreciation for the value of the river. There are also various opportunities for adults to go on board for a day or a longer cruise.

Sightseeing in Columbia County

Columbia County is rich in Shaker communities, including the first of their settlements in America at Watervliet, also called Niskayuna by the Indians. It is in the town of Colonie near Albany (see page 154). Mother Ann Lee was born in Manchester, England in 1736. She joined a sect of Quakers whose members would be aroused with "a mighty shaking" during their meetings. Ann Lee and eight others organized their community at Niskayuna in 1774. The Shakers lived by the Millennial Laws, which prescribed celibacy, required separate schools for boys and girls, restricted the clothing that could be worn, and prohibited private ownership of property.

WORD TO THE WISE
"Do all your work as though you had a thousand years to live and as you would if you knew you must die tomorrow" sums up the Shaker's attitude toward work.

Mount Lebanon Shaker Village, Route 20, New Lebanon, NY 12125, ☎ 518-794-9500. This was the second Shaker community in America; it was founded in 1785 and was home to 600 Shakers. Today there are 26 buildings on this site. We visited on a beautiful fall day with sunlight dappling through the trees onto historic buildings. You can visit the Granary, the 1859 Stone Barn ruins, the Brethren's Workshop, the Wash House and the Second Meeting House, which has a rainbow roof designed to shed snow.

Shaker Museum and Library, 88 Shaker Museum Road, Old Chatham, NY 12136, ☎ 518-794-9100. This complex displays a wealth of Shaker fur-

The Mid-Hudson

nishings that are very plain and simple, but supremely functional. It holds the most comprehensive collection in the country, including nearly 38,000 artifacts and archival materials. The collection was begun by John S. Williams, an Old Chatham resident who learned that the Mount Lebanon Shaker Village was very close to abandonment. He reacted quickly when he spotted two men attacking the community's double triphammer with sledgehammers. A five-dollar bill sent them down to the tavern while Williams went to find the Eldress. She told him that the building was about to be sold, within 48 hours, but he could take away the contents before that time. He did!

Outside of Columbia County, just across the state line in Massachusetts, is another Shaker village, the third in America:

Hancock Shaker Village, Routes 41 and 20, Pittsfield, MA 01202, ☎ 800-817-1137 or 413-443-0188. We were not surprised to find remarkable architecture, including the signature Round Stone Barn (1826) and five-story Brick Dwelling House (1830). The barn was ingeniously designed to stable 52 horned cattle, with hay and feed thrown down to the center from above, and to provide space for eight to 10 teams around the perimeter. Elder William Deming designed and supervised construction of the dwelling house, which accommodated nearly 100 members of the community for sleeping, eating and worship.

Tom Lewis, Professor of English at Skidmore College, collaborated with Ken Burns on the PBS documentary *The Shakers: Hands to Work, Hearts to God*, which is available in the Hancock Shaker Village museum store. It gives you a visual experience of 20th century Shakers as they describe life in a Shaker community.

■ Hudson

Olana, off Route 9G, Hudson, NY 12534, ☎ 518-828-0135. Frederic Edwin Church married Isabel Carnes in 1860 and they bought a 126-acre farm where he could paint. Richard Morris Hunt created a cottage for them, and Church had his studio up the hill. Church and his wife both liked Moorish architecture, so when they built their home this influence was the focus. The house was begun in 1870 and grew like Topsy, as Church designed and decorated his home. It was built around a Persian-style central hall with light entering from the surrounding windows and rooms.

Church was keen to plan his own landscaping and saw its design as a fine art. He wrote, "I can make more and better landscapes in this way than by tampering with canvas and paint in the studio."

■ Clermont

Clermont State Historic Site, 1 Clermont Avenue, Clermont, NY 12526, ☎ 518-537-4240. Robert Livingston, First Lord of Livingston Manor, developed a dynasty that endured into the 19th century. Although Clermont was burned by the British in 1777, by 1781 Mrs. Livingston was again entertaining friends, including Martha and George Washington. Robert Livingston was Minister to France in 1801. In France he became friends with Robert Fulton and together they built a steamboat named the *North River*, later known as the *Clermont*, which proved that the steam engine could become a practical source of power for ships.

HUDSON RIVER ICE YACHTS

During the 19th century, the Hudson River created a generation of famous ice yachts, used not only for pleasure and racing but sometimes for commuting. In an age before icebreakers mangled Hudson ice to keep it open for commerce, ice yachtsmen living in estates along the river would sometimes sail as far as they could to a train station that would bring them into Manhattan. The Roosevelt family was very much involved in ice yachting, owning some of the most famous boats. FDR's Uncle John owned the *Vixen* and the *Icicle II*, and FDR once owned the *Jack Frost* and the *Hawk*.

The largest of the Hudson River ice yachts was the *Icicle*, with a backbone 67 feet long and more than 1,000 square feet of sail. Somehow, in the late 1950s, a huge ice yacht purported to be the *Icicle* migrated to Lake Minnetonka, just west of Minneapolis, Minnesota. There, one of us had a chance to sail her on a windy day. Perched in a tiny cockpit at the stern, behind nearly 60 feet of undulating backbone, the ride was more than exhilarating, like riding a huge freight train downhill without brakes.

The Mid-Hudson

Sightseeing in Dutchess County

■ Annandale-on-Hudson

Montgomery Place, River Road, Route 103, Annandale-on-Hudson, NY 12504, ☎ 845-758-5461. After General Richard Montgomery died in 1775 in the battle for Quebec, his widow, Janet Livingston Montgomery, built a new home she called "Château de Montgomery." The home was intended to honor her husband's memory. Edward Livingston inherited the estate from his sister, and after his death his widow, Louise Livingston, added porches, wings and balustrades to the renamed Montgomery Place. After General John Ross Delafield inherited the place, his wife, Violetta White Delafield, concentrated on developing the gardens. She visited Italy every winter and brought back ideas for her own gardens. She also became a nationally recognized expert in *ikebana*, the art of Japanese flower arranging.

"There was not one of them who did not think, and sometimes say, that his or her country-seat was the choicest spot on the Hudson River; and that if there was nothing like it on the Hudson River, there was nothing like it in the world, for there was no river to compare with the Hudson." – Julia Livingston Delafield, 1877.

■ Rhinebeck

Wilderstein Preservation, Morton Road, Rhinebeck, NY 12572, ☎ 845-876-4818. In addition to the grand estate mansions, there are also fine, less pretentious country houses to visit. Thomas Suckley, who was descended from Robert Livingston and Henry Beekman, bought 32 acres in 1832 and built a two-story Italianate house overlooking the Hudson. In later years paths and trails were developed on the property toward the Hudson, the cove, and hills in the distance. In the 1920s Daisy Suckley renewed her friendship with Franklin Delano Roosevelt, a sixth cousin. She gave him Fala, his beloved little Scottie. In 1941 she undertook a job in the FDR Library at Springwood. She was with Roosevelt in Warm Springs, Georgia when he died in 1945.

Old Rhinebeck Aerodrome Museum, 44 Stone Church Road, Rhinebeck, NY 12572, ☎ 845-758-8610. This is the place to see a collection of antique aircraft and automobiles. Weekend air shows are held during the summer.

■ Staatsburg

Mills Mansion State Historic Site, Old Post Road, Staatsburg, NY 12580, ☎ 845-889-8851. Gertrude Livingston of Clermont, a great-granddaughter of the First Lord of the Manor, and her husband, General Morgan Lewis, were in residence in their brick home in 1795. The house burned in 1832 and was replaced by the current Greek Revival-style house with Doric porticos. In 1890 Ruth Livingston Mills inherited the house and moved in with her husband, Ogden Mills. By 1894 she was in the process of enlarging and redesigning her house, with Stanford White as the architect. Inside, you will see Beaux-Arts styles featured with gilt and marble.

"The fragrance of the late blossoms seemed an emanation of the tranquil scene, a landscape tutored to the last degree of rural elegance. In the foreground glowed the warm tints of the gardens. Beyond the lawn, with its pyramidal pale-gold maples and velvety firs, sloped pastures dotted with cattle; and through a long glade the river widened like a lake under the silver light of September." – Edith Wharton, *The House of Mirth*, 1905.

■ Hyde Park

Franklin D. Roosevelt Home National Historic Site, 519 Albany Post Road, Hyde Park, NY 12538, ☎ 800-967-2283. This house, **Springwood**, is the only place where a US president was born, raised, married, had children and is buried. Franklin's father, James Roosevelt, and his first wife, Rebecca, bought the property and lived there until her death in 1876. He then married Sara Delano, and their only child, Franklin Delano Roosevelt, was born in 1882 at Springwood. Young FDR loved the woods and fields around the estate and enjoyed ice-boating and fishing in the river. Franklin married Anna Eleanor Roosevelt in 1905; she was a great-great-great-granddaughter of Chancellor Robert Livingston.

However, Sara was the owner and head of Springwood until her death. She and FDR redesigned and enlarged the home to house his family. Eleanor remembered that "for over forty years I was only a visitor there." Eleanor was amused by a story about the visit of King George VI and Queen Elizabeth in 1939. Although Franklin offered them a cocktail, his mother Sara suggested a cup of tea. The King responded that although his mother would have preferred the latter, he would be happy with a cocktail. The King and Queen slept in the Pink Room, with English prints on the walls; the King was especially delighted to find that the prints were the same as those he had been brought up with at home.

"My husband always loved taking people he liked home with him. I think he felt he knew them better once they had been to Hyde Park." – Eleanor Roosevelt.

Franklin D. Roosevelt Library and Museum, Route 9, Hyde Park, NY 12538, ☎ 800-FDR-VISIT. This structure was the first Presidential Library and Museum. Roosevelt was aware that past presidents took their papers with them when they left office and that many were subsequently lost. He decided to create a repository next to his home where papers, photographs, books, ship models and family memorabilia could be displayed. Each room and display is tastefully arranged and visitors can spend as much time as they like there. We were touched by the Eleanor Roosevelt Gallery in the Museum, which features an engraved crystal flame to depict her invincible spirit.

Eleanor Roosevelt National Historic Site, Route 9G, Hyde Park, NY 12538, ☎ 800-229-9115. We felt at home here in Eleanor's retreat, Val-Kill. She was a respected woman in her own right and active as a humanitarian, traveling around the world to help others. She lived here with her friends, Nancy Cook and Marion Dickerman, relaxing away from the stress of her life out in the public world. In 1947 she bought out the interests of Nancy and Marion and continued to live here on her own. She enjoyed entertaining dignitaries in this unostentatious home, including Haile Selassie, Nikita Khrushchev, Marshal Tito, Jawaharlal Nehru, Walter Reuther, Adlai Stevenson and John F. Kennedy, among many others.

"Val-Kill is where I used to find myself and grow" – Eleanor Roosevelt.

Vanderbilt Mansion National Historic Site, Hyde Park, NY 12538, ☎ 800-967-2283. Walk into this mansion and you will think you're in Europe. Its elegant and ornate gilt furnishings are dazzling.

Frederick Vanderbilt, grandson of Commodore Cornelius Vanderbilt, purchased the estate in 1895, then proceeded to make extensive improvements. Upon discovering that the original Greek Revival house was not structurally sound, he built a new house on the site. The family moved in late in 1898; the basic amenities such as heating, plumbing and electricity were state-of-the-art for that time.

Stanford White, the architect of the new house, collected special pieces in Europe, and most of them are in the rooms on the first floor.

Louise Vanderbilt's bedroom is spectacular, done in Louis XV rococo style. A Paul Aubusson rug is said to weigh 2,000 pounds. The canopied bed and embroidered silk curtains define this version of imported elegance.

Hyde Park Railroad Station, River Road, Hyde Park, NY 12538, ☎ 845-331-9233. The station was based on a design shown at the Pan American World Exposition of 1898. Dating from 1914, the station has been restored.

■ Millbrook

Innisfree Garden, Tyrrel Road, Millbrook, NY 12545, ☎ 845-677-8000. The design of this garden relates to Chinese styles dating back 1,000 years, embellishing a lake, cliffs, hills, waterfalls and streams.

■ Poughkeepsie

Samuel F.B. Morse Historic Site, Locust Grove, 370 South Road, Route 9, Poughkeepsie, NY 12601, ☎ 845-454-4500. Samuel F.B. Morse bought Locust Grove in 1847 as a place to bring his children together after the death of his first wife.

Morse was a portrait painter before perfecting the electromagnetic telegraph and the Morse code. He was eventually remarried, this time to Sarah Elizabeth Griswold, a great-granddaughter of Henry Livingston Jr., and continued to live at Locust Grove. Morse embarked on a building program that included a park, lawns and flower gardens leading to the Hudson Rover. The house was converted into a Tuscan-style building under his direction.

Morse wrote to his brother about the house: "It is just such a place as in England could not be purchased for double the number of pounds sterling. Its 'capabilities,' as the landscape gardeners would say, are unequaled. There is every variety of surface, plain, hill, dale, glen, running stream and fine forest, and every variety of distant prospect; the Fishkill Mountains toward the south and the Catskills towards the north; the Hudson with its varieties of river craft, steamboats of all kinds, sloops, etc. constantly showing a varied scene."

Bardavon, 35 Market Street, Poughkeepsie, NY 12601, ☎ 845-454-3388. The Bardavon has been giving performances since 1869. They range from music, dance and theater to films.

Frances Lehman Loeb Art Center, Vassar College, 124 Raymond Avenue, Poughkeepsie, NY 12604, ☎ 845-437-5632. The permanent collection covers the history of art from ancient times to the present. Special exhibitions are held during the year.

The Mid-Hudson

SHOPPING FOR ANTIQUES

■ **Red Hook**

Annex Antiques Center, 23 East Market Street, ☎ 845-758-2843.

Cider Mill Antiques, 5 Cherry Street, ☎ 845-758-2599.

■ **Millbrook**

Millbrook Antique Center, Franklin Avenue, ☎ 845-677-3921.

Millbrook Antiques Mann, Franklin Avenue, ☎ 845-677-9311.

Village Antique Center, Franklin Avenue, ☎ 845-677-5160.

■ **Beacon**

Back In Time Antiques, 346 Main Street, ☎ 845-838-0623.

Cold Spring Galleries, 324 Main Street, ☎ 845-832-6800.

Early Everything, 468-470 Main Street, ☎ 845-838-3014.

Peale Center for Christian Living, 66 East Main Street, Pawling, NY 12564, ☎ 845-855-5000. Norman Vincent Peale's memorabilia are collected here in the Center for Positive Thinking. The **Isabelle Bacon Holy Land Museum** houses books, maps and costumes from the Holy Land.

Van Wyck Homestead Museum, Route 9 and I-84, Fishkill NY, 12524, ☎ 845-896-9560. This Dutch Colonial homestead dates from 1732. It was an important Revolutionary War Headquarters from 1777 to 1783.

Mount Gulian Historic Site, 145 Sterling Street, Beacon, NY 12508, ☎ 845-831-8172. The reconstructed 18th-century homestead was the Revolutionary War Headquarters of General von Steuben.

DUTCHESS WINE TRAIL

Cascade Mountain Winery, Flint Road, Amenia, NY 12501, ☎ 845-373-9021. Follow signs starting three miles north of the Amenia light on Route 22. Winery is four miles from Route 22. This is a farm winery, with free tours and tastings and a gourmet restaurant. Tours and tastings take place seven days a week. It is open all year.

Clinton Vineyards, Shultzville Road, Clinton Corners, NY 12514, ☎ 845266-5372. Take the Taconic Parkway to the Salt Point Turnpike exit, and proceed east through Clinton Corners to Schultzville Road. The winery is three miles from the Taconic. This is a farm winery and vineyard offering acclaimed white wines, champagne and dessert wines. Tours and tastings are offered year-round from Friday to Sunday.

Millbrook Winery, Wing and Shunpike Roads, Millbrook, NY 12545, ☎ 845-677-8383. Take the Taconic Parkway to Route 44 exit, proceed east on Route 44. Take Route 82 north three miles to Shunpike Road (Route 57). Go three miles and turn left on Wing Road. Winery is eight miles from the Taconic. This is a farm winery and vineyard with views of the Hudson Valley. It offers Chardonnay, Cabernet Sauvignon and Cabernet Franc. Tours and tastings are offered every day year-round.

Festivals & Events

▪ April

Country Folk Art, Dutchess County Fairgrounds, Route 9, Rhinebeck, ☎ 845-876-4001.

Wappingers Creek Water Derby, Pleasant Valley Recreation Center, Pleasant Valley, ☎ 845-635-3463.

▪ May

Apple Blossom Festival, Red Hook, ☎ 845-758-0824.

Canoe & Kayak Clinic, Webatuck Craft Village, Route 55, Wingdale, ☎ 845-832-6522.

Hudson River Striped Bass Derby. At various locations throughout the county, ☎ 845-297-9308.

Rhinebeck Antiques Fair, Dutchess County Fairgrounds, Route 9, Rhinebeck, ☎ 845-876-1989.

▪ June

Crafts at Rhinebeck, Dutchess County Fairgrounds, Route 9, Rhinebeck, ☎ 845-876-4001.

Fishkill Trolley Craft Fair, on sidewalks and greens in the Village of Fishkill, ☎ 845-897-6157.

Great Hudson Valley Balloon Race, Dutchess County Airport, Wappingers Falls, ☎ 800-445-3131.

Music in the Parks, Vanderbilt National Historic Site, Mills Mansion State Historic Site. Outdoor concert series runs from June through August, ☎ 845-229-8086.

■ July

Antique Car Show and Antique Show, Montgomery Place, River Road, Annandale-on-Hudson, ☎ 845-758-5461.

Children's Day, Samuel F.B. Morse Historic Site, Route 9, Poughkeepsie, ☎ 845-454-4500.

Golden Age Bi-Plane Fly-In, Old Rhinebeck Aerodrome, 44 Stone Church Road, Rhinebeck, ☎ 845-758-8610.

■ August

Bard Music Festival, Bard College, Annandale-on-Hudson, ☎ 845-758-7410.

Dutchess County Fair, Dutchess County Fairgrounds, Route 9, Rhinebeck, ☎ 845-876-4001.

Harlem Valley Artists Open Days, Artists' Studios in Pawling, Dover, Amenia, Pine Plains and Millerton, ☎ 845-877-3445.

■ September

A Celtic Day in the Park, Mills-Norrie State Park, Staatsburg, ☎ 845-889-8851.

Hudson River Arts Festivals, Riverfronts of Beacon and Poughkeepsie, ☎ 845-473-4ART.

International Wine & Hudson Valley Food Festival, Culinary Institute of America, Route 9, Hyde Park, ☎ 800-322-3735 or 800-662-WINE.

Pioneer Day Vintage Aircraft Show, Old Rhinebeck Aerodrome, 44 Stone Church Road, Rhinebeck, ☎ 845-758-8610.

Scenic Hudson's Poets' Walk Park Festival, Red Hook, ☎ 845-473-4440.

■ October

Clearwater's **Pumpkin Sail**, Hudson River Sloop *Clearwater*, various locations along the Hudson River, ☎ 845-454-7673.

Crafts at Rhinebeck Fall Festival, Dutchess County Fairgrounds, Route 9, Rhinebeck, ☎ 845-765-4001.

■ December

Holiday Performances at the Bardavon, Bardavon 1869 Opera House, 35 Market Street, Poughkeepsie, ☎ 845-473-5288.

Holiday Decorated Historic Sites. Franklin D. Roosevelt Home, Library & Museum, Eleanor Roosevelt National Historic Site, Vanderbilt Mansion, Mills Mansion, Montgomery Place, Wilderstein Preservation, Samuel F.B. Morse Historic Site, Madam Brett Homestead, Mount Gulian, Van Wyck Homestead and Amenia Library, ☎ 845-463-4000.

Where to Stay

ACCOMMODATIONS PRICE SCALE	
Prices for a double room for one or two persons, before taxes.	
$	Under $50
$$.	$50 to $100
$$$	$101 to $175
$$$$	Over $175

■ Red Hook

The Grand Duchess is a Victorian mansion bed & breakfast. You can also have afternoon tea on the porch. 50 North Broadway, Red Hook, NY 12571, ☎ 845-758-5818. $$-$$$.

Red Hook Inn was built by the local miller, Jeremiah Hendricks, in 1842. It was turned into an inn in the 1940s. The dining room serves three meals a day – lunch, brunch and dinner – to the public. The cuisine features contemporary American cuisine. 31 South Broadway, Red Hook, NY 12571, ☎ 845-758-8445. $-$$.

■ Rhinebeck

The Beekman Arms has been serving guests since the Revolutionary War. The lobby represents its history with a wide-planked floor, beamed ceiling and large stone fireplace. The associated Delamater House is a conference center with guest rooms decorated in Victorian style. The dining room and Tap Room serve both inns. Route 9, Rhinebeck, NY 12572, ☎ 845-876-7077 for Beekman Arms, 845-876-7080 for Delamater House. $$-$$$.

Belvedere Mansion is a 1900 building replacing the original 1760 home that burned. It is decorated in the "gilded age" style with 18th-century antiques, trompe l'oeil, silk and damask. Dining at the Belvedere is a special treat. We visited as they were preparing a feast for a graduating class of the Culinary Institute of America. Route 9, Rhinebeck, NY 12572, ☎ 845-889-8000. $-$$$$.

Hideaway Suites Bed & Breakfast offers seclusion in the woods, yet is close to Rhinebeck. Guest rooms have king-size four poster beds. Suites consist of a living room with fireplace, a bedroom, and a large bath with Jacuzzi and separate shower. 36 Lake Drive, Rhinebeck, NY 12572, ☎ 845-266-5673. $$-$$$.

Veranda House Bed & Breakfast is in an 1845 Federal-style house. It is on the National Register of Historical Places. The library houses a collection of books on art and architecture. 82 Montgomery Street, Rhinebeck, NY 12572, ☎ 845-876-4133. $$-$$$.

WhistleWood Farm Bed & Breakfast is located on a working farm. Guest rooms feature fireplaces and Jacuzzis, poster beds and decks. Two cottages are also available. 11 Pells Road, Rhinebeck, NY 12572, ☎ 845-876-6838. $$-$$$

■ Millerton

Simmons' Way Village Inn & Restaurant offers a library and fireplaces and is popular for weddings. The dining room is open to the public as well as guests. Main Street, Route 44, Millerton, NY 12546, ☎ 518-789-6235. $$$-$$$$.

■ Staatsburg

Half Moon Bed & Breakfast offers rooms with balconies, a pool and tennis courts. 284 Meadowbrook Lane, Staatsburg, NY 12580, ☎ 845-266-5296. $$$.

■ Stanfordville

Lakehouse Inn is a special secluded retreat in the country with birds calling and no sounds of traffic. Fireplaces, private decks and Jacuzzis are there for your relaxation, and you can take a rowboat out on the lake. A gourmet breakfast is delivered to your room in the morning. Shelley Hill Road, Stanfordville, NY 12581, ☎ 845-266-8093. $$$.

■ Amenia

The **Troutbeck Inn** was once a summer retreat for literary personalities in the 1920s. It looks like an English country house with woods all around. Activities include swimming in the indoor or outdoor pools, fishing, tennis, hiking, and a health facility. The cuisine is New American with a great variety of offerings. The chef will also provide healthy menus and the fish and vegetables are the freshest. Leedsville Road, Amenia, NY 12501, ☎ 845-373-9681. $$$.

■ Millbrook

A Cat in Your Lap Bed & Breakfast offers two rooms in the 1840 house and two suites in the barn with fireplaces. Old Route 82, Millbrook, NY 12545, ☎ 845-677-3051. $$.

■ Dover Plains

The **Old Drovers Inn** has been a gathering place for drovers, or Eastern cowboys, since the 1750s. It is one of the oldest inns in the country. The dining room offers seasonal game specialities as well as seafood and traditional dishes. The building looks like a farmhouse but the amenities are special. Each room is individually decorated. Old Route 22, Dover Plains, NY 12522, ☎ 845-832-9311. $$$.

■ Poughkeepsie

The modern **Inn at the Falls** offers the personal service of a small hotel with the charm of a country house. A European-style continental breakfast is delivered to each guest room. 50 Red Oaks Mill Road, Poughkeepsie, NY 12603, ☎ 845-462-5770, www.innatthefalls.com. $$$.

■ Hopewell Junction

Bykenhulle House Bed & Breakfast is a 15-room Georgian manor house on six acres. Some of the five guest rooms have a fireplaces or Jacuzzis. This 1841 house is listed in the National Register of Historic Places. 21 Bykenhulle Road, Hopewell Junction, NY 12533, ☎ 845-221-4182. $$-$$$.

Le Chambord is an inn and conference center in an 1863 Georgian Colonial mansion. The cuisine is sheer pleasure with four-star status. 2075 Route 52, Hopewell Junction, NY 12533, ☎ 845-221-1941. $$-$$$.

The Mid-Hudson

■ Camping

Rhinebeck

Interlake RV Park, 45 Lake Drive, Rhinebeck, NY 12572, ☎ 845-266-5387.

Millerton

Taconic State Park, **Rudd Pond Area**, Rudd Pond Road, Millerton, NY 12546, ☎ 518789-3069.

Staatsburg

Mills-Norrie State Park, Old Post Road Staatsburg, NY 12580, ☎ 845-889-4646.

Fishkill

Snow Valley Campground, Route 9, Fishkill, NY 12524, ☎ 845-897-5700.

Where to Eat

DINING PRICE SCALE
Prices include an entrée, which may come with vegetables and salad, but exclude beverage, taxes and tip.
$ . . . . Under $10
$$ . . . . $10 to $20
$$$. . . . . $21 to $50
$$$$. . . . . Over $50

■ Dover Plains

 The Old Drovers Inn offers seasonal game specialties as well as seafood and traditional dishes. Old Route 22, Dover Plains, NY, ☎ 845-832-9311. The restaurant is open for lunch and dinner and closed Tuesday and Wednesday. $$-$$$$.

■ Red Hook

Bois D'Arc offers American Progressive cuisine. 29 West Market Street, Red Hook, NY, ☎ 845-758-5992. $$.

Mariner's Harbor Inn offers live lobster, seafood, steaks and a raw bar. Route 9G, Red Hook, NY, ☎ 845-876-1331. $$.

■ Rhinebeck

The Beekman Arms is a 1766 tavern with lots of atmosphere serving New American cuisine. The chef takes pleasure in serving products from local farmers. Sunday brunch is a special treat. 4 Mill Street, Rhinebeck, NY, ☎ 845-871-1766. $$-$$$.

Calico Restaurant & Patisserie is a bistro serving eclectic American food with a European flare. Appetizers include smoked trout and salmon, wild mushroom risotto fritters, grilled polenta, pâté of chicken livers and gratinéed Vidalia onion soup. Entrées include filet of Black Sea bass, tenderloin of pork, bouillabaisse, Long Island duckling and swordfish. 9 Mill Street, Rhinebeck, NY, ☎ 845-876-2749. $$.

At **Cripple Creek Café**, appetizers include carmelized butternut squash and onion soup with pecan crème fraîche that melts in your mouth, smoked salmon plate, sea scallops with ginger-cilantro eggplant "caviar," Jonah crab, sweet corn and avocado salad with pepper coulis, and marinated grilled quail on mushroom mango salad. Dinner entrées include grilled parmesan-crusted lamb chops, maple-mustard glazed pork mignon, roasted duck, roasted halibut, seared rare yellowfin tuna and strip steak. 18 Garden Street, Rhinebeck, NY. 845-876-4355. $$.

Le Petit Bistro has knotty-pine panelling and mirrors for interest. Appetizers include Swiss cheese croquettes, smoked trout, house pâté and escargot. Entrées include sea scallops, Dover sole, frog's legs, veal scallopini and roast rack of lamb. 8 East Market Street, Rhinebeck, NY, ☎ 845-876-7400. $$-$$$.

Osaka Japanese Restaurant offers eat-in or take-out service. Appetizers include shrimp tempura, vegetable tempura, calamari tempura, fried bean curd with ginger sauce, pork dumplings, and octopus. Entrées include beef teriyaki, salmon teriyaki, sushi assortment, habachi vegetables with ginger sauce. Ask about their lunch specials. 18 Garden Street, Rhinebeck, NY, ☎ 845-876-7338. $$-$$$.

■ Staatsburg

Portofino Ristorante offers hot appetizers such as baked artichokes, deep fried calamari, escargot and potato ravioli and roasted portobello mushroom. Entrées include citrus and walnut seared sea bass, Mediterranean olive seared salmon, roasted scallops saltimbocca, trout à la Provençale, veal scallopine ala Marsala and chicken ala rosamarina. 57 Old Post Road, Staatsburg, NY, ☎ 845-889-4711. $$.

■ Bangall

The Stage Stop offers great appetizers including Maryland crab cakes and smoked salmon. Entrées include slow-roasted prime rib, marinated pork medallions, strip steak, roast duck, shrimp scampi, tortellini carbonara and baby back ribs. Hunns Lake Road, ☎ 845-868-1042. $$.

■ Hyde Park

Coppola's Italian American Bistro was formed by three brothers who arrived from Naples in 1954. They opened a restaurant in Poughkeepsie, then one in Hyde Park. Specialties include veal cutlet parmigiana, seafood ala Napolitano, chicken scaloppine ala Piemontese, veal scaloppine Oscar, scungilli fra diavolo, fried calamari, and chicken Marsala. Route 9, Hyde Park, NY, ☎ 845-229-9113. $$.

The Culinary Institute of America is the premier place for a meal in the Hudson River Valley. The Institute was founded in 1946 with 50 students, and today more than 2,100 students from every state and several foreign countries are involved in the program. The faculty is composed of 120 chefs and instructors from 15 countries. You can choose different types of cuisine in the **American Bounty** ($$-$$$), **Caterina de Medici** ($$$), and **Escoffier** ($$$), restaurants, as well as the **St. Andrew's Café** ($$). Each one serves a changing menu on the theme indicated by the name of the restaurant. Try to visit all of them! 433 Albany Post Road, Hyde Park, NY, ☎ 845-452-9600 for general information, 845-471-6608 for reservations.

Hyde Park Brewing Co. is just opposite the FDR home and library. It is a full-service restaurant and brewery. Lunch and dinner menus include steaks, seafood, pastas, sandwiches and pizza. Specialties include oven-fried catfish, wok-seared salmon, bourbon-glazed pork tenderloin, Irish stout braised short ribs and a number of innovative pastas. Desserts, breads and ice cream are made on-site. Route 9, Hyde Park, NY, ☎ 845-229-8277. $$.

■ Poughkeepsie

The Brass Anchor is a seafood restaurant and marina. Appetizers include gravlax (cured salmon), peel-your-own shrimp, smoked Idaho trout and baked stuffed clams. Popular entrées include filet mignon Mary

Powell, chicken and shrimp Champlain, Storm King veal, the Half Moon, Seafood Alfredo, shrimp brass anchor, Yankee John sole and mermaids delight. 31 River Point Road, Poughkeepsie, NY, ☎ 845-452-3232. $$.

Le Pavillon offers wine dinners monthly by reservation; each of five courses is served with a different wine. Appetizers on the menu include escargot simmered in pernod, herbs and garlic sauce, frog legs, sea scallops sautéed with ginger sauce, seafood crabcake with garlic/red pepper sauce and foie gras. Entrées include Maine lobster, rack of lamb, roast duck, coq au vin and squab. 230 Salt Point Turnpike, Poughkeepsie, NY, ☎ 845-473-2525. $$-$$$.

■ Wingdale

Guidetti's, featuring Northern Italian recipes, is owned by the third generation of the same family. Appetizers include sautéed mushrooms, anchovies on a bed of pimientos, calamari, eggplant Bolognese and artichokes vinaigrette. Entrées include penne paste, chicken Cordon Bleu, shrimp scampi, sole Meuniere, eggplant parmigiana, veal scaloppine ala Marsala and filet mignon. Pleasant Ridge Road, Wingdale, NY, ☎ 845-832-6721. $$.

■ Wappingers Falls

Greenbaum & Gilhooley's appetizers include shrimp cocktail, clams on the half-shell, shrimp scampi, herring in sour cream and a crock of baked onion soup. Entrées include filet mignon, pork chops, grilled swordfish, filet of sole, butterfly fried shrimp and twin lobster tails. Special desserts include mud pie and cheesecake. 1400 Route 9, Wappingers Falls, NY, ☎ 845-297-9700. $$.

■ Fishkill

The Inn at Osborne Hill features grilled quail salad, duck and pepper jack cheese spring rolls and andouille and smoked gruyere quesadilla for appetizers. Entrées include marinated stuffed loin of pork, gulf shrimp, roasted seafood brochette, center-cut filet mignon and beef and kidney pie. Dessert may be a chocolate pecan mousse cake or white chocolate mousse. 150 Osborne Hill Road, Fishkill, ☎ 845-897-3055. $$.

The Mid-Hudson

The Hudson Highlands
& Northern Palisades

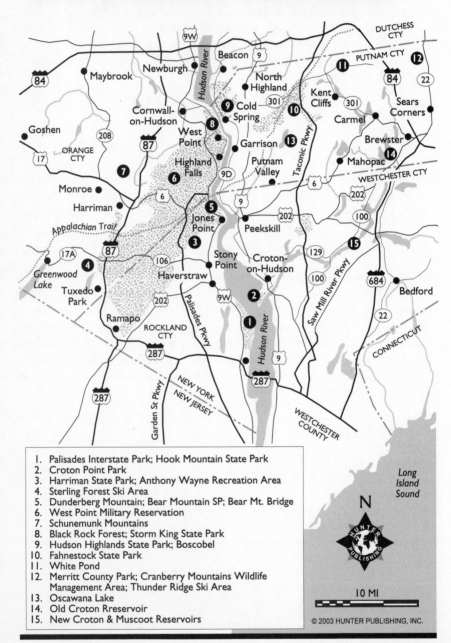

1. Palisades Interstate Park; Hook Mountain State Park
2. Croton Point Park
3. Harriman State Park; Anthony Wayne Recreation Area
4. Sterling Forest Ski Area
5. Dunderberg Mountain; Bear Mountain SP; Bear Mt. Bridge
6. West Point Military Reservation
7. Schunemunk Mountains
8. Black Rock Forest; Storm King State Park
9. Hudson Highlands State Park; Boscobel
10. Fahnestock State Park
11. White Pond
12. Merritt County Park; Cranberry Mountains Wildlife Management Area; Thunder Ridge Ski Area
13. Oscawana Lake
14. Old Croton Rreservoir
15. New Croton & Muscoot Reservoirs

Long Island Sound

N

10 MI

© 2003 HUNTER PUBLISHING, INC.

The Hudson Highlands & Northern Palisades

Just north of New York City and within easy reach of the metroplex lies one of the most beautiful regions of the Hudson River Valley. Still largely unspoiled in spite of its closeness to the urban center to the south, it stretches along the western shore of the river, protected in part by a rugged topography and large areas set aside as parkland. The New Jersey cliffs that front Manhattan are its southern terminus, and at Bear Mountain the high ground crosses the river on a northeasterly axis into Putnam County. Here the river carved its bed deep into the Highlands and spread into the broad reach flowing southward to Tappan Zee.

The Hudson Highlands

Along the western shore of the Hudson River, the Highlands extend from **Dunderberg Mountain** in the south, at Jones Point near Bear Mountain, to **Storm King Mountain** in the north; they continue on the eastern side in the region covered by the **Hudson Highlands State Park** and **Fahnestock State Park**. As the river breaks through the Appalachian Mountain chain at sea level, the rugged Highlands are majestic, with mountains rising up precipitously in cliffs above the river. The tides of the Atlantic swell up through this gut, and large vessels can sail through a mountain chain. Hikers on the Appalachian Trail must cross on the Bear Mountain Bridge to continue their trek.

In his novel, *The Spy*, James Fenimore Cooper wrote about November in the Hudson Highlands: "to be seen in their perfection, the Highlands must be passed immediately after the fall of the leaf. The scene is then the finest, for neither the scanty foliage, which the summer lends the trees, nor the snows of winter, are present to conceal the minutest objects from the eye. Chilling solitude is the characteristic of the scenery; nor is the mind at liberty, as in March, to look forward to a renewed vegetation that is soon to check, without improving the view."

THE DUNDERBERG

Washington Irving wrote about the Dunderberg (Thunder Mountain) in his 1832 *The Storm Ship*: "It is certain, nevertheless, that strange things have been seen in these highlands in storms... The captains of the river craft talk of a little bulbous-bottomed Dutch goblin, in trunk-hose and sugar-loafed hat, with a speaking-trumpet in his hand, which they say keeps about the Dunderberg. They declare that they have heard him, in stormy weather, in the midst of the turmoil, giving orders in Low Dutch for the piping up of a fresh gust of wind, or the rattling off of another thunder-clap."

History

 During the Revolutionary War the gut was of strategic importance because ships were exposed to gun batteries on shore in this narrow stretch. Here the Hudson River is only 3/8-mile wide – one of the narrowest sections below Albany – with depths up to 165 feet. The swift current, the fastest on the river, fostered its name, the "Devil's Horse Race."

Two miles downriver is the spot where the "chevaux-de-frise," or chains, were stretched across the Hudson to stop British ships. One was installed in 1776 between Bear Mountain and Anthony's Nose. This heavy iron chain was supported by wooden floats. However, the British, after seizing forts Clinton and Montgomery in 1777, took the chain apart and shipped it to Gibralter to protect that harbor.

ANTHONY'S NOSE

If you've wondered about the source of the name, "Anthony's Nose," Washington Irving has an answer. "The nose of Anthony the trumpeter was of a very lusty size, strutting boldly from his countenance like a mountain of Golconda, being sumptuously bedecked with rubies and other precious stones – the true regalia of a King of good fellows, which jolly Bacchus grants to all who bouse it heartily at the flagon. Now thus it happened, that bright and early in the morning, the good Anthony, having washed his burly visage, was leaning over the quarter railing of the galley, contemplating it in the glassy wave below. Just at this moment the illustrious sun, breaking in all his splendor from behind a high bluff of the Highlands, did dart one of his most potent beams full upon the refulgent nose of the sounder of brass – the reflection of which shot straightway down hissing hot into the water, and killed a mighty sturgeon that was sporting beside the vessel. This huge monster, being with infinite labour hoisted on board, furnished a luxurious repast to all the crew, being accounted of excellent flavour... "

For those of us who enjoy reckoning when the ice will go out on local lakes or rivers, it's pretty much guesswork. Nathaniel Parker Willis, who lived near West Point, described the importance of this event on March 25, 1854: "The most stirring bit of news, probably, in the whole year, for this neighborhood, is the breaking up of the ice at the mountain-lock, at West Point, and the passing of the first steamer through. 'A boat up yesterday' is this morning's announcement of suspended life re-begun. Our dock is once more noisy and lively, like returning voice and color to the Highland lip; and the wagons begin to come and go on the branching roads, like blood that has again found circulation in our veins. The trance is over... The rippled surface of the Hudson flows, *now*, where I was watching a trotting race of eight or 10 sleighs but *a few days ago*. The manly boys of my neighbor Roe's school-family skated to Newburgh, it hardly seems further off than yesterday, and, to-day, the sleep-prows are ploughing on the track of their skate-irons. We could take a walk where now we must take a boat."

 Carl Carmer, in his 1893 history, *The Hudson*, wrote about sailing the river and the need to plan for the tides: "Skippers learned to follow the tides as they glanced off the bank at a bend and to go with them even across midstream rather than sail shorter distances in straighter lines and slower time. It was safer to anchor than to lose ground when both wind and tide were set against them. Voyages came to be measured by tides – "two ebbs and a flood."

The river is no longer the only highway for commerce, and in a later era some roads were built for pure pleasure rather than transporting goods. **Storm King Mountain Highway** is is one of these; it is a striking four-mile road that was difficult to build. As sheer cliffs overhang the river by about 400 feet, building materials had to be moved into place by ingenious means. Some of the road was carved into the mountain and some was cantilevered out over the abyss.

Storm King Mountain also had a tumultuous period when Consolidated Edison, the power company, wanted to build a pumped-storage hydroelectric plant there in 1963. Residents were up in arms as they tried to preserve their mountain. The battle continued until 1980 when Con Ed gave up. This controversy has also raised awareness of the natural beauty in the area and the need to preserve it.

The Hudson Highlands

Getting Here & Getting Around

The Hudson Highlands and Northern Palisades are located in eastern Orange and western Putnam counties.

■ By Air

JFK International Airport . . . . ☎ 718-244-4444

Newark International Airport. . . . . ☎ 888-EWRINFO

La Guardia International Airport . . . . ☎ 718-533-4300

Westchester County Airport
in Harrison, five miles north of White Plains. . . . . ☎ 914-285-4860

■ By Car

I-84 and 684, Taconic State Parkway, Routes 6 and 9.

■ By Bus

Shortline. . . . . ☎ 800-631-8405

Putnam Area Rapid Transit (PART) . . . . ☎ 845-878-RIDE

Greyhound Lines. . . . . ☎ 800-231-2222

■ By Train

Metro-North. . . . . ☎ 800-METRO-INFO

Information Sources

Orange County Tourism, 30 Matthews Street, Suite 111, Goshen, NY 10924, ☎ 800-762-8687 or 845-291-2136, fax 845-291-2137, www.orange-tourism.org.

Putnam County Visitors Bureau, 110 Old Route 6, Building 3, Carmel, NY 10512, ☎ 800-470-4854 or 845-225-0381, fax 845-225-1421, www.visitputnam.org.

Adventures

■ On Foot

Hiking

Fahnestock State Park, RFD #2, Carmel, NY 10512, ☎ 845-225-7207. The park office is a half-mile west of the Taconic State Parkway on Route 301. The park has the most developed trail system in Putnam County. Part of the **Appalachian Trail** extends through the park. The **Nature Center** offers family film nights, children's puppetry, musical concerts and interpretive programs in summer. Trails for hiking, bicycling and horseback riding are marked. During the winter you can cross-country ski, snowshoe, skate and sled here.

Hudson Highlands State Park, Route 9D, Cold Spring, NY 10512, ☎ 845-225-7207, http://nysparks.state.ny.us/cgi-bin/cgiwrap/nysparks/parks.cgi?p+76. This undeveloped wilderness preserve offers 4,000 acres, with two sections of hiking trails. Try **Sugarloaf**, **Bull Hill** and **Breakneck Ridge** for great views.

Michael Ciaiola Conservation Area (formerly known as the Walter G. Merritt County Park), Haviland Hollow Road, Patterson NY, www.pattersonny.org/CountyPreserves.htm. This 600-acre park has gorges, waterfalls, and is open for hiking. Northeastern Putnam County off Route 22.

Cranberry Mountain Wildlife Management Area, Stagecoach Road, Patterson NY. This state facility is adjacent to Merritt Park. Hiking trails are available on 453 acres.

Manitoga, Garrison (off 9D), NY 10524, ☎ 845-424-3812, manitoga@ highlands.com. Known primarily as an industrial and residential designer, Russell Wright also designed walking trails through his own land near the Hudson River. He created paths "as a journey into the secrets of the forest." They begin in **Mary's Meadow**, past quarried rock, his home **Dragon Rock**, a plank bridge and **Boulders Osio**, which is a "framed window" shaped by trees. Continue on the old logging road and either cut off on **Deer Run** or continue on the main path to **White Pine** or **Lost Pond Path**. Lost Pond is fed by an underground spring and there are bullfrogs to listen to there. You can sit on log benches in **Four Corners Room** before heading to **Chestnut Oak Ridge Osio**. Some say that Henry Hudson moored the *Half Moon* there.

■ On Wheels

Scenic Drives

Route 9D is one to take for views of West Point, Storm King Mountain and fine river scenery up into Hudson Highlands State Park. From the east entrance to the Bear Mountain Bridge head north on Route 9D to a historic marker on the left side. This is the site of the iron chain put across the Hudson to foil the British. However, on October 6, 1777 the chain was destroyed by the British as they took command of Fort Clinton and Fort Montgomery. Continue a couple of miles farther to the entrance to the **Manitou Point Nature Preserve**. An Outward Bound school is now located there.

Head north again on Route 9D to the Manitoga Preserve and the Russell Wright house (see above). A little farther on Route 9D stands **Castle Rock**, an interesting landmark house that is privately owned and not open to the public.

The town of **Garrison** was the site where American troops were "garrisoned" during the Revolutionary War. To the north, **Boscobel** is a Federal-style mansion recovered from almost certain ruin by local residents. Just short of Hudson Highlands State Park, the town of **Cold Spring** stands below stunning peaks.

Bicycling

Putnam County is planning to develop more than 25 miles of paved trails for bicycling and walking, mostly along former railroad rights-of-way. These trails will connect Mahopac, Carmel and Brewster. For information on the progress of the trails call **Putnam County Planning Department**, ☎ 845-878-3480 or **Putnam Rail Trail Association**, ☎ 845-278-4990.

The **Tour de Putnam**, a road- and mountain-bike festival, takes place on the last Sunday in August every year. It begins at **Putnam County Veteran's Memorial Park** in Carmel. Call ☎ 800-470-4854 for information.

■ On Water

Boating

Boating is popular on lakes, ponds and the Hudson River.

White Pond, White Pond Road and Farmers Mills Road, Kent, NY 10512. This is a boat launch site.

Macdonald Marine, 1 Marina Drive, Mahopac, NY 10541, ☎ 845-628-2333. A boat launch site on Lake Mahopac.

Mahopac Marine, Route 6N, Mahopac, NY 10541, ☎ 845-628-6550. A boat launch site on Lake Mahopac.

Perry's Boats, Dunderberg Road, Putnam Valley, NY 10579, ☎ 845-526-2206. A boat launch site on Oscawana Lake.

Fishing

To fish in Putnam County you must have a New York State fishing license and a Watershed Permit, which you can obtain at 1 Belden Road on Route 6 in Carmel, ☎ 845-232-1309. Permits to use rowboats on the reservoirs are also issued there.

BAIT & TACKLE SHOPS

B & D Bait and Tackle, Putnam Avenue, Brewster, NY 10509, ☎ 845-279-7368.

Brewster Bait & Tackle, Route 22, Brewster, NY 10509, ☎ 845-279-2665.

Carmel Bait & Tackle, Route 6 at Lake Gleneida, Carmel, NY 10512, ☎ 845-225-3607.

Stewart Marine, Croton Falls Road, Carmel, NY 10512, ☎ 845-277-3143.

■ On Snow

Downhill Skiing

 Thunder Ridge, Route 22 and Birch Hill Road, Patterson, NY 12563, ☎ 845-878-4100, www.thunderridgeski.com. Thunder Ridge prides itself on being an accessible family ski area. With a vertical drop of 500 feet, it has 30 trails served by three chair-lifts and four surface tows. As you look uphill, the greens are on the left flank, the blues in the middle, and the blacks at the top and on the right flank. It's easily reached from suburbs in Westchester County and Connecticut and only 75 minutes from Manhattan. City folks who don't bother owning cars can ride the Metro-North Ski Train to the Patterson station and take a free shuttle from there.

Cross-Country Skiing

Fahnestock Winter Park, Cold Spring, NY 10516, ☎ 845-225-3998. The park has 15 km of marked and groomed trails for cross-country skiing, as well as a number of ungroomed wilderness trails.

■ Eco-travel

Taconic Outdoor Education Center, Clarence Fahnestock State Park, RFD #2, Carmel, NY 10512, ☎ 845-225-7207. This site is open year-round and offers environmental and recreational programs.

Sightseeing

■ Garrison

 Boscobel Restoration, Route 9D, Garrison, NY 10524, ☎ 845-265-3638. This house was almost lost during the 1950s when the federal government declared it in "excess." It was sold to a demolition contractor for $35. Preservationists dismantled the house and stored it; the house was rebuilt with financial backing from Lila Acheson Wallace. States Morris Dyckman began construction of the house in 1804. Sadly, only the foundation was complete when he died, but his widow, Elizabeth Corne Dyckman, finished the house and moved in by 1808. Decorative arts from the Federal period grace the house. The family's English china, silver, glass and some of the library have been saved. Guided tours take visitors through the house; then you can visit the spring house, orangery and herb garden, and gatehouse, as well as overlook the Hudson River from the belvedere.

Constitution Marsh Wildlife Sanctuary, Indian Brook Road, Garrison, NY 10524, ☎ 845-265-2601. The **National Audubon Society** operates this sanctuary. You can canoe here, stroll the boardwalk and look at exhibits in the Visitors Center.

■ Carmel

Chuang Yen Monastery, 2020 Route 301, Carmel, NY 10512, ☎ 845-225-1819. This is the largest Buddhist monastery in the eastern United States, containing the largest indoor statue of Buddha in Europe or the Americas. **Buddha Vairocana** is 37 feet tall. Small statues of Buddha encircle the statue on a lotus terrace. A large colored porcelain statue of Kuan-Yin Bodhisattva dates from the Ming Dynasty. A vegetarian lunch is served on Sundays from noon to 1 pm. A donation is requested for the vegetarian lunch.

Festivals & Events

■ March

St. Patrick's Day Parade, Route 6, Mahopac NY.

■ May

Memorial Day Parade, Route 6N, Mahopac NY.

■ July

Putnam County Old Fashioned Fair, Carmel NY, ☎ 845-278-7209.

■ October

Columbus Day Parade, Route 6, Mahopac NY.

The Hudson Highlands

Where to Stay

ACCOMMODATIONS PRICE SCALE	
Prices for a double room for one or two persons, before taxes.	
$	Under $50
$$.	$50 to $100
$$$	$101 to $175
$$$$	Over $175

■ Cold Spring

Eagle's Nest Bed & Breakfast is up on Breakneck Ridge. Guest rooms have river views. Route 9D, Cold Spring, NY 10516, ☎ 845-265-2484. $$$.

Hudson House is on the banks of the Hudson and dates from 1832. The dining room has a view of the river. 2 Main Street, Cold Spring, NY 10516, ☎ 845-265-9355. $$-$$$.

Plumbush Inn has three guest rooms. It is well known for its cuisine which is Continental fare with Swiss specialties. One of the five dining rooms has oak paneling from a château in France. Another is in a greenhouse. Route 9D, Cold Spring, NY 10516, ☎ 845-265-3904, www.pojonews.com. $$$.

■ Garrison

The Bird and Bottle Inn dates from 1761 and was once a stagecoach stop. The inn has fireplaces, wide-plank floors and antique furnishings. Old Albany Post Road, Garrison, NY 10524, ☎ 800-782-6837 or 845-424-3000, fax 845-424-3283. Guest room prices include a $75 discount for dinner in the inn. $$$$.

■ Camping

Clarence Fahnestock State Park, RFD #2, Carmel, NY 10512, ☎ 845-225-7207.

Putnam County Veterans Memorial Park, Gipsy Trail Road, Kent, NY 10512, ☎ 845-225-3650.

Where to Eat

DINING PRICE SCALE
Prices include an entrée, which may come with vegetables and salad, but exclude beverage, taxes and tip.
$ . . . . Under $10
$$ . . . . $10 to $20
$$$. . . . . $21 to $50
$$$$. . . . . Over $50

■ Cold Spring

Cathryn's Dolcigno Tuscan Grill offers Northern Italian cuisine including contemporary pasta dishes, lightly grilled meats and seafood. There is a Sunday brunch. 91 Main Street, Cold Spring, NY, ☎ 845-265-5582. $$.

Plumbush Inn offers Continental fare with Swiss specialties. One of the five dining rooms has oak paneling from a château in France. Another is in a greenhouse. You can choose prix fix or à la carte, ☎ 845-265-3904. The restaurant is open Wednesday through Sunday for dinner. $$$.

The Palisades

If you have driven along the Palisades Parkway, you may have stopped at an overlook to marvel at the sheer drop of the rocky mountain ridge into the water of the Hudson River. These spectacular cliffs are named for their appearance, not unlike a wooden palisaded fort. Today, **Henry Hudson Drive** (not to be confused with the Henry Hudson Parkway in Manhattan) runs for some distance below the cliffs; the **Palisades Interstate Parkway** on the top of the ridge continues northward all the way to Bear Mountain. It's a grand ride most of the time, with no trucks to contend with, but often clogged during commuting hours. Any fine road can turn into an ordeal under the worst conditions, and we remember one transit in the midst of a hurricane, when our car was making bow waves like a motorboat.

THE PALISADES

Henry Hudson sailed his *Half Moon* into the Hudson River, and Robert Juet annotated his journal to suggest what it might have looked like. Juet wrote: "On the fourteenth they glided past the pillared 12-mile wall of the Palisades and through the lake that would someday be known as Haverstraw Bay. The shadows of the Hill of Thunder lengthened over their white sails as they turned into the channel of the highlands and saw, beyond the swirling waters of the narrow race, the Mountain Bear crouching in the blue heavens."

Getting Here & Getting Around

■ By Air

JFK International Airport . . . . ☎ 718-244-4444

Newark International Airport. . . . . ☎ 888-EWRINFO

La Guardia International Airport . . . . ☎ 718-533-4300

Stewart International Airport. . . . . ☎ 845-564-7200

■ By Car

There are three options for approaching this area. From the north or south, take **I-87** to Exit 16 near Harriman. Then head west on **NY Route 17** to visit places to the west or go east to Bear Mountain. If you take Exit 17 near Newburgh, you can drive west on **I-84** or east on I-84 to reach places on the Hudson such as West Point. A third option is to drive **Palisades Interstate Parkway** north from the George Washington Bridge.

■ By Bus

Shortline . . . . ☎ 800-631-8405

New Jersey Transit . . . . ☎ 973-762-5100

Adirondack Trailways . . . . ☎ 800-858-8555

Greyhound Lines. . . . . ☎ 800-231-2222

■ By Train

Metro-North . . . . ☎ 800-638-7646 or 212-532-4900

NJ Transit. . . . . ☎ 973-762-5100

Information Sources

Orange Country Tourism, 30 Matthews Street, Suite 111, Goshen, NY 10924, ☎ 845-291-2136, 800-762-8687,www.orangetourism.org/sear.htm.

Rockland County Tourism, 10 Piermont Avenue, Nyack, NY 10960, ☎ 800-295 or 845-353-5533, www.rockland.org.

Adventures

■ On Foot

Hiking

THE APPALACHIAN TRAIL

This section of the trail offers views of **Greenwood Lake**, on the New York-New Jersey border, from its western shore. You walk over a series of glacial upthrusts until the last ridge, where you can look down on the lake. (For other sections of the Appalachian Trail west of the Hudson, pick up trail maps of **Harriman State Park** and **Bear Mountain State Park**. The trail crosses the Hudson on the Bear Mountain Bridge and continues through the Highlands into Fahnestock Memorial State Park.) Greenwood Lake, NY 10925, ☎ 212-685-9699.

Maps of the trails are available from the **New York-New Jersey Trail Conference, Inc.**, GPO Box 2250, New York, NY 10116. They are also available in shops in the area. Northern Harriman/Bear Mountain Trails are shown on *Trail Map 4*, southern ones on *Trail Map 3*.

ALONG THE HUDSON

Black Rock Forest, Route 9W, Cornwall-on-Hudson, NY 12518, ☎ 845-534-4517. A visitor center is located on Continental Road across from the 9W entrance to the forest. Marked and unmarked trails range from short walks to long hikes. The two main trails are **Stillman Trail** (yellow blazes), which leads to Black Rock, and **Scenic Trail** (white blazes), which takes you past Aleck Meadow Reservoir.

Trail Map 7 from the New York-New Jersey Trail Conference covers Black Rock Forest and Storm King State Park. *Trail Map 8* covers west Hudson Trails including Schunemunk Mountain, Long Path, Jessup Trail and Megaliths. The **Mountainville Conservancy of Storm King Art Center,** ☎ 845-534-3115, includes the northern part of Schunemunk Mountain.

Crow's Nest, Cornwall-on-Hudson, NY 12518, ☎ 845-786-5003. This is the Storm King section of the Palisades Interstate Parkway, Route 9W south of Storm King Mountain. There are no marked trails but good views.

West Point/Highland Falls Trail, Highland Falls, NY 10928, ☎ 845-938-2638. Normally, you can take a 5.5-mile historic tour through West Point and the village of Highland Falls. At this writing you cannot walk through West Point, however, because of security concerns following September 11. Call the above number as this may change. You can walk along part of the trail in Highland Falls. Park in the visitor center lot there.

Harriman State Park, Palisades Parkway, ☎ 845-786-2701. Harriman has 207 miles of trails. There are also 10 miles of cross-country ski trails. The Appalachian Trail and the 400-mile blue-blazed Long Path cut through this park, creating interesting hikes for those who want to do sections of the big ones. The Iron Mine Walk takes you by the Greenwood furnace, dating from 1810, which produced cannonballs during the War of 1812. Park in the lot at Lake Skannatati and follow the Long Path trail.

Bear Mountain State Park, Palisades Parkway, Bear Mountain, NY 10911, ☎ 845-786-2701. Bear Mountain offers 57 miles of hiking trails and one nature trail. There is a mountain-bike loop adjacent to the **Anthony Wayne Recreation Area** off Palisades Parkway. Cyclists may use any paved road open to automobile traffic except Palisades Parkway and Route 6. Some of the trails (a limited number) are designated for cross-country skiing in the winter.

For a visit to the **Trailside Museum and Zoo** (see *Sightseeing*, page 291), head north of the parking area for Bear Mountain Inn. Just east of the lake take the sharp right turn into the tunnel under 9W. There is also a walking path around **Hessian Lake**.

You can walk on Bear Mountain by taking **Perkins Drive** from Seven Lakes Drive to the parking lot at the top and walking to another overlook above the Bear Mountain Inn. **Perkins Tower** was named for George Perkins, one of the founders of Harriman Park.

To follow the route of the Hessian and British Troops take the **1777 Trail**, which was developed for the Bicentennial by the Palisades Interstate Park Commission, ☎ 845-786-5003. On October 6, 1777, 2,000 troops walked through this route and surprised the two American forts, **Fort Clinton** and **Fort Montgomery**. The 1777 Trail heads up through **Popolopen Gorge** to **Hell Hole** and the site of a fort, then passes through the pre-Revolutionary hamlet of **Doodletown**. Other trails on Bear Mountain include the **Cornell Trail**, **Ramapo-Dunderberg Trail**, the **Suffern-Bear Mountain Trail** and the **Timp-Torne Trail**.

SCHUNEMUNK MOUNTAINS AND WEST

Highlands Trail, NY/NJ Trail Conference, 232 Madison Avenue, New York, NY 10016, ☎ 212-685-9699. This 35-mile trail travels through parks, forests and natural areas in the Highlands. It traverses the Appalachian Trail, old railroad beds, lakes, over Schunemunk Mountain, through Black Rock Forest and to the top of Storm King Mountain. Call the above number for details as there are a number of access points along the 35 miles.

Mountainville Conservancy at Storm King Art Center, Schunemunk Mountain, Mountainville, NY 10953, ☎ 845-534-3190 or 212-685-9699. There are six marked trails ranging from 1.6 to 8.1 miles along Route 32 to Highland Mills. The **Howell Trail** leads to panoramic views both north and south. **Butter Hill** is also a popular walking area.

Sterling Forest, Route 17A West, Tuxedo Park, NY 10987, ☎ 845-351-5907. There is four-mile **Sterling Ridge Trail** and two-mile **Allis Trail**. One of the last operational fire towers in the state stands there.

Heritage Trail, Goshen, NY 10924, ☎ 845-344-8131. Another walk in the region takes you along the converted rail bed of the Erie Railroad. Park at the **Reeves Meadow Visitor Center** and head up on the Reeves Brook Trail. You can walk from Hartley road through Goshen to the old Chester railroad station. The next part of the trail will extend to **Museum Village** in Monroe.

■ On Wheels

Scenic Drives

 Old Storm King Highway, Route 218, Cornwall-on-Hudson, NY 12518. This drive is from Cornwall-on-Hudson to West Point, circling Storm King Mountain. The curving road has steep drops to keep the driver on his or her toes.

Perkins Memorial Drive, Bear Mountain, NY 10911. Take Exit 19 off Palisades Interstate Parkway. Then take Seven Lakes Drive past the Bear Mountain Inn, turning right at the sign for Perkins Drive. The drive leads you through forest on a curving road up to the tower. It is highly recommended for fall foliage (see *Sightseeing*, page 290, for information about Perkins Tower).

Bicycling

 Harriman-Bear Mountain Parks. Bicycles are allowed on paved park roads that are open to automobile traffic (except for Route 6 and Palisades Interstate Parkway). Mountain bikes are not allowed in the back country of Harriman-Bear Mountain Parks, except on a mountain bike loop trail adjacent to **Anthony Wayne Recreation Area**. Take Exit 17 from the Palisades Interstate Parkway and head for the Anthony Wayne Recreation Area. A mountain bike trail begins there and heads south on Beechy Bottom Road to Horn Hill. The road swings around and heads north to the parking area.

Black Rock Mountain Club offers great bicycling in the area, ☎ 914-534-2966.

■ On Water

Excursion Boats

 Hudson Highlands Cruises, Cornwall-on-Hudson, NY 12520, ☎ 845-534-SAIL. Narrated excursion cruises on the *Commander,* a ferry boat built in 1917, which is on the National Historic Register. It departs from **Haverstraw Marina** in Cornwall at 10 am and **West Point** at 12:30. Call for reservations.

Hudson River Adventures, Newburgh Landing, Newburgh, NY 12550, ☎ 845-782-0685. Two-hour narrated cruises on board the *Pride of the Hudson*. The vessel passes **Bannerman Castle** and there is a lecture and video on board. You'll also see **Mount Beacon, Storm King Moun-**

tain, **Breakneck Mountain**, the **Catskill Aqueduct**, **Cold Spring** and the northern part of **West Point Reservation**.

Canoeing & Rafting

Kittatinny Canoes, Barryville, NY 12719, ☎ 800-FLOAT-KC. Canoeing, rafting, kayaking, and tubing on the Delaware River are offered by Kittatinny. You can paddle through natural National Park Service lands. There is variety from wild whitewater to peaceful, gentle streams. They offer over 40 trips.

Lander's Delaware River Trips, Route 97, Narrowsburg, NY 12764, ☎ 800-252-3925 or 845-252-3925. Lander's offers river trips as well as canoeing and rafting on your own. They have 10 locations on the the Delaware River between Callicoon and Matamoras PA. Rafts must be checked in each night if taken by individuals who are not part of an organized trip.

Silver Canoe Raft Rentals, 37 South Maple Avenue, Port Jervis, NY 12771, ☎ 800-724-8342 or 845-856-7055. Raft, canoe and tube rentals on the Delaware in Orange County. A one-day trip paddles between Pond Eddy and Port Jervis. They also have one-person kayaks.

Whitewater Willie's, 17 West Main Street, Port Jervis, NY 12771, ☎ 800-233-RAFT or 845-856-2229. Inflatable canoes, rafts and tubes on the Delaware River.

Wild & Scenic River Tours and Rentals, 166 Route 97, Barryville, NY 12719, ☎ 800-836-0366 or 845-557-8783. Whitewater canoeing, rafting, tubing and kayaking trips on the Delaware River. On a family trip kids pay what they weigh. This company is now owned by Lander's (see above).

Boat Launching & Marinas

Bob's Marina, Sterling Road, Greenwood Lake, NY 10925, ☎ 845-477-2083.

City of Newburgh Boat Launching Site, Foot of Washington Street, Newburgh, NY 12550, ☎ 845-565-3230. Only for boats trailered with vehicles.

DeFeo's Marina, 672 Jersey Avenue, Greenwood Lake, NY 10925, ☎ 845-477-2552. This is a full-service marina, offering summer dock slips, launch ramp, boat sales and service, winter storage.

East Arm Boat Co., Sterling Road, Greenwood Lake, NY 10925, ☎ 845-477-3635. This company offers sailboat sales and service, summer dock rentals and winter storage.

Gull Harbor Marina, 2 Washington Street, Newburgh, NY 12550, ☎ 845-565-7110. The marina offers 200 slips and is open May 1 to October 15.

Hanaford's Marine Inc., 3032 Route 9W, New Windsor (near Newburgh), NY 12553, ☎ 845-561-2771. The launching ramp is on Front Street at the Hudson River.

Long Pond Marina, 634 Route 210, Jersey Avenue, Greenwood Lake, NY 10925, ☎ 845-477-8425. The marina offers launching, dockage, lake tours, WaveRunner and boat rentals.

North Shore Marina, Windermere Avenue, Greenwood Lake, NY 10925, ☎ 845-477-9320. Dock space and launching ramp, boat sales and service.

Olde Point Marina, Ten Eyck Avenue, Greenwood Lake, NY 10925, ☎ 845-477-8410. A ramp, snack stand, boat sales and service.

Public Boat Launching Site, Cornwall Landing Park, Cornwall-on-Hudson, NY 12520, ☎ 845-534-4200.

Rainbow Inn, Linden Avenue, Greenwood Lake, NY 10925, ☎ 845-477-9574. Motorboat and rowboat rentals.

Willow Point Marina, Route 210, Jersey Avenue, Greenwood Lake, NY 10925, ☎ 845-477-8063. Boat sales and service, dock space, picnic area and launching ramp.

Fishing

 The Delaware has small bass, chain pickerel and walleyes. Greenwood Lake offers large bass, small bass, chain pickerel, panfish and tiger musky. The lakes in Harriman State Park have large bass and panfish. The Hudson River has large bass, small bass, panfish and striped bass.

Bait Bucket, 313 Route 211 West, Middletown, NY 10940, ☎ 845-344-4774.

Ceely's Bait Bucket, 436 Shore Road, New Windsor, NY 12553, ☎ 845-534-3495.

O & H Bait Shop, 48 Main Street, Chester, NY 10918, ☎ 845-469-2566.

Delaware River Drift Trips, Goshen, NY 10924, ☎ 845-294-2588.

Reel 'Em In Guide Service, Fall Street, Port Jervis, NY 12771, ☎ 845-856-3009.

■ On Horseback

Borderland Farm, Route 94, Warwick, NY 10990, ☎ 845-986-1704. Lessons and trails are available on this 230-acre riding farm. Call for reservations.

J & E Ranch, 100 Union School Road, Montgomery, NY 12549, ☎ 845-361-4433. Trails and riding lessons available; off Route 17K west of Newburgh.

Juckas Stables, Pine Bush, NY 12566, ☎ 845-361-1429. Lessons and trails on 117 acres off Route 52 in northwestern Orange County. Call for reservations.

Pleasant Valley Farms, Farley Lane, Goshen, NY 10924, ☎ 845-294-8134. English and Western riding on 250 acres of trails. Call for reservations.

Silent Farms Stables, Axworthy Lane, Goshen, NY 10924, ☎ 845-294-0846. English and Western riding on trails and indoors.

■ On Snow

Downhill Skiing

Mount Peter Ski Area, Off Route 17A, Warwick, NY 10990, ☎ 845-986-4992, www.mtpeter.com. Founded in the 1930s, Mount Peter is one of the oldest ski areas in New York. It caters to skiing families living in New Jersey and New York suburbs west of the Hudson. The vertical drop is 400 feet, with 11 downhill slopes and trails served by two double chair lifts.

Sterling Forest, Route 17A West, Tuxedo, NY 10987, ☎ 800-843-4414 (NY & NJ in season). The vertical drop is 450 feet and there are four double chairlifts on seven slopes and trails. For snow conditions, call ☎ 845-351-4788.

■ In the Air

A Beautiful Balloon, 179 Intervale Road, Parsippany, NJ, ☎ 973-335-9799, www.balloon-rides.com. balloonsnj@aol.com. Reservations are required for hot air champagne flights in the Middletown and Poughkeepsie areas. Flights take place at sunrise and two hours before sunset. They are weather-dependent, of course. The sensation aloft is tranquil and romantic. The price is $225 per person.

Above the Clouds, Inc., Middletown, NY 10941, ☎ 845-692-2556, www.abovetheclouds.biz. Fully insured flight operations. The current charge is $199 per person, per hour. Call or visit the website (www.abovetheclouds.biz) for seasonal specials.

Fantasy Balloon Flights, Inc., 3 Evergreen Lane, Port Jervis, NY 12771, ☎ 845-856-7103. Hot air balloon rides over the lower Hudson River Valley. Flights depart from Randall Airport in Middletown, NY. Reservations are required. Packages include a one-hour flight for $199 per person, a gift certificate for $199, a one-hour flight for two at $599 and a half-hour flight for two at $399.

Sightseeing

■ Marlboro

 Gomez Mill House, 11 Millhouse Road, Marlboro, NY 12542, ☎ 845-236-3126. This is the oldest manor house in Orange County. The house was a fur-trading post and home to pioneers, merchants, patriots, farmers, craftsmen and statesmen. General George Washington attended Revolutionary War meetings in the house. It is on the National Register of Historic Places.

■ Cuddebackville

Delaware & Hudson Canal Park-Neversink Valley Area Museum, Hoag road (off Route 209 in western Orange County), Cuddebackville, NY 12729, ☎ 845-754-8870. The 300 acre D & H Canal Park is a National Historic Landmark. There is a self-guided audio walking tour of the canal, historical exhibitions, a children's **D & H Boat Activity Center** and an exhibition on blacksmithing. The park offers hiking, fishing and picnicking.

■ Newburgh

Crawford House, 189 Montgomery Street, Newburgh, NY 12550, ☎ 845-561-2585. This 1830 house looks like English country houses of the Palladian period. There is a collection of Hudson River sloop and steamboat models.

Washington's Headquarters State Historic Site, 84 Liberty Street, Newburgh, NY 12551, ☎ 845-562-1195. George Washington took half of his army and his wife Martha to Newburgh as he was trying to protect the Highlands. General and Mrs. Washington lived in **Hasbrouck House**

The Palisades

and the army camped at **New Windsor**. Washington wrote letters of dismay at the status of his army to the Secretary of War, Benjamin Lincoln. He also appealed to his men in his Newburgh Address. Years later, with the Revolution won, Washington issued the proclamation ending hostilities with the British from this house. The **Tower of Victory** monument stands for the peace achieved in 1783.

■ Vail's Gate

Knox's Headquarters State Historic Site, Forge Hill Road, Route 94, Vail's Gate, NY 12584, ☎ 845-561-5498. On several occasions during the Revolutionary War, Major General Henry Knox established military hedquarters at John Ellison's 1754 Georgian-style house, from which he commanded the artillery of George Washington's army. From October 1782 until the spring of 1783, as 7,000 soldiers and 500 "camp followers" were establishing winter quarters at the New Windsor Cantonment, and General Washington was lodged at Jonathan Hasbrouck's house in Newburgh, New York, Major General Horatio Gates occupied this elegant home from which he commanded the cantonment. Here the army awaited the end of the Revolutionary War that became effective when Washington issued the cease fire orders on April 19, 1783.

The Last Encampment of the Continental Army, Route 300, Vail's Gate, NY 12584, ☎ 845-561-5073 or 561-0902. Part of the campground (1782-83) is in this national military park. Two enlisted men's huts are on display. The nature trail has self-guided walks. General Henry Knox and officers of the Continental Army were here as the Revolutionary War concluded with the Treaty of Paris.

New Windsor Cantonment State Historic Site, Temple Hill Road, Route 300, Vail's Gate, NY 12584, ☎ 845-561-1765. During the Revolutionary War, Washington's Army camped here, with 7,000 soldiers and 500 civilians living in log huts. The (reconstructed) Temple was the army's first chapel, where George Washington spoke to rebellious officers. The original purple heart is on display. There are demonstrations on blacksmithing, open-hearth cooking, musket shooting and artillery drills.

■ Goshen

Goshen Historic Track, Park Place, Goshen, NY 10924, ☎ 845-294-5333. This is the oldest equestrian trotting track in the world. Visitors are welcome to watch the daily training. There are special events as well as harness racing.

Harness Racing Museum and Hall of Fame, 240 Main Street, Goshen, NY 10924, ☎ 845-294-6330. Housed in a building that was originally a stable, this museum traces the history of trotting, displays memorabilia, and provides interactive exhibits. The Hall of Fame honors key figures in the development of the sport.

■ Cornwall-on-Hudson

Museum of the Hudson Highlands, Cornwall-on-Hudson, NY 12520, ☎ 845-534-7781. This natural history museum is home to a variety of animals and birds, including the great horned owl, which thrives on a diet of white mice. Terrapin turtles live in a habitat where salt water meets fresh water. They do not have fungus on their shells because of the salt. Several turtles live in the Highland Pond display, including a wood turtle, spotted turtle, Eastern box turtle and painted turtle. Green frogs, eels, catfish and a musk turtle round out the residents. Visitors can walk around the area on almost a mile of walking paths. You will see ponds, trees, a marsh and some of the animals that live here.

Kendridge Farm is also owned by the Hudson Highlands museum (above). There is a gallery in the house and the barn is full of displays. A walking trail provides numbered signs along the way, with information on forest regeneration, a sheep lane, an amphibian pond, a muskrat pond, a goose pond and a Storm King vista.

■ Mountainville

Storm King Art Center, Old Pleasant Hill Road, Mountainville, NY 10953, ☎ 845-534-3115. Storm King Art Center is familiar to anyone who drives I-87 north from New York City. We had admired fleeting glimpses of the sculptures standing in fields near the Thruway not far north of Harriman for years. Curiosity eventually led us to get off the Thruway and explore this extraordinary museum, with 120 outdoor sculptures spread over 500 acres and indoor galleries in an elegant mansion.

Thirteen large sculptures by David Smith anchor the collection. Take a map as you drive in and walk around outside to see works by Alexander Calder, Henry Moore, Louise Nevelson and many more world-famous sculptors. This is a truly marvelous place where landscape and sculpture merge to create an unforgettable aesthetic experience.

In 1997 the museum commissioned Andy Goldsworthy's *The Wall That Went for a Walk*. Walls were a part of Goldsworthy's life as he was growing up in Yorkshire. He found a fallen wall and a straight row of trees that could lend themselves to a wandering scalloped wall around and through the trees. Like a serpent, the wall headed downhill, into a pond and out the other side. A group of skilled British "wallers" arrived to construct the wall and proceeded to lay large stones on the bottom and long ones through the middle in patterns that fit the topography. The rocks are not dressed but pieces were skillfully chopped off, and large flat pieces were saved for the top.

■ West Point

US Military Academy, West Point, NY 10996, ☎ 845-938-2638. Head for the **Visitor Center** where you can see displays and get information. West Point Tours, ☎ 845-446-4724 operate on scheduled trips around the Academy. The West Point Museum, ☎ 845-938-2203/3590, has an extensive collection of military artifacts. You will see displays on land warfare from ancient times to the present.

One of the most scandalous events that took place at West Point was the collusion of former war hero General Benedict Arnold and British Major John André. James Thacher's military journal from 1775-1783 details his observation as a witness to the treason of General Arnold.

JAMES THACHER'S MILITARY JOURNAL

"September 26th – A British sloop-of-war, called the *Vulture*, came up the North river, and anchored near King's ferry, about twelve miles below West Point. On board of this vessel were a Colonel Robinson, and Major André, under the assumed name of John Anderson. A communication was now maintained between Arnold and the persons on board the *Vulture*, without exciting the least suspicion of treasonable designs... Joshua Smith, by the desire of Arnold, went with a boat, rowed by some men employed on his farm, and brought Major André, *alias* John Anderson, on shore, where he was received by Arnold... when he became extremely anxious to return on board the *Vulture* [but the vessel had been driven from her station by a cannon on shore]... it was resolved that André should return to New York by land... Having arrived at Tarrytown near the lines of the royal army, André was arrested... the captors now very properly delivered their prisoner, with the papers found on him, into the hands of Lieutenant-Colonel Jameson.

October 1st – I went this afternoon to witness the execution of Major Andre... the execution is postponed till tomorrow.

October 2nd – Major André is no more among the living."

Constitution Island, US Military Academy, West Point, NY 10996, ☎ 845-446-8676. This tour offers a boat ride to and from the island, as well as a guided tour of Revolutionary War fortifications and the 17-room Warner House. Reservations are required.

Famous Visitors to West Point

Edgar Allan Poe attended West Point for a short period of time until he was dismissed in January 1831. He was noted for various escapades on campus as well as telling tall tales. He enjoyed lampooning officers and tacked some of his efforts up where others would see them. He also spent earlier summers in a camp at Fort Clinton. He probably picked up some of the legends about Captain Kidd while there. Some say there is treasure buried in the area, and others say that the ghost of Captain Kidd guards the treasure.

The **Marquis de Lafayette** also spent time in the Hudson River Valley, along with his son, **George Washington Lafayette**, in 1824. After a dinner in New York he sailed on the steamboat *James Kent*, encountered fog at Tarrytown but kept on to West Point. People gathered all along the shore to greet him, including the Cadets in line when the vessel pulled up to the dock.

Anthony Trollope made a trip to America in 1861. He wrote at length about the strictness of discipline at West Point, including this ironic observation: "Let us fancy an English mess of young men from seventeen to twenty-one, at which a mug of beer would be felony, and a glass of wine high treason!"

Mark Twain visited West Point in 1890 and his lecture and reading included sections from his *A Connecticut Yankee in King Arthur's Court*. He found its customs very similar to those at West Point, which replicate some of the rules of conduct in medieval England.

▪ Harriman Park

Perkins Tower, Perkins Memorial Drive, Bear Mountain, NY 10911, ☎ 845-942-5873. Perkins Tower is the place to go for great views of the Hudson and the surrounding countryside. We walked up the 56 steps inside, pausing to answer 20 questions on the wall tiles. Historical tiles with photos decorate landings and walls. At the top there is a panoramic photo map with sites in the view identified.

▪ Arden

Clove Furnace Historic Site, 21 Clove Furnace Drive & Route 17, Arden (south of Harriman), NY 10910, ☎ 845-351-4696. The museum has iron mining displays, an iron-making furnace and exhibits related to county history. The iron-making furnace was one of the two furnaces of the **Greenwood Iron Works**. Peter Parrott and his brother Robert developed the Parrot Civil War artillery pieces.

■ Monroe

Museum Village in Orange County, Route 17M, Monroe, NY 10950, ☎ 845-782-8247, ☎ 845-782-8247. This is the largest living history museum in New York. You will catch a glimpse of daily life and work in the 19th century. Walk around through the 30 buildings, each with a different theme. Costumed interpreters give demonstrations of various kinds of work and crafts.

■ Warwick

Historic Warwick Village, Warwick (Route 17A west of Harriman State Park), NY 10990, ☎ 845-986-2720. Warwick Historical Society Buildings include **Baird's Tavern**, dating from 1766; **Shingle House**, which was the first home in Warwick in 1764; and **Ketchum House**.

■ Bear Mountain

Trailside Museum, Bear Mountain, NY 10911. The museum is just a short walk from Bear Mountain Inn. Displays explain Indian myths such as creation, false-face societies, and gods, including those of corn, fire, sea, wind, day and night. A map shows man entering North America across a land bridge from Siberia. Another exhibit details the construction of Forts Clinton and Montgomery before their capture and destruction by the British in 1777.

■ Stony Point

Stony Point Battlefield, Box 182, Stony Point, NY 10980, ☎ 845-786-2521. In May 1779 the British had captured Stony Point but George Washington had a plan to displace them. Brigadier General Anthony Wayne led a surprise midnight attack, with his men wearing pieces of white paper in their hats to identify them in the dark. They also carried unloaded muskets and fixed bayonets. Silence was the key to this attack and an accidental shot could reveal their presence. The British surrendered and never tried to threaten the Hudson Highlands again.

During the summer, military encampments as well as musket/artillery and camplife/cooking demonstrations are held. Battlefield Evening Tours include a narrated walk as men fire muskets and cannon in the distance to give visitors a chance to feel what it must have been like during the Revolutionary War.

THE BATTLE OF STONY POINT

Bernard Lossing, in his 1866 volume, *The Hudson, From the Wilderness to the Sea,* describes Stony Point after battles had finished: "The whole Point is a mass of granite rock with patches of evergreen trees and shrubs, excepting on its northern side where may be seen a black cliff of magnetic iron ore... that peninsula, clustered with historic association, will ever remain almost unchanged in form and feature."

Stony Point Lighthouse, dating from 1826, has been restored with a Fresnel lens and the light shines again. It is the oldest lighthouse on the Hudson River.

■ New City

The Jacob Blauvelt Farmhouse, 20 Zukor Road, New City, NY 10956, ☎ 845-634-9629. This 1832 restored house shows Flemish Vernacular architecture with Greek Revival ornamentation. The furnishings are in period style to depict the homes of farming families in this region during the first half of the 19th century. Exhibitions in the house as well as the barn further illustrate farm life. Special events include candlelight tours, 19th-century country dancing and an annual dollhouse show.

■ Nyack

Edward Hopper House, 82 North Broadway, Nyack, NY 10960, ☎ 845-358-0774. Edward Hopper was a realist painter; one of the rooms in his boyhood home focuses on his work. Monthly exhibits by local artists are mounted in other rooms. Jazz concerts are held in the restored garden during the summer.

Hudson Valley Children's Museum, 21 Burd Street, Nyack, NY 10960, ☎ 845-358-2314. This museum appeals to children of all ages with a range of programs, from preschool activities such as Toddler Time, Toddler Dance and Cooking for Kids, to the Kinetic Ball Machine for middle and high school students. In 1998 the Hudson River Dive exhibit opened. There are weekend and weekday workshops as well as summer minicamp programs.

■ Woodbury

Woodbury Historical Society & Cemetery of the Highlands, Main Street (Route 32), Woodbury, NY 10930, ☎ 845-928-6770. Mount Rushmore was named after Charles E. Rushmore, whose family gave the Historical Society building to the town of Woodbury.

WINERIES

Adair Vineyards, 52 Alhusen Road, New Paltz, NY 12561, ☎ 845-255-1377. It is open in April, Friday-Sunday, 11-6; May-October, open daily, 11-6; November-December, open Friday-Sunday, 11-5.

Applewood Winery, Four Corners Road, Warwick, NY 10990, ☎ 845-988-9292. It is open July to October from Friday to Sunday; April to December, Saturday and Sunday.

Baldwin Vineyards, 110 Hardenburgh Road, Pine Bush, NY 12566, ☎ 845-744-2226. Tours and tastings are available daily from May to November, 10-5:30; January to March, 11:30-4:30, Saturday and Sunday. In December and April they are open 11-5, Friday to Monday.

Brimstone Hill, 61 Brimstone Hill Road, Pine Bush, NY 12566, ☎ 845-744-2231. From May to October it is open daily, 11:30-5:30. From November to April it is open weekends.

Brotherhood Winery, 35 North Street, Washingtonville, NY 10992, ☎ 845-496-3661. The winery is open daily, May to October; and weekends only, November to April. It is open year-round for wine purchases. Tastings are available on weekends.

Demarest Hill, 81 Pine Island Turnpike, Warwick, NY 10990, ☎ 845-986-4723. It is open November to May, 11-5; June to October, 11-6.

Rivendell, 714 Albany Post road, New Paltz, NY 12561, ☎ 845-255-2494. It is open every day except Christmas, New Years Day and Thanksgiving.

Warwick Valley Winery and Orchards, 114 Little York Road, Warwick, NY 10990, ☎ 845-258-4858. Try Doc's Hard Apple Cider, Raspberry Cider, Chardonnay, Riesling and fruit wines, which are available for tasting. The winery is open summer and fall on Friday, Saturday and Sunday; in winter, Saturday and Sunday.

Whitecliff Vineyard, 331 McKinstry Road, Gardiner, NY 12525, ☎ 845-255-4613. It is open Thursday, Friday and Sunday, 12-5, Saturday, 11:30-6, Memorial Day Weekend through October. Open weekends only in November and December.

Festivals & Events

■ February

 George Washington's Birthday Celebration at Washington's Headquarters, Newburgh, ☎ 845-562-1195.

■ March

Easter Egg Hunt, Thomas Bull Park, ☎ 845-457-4900.

Maple Sugaring on the Farm at Museum of the Hudson Highlands, ☎ 845-534-7781.

St. Patrick's Day Parade at Port Jervis, ☎ 845-856-6694.

■ April

Earth Day at Bear Mountain State Park, ☎ 845-786-8247.

Easter Parade at Greenwood Lake, ☎ 845-477-0112.

Springfest at Nyack. Open-air festival of crafts and food, ☎ 845-353-2221.

■ May

Delaware River Run at Port Jervis, ☎ 845-856-4045.

Spring Crafts Fair at Sugar Loaf Craft Village, ☎ 845-469-9181.

Rocklandfest at Thiells. Rides, food, games, live music, children's activities, country western night, fireworks and 4H Youth Fair, ☎ 845-429-7085.

Antiques and Collectibles Street Fair at Nyack, ☎ 845-353-6981.

Pow Wow at Bear Mountain. Dancing, exhibits, food and presentations, ☎ 845-786-2731.

■ June

Greek Festival at West Nyack, ☎ 845-623-4023.

Around the World in 60 Miles on the Shawangunk Wine Trail, ☎ 845-496-3661.

Orange Classic 10K at Middletown, ☎ 800-295-2181, extension 1500.

Riverfront Festival at Cornwall-on-Hudson, ☎ 845-534-4200.

■ July

General Knox's Birthday Celebration at Knox's Headquarters, ☎ 845-561-1765.

Great American Weekend at Goshen, ☎ 845-294-7741.

Irish Festival at Stony Point, ☎ 845-942-2358.

Heritage Days at Port Jervis, ☎ 845-856-6694.

New York Renaissance Faire at Sterling Forest, ☎ 845-351-5171.

Orange County Fair in Middletown, ☎ 845-343-3134.

■ August

Kids Day at the Cantonment at New Windsor Cantonment. This was the last encampment of the Continental Army during the Revolution, in 1782-83. The site includes a meeting hall and features living history demonstrations during its April-to-October season, ☎ 845-561-1765.

Kites of the Hudson at Washington's Headquarters at Newburgh, ☎ 845-562-1195.

New Windsor Cantonment by Candlelight at Vail's Gate, ☎ 845-561-1765.

Old Fashioned Children's Festival at Museum Village (see *Sightseeing*, page 291), ☎ 845-782-8247.

Shawangunk Wine Trail, a tour of seven wineries, ☎ 845-496-3661.

■ September

Septemberfest, an open-air festival of crafts and food at Nyack, ☎ 845-353-2221.

Egyptian Festival at Spring Valley, ☎ 845-356-5257.

Civil War Weekend at Museum Village, ☎ 845-782-8247.

Waterfront Festival at Newburgh, ☎ 845-562-5100.

■ October

18th-Century Market Days at New Windsor Cantonment, ☎ 845-561-1765.

Fall Foliage Festival at Port Jervis, ☎ 845-856-4717.

Oktoberfest at Bear Mountain, ☎ 845-786-2731.

■ November

Holiday Trimming Time at Museum Village, ☎ 845-782-8247.

■ December

Candlight Tour of Newburgh Homes at Crawford House, ☎ 845-291-2154.

Christmas in the Village in Museum Village, ☎ 845-782-8247.

Washington's Headquarters by Candlelight in Newburgh, ☎ 845-562-1195.

Where to Stay

ACCOMMODATIONS PRICE SCALE	
Prices for a double room for one or two persons, before taxes.	
$	Under $50
$$	$50 to $100
$$$	$101 to $175
$$$$	Over $175

■ Campbell Hall

Point of View is located near Goshen Village in the country; perfect for strolling, running or biking. Great views in a pastoral setting. 253 Ridge Road, Campbell Hall (north of Goshen on Route 207), NY 10916, ☎ 845-294-6259. $$-$$$.

■ Cornwall-on-Hudson

Cromwell Manor Inn Bed & Breakfast is a restored 1820s Greek Revival mansion located on seven acres. It is listed on the National Register of Historic Places. 174 Angola Road, Cornwall-on-Hudson, NY 12518, ☎ 845-534-7136, www.cromwellmanor.com. $$$.

■ Mountainville

The Storm King Lodge is an 1800s lodge located between Storm King and Schunemunk mountains. Two rooms have fireplaces. 100 Pleasant Hill Road, Mountainville, NY 10953, ☎ 845-534-9421, fax 845-534-9416, www.stormkinglodge.com. $$-$$$.

■ Salisbury Mills

The Caldwell House is a restored 1803 Colonial home. It is located on three acres. 25 Orrs Mill Road, Salisbury Mills (west of Cornwall-on-Hudson on Route 94), NY 12577, ☎ 845-496-2954, www.caldwellhouse.com. $$.

■ West Point

Hotel Thayer has been recently restored and is very attractive; it is located on the grounds of the US Military Academy at West Point. 674 Thayer Road, West Point, NY 10996, www.hotelthayer.com, ☎ 800-247-5047 or 845-446-4731. $$$.

■ Goshen

Anthony Dobbins Stagecoach Inn was once a stagecoach stop. It is furnished with family heirlooms and other antique pieces. The owners are descended from "Wild Bill" Hickok and William Penn. 268 Main Street at Maplewood Terrace, Goshen, NY 10924, ☎ 845-294-5526, www.dobbinsinn.com, dobbins@warwick.net. $$-$$$.

■ Sugar Loaf

Sugar Loaf Village Bed & Breakfast is filled with antiques. The house has pine floors, hand-hewn beams and fireplaces. POB 23, Pine Hill Road, Sugar Loaf, NY 10981, ☎ 845-469-2717. $$$.

■ Warwick

Château Hathorn has eight rooms. The restaurant is especially notable with continental cuisine. 33 Hathorn Road, Warwick, NY 10990, ☎ 845-986-6099. $$-$$$.

Peach Grove Inn is an antebellum Greek Revivial home furnished with antiques. It overlooks a 200-acre farm in the Warwick Valley. 205 Route 17A, Warwick, NY 10990, ☎ 845-986-7411. $$-$$$.

Warwick Valley Bed and Breakfast offers four rooms decorated with antiques and country furnishings. The 1900 Colonial Revival home is in the historic district. 24 Maple Avenue, Warwick, NY 10990, ☎ 845-987-7255. $$-$$$.

■ Bear Mountain

Bear Mountain Inn is located right in the park on a lake with all sorts of activities available. Guests can stay in the main building or in the nearby lodge. Route 9W, Bear Mountain, NY 10911, ☎ 845-786-2731. $$-$$$.

■ Pearl River

Pearl River Hilton has a style reminiscent of a French château. 500 Veterans Memorial Drive, Pearl River, NY 10965, ☎ 800-445-8667 or 845-735-9000, fax 845-735-9005, www.pearlriver.hilton.com. $$$$.

■ Camping

Cuddebackville

Oakland Valley Campground, 399 Oakland Valley Road, Cuddebackville, NY 12729, ☎ 845-754-8732.

Middletown

Korn's Campgrounds, 60 Meyer Road, Middletown, NY 10940, ☎ 845-386-3433.

Montgomery

Winding Hills Park, Route 17K, Montgomery, NY 12549, ☎ 845-457-4918.

Godeffroy

American Family Campground, 110 Guymard Turnpike, Godeffroy (western Orange County on Route 209), NY 12739, ☎ 800-CAMP AFC.

Port Jervis

Inn at Twin Lakes, 219 Old Mountain Road, Port Jervis, NY 12771, ☎ 845-856-8326.

The Palisades

Florida

Black Bear Campground, 197 Wheeler Road, Florida (north of Warwick on Route 17A/94), NY 10921, ☎ 888-867-2267 or 845-651-7717.

Bear Mountain

Beaver Pond Campground, Harriman State Park, Bear Mountain, NY 10911, ☎ 845-947-2792.

Sebago Cabins, Harriman State Park, Bear Mountain, NY 10911, ☎ 845-351-2360.

Where to Eat

■ Campbell Hall

Bull's Head Inn offers lunch from Wednesday to Friday; and dinner, Tuesday to Sunday. Sarah Wells Trail, ☎ 845-496-6758. $$.

■ Newburgh

Yobo's offers cuisine from China, Japan, Korea, and Thailand. 1297 Route 300, ☎ 845-564-3848. $$-$$$.

■ Port Jervis

Cornucopia's specialty is rack of lamb. 175 Route 209, ☎ 845-856-5361. $$.

■ Salisbury Mills

Loughran's has an Irish pub atmosphere. Route 94, ☎ 845-496-3615. $$.

■ Highland Mills

Black Forest Mill offers German-American fare. Route 32, ☎ 845-928-9895. $$.

■ West Point

Hotel Thayer offers three meals a day plus a champagne brunch on Sunday, ☎ 845-446-4731. $$.

■ Goshen

Oliver's of Goshen offers American cuisine with a British accent. 40 Park Place, ☎ 845-294-5077. $$.

■ Sugar Loaf

Sugar Loaf Inn offers New American cuisine, ☎ 845-469-2552. $$.

■ Warwick

Château Hathorn has Continental cuisine. Route 94 and County Route 1, ☎ 845-986-6099. $$.

■ Bear Mountain

Bear Mountain Inn offers breakfast, lunch, dinner and Sunday brunch. Entrées include chicken Sorrentino, seared salmon, Black Angus shell steak and pasta. Route 9W, ☎ 845-786-2731. $$.

■ Haverstraw

Civiles Venice on the Hudson offers salmon Delle Rose with incredible Hudson River Views. 16 Front Street, ☎ 845-429-3891. $$-$$$.

■ Suffern

Marcello's Ristorante has roasted filet mignon in a red barolo wine sauce. 21 Lafayette Avenue (in Rockland County near the New Jersey border), ☎ 845-357-9108. $$.

■ Congers

Restaurant X & Bully Boy Bar offers Wasabi Crusted Pacific Ahi Tuna and Classic Beef Wellington. 117 North Route 303, ☎ 845-268-6555. $$.

■ Nyack

The specialty at **Heather's Open Cucina** is lobster Arribiata. 13 North Broadway, ☎ 845-358-8686. $$-$$$.

Lanterna Tuscan Bistro has old-fashioned home-made ravioli. 3 South Broadway, ☎ 845-353-8361. $$-$$$.

■ Tappan

Giulio's Restaurant of Tappan offers Northern Italian cuisine including Valdostana di Vitello. 154 Washington Avenue (in Rockland County near the New Jersey border), ☎ 845-359-3657. $$.

The Old 76 House is an historic restaurant with Yankee pot roast a specialty. 110 Main Street. $$-$$$.

Sleepy Hollow Country

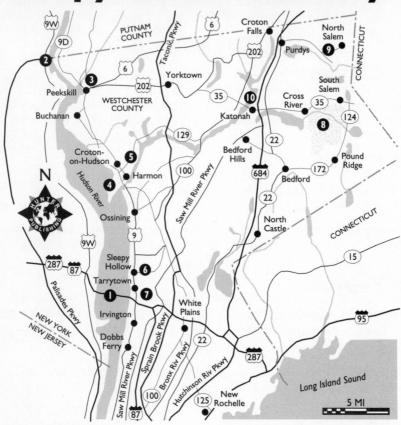

1. Tappan Zee Bridge
2. Bear Mountain State Park & Bridge (Appalachian Trail)
3. Paramount Center for the Arts
4. Croton Point Park
5. Van Cortlandt Manor; Croton Dam; Old Croton Aqueduct Trailway
6. Kykuit; Old Dutch Church; Philipsburg Manor; Union Church of Pocantico Hills
7. Lyndhurst; Sunnyside; Tarrytown Music Hall
8. Ward Pound Ridge Reserve
9. North Salem Vineyard
10. Caramoor Center for Music & Art

Sleepy Hollow Country

Sleepy Hollow legends are favorites among visitors who would like to see the places where Ichabod had his adventures. The Sleepy Hollow region centers on Tarrytown and north along the Hudson River. It is all in Westchester County, which shares a southern boundary with New York City and the northern boundary with Putnam County. The Hudson River flows on the west side and Long Island and Fairfield County in Connecticut on the east side. In this chapter we cover Croton-on-Hudson, Sleepy Hollow and Tarrytown.

Even if it's not close to Halloween we can shiver as we remember the "headless horseman" of Sleepy Hollow. Ichabod Crane tried to outrun the horseman, kicking his steed, "Old Gunpowder," to make him run faster. Washington Irving is quite specific about the site of this misadventure:

"In the bosom of one of the spacious coves which indent the eastern shore of the Hudson, at that broad expansion of the river denominated by ancient Dutch navigators the Tappen Zee... there lies a small market town or rural port, which by some is called Greensburgh, but which is more universally and properly known by the name of Tarry Town... Not far from this village, perhaps about three miles, there is a little valley, or rather lap of land among high hills, which is one of the quietest places in the whole world." Here the action of *The Legend of Sleepy Hollow* takes place.

THE HEADLESS HORSEMAN

You can find the Headless Horseman bridge and think of Ichabod as he mopes along after being rejected by Katrina Van Tassel. "It was the very witching time of night that Ichabod, heavy-hearted, and crestfallen, pursued his travel homewards, along the sides of the lofty hills that rise above Tarry Town... All the stories of ghosts and goblins that he had heard in the afternoon, now came crowding upon his recollection... In the dark shadow of the grove, on the margin of the brook, he beheld something huge, misshapen, and mounted on a black horse of powerful frame... Ichabod was horror-struck on perceiving that he was headless."

The headless horseman threw his "head" at Ichabod before he could reach the safety of the bridge. But the next morning a pumpkin was found in the road and Gunpowder was wandering there alone. – Washington Irving, *The Legend of Sleepy Hollow*

Washington Irving composed wondrous stories of life along the Hudson River, including the one about Rip Van Winkle, who fell asleep for 20 years in the Catskills. Visitors to his home, Sunnyside, can become immersed in his life there.

DID YOU KNOW?

Washington Irving's *Diedrich Knickerbocker's History of New York* led to New Yorkers being called "Knickerbockers."

Getting Here & Getting Around

■ By Air

JFK International Airport, ☎ 718-244-4444.

Newark International Airport, ☎ 888-EWRINFO.

La Guardia International Airport, ☎ 718-533-4300.

Westchester County Airport, in Harrison, five miles north of White Plains, ☎ 914-285-4860.

■ By Car

New York State Thruway (I-87), Interstate 95 (New England Thruway) and I-287 (the Cross-Westchester Expressway).

■ By Bus

Bee-Line, ☎ 914-682-2020.

Adirondack, ☎ 800-858-8555.

Greyhound Lines, ☎ 800-231-2222.

Leprechain, ☎ 800-624-4217.

Shortline, ☎ 800-631-8405.

■ By Train

Metro-North Railroad operates three lines (Hudson, Harlem, and New Haven) that run through Westchester County.

Amtrak serves the Yonkers and Croton-Harmon stations on its Empire Service, and New Rochelle on its Metroliner Service, for points north (upstate New York, Boston, Canada) and points south (Washington, DC), ☎ 800-872-7245.

Information Sources

Westchester Convention & Visitors Bureau, 235 Mamaroneck Avenue, White Plains, NY 10605, ☎ 800-833-WCVB (9282) or 914-948-0047, fax 914-948-0122.

Historic Hudson Valley, 150 White Plains Road, Tarrytown, NY 10591, ☎ 914-631-8200.

Adventures

■ On Foot

Old Croton Aqueduct Trailway is a popular place to walk and cycle. It extends for 26 miles from Van Cortlandt Park in the Bronx to Croton Dam. Water was carried on the aqueduct into New York City from 1842 to 1955. The trailway goes through 11 communities and wonderful views of the Hudson River are visible in sections. The part from Philipse Road to Croton-on-Hudson is also part of the Greenway Conservancy's Hudson River Trail.

 If you would like a trail map of the Old Croton Aqueduct Trailway, send $5.25 and a stamped, self-addressed envelope to Friends of the Old Croton Aqueduct, 15 Walnut Street, Dobbs Ferry, NY 10522, ☎ 914-693-5259.

The **Ossining Visitor Center**, 95 Broadway, Ossining, NY 10562, ☎ 914-941-3189, has an exhibit on the Aqueduct. The double arch of the aqueduct bridge is hard to miss.

When you reach the end of the trailway you will see Croton Dam, just off Route 129. It is the second largest hand-hewn structure in the world, only topped by Egypt's Great Pyramid. The new dam was begun in 1892 and completed in 1906. It is 297 feet high and 2,168 feet long with a capacity of 30 billion gallons of water. Croton Gorge was used in the cinema production of *Tarzan* and also *The Perils of Pauline*.

Croton Point Park is the largest park in the area with 504 acres. It is located on a peninsula and is open for camping, fishing, picnicking and walking. There are vacation cabins, lean-to facilities, and tent and trailer camping sites. Call for reservations: ☎ 914-271-3293.

North County Trailway runs for 22.1 miles from Eastview in the town of Mount Pleasant to Baldwin Place in the Town of Somers. It is a paved cycle/pedestrian path on right-of-way lands of the former Putnam Division of the New York Central Railroad.

DID YOU KNOW?

The "Old Put," well known to commuters, provided service from 1881 to 1958 from Brewster in Putnam County to New York City.

The **Westchester County Department of Parks**, 25 Moore Avenue, Mount Kisco, NY 10549, ☎ 914-242-PARK, maintains the 90-mile countywide trailway system that includes **North County Trailway**, **Bronx River Pathway**, **Briarcliff-Peekskill Trailway** and **South County Trailway**.

Blue Mountain Reservation, Welcher Avenue, Peekskill NY, ☎ 914-737-2194. This area offers swimming, camping and hiking. Mountain bikers will appreciate the bike trail system here.

Briarcliff-Peekskill Trailway, ☎ 914-242-PARK. Bicycles are not allowed. This park runs for 12 miles from Ossining to the Blue Mountain Reservation in Peekskill. In Ossining begin at Route 9A at **Ryder Road** and follow a wooded road to **Teatown Lake Reservation**. The trail follows Bailey Brook north for a half-mile and then turns west toward Croton Dam. The trail continues northwest near Colabaugh Pond to Blue Mountain Reservation. Then it climbs 560 feet on Spitzenberg Mountain with great views of the Hudson River.

Cranberry Lake Preserve, Old Orchard Street, North White Plains NY, ☎ 914-428-1005. The preserve offers hiking, cross-country skiing and fishing on 135 acres.

Teatown Lake Reservation, Spring Valley Road, Ossining NY, ☎ 914-762-2912. This nature preserve has walking trails as well as animal displays. A favorite trail is the Hidden Valley Trail.

Ward Pound Ridge Reservation, Routes 35 & 121, Cross River NY, ☎ 914-763-3993. Nature preserve with nearly 5,000 acres of hiking and horseback-riding trails.

Westmoreland Sanctuary, 260 Chestnut Ridge Road, Bedford Corners NY, ☎ 914-666-8448. The 625-acre nature sanctuary has eight miles of hiking trails.

■ On Wheels

Scenic Drives

Croton Dam. Take Route 129 from Croton-on-Hudson and follow along to this scenic wonder (see page 306).

Sleepy Hollow. For a jouney into the legends, and facts, of Sleepy Hollow visit the home of Washington Irving. His home, **Sunnyside**, is located on Route 9 and will set the stage for many of the stories. Then head north on Route 9 to visit **Sleepy Hollow Cemetery** where Irving is buried. The bridge near the **Old Dutch Church** on the Pocantico River is the site of Ichabod Crane's ride.

Bicycling

Sundays in May, June and September are motor-vehicle free on the Bronx River Parkway. Begin at the **Westchester County Center** in White Plains and cycle to **Scarsdale Road** in Yonkers, a distance of 14 miles round-trip. Cyclists are also welcome in all Westchester parks and trails. See *On Foot,* above. There are seven miles of color-coded mountain bike trails at **Blue Mountain Reservation**. The mountain bike trail at **Graham Hills** is meant for experienced riders.

BLUE MOUNTAIN CYCLIST
RESPONSIBILITY CODE

- Always wear a helmet and keep your bicycle in good condition.

- Control your speed at all times.

- Slow down and pass with care (on the left).

- Stay on designated trails.

- Do not disturb wildlife.

- Minimize your impact on trail erosion.

- Please do not litter.

- Respect public and private property.

- Know park rules by checking with the park office for current trail status and park regulations.

- Plan ahead, remembering weather and trail conditions.

- Never ride alone.

- Obey park rules.

On Rails

MTA Metro-North Railroad, ☎ 800-METRO-INFO (when outside New York City) or 212-532-4900. This is a commuter railroad with 43 station stops in Westchester. Ask for "One-Day Getaway" packages.

Amtrak, ☎ 800-872-7245. Amtrak offers service from New York to stations on the Boston-Washington Northeast Corridor, including Metroliner service. Passengers can also take Amtrak to upstate New York, Montreal, Chicago and points west. We have enjoyed the waterline trip from Albany to New York City, craning our necks to get a glimpse of passing Hudson River landmarks such as Washington Irving's "Sunnyside" and other mansions, many of which loom above the tracks. There are also wonderful spreads of the western shore to enjoy.

■ On Water

 Westchester County is surrounded on the south and west by two bodies of water, Long Island Sound and the Hudson River. Visitors can enjoy the water on cruises, learning to sail, renting a boat or launching your own.

 *We ran a sailing school on Lake George for 10 years and know the pleasure we shared with visitors who came to love the water. Some people had sailed for years and wanted to perfect such skills as recognizing wind shifts on a mountain lake. Others had never sailed before. One of our mottos was, "when the going gets rough where would you rather be?" Answer: at the tiller, rather than up in the bow handling the sails.*

Excursion Boats

Hudson Highlands Cruises, ☎ 914-534-7245. A three-hour cruise is scheduled on the last Saturday of every month from May through October. It heads upriver from Peekskill to the Hudson Highlands on a three-hour narrated excursion. You'll pass West Point, Cold Spring, Constitution Island and Bear Mountain Bridge. The scenery is varied and beautiful.

NY Waterway, ☎ 800-53-FERRY. Sightseeing cruises are offered from New York City to Sleepy Hollow. They run from mid-May until November 1. The excursion lasts for two hours and box lunches are available. Here's the chance to see historic sites such as Lyndhurst, Kykuit, Sunnyside and Philipsburg Manor.

Hudson River Yacht Tours, ☎ 914-925-1128. Cruises are offered from Playland Parkway, Rye NY.

Kayaking

Hudson River Recreation, Tarrytown, ☎ 888-321-HUDSON. This company offers seasonal guided kayak tours of various lengths for all ability levels. If you've never kayaked before, you can still enjoy the trip. Tours on the Hudson River take off both north and south from Sleepy Hollow and there is focus on the history of the area. Tours on Long Island Sound leave from New Rochelle.

Sailing

Croton Sailing School, Senesqua Park, Croton-on-Hudson NY, ☎ 914-271-6868.

Boat Rentals

New York Sailing School, ☎ 914-235-6052, www.nyss.com. You can rent a sailboat from 22 to 40 feet long from April through November. Departures are from New Rochelle. Skill certification and reservations are required. Sunset cruises are available beginning at 6:30 pm. You can also choose an overnight cruise.

Mountain Lakes, Hawley Road, North Salem NY, ☎ 914-669-5793, www.westchestergov.com/parks. Rowboats and canoes are available in spring, summer and fall. Advance reservations are required.

Boat Launching

Croton Point Park, Croton-on-Hudson NY, ☎ 914-271-3293.

Croton Sailing School, Senesqua Park, Croton-on-Hudson NY, ☎ 914-271-6868.

George's Island Park, Montrose NY, ☎ 914-737-7530.

Ossining Boat & Canoe Club, Westerly Road, Ossining NY, ☎ 914-762-9724.

■ On Snow

Cross-Country Skiing

 Rockefeller Preserve, Route 117, Tarrytown NY, ☎ 914-631-1470. Here you can enjoy cross-country skiing or showshoeing on 20 miles of carriage roads and other trails in this 850-acre preserve.

For information on any of the areas below, ☎ 914-242-PARK.

- **Blue Mountain Reservation**, Welcher Avenue, Peekskill

- **Cranberry Lake Preserve**, Old Orchard Street, North White Plains

- **Croton Gorge**, Route 129, Cortlandt

- **Maple Moor Golf Course**, North Street, White Plains

- **Mountain Lakes Park**, Hawley Road, North Salem

- **Saxon Woods Park**, Mamaroneck Avenue, White Plains

Sightseeing

■ Croton-on-Hudson

 Van Cortlandt Manor, South Riverside Avenue, Croton-on-Hudson NY, ☎ 914-631-8200. This National Historic Landmark is an 18th-century estate on the banks of the Croton River. Inside, the house contains many of the original Van Cortlandt furnishings. The parlor furniture includes Queen Anne, Chippendale and Federal-style pieces. Delft biblical tiles around the fireplace are original to the house. Handsome Chelsea and Chelsea-Derby figurines on the mantel belonged to Cornelia Van Cortlandt Beekman.

There's an 18th-century tavern located where the ferry crossed over the Croton River along the original Albany Post Road. The "common room" was more exclusive than the bar room, where anyone could pop in for a drink. The house also had a ladies' parlor and a ladies bedroom, which allowed some privacy. Visitors can enjoy open hearth cooking demonstrations as well as weaving and spinning in the nearby 18th-century tenant house.

WINERY TOUR

North Salem Vineyard, Hardscrabble Road, North Salem NY, ☎ 914-669-5518. Grapes have been grown here for 34 years, producing champagne and table wines. Tours and tastings are available year-round on Saturday and Sunday or by appointment.

■ Sleepy Hollow

Kykuit, Sleepy Hollow NY, ☎ 914-631-9491 or 631-8200. Four generations of Rockefellers lived in this exquisite Beaux Arts Mansion before it opened to the public in 1994. *Kykuit* means "lookout" in Dutch and it has a wonderful view of the Hudson River and the Palisades.

You begin by parking at Philipsburg Manor on Route 9 in North Tarrytown, where a shuttle will take you to tour Kykuit. It is preferable to make a reservation in advance as there may not be space available. You can choose to take either The House and Garden Tour or The Special Garden and Sculpture Tour; we recommend the former for the first visit.

John D. Rockefeller, Jr. had the responsibility of building the house for his parents in 1913. Then he lived there with his wife, Abby Aldrich Rockefeller, beginning in 1937. Governor Nelson A. Rockefeller and his wife, Happy, lived there beginning in 1960.

Outside, the landscaping and classical sculpture is a tour in itself. The collection includes pieces by Henry Moore, Alexander Calder, Louise Nevelson and others. And the Hudson River is there as a magnificent backdrop.

Inside, the house is elegant and filled with works of art as well as family memorabilia. Yet the rooms seem comfortable and one can imagine a family relaxing there.

Old Dutch Church, Route 9 & Sleepy Hollow Avenue, Sleepy Hollow NY, ☎ 914-631-1123. This church is thought to be the oldest church in New York State that is still in use. Frederick Philipse built it in the 1680s and the sturdy 30 inch-thick stone walls were meant to forestall Indian attacks. Washington Irving admired the church and is buried behind it. He is in good company with William Rockefeller, Walter Chrysler, Andrew Carnegie and Robert Ingersoll.

Philipsburg Manor, Route 9, Sleepy Hollow NY, ☎ 914-631-8702. Frederick Philipse rose from his life as a carpenter to become the wealthiest man in New York. King William and Queen Mary of Great Britain granted him a charter for 52,000 acres on the Hudson River in 1693. Philipsburg Manor is a working 18th-century farm with a stone manor house, a working water-powered grist mill and millpond, an 18th-century barn and an herb and kitchen garden.

The parlor contains a handsome painted Dutch cupboard. The Adolph Philipse inventory of 1750 lists three framed maps, which were important for those who were traders. Adolph Philipse's bedroom inventory lists a bed that can be folded up against the wall so the room could be used for other purposes – a common practice in colonial times.

His descendants left for England during the American Revolution and their estate was sold at auction. John D. Rockefeller, Jr. saved and restored the property in the 1940s. **Historic Hudson Valley**, ☎ 914-631-8200, now operates the site and tours are available from 18th-century costumed interpreters. We crossed the bridge and felt transplanted into the 18th century. Ducks and geese were active in the pond and the mill wheel swished around and around. Demonstrations are given in the grist mill.

Union Church of Pocantico Hills, Route 448, Bedford Road, Sleepy Hollow NY, ☎ 914-631-8200. If you love stained-glass windows, this church is a jewel. Henri Matisse worked on the windows, which were finished just two days before his death. He created a rose window in memory of Abby Aldrich Rockefeller, choosing the colors and the type of glass before he died. His daughter had the window finished and it was dedicated on Mothers Day, 1956.

Marc Chagall designed the "Good Samaritan" window in memory of John D. Rockefeller, Jr., and it was installed in 1965. Chagall also created eight side windows, the first seven focused on the Old Testament. The eighth window, "The Crucifixion," is a memorial to Michael Rockefeller who was lost in New Guinea.

■ Tarrytown

Lyndhurst, 635 South Broadway, Tarrytown NY, ☎ 914-631-4481. This 1838 Gothic Revival mansion was designed by Alexander Jackson Davis. William Paulding, a former New York congressman and ex-mayor of New York City, was the first owner. George Merritt bought the house and proceeded to enlarge it beginning in 1865. The new north wing almost doubled the size of the house and a tower enhanced it on the western side. Sing Sing marble was used and the stained glass windows are dazzling. The last owner was railroad magnate Jay Gould. The 67-acre estate is a property of the **National Trust for Historic Preservation**, ☎ 202-588-6166.

Sunnyside, West Sunnyside Lane, Tarrytown NY, ☎ 914-631-8702. Visitors are entranced by the romance of Washington Irving's stories, some of which were written here. After the visit we almost felt as if we knew him. He loved his "little old-fashioned stone mansion all made up of gable ends, and as full of angles and corners as an old cocked hat."

The house was built by Wolfert Ecker in the 17th century and during the Revolution it was owned by Jacob Van Tassel. The Van Tassel name is featured in some of Irving's work.

As you approach the house look at the wisteria vine, which Irving planted himself. The door may be opened by a costumed interpreter who loves telling Washington Irving stories. Inside, his study looks as if he left in a hurry and planned to return. The books are original to Irving. One can almost see him having a snooze on the couch there. His favorite chair is still by the window in the dining room where he could enjoy the view. Irving died in his bedroom in 1859. He brought the Federal-style bed from New York City when he arrived at Sunnyside.

Performing Arts

Paramount Center for the Arts, 1008 Brown Street, Peekskill NY, ☎ 914-739-2333. This restored historic vaudeville theater offers music, dance, theater and film year-round.

Caramoor Center for Music and the Arts, Girdle Ridge Road, Katonah NY, ☎ 914-232-5035. Open year-round for musical events and lectures. The museum has an extensive collection of fine and decorative arts from Europe and China, and the gardens are magnificent.

The Tarrytown Music Hall, 13 Main Street, Tarrytown NY, ☎ 914-631-3390. The program includes the Jazz Forum Arts Series, classical music and musical theater.

Festivals & Events

■ April

Christie's Vintage Car Auction, Tarrytown, at Lyndhurst, ☎ 914-631-4481.

■ June

Caramoor International Music Festival (through August), Katonah, ☎ 914-232-1252. World-renowned outdoor music festival, featuring classical, opera and jazz performances, with picnicking on the grounds.

The Great Hudson River Revival, Croton-on-Hudson, ☎ 914-454-7673. The festival features an eclectic gathering of crafts, ethnic food and educational displays with an ecological slant. Musicians and other performers appear on six solar-powered stages.

■ July

Asian Festival at the Japanese Stroll Garden, North Salem, ☎ 914-669-5033. Annual family festival featuring Chinese Lion Dancers, Japanese drummers, Korean musicians, childrens' crafts and Asian food.

■ August

Sunnyside Jazz Festival, Tarrytown, ☎ 914-631-8200. Spread out a blanket and enjoy continuous open-air jazz performances beside the Hudson River.

■ September

Hudson Heritage Festival (through October), Yonkers to Peekskill, ☎ 914-948-0047. Two months of events in every riverside community, including fairs, parades, concerts, farmers' markets, special exhibits, trolley tours.

RiverFair, Croton Point, Croton-on-Hudson. A celebration of the bounty of the Hudson including crafts, farmers' market, wine tasting, blue grass music, and children's activities.

Where to Stay

ACCOMMODATIONS PRICE SCALE
Prices for a double room for one or two persons, before taxes.
$ . . . . Under $50
$$. . . . . $50 to $100
$$$ . . . . $101 to $175
$$$$ . . . . Over $175

■ Croton-on-Hudson

 Alexander Hamilton House is an 1889 Victorian B&B furnished with antiques. Some of the guest rooms have wood-burning fireplaces and/or whirlpool tubs. There's even a bridal chamber with an entertainment center and five skylights. 49 Van Wyck Street, Croton-on-Hudson, NY 10520, ☎ 914-271-6737, fax 914-271-3927, www.alexanderhamiltonhouse.com. $$.

■ Tarrytown

The Castle is a handsome stone mansion overlooking the Hudson River. Each room is beautifully and individually decorated. This is the place to go if you want to be pampered. Dining is spectacular (see page 316). 400 Benedict Avenue, Tarrytown, NY 10591, ☎ 914-631-1980, fax 914-631-4612. $$$.

Tarrytown House is a hotel and conference center in two historic mansions. East Sunnyside Lane, Tarrytown, NY 10591, ☎ 800-553-8118 or 914-591-8200, fax 914-591-7118. $$$.

■ Camping

Peekskill

The Trail Lodge at Blue Mountain Reservation, Welcher Avenue, Peekskill NY, ☎ 914-737-2194.

North Salem

Mountain Lakes Park, Hawley Road, North Salem NY, ☎ 914-669-5793 or 763-3493.

Croton-on-Hudson

Croton Point Park, Croton Point Avenue, Croton-on-Hudson NY, ☎ 914-271-3293.

Cross River

Ward Pound Ridge Reservation, Routes 35 and 121, Cross River NY, ☎ 914-763-3493.

Sleepy Hollow Country

Where to Eat

DINING PRICE SCALE	
Prices include an entrée, which may come with vegetables and salad, but exclude beverage, taxes and tip.	
$	Under $10
$$	$10 to $20
$$$.	$21 to $50
$$$$.	Over $50

■ Peekskill

 Crystal Bay, in the Charles Point Marina, has plenty of seafood and a Sunday brunch, ☎ 914-737-8332. $$.

■ Ossining

Guida's offers Northern Italian cuisine. 199 Main Street, Ossining, NY, ☎ 914-941-2662. $$-$$$.

■ Chappaqua

Crabtrees Kittle House dates from 1790. The cuisine is Progressive American and they have an award-winning wine list. Sunday brunch is popular. 11 Kittle Avenue, Chappaqua, NY. $$-$$$.

■ Tarrytown

Equus (at The Castle, see page 315) features a gourmet menu with classical music playing softly. Terrace dining overlooks the Hudson River. 400 Benedict Avenue, Tarrytown, NY, ☎ 914-631-1980. $$-$$$.

Horsefeathers features health conscious cuisine as well as homemade desserts. Brunch is popular on Saturday and Sunday. 94 N Broadway, Tarrytown, NY 10601, ☎ 914-631-6606. $$.

Sunset Cove is located on the Hudson River and offers Continental cuisine with a Mediterranean flair. 238 Green Street, Tarrytown, NY, ☎ 914-366-7889. $$.

Index

Butternut, skiing, 173

Calvin Coolidge State Forest, 66
Calvin Coolidge State Park, 43
Camping: Adirondacks, 108-110;
Berkshires, 181; Capital District,
162; Catskills, 221-222; Dutchess
and Columbia counties, 262; Green
Mountains, 66-67; Hudson High-
lands, 276; Lake Champlain (New
York side), 37-38; Lake Champlain
(Vermont side), 23; Palisades, 298-
299; Sleepy Hollow Country, 315;
Taconics, 195; Ulster County, 238-
239; Upper Hudson, 138-139
Camp Plymouth State Park, 43-44
Canal boats, 124-125, 235
Canoeing: Adirondacks, 90-94;
Berkshires, 171; Capital District,
150; classes of difficulty, 93-94;
Green Mountains, 49-50; Palisades,
283; Taconics, 189; Upper Hudson,
125-126
Capital District, 142-163; accommodations, 160-162; adventures, 147-
152; camping, 162; dining, 162-163;
festivals and events, 158-160; getting here and getting around, 146;
history, 143-146; information
sources, 147; map, 142; sightseeing,
152-158
Carmel, monastery, 275
Castleton, sightseeing, 59
Catamount, 151, 173
Catskill, New York, 208; accommodations, 221; dining, 224; sightseeing,
217
Catskills, 197-225; accommodations,
219-222; adventures, 203-215;
camping, 221-222; dining, 223-225;
festivals and events, 217-219; getting here and getting around, 202;
history, 197-201; information
sources, 202-203; map, 198; sightseeing, 215-217
Champlain Canal, 123, 124, 144
Champlain-Hudson waterway, 1-6;
climate, 5; ecology, 5-6; geology, 3;
history, 2-3; information sources, 9-
10; map, 4; travel information, 7-9
Champlain Islands, 15
Chappaqua, dining, 316
Charlotte, camping, 23

Chestertown: accommodations, 105;
dining, 111-112
Clermont, sightseeing, 251
Clothing and gear, 8
Cold Spring: accommodations, 276;
dining, 277
Columbia County, see Dutchess and
Columbia counties
Connecticut: information sources,
184, 189; Taconics, 183-196
Corinth, camping, 139
Cornwall Bridge: hiking, 186-187;
scenic drive, 188
Cornwall-on-Hudson: accommoda-
tions, 296; sightseeing, 288
Cornwallville, sightseeing, 215
Coxsackie, sightseeing, 216
Cross-country skiing: Adirondacks,
96-97; Berkshires, 172-174; Capital
District, 151-152; Catskills, 214;
Green Mountains, 57-59; Hudson
Highlands, 274; Mid-Hudson, 233;
Sleepy Hollow Country, 310;
Taconics, 190; Upper Hudson, 126
Croton-on-Hudson: accommodations,
315; camping, 315; sightseeing, 310-
311
Crown Point, sightseeing, 35-36, 100

D&H Canal, 231, 232, 235, 286
Delaware River, fishing, 284
Diamond Point, accommodations, 107
Dining: Adirondacks, 111-113;
Berkshires, 181-182; Capital Dis-
trict, 162-163; Catskills, 223-225;
Dutchess and Columbia counties,
262-265; Green Mountains, 67-69;
Hudson Highlands, 277; Lake
Champlain (New York side), 38-39;
Lake Champlain (Vermont side), 24;
Palisades, 299-301; price scale, 9;
Sleepy Hollow Country, 316;
Taconics, 195-196; Ulster County,
240-241; Upper Hudson, 140-141
Diving, 18-19
Dorset: accommodations, 64-65; din-
ing, 68
Dover Plains: accommodations, 261;
dining, 262
Downhill skiing: Adirondacks, 96;
Berkshires, 172-173; Capital Dis-
trict, 151; Catskills, 212-214; Green
Mountains, 52-57; Hudson High-

Index

DATE DUE

10/14			
AP 25 '06			
5/4/6			
OC 2 ? '09			

DEMCO 38-296